IN THEIR OWN WORDS

# WARRIORS
# AND
# PIONEERS

Collected and Edited by
## T. J. Stiles

*With an Introduction by Richard Maxwell Brown*

A PERIGEE BOOK

A Perigee Book
Published by The Berkley Publishing Group
200 Madison Avenue
New York, NY 10016

First edition: March 1996

Published simultaneously in Canada.

The Putnam Berkley World Wide Web site address is http://www.berkley.com

Library of Congress Cataloging-in-Publication Data
Warriors and pioneers / collected and edited by T. J. Stiles ; with an
    introduction by Richard Maxwell Brown.—1st ed.
        p.    cm.—(In their own words)
    Includes bibliographical references.
    ISBN 0-399-51988-2
    1. West (U.S.)—History—Sources.   2. Frontier and pioneer life—West (U.S.)—
Sources.   3. Pioneers—West (U.S.)—Biography.   4. Soldiers—West (U.S.)—
Biography.   5. Indians of North America—West (U.S.)—Biography.   I. Stiles,
T. J.   II.   Series: In their own words (Berkley Publishing Group)
F591.W29   1996
978—dc20                                                                         95-38327

Printed in the United States of America

10   9   8   7   6   5   4

# CONTENTS

List of Maps  viii

Preface  ix

Sources  xiii

The Writers and Their Positions at the Time  xv

Introduction by Richard Maxwell Brown  xvii

A Note to the Reader  xxii

**I. The Great Flood:**
THE FAR WEST, 1843–1863  1

1. The Oregon Trail                                              5
   *Across the Great Plains: Francis Parkman, Jr.*
   *Settling Oregon: Jesse A. Applegate*
2. The California Gold Rush                                     28
   *The California Gold Rush: General William T. Sherman*
3. The Nez Percé Resistance                                     41
   *The Struggle of Old Joseph: Chief Joseph*

**II. The Burning Prairie:**
THE GREAT PLAINS, 1864–1878  47

4. A Tale of the Northern Plains                                51
   *The Pioneers: Fanny Kelly*
   *The Invaders: Generals Henry H. Sibley and Alfred Sully*
   *The Captive: Fanny Kelly*
5. The Closing Vise: The Central Plains, 1864–1868              82
   *The Sand Creek Massacre: William M. Breakenridge*
   *Railroad Building and Buffalo Killing: Buffalo Bill Cody*
6. War for the Southern Plains, 1868–1869                       92
   *A Winter Campaign: General Philip H. Sheridan*
   *The Battle of the Washita: General George A. Custer*
   *The Vanquished: General Philip H. Sheridan*

7.  Kansas Cowtowns and Texas Badmen: The Other Plains War     127
       *Wild Bill Hickok: General George A. Custer*
       *Up the Chisholm Trail: John Wesley Hardin*
       *The Rangers Clean Up Kimble County: J.B. Gillett*


### III. The Conflagration:
THE CONQUEST OF THE NORTHERN PLAINS, 1875–1886    151

8.  War for the Black Hills: The Great Sioux War of 1876        155
       *Out of the Black Hills: Wooden Leg*
       *Battle of the Rosebud: John F. Finerty*
       *Custer's Last Stand: Two Moons*
       *After the Victory: Wooden Leg*
       *Chasing Sitting Bull: General Nelson A. Miles*
       *Last Days of the Northern Cheyennes: Wooden Leg*
9.  Refugees of Conquest                                         201
       *The Great Trek of the Nez Percés: Chief Joseph*
10.  Cattle Barons and Horse Thieves                             213
       *The Making of the Cattle Country: Theodore Roosevelt*
       *The Sheriff of Johnson County: Frank M. Canton*


### IV. The Mountains and the Desert:
BATTLES OF THE SOUTHWEST, 1861–1884    227

11.  The Long Fight of the Apaches                               231
       *Our First Fight with the Apaches: J.B. Gillett*
       *The Making of a Warrior: Geronimo*
       *The Coming of the White Men: Geronimo*
       *Bringing in Geronimo: Lieutenant Britton Davis*
12.  The Lincoln County War                                      263
       *A Civil War in New Mexico: George W. Coe*
       *The Five-Day Battle: George W. Coe*
       *The Hunt for Billy the Kid: Pat F. Garrett*


### V. Conquered Ground:
LAST EPISODES ON THE FRONTIER, 1885–1892    297

13.  The Geronimo Campaign                                       301
       *The Final Outbreak: Lieutenant Britton Davis*
       *The Chase: Lieutenant Marion P. Maus*

*Surprise Attack: Tom Horn*
*Miles Takes Command: Lieutenant Britton Davis*
*On the Run: Geronimo*
*The Last Surrender: Lieutenant Britton Davis*
14. The Daltons Ride for the Last Time 321
*The Final Reckoning: Emmett Dalton*
Epilogue 337

# MAPS

United States Territorial Expansion, 1845-1858          Frontispiece
Part I: The Great Flood                                           4
Part II: The Burning Prairie                                    50
Part III(A): The Conflagration, Chapters 8 & 9                 154
Part III(B): The Conflagration, Chapter 10                     212
Parts IV & V: The Mountains and the Desert &
   Conquered Ground                                            230

All maps designed by Nora Wertz.

# PREFACE

Personal history is almost always history at its most gripping. That simple realization is the idea behind *Warriors and Pioneers*, the second book of *In Their Own Words*, a three-part series of narrative anthologies on critical periods in America's past. Historians have long known the fascination of reading first-person accounts of great events—the excitement of hearing the thoughts of those who actually shaped and experienced ages long past. This series brings these gripping personal narratives to the general public—and the reader of this volume will not be disappointed: here figures such as Chief Joseph and George Custer, Geronimo and John Wesley Hardin, and a remarkable pioneer woman named Fanny Kelly describe the climactic episodes of their adventurous lives.

But *Warriors and Pioneers* is far more than a simple reader—it is no mere collection of excerpts rattling around loosely like so many aspirin in a bottle. These first-person accounts have been carefully edited and footnoted, and placed in a chronological, narrative, and *interpretive* framework to form a cohesive whole. The epic history of the nineteenth-century West unfolds in these pages—each selection telling its story within the wider context of the era. Of course, that history is so epic that I have had to carefully focus the theme of this volume, selecting individual episodes to move along a larger story. And that theme, that story, is conflict and conquest.

There are countless stories that could be told about the history of the American frontier; there is probably one for every hoofprint or fence post ever driven into Western soil. In the search for an ever-deeper understanding of the Western past, historians have researched countless topics over the last few decades: the many Indian cultures and languages; the lives of black, Chinese, and Hispanic communities; economic development and labor conflict; the role of women; and much more. The result has been a much richer understanding of life in the Old West. But this volume returns to a subject that seems almost old-fashioned in light of the changing historiography—and yet one that remains absolutely fundamental to the history of the region. The overwhelming fact of the nineteenth-century West (meaning, in this book, the lands west of Minnesota, Iowa, Missouri, and Arkansas, from 1843 to 1892) is that it was utterly transformed by invasion and conquest by an outside people—the citizens of the United States.

That invasion began with the first large-scale use of the Oregon Trail in 1843, when settlers from the United States initiated an infiltration of the vast Western wilderness. A few whites already lived there—mainly French

Canadian trappers and fur traders—but until the pioneers arrived, the West was governed by Indian peoples who thrived on an ecosystem unlike that of the settled parts of the United States. The land those first wagon trains ventured into was far more different from the Eastern states than, say, France at the time was from Spain or Prussia.

To describe the impending conflict in simplified terms, it is accurate to say that the pioneers brought with them an entirely different culture that was irreconcilable with the native societies they encountered. The Americans thought in terms of transforming the land to make it more productive through farming, ranching, and mining; most of the Indians relied on harvesting wild game and vegetation, without engineering changes in the earth. The pioneers formed fixed settlements; most Indians moved their villages in response to the demands of nature. The pioneers erected permanent structures; many Indians lived in carefully designed lodges that could be broken down for travel in a few minutes. The pioneers came from an economy driven by money, capital, manufactured goods, and wages; the Indians created what they needed, or bartered with the fur traders for weapons and products that they wanted. Most important, the pioneers believed in private land ownership, where most Indians believed in communal rights to a region. And, since the settlers thought in terms of legal ownership, they sought to "extinguish Indian title" to gain access to Native American lands—which sometimes meant provoking wars.

The clash between the two cultures was clear and unavoidable. As Wooden Leg, a Northern Cheyenne warrior, so aptly put it: "All of our teachings and beliefs were that land was not made to be owned in separate pieces by persons and that the plowing up and destruction of vegetation placed by the Great Spirit and the planting of other vegetation according to the ideas of men was an interference with the plans of the Above." The two systems of life could not coexist in the same territory—and both the native and the newer Americans were heavily armed, with long traditions of warfare and personal violence. The result of the white invasion, then, was the first stage of a two-part war for the West.

In the introduction to this volume, historian Richard Maxwell Brown describes this war—a "Western Civil War of Incorporation," as he names it. Due to the far smaller numbers of combatants, and their extreme dispersion on the broad frontier, the casualties never amounted to those of that other, and better-known Civil War—yet it was war nonetheless.[1] And

---

[1] The conquest and control of the Indians tied down well over 60 percent of the army in the decades following the Civil War, involving 20,000–23,000 troops annually. They faced approximately 100,000 hostile Indians as of 1870 (including noncombatants). From 1865 to 1890, the army fought over a thousand separate engagements, with an official loss of 948 dead—not including hundreds of casualties among civilians and Indian warriors fighting for the military. Native American combat casualties are impossible to estimate accurately, but they undoubtedly run into the thousands.

# SOURCES

Applegate, Jesse A., *Recollections of My Boyhood* (Roseburg, Ore.: Press of Review Publishing, 1914)

Barrett, S.M., *Geronimo's Story of His Life* (New York: Duffield & Co., 1906)

Breakenridge, William M., *Helldorado: Bringing Law to the Mesquite* (Boston: Houghton Mifflin Co., 1928). By permission of Houghton Mifflin Co.

Canton, Frank M., *Frontier Trails: The Autobiography of Frank Canton*; edited by Edward Everett Dale (Boston: Houghton Mifflin Co., 1930; new edition copyright 1966, University of Oklahoma Press). By permission of the University of Oklahoma Press.

Cody, William F., *An Autobiography of Buffalo Bill* (New York: Farrar & Rinehart, 1920)

Coe, George W., *Frontier Fighter: The Autobiography of George W. Coe, as Related to Nan Hillary Harrison* (Boston: Houghton Mifflin Co., 1930). By permission of the Perry Ranch, Inc.

Custer, George Armstrong, *My Life on the Plains, or Personal Experiences with Indians* (New York: Heldon & Co., 1874)

Dalton, Emmett (in collaboration with Jack Jungmeyer), *When the Daltons Rode* (Garden City, N.Y.: Doubleday, 1931)

Davis, Britton, *The Truth About Geronimo* (New Haven, Conn.: Yale University Press, 1929). By permission of Yale University Press.

Finerty, John F., *War-Path and Bivouac, or The Conquest of the Sioux*, Second Edition (Chicago: 1890?)

Garland, Hamlin, "General Custer's Last Fight as Seen by Two Moons," *McClure's Magazine*, Vol. 11, 1898

Garrett, Pat F., *Pat F. Garrett's Authentic Life of Billy the Kid* (Santa Fe, N.Mex.: New Mexican Printing and Publishing, 1882)

Gillett, James B., *Six Years with the Texas Rangers, 1875–1881* (Austin, Tex.: Von Boeckmann-Jones Co., 1921)

Hardin, John Wesley, *The Life of John Wesley Hardin, from the Original Manuscript, as Written by Himself* (Seguin, Tex.: Smith & Moore, 1896)

Horn, Tom, *Life of Tom Horn, Government Scout and Interpreter, Written by Himself: A Vindication* (Denver: Louthan Book Co., 1904)

Chief Joseph, "An Indian's View of Indian Affairs," *North American Review*, 1879

Kelly, Fanny, *Narrative of My Captivity Among the Sioux Indians* (Hartford, Conn.: Mutual Publishing Co., 1871)

Marquis, Thomas B., *A Warrior Who Fought Custer* (Minneapolis: The Midwest Co., 1931)

Miles, Nelson A., *Personal Recollections of General Nelson A. Miles* (Chicago: The Werner Co., 1897)

Parkman, Francis, Jr., *The Oregon Trail: Sketches of the Prairie and Rocky-Mountain Life* (Boston: Little, Brown, and Co., 1892)

Roosevelt, Theodore, "Ranch Life in the Far West: In the Cattle Country," *Century Magazine*, February 1888.

Sheridan, Philip H., *Personal Recollections of P.H. Sheridan* (New York: C.L. Webster & Co., 1888)

Sherman, William T., *Memoirs of General William T. Sherman* (New York: D. Appleton & Co., 1875)

*The War of Rebellion: A Compilation of the Official Records of the Union and Confederate Armies*, Series I (Washington, D.C.: 1880–1901)

# THE WRITERS AND THEIR POSITIONS
# AT THE TIME

## Native Americans

**Chief Joseph** (also called Young Joseph or Thunder Traveling Over the Mountains), chief of the Wallowa band of Nez Percés
**Geronimo** (also called Goyakla), Chiricahua Apache war leader
**Two Moons**, minor chief in the Fox warrior society of the Northern Cheyennes
**Wooden Leg**, young warrior of the Northern Cheyennes

## Soldiers

**William M. Breakenridge**, private in the 3rd Colorado Cavalry
**General George A. Custer**, lieutenant colonel of the 7th Cavalry
**Lieutenant Britton Davis**, second lieutenant, 3rd Cavalry, and commander of the Apache Scouts at the San Carlos Reservation, Arizona Territory
**Lieutenant Marion P. Maus**, lieutenant of the 3rd Cavalry and officer of the 2nd Battalion of Apache Scouts
**General Nelson A. Miles**, colonel of the 5th Infantry Regiment, later commander of the Department of Arizona
**General Philip H. Sheridan**, commander of the Department of the Missouri, later commander of the U.S. Army
**General William T. Sherman**, assistant to Colonel R.B. Mason, military governor of California, later commander of the U.S. Army
**General Henry H. Sibley**, commander of the 6th Minnesota Regiment
**General Alfred Sully**, commander of the Military District of Iowa

## Scouts

**William F. ("Buffalo Bill") Cody**, buffalo hunter for the Kansas Pacific Railroad and later a civilian scout for the army
**Tom Horn**, civilian Chief of Scouts for the 2nd Battalion of Apache Scouts

## Settlers & Travelers

**Jesse A. Applegate**, early settler in Oregon
**John F. Finerty**, war correspondent for the *Chicago Times*
**Fanny Kelly**, anti-slavery pioneer in Kansas and emigrant to Idaho
**Francis Parkman, Jr.**, writer and historian
**Theodore Roosevelt**, rancher in the Little Missouri Badlands, Dakota
  Territory

## Gunfighters

**Frank M. Canton**, detective for the Wyoming Stockgrowers' Association
  and sheriff of Johnson County, Wyoming Territory
**George W. Coe**, member of the Regulators in the Lincoln County War,
  Lincoln County, New Mexico Territory
**Emmett Dalton**, member of the Dalton Gang, Oklahoma Territory
**Pat F. Garrett**, sheriff of Lincoln County, New Mexico Territory
**J.B. Gillett**, corporal in Company E and later first sergeant in Company C,
  Frontier Battalion, Texas Rangers
**John Wesley Hardin**, Texas cowboy and gunslinger

# INTRODUCTION

Americans are well aware of the Civil War between the North and the South from 1861 to 1865. Less well known is a second civil war that took place in the Old West in the nineteenth century. As I have termed it elsewhere, this was the "Western Civil War of Incorporation"[2] that erupted as the frontier was absorbed—or "incorporated"—into the social, economic, and political system of the rest of the United States. The polarizing antagonism resulting from the trend of incorporation produced a civil war in the West—one fought in many places and on many fronts in almost all of the Western territories and states from the 1850s into the 1910s.

This war—described in *Warriors and Pioneers* by those who fought it— broke down into two parts. In the first, the U.S. Army intervened in the conflict between settlers and Indians and eventually broke the military power of the Native American tribes. Hand in hand with this warfare was the transformation of the land itself by pioneers that gradually eliminated the buffalo and the hunting grounds that perpetuated Indian culture. Stripped of their arms, lands, and sustenance after decades of struggle, the Indians were shunted into a life of total dependence on scattered reservations. Within one generation, the ecosystem and population of the West was revolutionized—often by naked force.

The second phase of the Western Civil War of Incorporation came in the aftermath of the Indians' defeat. Frontier communities of whites, Hispanics, and blacks faced pressure from conservative economic and political powers, igniting a struggle for supremacy in the West. To roughly sketch the conflict, the frontier hosted homesteaders, ranchers, and miners— along with scores of violent drifters—who were fiercely democratic (or at least individualistic) in their beliefs, well sustaining themselves through individual effort with little respect for large wealth and property. Many

[2] Richard Maxwell Brown, *No Duty to Retreat: Violence and Values in American History and Society* (New York: Oxford University Press, 1991; paperback reprint, Norman: University of Oklahoma Press, 1994), chapters 2–3, and chapter 11, "Violence," in *The Oxford History of the American West*, ed. Clyde A. Milner II, Carol A. O'Connor, and Martha A. Sandweiss (New York: Oxford University Press, 1994). For the concept of incorporation applied to late nineteenth-century American society as a whole, see Alan Trachtenberg, *The Incorporation of America: Culture and Society in the Gilded Age* (New York: Hill and Wang, 1982).

were from Texas or elsewhere in the South and had a taste for rebellion, thanks to the Civil War. They were also heavily armed and cherished the famed "Code of the West"—a belief that everyone had the right to stand his ground in a dispute and resort to firearms if both parties were on reasonably equal footing. This violent lifestyle was intertwined with a strong loyalty to kin and local community that was much tighter than their allegiance to the laws and formal government.

As wealthy and powerful men and corporations expanded into the West, they faced opposition from local gunslingers. Cattle barons such as Granville Stuart in Montana and John Chisum in New Mexico; corporations such as the various railroad companies, the Maxwell Land Grant Company in New Mexico, and the XIT ranching syndicate in Texas; smaller-scale businessmen in places such as Abilene and Tombstone; and corrupt political networks such as the Santa Fe and Tucson rings all tried to enforce their will on independent-minded frontiersmen who lived by different rules. Sometimes the resisters—very often Democrats and Southerners— engaged in conscious, focused opposition, using violence with the specific aim of stopping the advance of the incorporating powers. Sometimes they simply made their haunts ungovernable through flagrant outlawry and personal killings.[3]

Either way, these fierce fighters against incorporation posed a political problem for the conservative interests of money and government—which responded by hiring gunmen of their own. Some were famous, such as Wild Bill Hickok, Wyatt Earp, and Pat Garrett. Others, such as Frank Canton and Texas Ranger J.B. Gillett, are forgotten by all but specialists. Usually they were aligned with the conservative powers because of politics (most were Republicans, including Hickok, Earp, and Garrett[4]) and regional origin— many were Northerners and, often, like Hickok and the older brothers of Earp, Union army veterans (Wyatt himself had been too young to fight).

Countless battles—between organized groups as well as individual gunslingers—erupted between men who took the side of the incorporators or the resisters. A noted resister outlaw and gunfighter, Emmett Dalton of the bank-robbing Dalton brothers, put the situation in his own words as he wrote of the Western Civil War of Incorporation roaring to a climax in the 1890s: "There was widespread corruption in business and government. Predatory rings multiplied. Legislatures abetted notorious

[3] Often, however, these resisting gunmen turned their weapons on blacks, Hispanics, Chinese, and Indians—groups that were also without power. The frontier atmosphere was heavy with racism of the worst sort, something important to keep in mind when one's tendency to root for the underdog whites in the Western Civil War of Incorporation surfaces.

[4] A Texas migrant to New Mexico, Garrett had been a Democrat, but in line with his conservative convictions and political connections he changed his party allegiance to Republican.

pillage. [It was] a time when men were inclined to take back their delegated powers, turning again to the personal force of wit or gun. It was an outstanding example of how easily crime can become democratic. . . . In the West it incubated a large nest of outlaws. On the one side [were] railways, banks, and great corporations, many of which were lawlessly maneuvering for privileged booty; on the other side [were] train and bank robbers who lobbied with six-shooters."[5]

On October 5, 1892, in Coffeyville, Kansas, the Dalton brothers' bandit career was shot to pieces, and in general throughout the West the incorporators were the big winners. They had violently broken the resistance of independent, law-defying frontiersmen, and planted a new set of values: respect for wealth, property, and legal authority. Thus, the twice-conquered West was successfully integrated into American society.

Whether whites fought whites or whites fought Indians, this Western conflict was America's great war at the grass roots, with frontline battles occurring in such typical locations as peaceful Indian villages under army attack, civilian wagon trains suddenly ambushed, boomtown streets spattered with blood and spent bullets, and cattle ranges where frequent shootouts blasted away the silence of the Big Sky country.

Punctuating the overall pattern of the Western Civil War of Incorporation were wondrous acts of heroism and ignoble feats of villainy, of death and survival at the grass roots—all represented in the words of the settlers, soldiers, and Native Americans so astutely compiled and ably edited by T.J. Stiles in this book aptly entitled *Warriors and Pioneers*. These words range from the polished narrative prose of Francis Parkman, Jr., one of America's greatest historians of the nineteenth century, who encountered the living history of the westward-moving settlers and described it in his classic book, *The Oregon Trail*, through the suspenseful account of the pioneer Fanny Kelly's ordeal of captivity by plains Indians, to the tragic nobility and understated but enduring eloquence of the Nez Percé Chief Joseph's tribal autobiography.

The words we read in this volume are written by both the famous and the obscure. They illustrate the rich humanity and complexity of the Western experience. Included among the famed, in addition to Parkman and Chief Joseph, are the generals Sherman, Sheridan, and Custer; the mighty hunter and living legend Buffalo Bill; the fearsome gunfighters John Wesley Hardin and Pat Garrett; the future president Theodore Roosevelt, on his youthful Western ranching days; and the Apache war chief Geronimo, whose name alone struck fear into the hearts of Southwestern settlers. Among the obscure are, besides Fanny Kelly, Jesse A. Applegate, with his memoir of childhood days in frontier Oregon; the Indians Wooden Leg and Two Moons, with their eyewitness accounts of the Great

[5] Emmett Dalton, "The Final Reckoning," in Chapter 14, below.

Sioux War of 1876; and Lieutenant Britton Davis, a straightforward reporter of the U.S. Army's campaign against Geronimo.

As edited by T.J. Stiles, *Warriors and Pioneers* is an absorbing but rigorously realistic account of conflict and conquest in the Old West, yet the reader's approach to it is likely to be tinged with romance. I say "likely," because, despite a century of scholarship by academic historians, the predominant American understanding of the West clusters around its mythic dimension—a medley of cowboys and Indians, gunfighters and outlaws, "soiled doves" and pioneer madonnas, all merged into an emotionally resonant image of the legendary West. For almost every type of episode recorded in *Warriors and Pioneers* there is a romantic version that is more or less known to the public through nineteenth-century dime novels and through formula fiction, films, and television scenarios of the twentieth century.

Whether recounted in the authoritative pages of research historians or told by purveyors of myth, the nineteenth-century war between whites and Indians in the West rivals the Civil War of North vs. South as the American *Iliad*. It can reasonably be argued that Sitting Bull and George A. Custer—both prominent in this book—are even more important as figures of myth than of reality. Yet, it seems that virtually every myth of lasting power goes back to some sort of urtext of historical reality, and one of the most valuable contributions of *Warriors and Pioneers* is to present the reality behind the myth.

Scholars have been no less fascinated by the Western myth than has the public. Indeed, some of the finest critical scholarship about the West has been written to explain the meaning of its myth rather than the record of its reality. One perceptive view of what the critic John G. Cawelti calls "the six-gun mystique" holds that popular Western fiction in print or film embodies a deep formula in which the hero mediates between civilization and savagery or, in similar terms, between order and chaos.[6] In this deep formula, the gunfighting hero (played on the screen by the likes of Gary Cooper or John Wayne) is a transitional figure in Western society—one who reluctantly and paradoxically employs six-gun violence against villainy to establish the peaceable civilized values of the Western future.

The Western Civil War of Incorporation is strikingly reflected in Western mythology through a cognitive split in the legend of the gunfighter. On one hand, the conservative winning side in the Western Civil War of Incorporation bred a socially conservative myth of the Western hero in which real-life figures personify the successful struggle for the goal of incorporated order and law. On the other hand, there is a competing

[6] John G. Cawelti, *The Six-Gun Mystique* (Bowling Green, Ohio: Bowling Green State University Press, 1975). A massive study of Western fiction and film (especially the latter) is Richard Slotkin, *Gunfighter Nation: The Myth of the Frontier in Twentieth-Century America* (New York: Atheneum, 1992).

Western mythology in which those heroes are not law-enforcing agents of society but those who exemplify the scholar E.J. Hobsbawm's concept of the "social bandit"—an outlaw admired by aggrieved but law-abiding folk for his blows against oppressive wealth and power.[7] The classic example of the American social bandit is the globally famous Billy the Kid. Thus, in the mythology of the West the socially conservative Western hero vies with the dissident social-hero bandit.

This conflict in mythology has long thrived, because each image appeals to a contemporary side of the American character. The side that values order and security heartily responds to the reassuring conservative myth of the hero always besting evil. The other side of the American character distrusts established power and glories in the ideal of social protest romanticized in the figure of the bandit hero of the West. Oddly enough, these contradictory mythologies are an important unifying factor in our culture, because most Americans believe in both the conservative values of order and security and the progressive values of protest and reform, emphasizing one and then the other as conditions seem to require.

Having long been indoctrinated in the mythology, readers of this book will, however, seek the reality of the subject. In *Warriors and Pioneers* they will get it.

—Richard Maxwell Brown

[7] E.J. Hobsbawm, *Social Bandits and Primitive Rebels* (Glencoe, Ill.: Free Press, 1959). See, also, the editor's afterword to chapter 12, below.

# A NOTE TO THE READER

In addition to providing introductions to the first-person accounts in this book, the editor has included original narrative to connect the selections and offer critical commentary. A heavy line appears at the beginning and end of these sections, marking off the editor's words from those of the historical writers. Within the first-person accounts, of course, the editor's insertions appear in brackets.

# I

# THE GREAT FLOOD

## THE FAR WEST
## 1843–1863

| | |
|---|---|
| 1803 | · Louisiana Purchase |
| 1804–06 | · Lewis and Clark expedition |
| 1811 | · Founding of Astoria, a trading post of John Jacob Astor's American Fur Company, in Oregon Country |
| 1821 | · Opening of the Santa Fe Trail |
| 1834 | · First Protestant missionaries in Oregon |
| | · Indian Territory established on the Great Plains |
| 1836 | · Texas wins independence from Mexico |
| 1843 | · The Great Migration travels up the Oregon Trail |
| 1844 | · Presidential campaign focuses on dispute with Great Britain over the ownership of Oregon, with the slogan "Fifty-four-forty or fight!" |
| 1845 | · James Polk (Democrat) takes office as president |
| | · The Texas Republic annexed by the United States |
| 1846 | · Oregon dispute settled with Britain; boundary set at 49th parallel |
| 1846–48 | · Mexican War |
| 1847 | · Brigham Young establishes Salt Lake City, a Mormon colony, in Utah |
| | · Whitman Massacre in Oregon leads to Cayuse War |
| | · Zachary Taylor (Whig) takes office as president |
| 1848 | · Gold discovered in California; non-Indian population 15,000 |
| | · Oregon Territory organized by Congress |
| 1849 | · Mormons declare a vast area the (unrecognized) State of Deseret |
| 1850 | · Millard Fillmore (Whig) takes office as president |
| | · California becomes 31st state; non-Indian population 250,000 |
| | · Utah Territory organized by Congress; Brigham Young named governor |
| 1853 | · Franklin Pierce (Democrat) takes office as president |
| | · Washington Territory organized by Congress |
| | · California's non-Indian population 250,000 |
| 1855–56 | · Rogue River and Yakima wars in Oregon and Washington territories |
| 1857 | · James Buchanan (Democrat) takes office as president |
| | · U.S. troops march to Utah to suppress the Mormon Rebellion |
| 1858 | · Renewed Yakima War leads to Indian defeat |
| | · Butterfield stage company begins regular overland transportation from the East to the Pacific coast |
| 1859 | · Oregon becomes 33rd state |
| | · Comstock Lode of silver found in Nevada; Virginia City mining boom |

| | |
|---|---|
| **1861** | · Abraham Lincoln takes office as president; Civil War erupts |
| | · Nevada Territory organized by Congress |
| **1863** | · Idaho Territory organized by Congress |
| | · Nez Percé treaty creates Lapwai reservation |
| **1864** | · Nevada becomes 36th state |

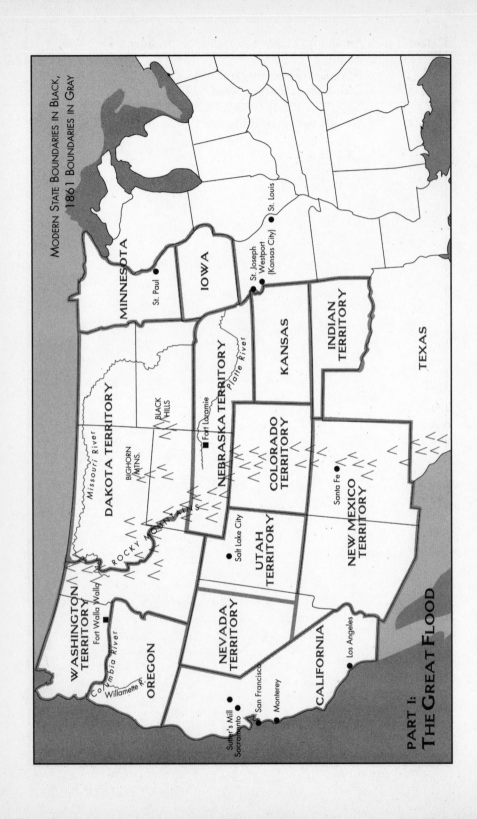

MODERN STATE BOUNDARIES IN BLACK,
1861 BOUNDARIES IN GRAY

MINNESOTA

St. Paul

IOWA

St. Louis

St. Joseph
Westport
(Kansas City)

DAKOTA TERRITORY

Missouri River

BLACK
HILLS

BIGHORN
MTNS.

Fort Laramie

Platte River

NEBRASKA TERRITORY

KANSAS

INDIAN
TERRITORY

ROCKY MOUNTAINS

COLORADO
TERRITORY

UTAH
TERRITORY

Salt Lake City

Santa Fe

NEW MEXICO
TERRITORY

TEXAS

WASHINGTON
TERRITORY

Fort Walla Walla

Columbia River

Willamette R.

OREGON

NEVADA
TERRITORY

CALIFORNIA

Los Angeles

Sutter's Mill
Sacramento

San Francisco

Monterey

PART I:
THE GREAT FLOOD

# 1
# THE OREGON TRAIL

Come, my tan-faced children
Follow well in order, get your weapons ready,
Have you your pistols? have you your sharp-edged axes?
Pioneers! O pioneers!

For we cannot tarry here,
We must march my darlings, we must bear the brunt of danger
We the youthful sinewy races, all the rest on us depend,
Pioneers, O pioneers!

—from "Pioneers! O Pioneers!" by Walt Whitman

The conquest of the West began not with the tramp of cavalry or the crack of a rifle, but with the creak of wagon wheels. The year was 1843, a time when hundreds of wagons rolled and wobbled out of the state of Missouri, bearing the weight of more than nine hundred men, women, and children bound for Oregon. That train of pioneers came to be known as the Great Migration—the first sizeable body of settlers to cross the Great Plains and settle in the Pacific Northwest.

They did not seem much like a conquering army: they had little or no sense that they were carrying out that grand historical mission that would soon be dubbed "Manifest Destiny"—the march of the United States to the Pacific shore. They barely resembled the "tan-faced children," the "youthful sinewy races" of Walt Whitman's poem; they were a poor, loosely organized set of farmers, wearing homespun clothing and carrying everything they owned in the backs of their wagons. Far from carrying the American republic west, they were actually leaving it far behind, as they marched toward a life of remoteness on rich, free land.

Nor were they even the first Anglo-Americans to journey from Missouri to the Northwest: the famous Oregon Trail they followed had been established by trappers working for the Hudson Bay and American Fur companies, and a handful of adventurers and missionaries who had already settled in Oregon's Willamette Valley. But those nine hundred were the beginning of an American *community* in the West—they had begun an infiltration of that vast, alien country, which they would remake in the

5

image of the nation they had left behind. Over the next several years, thousands more pioneers would follow in their wake, as wagon train after wagon train rolled up that broad path known as the Oregon Trail. To that extent, these first nine hundred were the truth in Whitman's poem: on them all the rest of Western history depended. They earned the title "the Great Migration."

The wilderness they entered was a far different place from what it would be just four decades later, in terms of borders alone. To the south, Texas was an independent nation whose American settlers had rebelled against Mexican rule a few years before. The Southwest (including California, Arizona, New Mexico, Nevada, Utah, and much of Colorado) was a province of Mexico, sprinkled with Hispanic ranchers and settlers. The Oregon country itself was disputed between Great Britain (which ruled Canada) and the United States.

The federal government held title to the vast country obtained in the Louisiana Purchase—the Great Plains and much of the Rocky Mountains—but it was an ownership on paper only. A decade earlier, the region had been officially designated the Permanent Indian Frontier. To one part of it, modern-day Oklahoma, President Andrew Jackson and an act of Congress had banished the so-called Five Civilized Tribes of Native Americans—the Cherokee, Chocktaw, Chickasaw, Creek, and Seminole—who were driven out of their homes in Georgia and the Gulf States along a route the Indians called the Trail of Tears. "It will separate the Indians from immediate contact with the settlements of whites," Jackson told Congress, "free them from the power of the States; enable them to pursue happiness in their own way and under their own rude institutions . . . and perhaps cause them gradually, through the influence of good counsels, to cast off their savage habits and become an interesting, Christian, and civilized community."

The Permanent Indian Frontier was also a tidy solution to the problem that the government simply did not have the resources to control the enormous western wilderness in the 1830s and '40s, or the numerous peoples who thrived there. The West was indeed a hostile, alien country, differing far more from the settled states of the East than France, for instance, did from Prussia. The many Native American cultures that flour-ished beyond the Missouri border arose from completely different beliefs about how humanity should live with nature, about the purpose of society, and the nature of community.

East of the town of Westport (the starting point of the Oregon Trail[1]), the land was divided into privately owned plots, and the owners had the right to do with it what they chose. Agriculture and development—the

---

[1] Westport was located within the modern-day limits of Kansas City, on Missouri's western border.

process of altering the landscape to make it more productive—was the basis of life in the United States; and so the earth was plowed under, mined into, and wrapped with fences. On the other side of Westport, an enormous variety of Native American cultures generally hunted and gathered, tapping the land but altering it far less drastically than did white farmers. Few in number, most Indian bands drew what they needed and moved on—thanks especially to the arrival of the horse in the early 1700s. Given this semi-nomadic lifestyle, the community took on tremendous importance—made even greater by the emphasis on warfare among most Plains tribes.[2]

The Great Migration shattered the Permanent Indian Frontier, and brought these contradictory cultures into direct conflict. Unlike the fur trappers of the passing era, the pioneers could reach no long-term accommodation with the Indians in the areas they settled. The conflict was not just one of a lack of space: it was a collision of irreconcilable social and economic systems. The settlers not only claimed possession of the land, they sought to change it; and, since they thought in terms of ownership, they often sought to "extinguish Indian title" to the lands they occupied—often through treaties the Native Americans could barely comprehend, or through outright violence, dragging in the U.S. Army as a result.

The pioneers, then, were the thin edge of the great wedge about to be driven into the Native American West. Under no orders from any official, with no plans other than making new homes for themselves, the first settlers unwittingly began the massive process of conquest—the remaking of the wilderness, the crushing of Native American independence, and the absorption of half a continent into American society. In the creaking of the ox-drawn wagon was a prophetic echo of ferocious fighting to come.

In 1846, a young scholar named Francis Parkman decided to observe the emigration to Oregon that had been initiated by the Great Migration three years earlier. He was a well-bred Boston boy, destined to become one of the first great American historians, and he left us a remarkable record of the great flood that was transforming the West. By the time he reached St. Louis, the Oregon Trail was booming—and Parkman captured it all, from the multicultural madhouse of western Missouri (where Mexicans, African Americans, Indians, and whites mingled on the frontier) to the hardships and epic, unspoiled beauty of the Great Plains.

The young writer had a keen, occasionally scathing eye. His account reveals, for example, the abiding stamp left on the West by the French Canadians, who had forged the western fur trade, and he offers glimpses of the flourishing commerce between the United States and Santa Fe (then a

---

[2] Some Indian nations, especially in the Southwest, were far more settled and engaged in agriculture.

city of Mexico). He also depicted the pioneers as quarreling, usually impoverished, and often thick-headed—a telling counterpoint to Whitman's romantic vision. Yet Parkman could not conceal his astonishment at their bravery and determination in making a new life in an unknown country.

At the height of his trip (which only reached to the fur-trading post of Fort Laramie, halfway along the Trail), he joined up with a very different community, a band of Oglala Sioux Indians. His time among them left him with a feeling little short of awe. Somehow, this son of New England achieved profound insight into the minds and lives of these people, just a couple of decades before a new wave of pioneers would move onto their lands and change their lives forever. His is a portrait to be remembered—especially when, in chapters to come, the Oglala ride forward to help lead the fight against the conquest of the West.

## Across the Great Plains
*by Francis Parkman, Jr.*

Last spring, 1846, was a busy season in the city of St. Louis. Not only were emigrants from every part of the country preparing for the journey to Oregon and California, but an unusual number of traders were making ready their wagons and outfits for Santa Fe. Many of the emigrants, especially those bound for California, were persons of wealth and standing. The hotels were crowded, and the gunsmiths and saddlers were kept constantly at work in providing arms and equipment for the different parties of travellers.

Almost every day steamboats were leaving the levee and passing up the Missouri, crowded with passengers. In one of these, the *Radnor*, my friend and relative, Quincy A. Shaw, and myself, left St. Louis on the 28th of April on a tour of curiosity and amusement to the Rocky Mountains. The boat was loaded until the water broke alternately over her guards. Her upper deck was covered with large wagons of a peculiar form for the Santa Fe trade, and her hold was crammed with goods for the same destination. There were also the equipment and provisions of a party of Oregon emigrants, a band of mules and horses, piles of saddles and harness, and a multitude of nondescript articles, indispensable on the prairies. . . .

The passengers on board the *Radnor* corresponded with her freight. In her cabin were Santa Fe traders, gamblers, speculators, and adventurers of various descriptions, and her steerage was crowded with Oregon emigrants, "mountain men," negroes, and a party of Kansas Indians who had been on a visit to St. Louis.

Thus laden, the boat struggled upward for seven or eight days against the rapid current of the Missouri, grating upon snags, and hanging for two or three hours at a time upon sandbars. We entered the mouth of the Missouri in a drizzling rain, but the weather soon became clear, and showed distinctly the broad and turbid river, with its eddies, its sandbars, its ragged islands, and forest-covered shores. . . .

In five or six days we began to see signs of the great western movement that was then taking place. Parties of emigrants, with their tents and wagons, would be encamped on open spots near the bank, on their way to the common rendezvous at Independence. On a rainy day, near sunset, we reached the landing of this place, which is situated some miles from the river, on the extreme frontier of Missouri. The scene was characteristic, for here were represented at one view the most remarkable features of this wild and enterprising region. On the muddy shore stood some thirty or forty dark slavish-looking Spaniards, gazing stupidly out from beneath their broad hats. They were attached to one of the Santa Fe companies, whose wagons were crowded together on the banks above. In the midst of these, crouching over a smoldering fire, was a group of Indians, belonging to a remote Mexican tribe.

One or two French hunters from the mountains, with their long hair and buckskin dress, were looking at the boat; and seated on a log close at hand were three men with rifles laying across their knees. The foremost of these, a tall, strong figure, with a clear blue eye and an open, intelligent face, might well represent that race of restless and intrepid pioneers whose axes and rifles have opened a path from the Alleghenies to the western prairies. He was on his way to Oregon, probably a more congenial field to him than any that now remained on this side of the great plains.

Early on the next morning we reached Kansas, about five hundred miles from the mouth of the Missouri. Here we landed, and leaving our equipment in charge of my good friend Colonel Chick, whose log house was the substitute for a tavern, we set out in a wagon for Westport, where we hoped to procure mules and horses for the journey. It was a remarkably fresh and beautiful May morning. The rich and luxuriant woods through which the miserable road conducted us, were lighted by the bright sunshine and enlivened by a multitude of birds. . . .

Westport was full of Indians, whose little shaggy ponies were tied by dozens along houses and fences. Sauks and Foxes, with shaved heads and painted faces, Shawnees and Delawares, fluttering in calico frocks and turbans, Wyondots dressed like white men, and a few wretched Kansas wrapped in old blankets, were strolling about the streets, or lounging in and out of the shops and houses. . . .

The emigrants . . . were encamped on the prairie about eight or ten miles distant, to the number of a thousand or more, and new parties were constantly passing out from Independence to meet them. They were in great confusion, holding meetings, passing resolutions, drawing up regulations, but unable to unite in the choice of leaders to conduct them across the prairie.

Being at leisure one day, I rode over to Independence. The town was crowded. A multitude of shops had sprung up to furnish the emigrants and Santa Fe traders with necessaries for their journey, and there was an incessant hammering and banging from a dozen blacksmiths' sheds, where the heavy wagons were being repaired and the horses and oxen shod. The streets were thronged with men, horses, and mules. While I was in the town, a train of emigrant wagons from Illinois passed through, to join the camp on the prairie, and stopped in the principal street. A multitude of healthy children's faces were peeping out from under the covers of the wagons. Here and there a buxom damsel was seated on horseback, holding over her sunburnt face an old umbrella or parasol, once gaudy enough, but now miserably faded. The men, very sober-looking countrymen, stood about their oxen, and as I passed I noticed three old fellows, who with their long whips in their hands were zealously discussing the doctrine of regeneration. The emigrants, however, are not all of this stamp. Among them are some of the vilest outcasts in the country.

I have often perplexed myself to divine the various motives that give impulse to this strange migration, but whatever they may be, whether an insane hope of a better condition in life, or a desire of shaking off restraints of law and society, or mere restlessness, certain it is, that multitudes bitterly repent the journey, and after they have reached the land of promise, are happy enough to escape from it. . . .

Our preparation being now complete, we attempted one fine morning to commence our journey. The first step was an unfortunate one. No sooner were our animals put in harness, than the shaft mule reared and plunged, burst ropes and straps, and nearly flung the cart into the Missouri. . . . This foretaste of prairie experience was very soon followed by another. Westport was scarcely out of sight when we encountered a deep muddy gully, of a species that afterward became but too familiar to us; and here for the space of an hour or more the cart stuck fast. . . .

Escaping from the mudhole . . . we pursued our way for some time along the narrow track, in the checkered sunshine and shadow of the woods, till at length, issuing forth into the broad light, we left behind the farthest outskirts of that great forest, that once spread unbroken from the western plains to the shore of the Atlantic. Looking over an intervening belt of shrubbery, we saw the green, ocean-like expanse of prairie, stretching swell over swell to the horizon. . . .

Foremost [among us] rode Henry Chatillon, our guide and hunter, a fine athletic figure, mounted on a hardy gray Wyondot pony. He wore a white blanket coat, a broad hat of felt, moccasins, and pantaloons of deerskin, ornamented along the seams with rows of long fringes. His knife was stuck in his belt, his bullet pouch and powder horn hung at his side, and his rifle lay before him, resting against the high pommel of his saddle—which, like all his equipment, had seen hard service and was much the worse for wear.

Shaw followed close, mounted on a little sorrel horse, and leading a larger animal by a rope. His outfit, which resembled mine, had been provided with a view to use rather than ornament. It consisted of a plain, black, Spanish saddle, with holsters of heavy pistols, a blanket rolled up behind it, and the trail rope attached to his horse's neck hanging coiled in front. He carried a double-barreled smooth-bore, while I boasted a rifle of some fifteen pounds weight. At that time, our attire, though far from elegant, bore some marks of civilization, and offered a very favorable contrast to the inimitable shabbiness of our appearance on the return journey. A red flannel shirt, belted around the waist like a frock, then constituted our upper garment; moccasins had supplanted our failing boots; and the remaining essential portion of our attire consisted of an extraordinary article, manufactured by a squaw out of smoked buckskin.

Our muleteer, Delorier, brought up the rear with his cart, wading ankle-deep in the mud, alternately puffing at his pipe, and ejaculating in his prairie patois: "Sacre enfant de grace!" as one of the mules would seem to recoil before some abyss of unusual profundity. . . .

We were in all four men with eight animals, for besides the spare horses led by Shaw and myself, an additional mule was driven along as a reserve in case of accident. . . .

On the evening of the 23rd of May we encamped near its [St. Joseph's Trail] junction with the old legitimate trail of the Oregon emigrants. We had ridden long that afternoon, trying in vain to find food and water, until at length we saw the sunset sky reflected from a pool encircled by bushes and a rock or two. The water lay in the bottom of a hollow, the smooth prairie gracefully rising in ocean-like swells on every side. We pitched our tents by it—not, however, before the keen eye of Henry Chatillon had discerned some unusual object upon the faintly defined outline of the distant swell. But in the moist, hazy atmosphere of the evening nothing could be clearly distinguished.

As we lay around the fire after supper, a low and distant sound, strange enough amid the loneliness of the prairie, reached our ears: peals of laughter and the faint voices of women. For eight days we had not encountered a human being, and this singular warning of their vicinity had an effect extremely wild and impressive. About dark, a sallow-faced fellow descended the hill on horseback and, splashing through the pool, rode up to the tents. He was enveloped in a huge cloak, and his broad felt hat was weeping about his ears with the drizzling moisture of the evening. Another followed, a stout, square-built, intelligent-looking man, who announced himself the leader of the emigrant party, encamped a mile in advance of us. About twenty wagons, he said, were with him; the rest of his party were on the other side of the Big Blue [River], waiting for a woman who was in the pains of childbirth and quarrelling meanwhile among themselves.

These were the first emigrants that we had overtaken, although we had found abundant and melancholy traces of their progress throughout the whole course of the journey. Sometimes we passed the grave of one who had sickened and died on the way. The earth was usually torn up, and covered thickly with wolf-tracks. Some had escaped this violation. One morning, a piece of plank, standing upright on the summit of a grassy hill, attracted our notice, and riding up to it we found the following words very roughly traced upon it, apparently by a piece of red-hot iron:

MARY ELLIS
DIED MAY 7TH, 1845
AGED TWO MONTHS

Such tokens were of common occurrence. Nothing could speak more for the hardihood, or rather infatuation, of the adventurers, or the sufferings that await them upon their journey.

We were late in breaking up our camp on the following morning, and scarcely had we ridden a mile when we saw, far in advance of us, drawn against the horizon, a line of objects stretching at regular intervals along the level edge of the prairie. An intervening swell soon hid them from sight, until, ascending it a quarter of an hour after, we saw close before us the emigrant caravan, with its heavy white wagons creeping on in their slow procession, with a large drove of cattle following behind. Half a dozen yellow-visaged Missourians, mounted on horseback, were cursing and shouting among them; their lank angular proportions enveloped in brown homespun, evidently cut and tailored by the hands of a domestic female tailor. As we approached, they greeted us with the polished salutation: "How are ye, boys? Are ye for Oregon or California?"

As we pushed rapidly past the wagons, children's faces were thrust out from the white coverings to look at us; while the care-worn, thin-featured matron, or the buxom girl, seated in front suspended the knitting on which most of them were engaged to stare at us with wondering curiosity. By the side of each wagon stalked the proprietor, urging on his patient oxen, who shouldered heavily along, inch by inch on their interminable journey. It was easy to see that fear and dissension prevailed among them. Some of the men—but these, with one exception, were bachelors—looked wistfully upon us as we rode lightly and swiftly past, and then impatiently at their own lumbering wagons and heavy-gaited oxen. Others were unwilling to advance at all, until the party they had left behind should have rejoined them. Many were murmuring against the leader they had chosen, and wished to depose him, and this discontent was fomented by some ambitious spirits who had hopes of succeeding in his place. The women were divided between regrets for the homes they had left and apprehension of the deserts and the savages before them.

We soon left them far behind, and fondly hoped that we had taken a final leave; but unluckily our companions' wagon stuck so long in a deep muddy ditch, that before it was extricated the van of the emigrant caravan appeared again, descending a ridge close at hand. Wagon after wagon plunged through the mud; and as it was nearly noon, and the place promised shade and water, we saw with much gratification that they were resolved to encamp. Soon the wagons were wheeled into a circle; the cattle were grazing over the meadow, and the men, with sour, sullen faces, were looking about for wood and water.

They seemed to meet with but indifferent success. As we left the ground, I saw a tall, slouching fellow, with the nasal accent of "down east," contemplating the contents of his tin cup, which he had just filled with water. "Look here, you," said he, "it's chock full of animals!" The cup, as he held it out, exhibited in fact an extraordinary variety and profusion of animal and vegetable life. . . .

We had passed the more toilsome and monotonous part of our journey, but four hundred miles still intervened between us and Fort Laramie—and to reach that point cost us the travel of three additional weeks. During the whole of this time, we were passing up the center of a long narrow sandy plain, reaching like an outstretched belt nearly to the Rocky Mountains. Two lines of sand hills, broken often into the wildest and most fantastic forms, flanked the valley at the distance of a mile or two on the right and left; while beyond them lay a barren, trackless waste—The Great American Desert—extending for hundreds of miles to the Arkansas [River] on the one side and the Missouri on the other.

Before and behind us, the level monotony of the plain was unbroken as far as the eye could reach. Sometimes it glared in the sun, an expanse of hot, bare sand; sometimes it was veiled by long coarse grass. Huge skulls and whitening bones of buffalo were scattered everywhere; the ground was tracked by myriads of them, and often covered with the circular indentations where the bulls had wallowed in the hot weather. From every gorge and ravine, opening from the hills, descended deep, well-worn paths, where the buffalo issue twice a day in regular procession down to drink in the Platte. The river itself runs through the midst, a thin sheet of rapid, turbid water, half a mile wide and scarce two feet deep. Its low banks, for the most part without a bush or a tree, are of loose sand, with which the stream is so charged that it grates on the teeth in drinking. The naked landscape is of itself dreary and monotonous enough, and yet the wild beasts and wild men that frequent the valley of the Platte make it a scene of interest and excitement to the traveller. . . .

[Upon finally reaching Fort Laramie,] we were met at the gate, but by no means cordially welcomed. Indeed, we seemed objects of some distrust and suspicion, until Henry Chatillon explained that we were not traders, and we, in confirmation, handed to the *bourgeois* a letter of introduction from his principals. He took it, turned it upside down, and tried hard to read it, but his literary accomplishments not being adequate to the task, he applied for relief to the clerk, a sleek, smiling Frenchman named Montalon. . . .

Our arrangements made, we stepped out to the balcony [of the room assigned to them] to take a more leisurely survey of the long-looked-for haven at which we had arrived at last. Beneath us was the square area surrounded by little rooms, or rather cells, which opened up on it. These were devoted to various purposes, but served chiefly for the accommodation of the men employed at the fort, or of the equally numerous squaws whom they were allowed to maintain in it. Opposite to us rose the blockhouse above the gateway. It was adorned with a figure which even now haunts my memory: a horse at full speed, daubed upon the boards with red paint, and exhibiting a degree of skill which might rival that displayed by the Indians in executing similar designs upon their robes and lodges. A busy scene was enacting in the area. The wagons of Vaskiss, an old trader, were about to set out for a remote post in the mountains, and the Canadians were going through their preparations with all possible bustle, while here and there an Indian stood looking on with imperturbable gravity.

Fort Laramie is one of the posts established by the American Fur Company, who well-nigh monopolize the Indian trade of this whole region.[3] Here their officials rule with an absolute sway. The arm of the United States has little force, for when we were there the extreme outposts of her troops were about seven hundred miles to the eastward. The little fort is built of bricks dried in the sun, and externally is of an oblong form, with bastions of clay in the form of ordinary blockhouses, at two of the corners. The walls are about fifteen feet high, and surmounted by a slender palisade. . . .

I had come into the country almost exclusively with a view of observing the Indian character. Having from childhood felt a curiosity about this subject, and having failed completely to gratify it by reading, I resolved to have recourse to observation. I wished to satisfy myself with regard to the position of the Indians among the races of men; the vices and the virtues that have sprung from their innate character and from their modes of life, their government, their superstitions, and their domestic situation. To accomplish my purpose it was necessary to live in the midst of them, and

[3] The American Fur Company was founded by John Jacob Astor in 1808, when beaver pelts were in tremendous demand. By the 1830s it did indeed monopolize trade with the Indians in the northern Rockies—though the near-extinction of the beaver, along with declining demand, steadily made buffalo skins the most sought-after commodity.

become, as it were, one of them. I proposed to join a village, and make myself an inmate of one of their lodges. . . .

We resolved on no account to miss [the widely rumored] rendezvous [of Oglala and other Sioux Indians] at "La Bonte's Camp." Our plan was to leave Delorier at the fort in charge of our equipage and the better part of our horses, while we took with us nothing but our weapons and the worst animals we had. . . .

[Parkman and his guide, Henry Chatillon, travelled to the spot known as La Bonte's Camp to wait the arrival of the Sioux—all members of the western tribes of that nation, known in their own language as the Lakota. A war between the Oglala—a Lakota tribe—and the Snake Indians was rumored to be impending, and the Sioux were said to be headed for La Bonte's Camp to unite for the planned offensive. The two men waited for several days until Chatillon saw the first signs of the Native Americans.]

"There comes Bull Bear," said Henry Chatillon, as we sat on the grass for dinner. Looking up, we saw several horsemen coming over the neighboring hill, and in a moment four stately young men rode up and dismounted. One of them was Bull Bear, or Mahto-Tatonka, a compound name which he inherited from his father, the most powerful chief in the Oglala band. One of his brothers and two other young men accompanied him. We shook hands with the visitors, and when we had finished our meal—for this is the orthodox manner of entertaining Indians, even the best of them—we handed to each a tin cup of coffee and a biscuit, at which they ejaculated from the bottom of their throats, "How! How!" a monosyllable by which an Indian contrives to express half the emotions that he is susceptible of. Then we lighted the pipe and passed it to them as they squatted on the ground.

"Where is the village?"

"There," said Mahto-Tatonka, pointing southward, "it will come in two days."

"Will they go to war?"

"Yes." . . .

For that and several succeeding days, Mahto-Tatonka and his friends remained our guests. They devoured the relics of our meals; they filled the pipe for us, and also helped us to smoke it. Sometimes they stretched themselves side by side in the shade, indulging in raillery and practical jokes, ill-becoming the dignity of brave and aspiring warriors, such as two of them in reality were. . . .

[Four days] passed, and Indians began rapidly to come in. Parties of two or three or more would ride up and silently seat themselves on the grass. The fourth day came at last, when about noon horsemen suddenly appeared into view on the summit of the neighboring ridge. They descended, and behind them followed a wild procession, hurrying in haste and disorder down the hill and over the plain below. Horses, mules, dogs, heavily burdened travaux, mounted warriors, squaws walking amid the throng, and a host of children.

For a full half-hour they continued to pour down, and keeping directly to the bend of the stream, within a furlong of us, they soon assembled there, a dark and confused throng, until, as if by magic, a hundred and fifty lodges sprung up. On a sudden the lonely plain was transformed into the site of a miniature city. Countless horses were soon grazing over the meadows around us, and the whole prairie was animated by restless figures careering on horseback, or sedately stalking in their long white robes. . . .

The Dakota (I prefer this national designation to the unmeaning French name, Sioux[4]) range over a vast territory, from the river St. Peter's[5] to the Rocky Mountains themselves. They are divided into several independent bands, united under no central government, and acknowledging no common head. The same language, usages, and superstitions form the sole bond between them. They do not unite even in their wars. The bands of the east fight the Ojibwas on the Upper [Great] Lakes; those of the west make incessant war upon the Snake Indians in the Rocky Mountains.

As the whole people is divided into bands, so each band is divided into villages. Each village has a chief, who is honored and obeyed only so far as his personal qualities may command respect and fear. Sometimes he is a mere nominal chief; sometimes his authority is little short of absolute, and his fame and influence reach beyond even his own village, so that the whole band to which he belongs is ready to knowledge him as their head. This was, a few years since, the case with the Oglala. Courage, address, and enterprise may raise any warrior to the highest honor, especially if he be the son of a former chief, or a member of a numerous family to support him and avenge his quarrels; but when he has reached the dignity of chief, and the old men and warriors by a peculiar ceremony have formally installed him, let it not be imagined that he assumes any outward semblances of rank and honor. He knows too well on how frail a tenure he holds his station. He must conciliate his uncertain subjects. Many a man in the village lives better, owns more squaws and more horses, and goes better clad than he. . . . Very seldom does it happen, at least among these western bands,

[4] The many names of the Sioux can be confusing. "Sioux" is a French corruption of the Ojibwa word for "enemy." It will appear frequently in this book, since it is convenient and remains an accepted term. The Sioux were divided into three branches, each composed of separate tribes (such as the Oglala): the Santee, the Minnesota (eastern) branch of the Dakota; the Yankton and Yanktonai, the central branch of the Dakota, who lived east of the Missouri River; and the Lakota, or western branch, also called the Teton Sioux. The Lakota speak a different dialect from the central and eastern Sioux, but they have often been included in the term "Dakota".

[5] Now known as the Minnesota River. The Sioux were forced out of central and northern Minnesota by the Ojibwa in the eighteenth century, adding to a westward pressure that resulted in the Lakota driving the Crow out of the Black Hills and the Powder River country probably in the early nineteenth century.

that a chief attains much power, unless he is the head of a numerous family. Frequently the village is principally made up of his relatives and descendants, and the wandering community assumes much of the patriarchal character. A people so loosely united, torn, too, with rankling feuds and jealousies, can have little power or efficiency.

The western Dakota have no fixed habitations. Hunting and fighting, they wander incessantly, through summer and winter. Some are following the herds of the buffalo over the waste of prairie; others are traversing the Black Hills, thronging, on horseback and on foot, through the dark gulfs and somber gorges, beneath the vast splintering precipices, and merging at last upon the Parks, those beautiful but most perilous hunting grounds.

The buffalo supplies them with almost all the necessaries of life; with habitations, food, clothing, and fuel; with strings for their bows, with thread, cordage, and trail ropes for their horses, with coverings for their saddles, with vessels to hold water, with boats to cross streams, with glue, and with the means of purchasing all that they desire from the traders. When the buffalo are extinct, they too must dwindle away.

War is the breath of their nostrils. Against most of the neighboring tribes they cherish a deadly, rancorous hatred, transmitted from father to son, and inflamed by constant aggression and retaliation. Many times a year, in every village, the Great Spirit is called upon, fasts are made, the war parade is celebrated, and the warriors go out by handfuls at a time against the enemy. This fierce and evil spirit awakens their most eager aspirations, and calls forth their greatest energies. . . . The Dakota warrior can sometimes boast of heroic virtues. It is very seldom that distinction and influence are attained among them by any other course than that of arms. . . .

One morning we were summoned to the lodge of an old man, in good truth the Nestor of his tribe. We found him half sitting, half reclining on a pile of buffalo robes. His long hair, jet black even now, though he had seen some eighty winters, hung on either side of his thin features. Those most conversant with Indians in their homes will scarcely believe me when I affirm that there was dignity in his countenance and mien. His gaunt but symmetrical frame did not more clearly exhibit the wreck of bygone strength, than did his dark, wasted features, still prominent and commanding, bear the stamp of mental energies. . . . Opposite the patriarch was his nephew, the young aspirant Mahto-Tatonka; and besides these, there were one or two women in the lodge.

The old man's story is peculiar, and singularly illustrative of a superstitious custom that prevails in full force among many of the Indian tribes. He was one of a powerful family, renowned for their warlike exploits. When a very young man, he submitted to the singular rite to which most of the tribe subject themselves before entering upon life. He painted his face black; then seeking out a cavern in a sequestered part of the Black Hills, he lay for several days, fasting and praying to the Great Spirit. In the dreams and visions produced by his weakened and excited state, he fancied, like all Indians, that he saw supernatural revelations. Again and again the form of an antelope appeared before him. The antelope is the graceful peace spirit of the Oglala, but seldom is it that such a gentle visitor presents itself during the initiatory fasts of their young men. The terrible grizzly bear, the divinity of war, usually appears to fire them with martial ardor and thirst for renown.

At length the antelope spoke. He told the young dreamer that he was not to follow the path of war, that a life of peace and tranquility was marked out for him, that thence forward he was to guide the people by his counsels and protect them from the evils of their own feuds and dissensions. Others were to gain renown by fighting the enemy; but greatness of a different kind was in store for him.

The visions beheld during the period of this fast usually determine the whole course of the dreamer's life, for an Indian is bound by iron superstitions. From that time, Le Borgne, which was the only name by which we know him, abandoned all thoughts of war, and devoted himself to the labors of peace. He told his vision to his people. They honored his commission and respected him in his novel capacity.

A far different man was his [late] brother, Mahto-Tatonka, who had transmitted his names, his features, and many of his characteristic qualities to his son [of the same name, introduced earlier]. He was the father of Henry Chatillon's squaw, a circumstance which proved of some advantage to us, as securing for us the friendship of a family perhaps the most distinguished and powerful in the whole Oglala band. Mahto-Tatonka, in his rude way, was a hero. No chief could vie with him in warlike renown, or in power over his people. He had a fearless spirit, and a most impetuous and inflexible resolution. His will was law. He was politic and sagacious, and with true Indian craft he always befriended the whites, well knowing that he might thus reap great advantages for himself and his adherents.

When he had resolved on any course of conduct, he would pay to the warriors the empty compliment of calling them together to deliberate upon it, and when their debates were over, he would quietly state his own opinion, which no one ever disputed. The consequences of thwarting his imperious will were too formidable to be encountered. Woe to those who incurred his displeasure! He would strike them or stab them on the spot; and this act, which if attempted by any other chief would instantly have cost him his life, the awe inspired by his name enabled him to repeat again and again with impunity. In a community where, from immemorial time, no man has acknowledged any law but his own will, Mahto-Tatonka, by the force of his dauntless resolution, raised himself to power little short of despotic.

His haughty career came at last to an end. He had a host of enemies only waiting for their opportunity of revenge, and our old [Indian] friend

Smoke, in particular, together with all his kinsmen, hated him most cordially. Smoke sat one day in his lodge, in the midst of his own village, when Mahto-Tatonka entered it alone, and approaching the dwelling of his enemy, called on him in a loud voice to come out if he were a man and fight. Smoke would not move. At this, Mahto-Tatonka proclaimed him a coward and an old woman, and standing close to the entrance of the lodge, stabbed the chief's best horse, which was picketed there. Smoke was daunted, and even this insult failed to call him forth. Mahto-Tatonka moved haughtily away; all made way for him, but his hour of reckoning was near.

One hot day, five or six years ago, numerous lodges of Smoke's kinsmen were gathered around some of the Fur Company's men, who were trading in various articles with them, whiskey among the rest. Mahto-Tatonka was also there with a few of his people. As he lay in his own lodge, a fray arose between his adherents and the kinsmen of his enemy. The war-whoop was raised, bullets and arrows began to fly, and the camp was in confusion. The chief sprang up, and rushing in a fury from the lodge, shouted to the combatants on both sides to cease. Instantly—for the attack was preconcerted—came the reports of two or three guns, and the twanging of a dozen bows, and the savage hero, mortally wounded, pitched forward headlong to the ground. Rouleau was present, and told me the particulars. The tumult became general, and was not quelled until several had fallen on both sides. When we were in the country the feud between the two families was still rankling, and not likely soon to cease.

Thus died Mahto-Tatonka, but he left behind him a goodly army of descendants to perpetuate his renown and avenge his fate. . . . Of these, our visitor, young Mahto-Tatonka, was the eldest, and some reported him as likely to succeed to his father's honors. Though he appeared not more than twenty-one years old, he had oftener struck the enemy, stolen more horses and more squaws than any young man in the village. We of the civilized world are not apt to attach much credit to the latter species of exploit; but horse-stealing is well known as an avenue to distinction on the prairies, and the other kind of depredation is esteemed equally meritorious. Not that the act can confer fame from its own intrinsic merits. Anyone can steal a squaw, and if he chooses afterward to make an adequate present to her rightful proprietor, his vengeance falls asleep, and all danger from that quarter is averted. Yet this is esteemed but a pitiful and mean-spirited transaction. The danger is averted, but the glory of the achievement also is lost.

Mahto-Tatonka proceeded after a more gallant and dashing fashion. Out of several dozen squaws whom he had stolen, he could boast that he had never paid for one, but snapping his fingers in the face of the injured husband had defied the extremity of his indignation, and no one yet had dared to lay the finger of violence upon him.

He was following close in the footsteps of his father. The young men and the young squaws, each in their way, admired him. The one would always follow him to war, and he was esteemed to have unrivalled charm in the eyes of the other. . . . Though he found such favor in the eyes of the fair, he was no dandy. As among us, those of highest worth and breeding are most simple in manner and attire, so our aspiring young friend was indifferent to the gaudy trappings and ornaments of his companions. He was content to rest his chances of success upon his own warlike merits. . . .

See him now in the hour of his glory, when at sunset the whole village empties itself to behold him, for tomorrow their favorite young partisan goes out against the enemy. His superb head-dress is adorned with a crest of the war-eagle's feathers, rising in a waving ridge above his brow and sweeping far behind him. His round white shield hangs at his breast, with feathers radiating from the center like a star. His quiver is at his back; his tall lance in his hand, the iron point flashing against the declining sun, while the long scalp-locks of his enemies flutter from the shaft. Thus, gorgeous as a champion in his panoply, he rides round and round within the great circle of lodges, balancing with beautiful buoyancy to the free movements of his warhorse, while with a sedate brow he sings his song to the Great Spirit. Young rival warriors look askance at him; vermillion-cheeked girls gaze in admiration; boys whoop a scream in a thrill of delight; and old women yell forth his name and proclaim his praises from lodge to lodge. . . .

I recall these scenes with a mixed feeling of pleasure and pain. At this time, I was so reduced by illness that I could seldom walk without reeling like a drunken man, and when I rose from my seat upon the ground the landscape suddenly grew dim before my eyes. . . . I used to lie languid and dreamy before our tent, and muse on the past and the future, and when most overcome with lassitude, my eyes turned always toward the distant Black Hills. There is a spirit of energy and vigor in mountains, and they impart it to all who approach their presence. At that time I did not know how many dark superstitions and gloomy legends are associated with those mountains in the minds of the Indians, but I felt an eager desire to penetrate their hidden recesses, to explore the awful chasms and preci-pices, the black torrents, the silent forests that I fancied were concealed there.

---

TO PARKMAN'S LASTING disappointment, the band he joined never went to war during his stay with them; perhaps they failed to reach a consensus, or perhaps they were following the advice of Le Borgne, the old man of peace who was his host. But this opinionated young writer man-aged to absorb something of the Oglala character: the pride, disunity, love of war, and reverence for the Black Hills that would later place this tribe at the center of wars yet to come. He even glimpsed a foreshadowing of the Lakota's impending apocalypse, as he mused upon their utter dependence on the buffalo and the mystical allure of the Black Hills. Only thirty years later, the temptation of the Hills would spark the final conflict for Parkman's proud hosts—the climax of almost two centuries of dramatic change in Lakota life.

Europeans sparked the first great transformation by introducing the horse to Central America in the 1500s. By the eighteenth century, horses had spread from Mexico to the Great Plains; from the Comanches to the Lakota, Plains Indians adopted a horse-centered culture with astonishing speed. Before, the buffalo provided only a supplemental source of food, clothing, and supplies: it was simply too hard to hunt on foot, and some crop raising was often necessary. The arrival of the horse, however, allowed many Indians to discard their limited agriculture and take up pure hunting nomadism. Warfare became far-reaching: the Sioux quickly expanded west from Minnesota in the 1700s, occupying the Black Hills and carrying their battles all the way to the Rocky Mountains. Around 1830, the Cheyennes split into two tribes; the southern branch conducted a trek of hundreds of miles, meeting and fighting new enemies.

The horse, then, was a recent and mixed blessing. On one hand, it probably increased the friction between scattered bands, and ensured that warrior values would occupy the center of the cultures of most Plains tribes. It also made them completely dependent on the buffalo for survival, as Parkman observed. On the other hand, the generations of Native Americans raised on horseback acquired the mobility and fighting skills necessary to fiercely resist the U.S. Army, in battles looming only a decade or two over the horizon—battles destined to end in a climactic struggle for the Black Hills.

Meanwhile, the emigrants continued their journey west. All were bound for the Pacific coast; the Rocky Mountains and Great Plains would remain unsettled by whites for years to come. Some of the settlers made for California, a newly popular destination, though still a Mexican province. Still more made for Oregon, following in the footsteps of the Great Migration.

One of the nine hundred who made that original, epic journey of 1843 was a young boy named Jesse A. Applegate (whose uncle of the same name was a prominent leader of the Great Migration, along with young Jesse's father, Lindsay, and other uncle, Charles). In the passage that follows, young Applegate recalls the end of his six-month trip across the continent. Tracing the path taken by many later emigrants, he describes his party's arrival at Fort Walla Walla (in what was then the eastern Oregon country), their journey down the Columbia River, and his family's first years in the wild Willamette valley. Applegate tells his tale simply and directly, recalling the wild country, the scattered traders and posts of the Hudson Bay

Company, the early missionaries, and the ingenuity of the pioneers as they made a life in a world without manufactured goods or trade.

As a young boy, he had no idea that the trek of his fellow settlers would land them in the center of a fierce dispute between Great Britain and the United States over ownership of the vaguely defined territory of Oregon—a dispute that became a central issue of the 1844 presidential campaign.[6] Nor did he know that his ragged band of pioneers carried the hopes of millions of expansion-minded Americans, who believed the nation should extend all the way to the Pacific Ocean. In 1845, less than two years after the Great Migration reached Oregon, journalist John L. O'Sullivan coined the phrase "Manifest Destiny" to capture the idea that the entire continent belonged to the United States by right. The expression became the magic spell of American politics, as a proud and restless people demanded the Pacific coast for their own.

Most of this tumult passed by the few thousands who actually went through the hardships of the journey west. The difficulties of life in Oregon demanded their full attention. But little Jesse A. Applegate was well aware of a conflict much closer to home: the tensions between his fellow whites and the Indians, foreshadowing brutal events only a few years off.

## Settling Oregon
*by Jesse A. Applegate*

A train of wagons with their once white, now torn, grease- and dust-stained covers, parked on the bank of the Columbia River was a novel spectacle. Such had never been seen there before. The faithful oxen, now sore-necked, sore-footed, and jaded, which had marched week after week, and month after month, drawing those wagons with their loads from the Missouri River to the Columbia, had done their task, and were unhitched for the last time—and I hope all recovered from their fatigue and lived to enjoy a long rest on the banks, "Where rolls the Oregon and hears no sound save his own dashing."

Mr. McKinlay was in charge of the post of Walla Walla, and was very kind and accommodating to the emigrants. There were many Indians here; bucks, squaws, and papooses. . . . The Indians' tribal names were Cayuse, Nez Percés, and Walla Walla, and we had many visitors from all these tribes. I think there was no hostile feeling among these people

6 In 1846, the conflict over the ownership of Oregon was resolved peacefully, as the U.S.–Canadian boundary was extended to the Pacific along the same line it followed from Minnesota west.

against us, but some of the emigrants were prejudiced against Indians of whatever kind, and were annoyed by the familiarity assumed by them in their intercourse with whites. . . . One of our young men, who did not like Indians, gave a buck a push to get him out of his way, and when the Indian resisted, seized a brand from the fire and struck him a severe blow on the shoulders. I heard the blow and saw the sparks fly. The blow was probably aimed at the Indian's head, but he ducked and saved his cranium. This somewhat rough affair, coming up so unexpectedly, created some excitement in the camp for a moment, but it was soon over. . . .

Probably the next day, the commander of the fort, McKinlay, visited our camp and remained quite a while. I understood afterwards that he invited, or rather advised, us to sleep in the fort, as the Indians were not well disposed toward us. . . .

During the time we remained at Walla Walla, probably two weeks, the men were busy sawing lumber and building small boats. They called them skiffs, and one of average size would carry a family of eight or ten persons. The lumber was sawed by hand with a pit saw or whip saw, from timber that had drifted to that place when the river was very high. To carry out the plan of descending the Columbia River to the Willamette country in those small boats, it was, of course, necessary to leave the wagons and cattle behind. The cattle and horses were branded with the Hudson Bay Company's brand, H.B., and the property was understood to be under the protection of that company.

I well remember our start down the river, and how I enjoyed riding in the boat, the movement of which was like a grape vine swing. Shoving out from the Walla Walla canoe landing about the first of November, our little fleet of boats began the voyage down the great River of the West. Whirlpools looking like deep basins in the river, the lapping, splashing, and rolling of the waves, crested with foam sometimes when the wind was strong, alarmed me for a day or two on the start. But I soon learned that the motion of the boat became more lively and gyratory, rocking from side to side, leaping from wave to wave, or sliding down into a trough and then mounting with perfect ease to the crest of a wave, dashing the spray into our faces when we were in rough water, the sound of rapids and the sight of foam and white caps ahead occasioned only pleasant anticipation. Often when the current was strong, the men would rest on their oars and allow the boats to be swept along by the current. . . .

Robert Shortes met us at the Dalles with supplies. He came in a canoe with two Indians. He lived at Tumchuk, now Oregon City. . . . Shortes did not come as a speculator, but as a "friend indeed to friends in need." He had made his home with the Applegate families before he came to Oregon. He had written letters from Oregon to his friends, advising them to come to the new country, giving as reasons the healthful climate and mild winters of the northwest coast. His letters were published in the newspapers and widely read with that deep interest we always feel when we hear tidings of a better land. The Oregon Fever followed.

When we passed the Cascades the water was at the lowest stage and the water covered only a part of the river bed. . . . Getting past this obstacle was called the Portage of the Cascades. The boats had to be drawn or carried over the rocks a considerable distance. . . .

When the boats had been launched below the Cascades we had navigated the river from old Fort Walla Walla to the head of navigation, and had an open and safe waterway to the sea. . . .

Dr. McLoughlin, of the Hudson Bay Company at Vancouver, had not known of our arrival until he visited our camp [at the mouth of the Columbia]. . . . The Doctor invited the immigrants to visit him at the fort, and some of them did so. He was a valuable friend to the needy. . . .

We were at this camp one day, and discovered that the river rose and fell two feet. We had reached tidewater and were on the western margin of the continent. Our small fleet of boats had kept within supporting distance of each other on the way down the river, but there was a parting of the ways.

The Applegate families, with the Straits and the Naylors, started across the river from the camp at Vancouver intending to go direct to the mouth of the Willamette River. But there came on such a storm of wind and rain it was thought best to land the boats at Sauvie's Island, where two or three deserted houses accorded shelter. . . .

The Straits and Naylors parted company with us at Sauvie's Island, where we remained three or four days. Passing across from Sauvie's Island and near a low point of land on our left, our boats entered the mouth of the Willamette River. Continuing up the stream we passed the place where Strait and Naylor had established a camp on the west bank of the river. They called the place Linnton. . . .

Where should we locate? was the all-absorbing topic of conversation at [our] camp in the woods. It seemed to be difficult to decide where to settle down in such a vast unappropriated wilderness. We were then actually encamped on the site of the city of Portland, but there was no prophet with us to tell of the beautiful city that was to take the place of that gloomy forest.

From this camp we were two days getting up the river to Tumchuck, now Oregon City. . . . The boats were hauled around the falls to the river above by a French Canadian with one yoke of long-horned steers. We made camp on the east shore nearly opposite the main cataract. There were less than a dozen houses at Tumchuk, including a tinshop, blacksmith shop, sawmill, and probably a grist mill. We spent one night at this place. In the morning two or three Kanakas helped to launch the boats above the falls and to clear the rapids. In the evening of the same day we landed at Champoeg . . .

From Champoeg we traveled by land. The baggage was hauled on a cart drawn by one yoke of oxen. I think the cart was hired from a French settler. Mrs. Charles Applegate and four small children rode in the cart while the rest of our party followed on foot. All day we traveled and it was quite dark when we saw a light. The light was in a window at Doctor White's house. . . .

From Doctor White's house we had to travel another mile and our long journey was ended. We called this place the Old Mission. It was at this place that the first Methodist mission in the Willamette Valley was located. The missionaries must have lived here two or three years, for there were peach trees there in blossom the next spring. When another location, called The Mill, now the city of Salem, had been made higher up the river this place was abandoned. . . . There were three log cabins under one roof at this place. We went into them on the 29th day of November, 1843, and here we passed our first winter in Oregon. It was our home until after harvest the following summer.

The absorbing thought of this winter was keeping up the food supply. The men were out at work in all kinds of weather, not for money, but for food. Father built a ferry boat for A. Beers and James O'Neil. . . . For building the boat, father took his pay in provisions: pork and peas constituted the greater part of these provisions. The French settlers seem to have grown peas extensively. . . .

There were no dry goods or clothing stores nearer than Fort Vancouver. There was no place where shoes could be gotten. The older people wore buckskin moccasins purchased from the Indians, while the young people went barefooted. Fortunately this proved to be a warm winter, but wet, as a Willamette winter usually is. . . .

I had already learned a number of Indian proper names. We saw Indians on the Columbia River who said they were Spokane. Others said they were Waskopum, Walla Wallas, Kince-Chinook, Klackamas, Klickitat, and Chemomachat. After we had settled in the valley we had visitors from the tribes living on the Columbia. . . . We learned to speak the Chinook Wa-Wa[7] that winter. The mission children spoke it as habitually as they did the mother tongue. We talked Chinook every day with the Indians and half-bloods. . . . There were a few missionaries and Canadian families in the neighborhood. There was a school kept during the winter near where we lived. The children of the three Applegate families, with the French and mission children, made up a school of about twenty-five pupils. No Indian children attended this school. A pious young man, Andrew Smith by name, presided over this religious training school. . . .

---

[7] According to Richard Maxwell Brown, who has written about the Chinook Wa-Wa, it was a hybrid tongue (he calls it a "jargon") that included a core of Chinook words, as well as words from other Indian languages and English and French. The Applegates were all fluent in Chinook jargon.

Our people harvested on the mission farm, using sickles and scythes to cut the grain, which was afterwards formed into bundles or sheaves. My work was to stack the sheaves into shocks. A vine known as the ground blackberry was grown with the grain. When they cut the grain they failed to separate it from the vines, which were bent and twisted into loops all through the stubble, and were also in and around the bunches of bound-up wheat and oats. My poor, bare feet had to wander in thorny paths and the scratches made me forget that I was tired and hungry . . . By harvesting this crop our people supplied themselves with grain to take to the new settlement. The wheat was the red bearded variety. . . .

The pioneers in the beginning had to make their own agricultural implements, such as plows, harrows, and all kinds of implements to clear and cultivate the ground. My father, Lindsay Applegate, was handy with carpenter's tools of the few and simple kinds they had, and Uncle Charles was a rough blacksmith, who shod horses when it was necessary, made bars, shears, coulters, and clevises for plows; rings and clevises for ox yokes; and repaired broken ironings of wagons; and, generally speaking, did all kinds of frontier blacksmithing. Father did the wood work in making plows and harrows and in repairing wagons. Every part of the plow was wood except the bar, shear, coulter, and clevis. Tough oak was used in the beam and the mould-board was of ash timber. Ash was also generally used in ox yokes.

The prairie lands fenced for cultivation were more or less heavily sodded and set with tufts of brushwood and strong roots of various kinds, and it was necessary to have very strong plows to break the lands. A strong two-wheeled truck, with a large strong plow attached to it, drawn by four yoke of oxen, was an outfit often seen breaking prairie. . . .

When we arrived at the place where we settled on Salt Creek in September, we had no time to spare from the building of cabins and other preparations for winter to make plows, and so it happened that the first plow to break ground in that country was one brought by Lindsay Applegate from the Old Mission where we had passed our first winter in Oregon. This plow was probably purchased from a missionary or French Canadian settler. . . .

Father built his first cabin on the point of a ridge a hundred and fifty feet above the valley. He said that in the river bottom where we lived in Missouri we had chills and fever. He wanted to build where we could get plenty of fresh air. In this he was not disappointed, for the sea breeze kept the boards on the roof rattling all through the autumn season, and the first storm of winter blew the roof off. . . .

In the course of three or four years after we began life in the wilderness of Salt Creek, we had pastures fenced, grain fields and gardens, small apple and peach orchards grown from the seed, comfortable log cabins, barns, and other outhouses, and quite a number of cattle, horses, hogs, and chickens. We had grain growing and in store and vegetables in abundance.

But many things we had always considered necessities were not to be had in the wilderness where we lived. Coffee, tea, and sugar were among these. Having an abundance of good milk, a family could do without tea or coffee, and even an old coffee drinker could be consoled by a beverage made by roasted peas crushed in a buckskin bag. Habitual tea drinkers soon became reconciled to what was generally known as "mountain tea," a drink of a spicy odor made from the leaves of a vine found growing in the woods. Many people came to prefer this tea to any tea of commerce. But there was no substitute for sugar. Father and mother had been in the sugar camps in Kentucky and Tennessee and knew how sugar was made from the sap of maple trees. Our spring was surrounded by a grove of maple trees and though the sap was not as sweet as the sap of the sugar maple, they believed sugar could be made from it. The experiment was tried and proved a success, and we had plenty of sugar, syrup, and candy.

---

WITH THE AMERICAN flag firmly planted in the Pacific Northwest, dozens of wagon trains followed the Great Migration up the Oregon Trail. In an age before railroads and telegraph lines spanned the continent, however, the journey was hard and the connections to the East strained. The federal government established the Oregon Territory in 1848, but the scant ten thousand white settlers in the region had little intercourse with the rest of the country. Money, especially American money, was scarce for years; the settlers sold most of the grain they grew to the Russians in Alaska, and much of the trade was in barter. The promised land of Oregon demanded the utmost out of its pioneers.

Meanwhile, tensions between the settlers, missionaries, and Native Americans of the Northwest rose higher. As Jesse A. Applegate vividly described, many of the emigrants felt pure hatred for Indians.[8] The missionaries, too, bred divisions in the Native American societies, converting some and alienating others as they demanded adherence to white, Christian ways. War loomed ever closer.

Before it could erupt, war of another kind exploded to the south. After a decade of rising hostilities with Mexico, the United States government decided to make Manifest Destiny national policy by declaring war on its southern neighbor. The victory that followed would give the American republic vast new lands—including mountains of gold.

---

[8] The Applegates themselves were quite sympathetic to the Indians.

## 2

# THE CALIFORNIA GOLD RUSH

It was war that altered the history of the West—war against Mexico, a nation often hailed as America's "sister republic." The changes it brought about were staggering: Before the hostilities, the U.S. population lived almost entirely east of the Mississippi, and was represented on the Pacific coast by barely ten thousand settlers in Oregon. Not long after, hundreds of thousands made their way to California, anchoring an empire that fell into America's lap almost overnight.

The war was not universally popular. Despite the political ferment over Manifest Destiny—the political campaigns won by expansionist politicians, the territorial demands made by jingoistic newspapers—the attack on Mexico was opposed by many men of principle (including then-Congressman Abraham Lincoln). The war was "one of the most unjust ever waged by a stronger against a weaker nation," according to General Ulysses S. Grant (who fought in the conflict as a young man). Slavery was the true cause, he wrote; and the seeds spilled by the war would eventually grow through the cracks in American society and split it apart in the Civil War.

The most immediate cause of the war was Texas—the Republic of Texas since 1836. Until that time, the region had been a part of Mexico. Few non-Indian Mexicans lived there, however; in the years since Stephen F. Austin led the first pioneers across the border in 1821, American settlers had come to outnumber Mexicans by three to one. Attempts by the Mexican government to assert its authority led to a war of independence, which the Texans won with the Battle of San Jacinto on April 21, 1836. Texas promptly declared its independence and petitioned for permission to join the United States.

The fate of Texas, however, became the center of a fierce debate in Congress over the extension of slavery to new states. The balance between the North and South dominated much of the political maneuvering in the United States before the Civil War, and the possibility that Texas would enter the union as a slave state created a political storm. Texas, after all, had been settled by Southerners, who had brought slaves with them; Texas annexation was strongly supported in the South, where politicians were pushing hard to expand the territories where slavery was legal. The issue went unresolved for almost a decade, and the Lone Star republic continued to function as an independent, though sparsely populated, country.

The crisis came in 1845. Nationalist expansionism—termed "Manifest Destiny" that year—finally drove Congress to annex Texas. Tensions with Mexico rose rapidly, especially as American politicians began to covet California. A young officer named John Charles Frémont was dispatched to explore routes through the Rockies to the region, while President Polk sent John Slidell to Mexico, authorizing him to pay up to forty million dollars for what is now the American Southwest. Meanwhile, the Americans declared the southern Texas border to be the Rio Grande—while the Mexicans placed it on the Nueces River, farther north.

A blur of events unfolded in 1846 (the year Francis Parkman set out on the Oregon Trail). A tightly organized religious group, calling themselves the Latter-day Saints but known to all as the Mormons, left their settlement in Illinois and headed for the southern Rocky Mountains; they had been victims of numerous armed attacks by mainstream Christians, and their leader, Brigham Young, thought Mexican territory might prove more friendly. On the west coast, Frémont made contact with American settlers in California, bearing news that the United States government would look kindly upon a rebellion against Mexico. And General Zachary Taylor was dispatched with an army to the Rio Grande, in hopes that the Mexicans might be tempted into launching the first attack in the looked-for war.

On May 1, 1846, the Mexican army took the bait, assaulting Taylor's force at the site of today's Brownsville, Texas. War immediately followed. In the end, it would be won by a skillful campaign by General Winfield Scott, who landed an army at Vera Cruz and marched to Mexico City, which he captured on September 13, 1847.

In the Southwest, far removed from the main theaters of war in Texas or Mexico, events took on a life of their own. General Stephen Watts Kearny marched into New Mexico and captured Santa Fe on August 18. He promptly set out across the mountains and desert for California. Frémont, however, was already there; he organized a motley force of American settlers and started a revolt, declaring California to be an independent republic. To make matters even more complicated, Commodore John Sloat appeared off the coast of California with a naval force and a unit of troops that included a young, no-nonsense lieutenant named William Tecumseh Sherman. These forces swiftly conquered California, and all three commanders—Kearny, Frémont, and Sloat's replacement, Commodore Robert Stockton—fell to arguing over who was in charge.

Chaos reigned in the Southwest in 1847. In California, no one seemed to be in charge. To the east, the Mormons reached Great Salt Lake, where Brigham Young decided they would found a colony, which he ran like an independent country for the next decade. A special battalion of Mormons had enlisted during the war and found itself stationed in California, waiting for discharge so the men could join their community in its new home. In New Mexico, an Indian revolt took the life of Governor Charles Bent. And while all these events seem sweeping and momentous on paper, vast areas existed beyond the control of the American authorities: countless miles of wilderness, where Indians—both warriors and peaceful pueblo farmers—reigned.

In California, matters settled down when all three commanders were recalled. The White House replaced General Kearny with Colonel Richard Mason, naming him military governor of the newly conquered province. Though the insubordinate and politically connected Frémont continued to intrigue, he too took his leave. Colonel Mason made Lieutenant Sherman his assistant, and the two men set about organizing the affairs of the vast, lightly settled country.

Sherman was in the hamlet of Los Angeles together with Kearny in 1847, when the word came that the general was to return to the East. Sherman then made his way back to Monterey, where Colonel Mason set up his bare-bones government. California was not completely empty: in addition to numerous Indians, many living barely at subsistence level, and a few Mexican residents, the region was home to a number of American settlers. Perhaps the most prominent was John Sutter, who was building a large complex inland from San Francisco Bay. Labor was hard to find, so Sutter turned to the still-waiting Mormon battalion to recruit workers for his backwoods barony.

As Sutter expanded his operations, he relied heavily on James Marshall, his head carpenter. To provide wood for the new buildings, Marshall took his Mormon employees into the Coloma Valley, up the American River, where he began to build a sawmill. But then he found something far more interesting than wood—and California was never the same again.

## The California Gold Rush
*by General William T. Sherman*

At the time of our visit, General Kearny was making his preparations to return overland to the United States, and he arranged to secure a volunteer escort out of the battalion of Mormons that was then stationed at San Luis Rey, under Colonel Cooke and a Major Hunt. This battalion was only enlisted for one year, and the time for their discharge was approaching, and it was generally understood that the majority of the men wanted to be discharged so as to join the Mormons who had halted at Salt Lake, but a lieutenant and about forty men volunteered to return to Missouri as the escort of General Kearny. These were mounted on mules and horses, and I was appointed to conduct them to Monterey by land.

Leaving the party at Los Angeles to follow by sea in the *Lexington*, I started with the Mormon detachment and traveled by land. We averaged about thirty miles a day. . . . This gave me the best kind of an opportunity for seeing the country, which was very sparsely populated indeed, except by a few families at the various missions. We had no wheeled vehicles, but packed our food and clothing on mules driven ahead, and we slept on the ground in the open air, the rainy season having passed.

Frémont followed me by land in a few days, and, by the end of May, General Kearny was all ready at Monterey to take his departure, leaving to succeed him in command Colonel R.B. Mason, First Dragoons. . . . Colonel Mason selected me as his adjutant-general. . . .

Frémont also left California with General Kearny, and with him departed all cause of confusion and disorder in the country. From that time forth no one could dispute the authority of Colonel Mason as in command of all the United States forces on shore, while the senior naval officer had a like control afloat. . . .

Colonel R. B. Mason, First Dragoons, was an officer of great experience, of stern character, deemed by some harsh and severe, but in all my intercourse with him he was kind and agreeable. He had a large fund of good sense, and, during our long period of service together, I enjoyed his utmost confidence. He had been in his day a splendid shot, and often entertained me with characteristic anecdotes of Taylor, Twiggs, Worth, Harney, Martin, Scott, etc., etc., who were then in Mexico, gaining a national fame. California had settled down to a condition of absolute repose, and we naturally repined at our fate in being so remote from the war in Mexico, where our comrades were reaping large honors. . . .

I had a single clerk, a soldier named Baden; and William E.P. Hartnell, citizen, who also had a table in the same room. He was the government interpreter, and had charge of the civil archives. After Halleck's return from Mazatlán, he was, by Colonel Mason, made Secretary of State; and he then had charge of the civil archives, including the land titles, of which Frémont first had possession but which had reverted to us when he left the country.

I remember one day, in the spring of 1848, that two men, Americans, came into the office and inquired for the Governor. I asked their business, and one answered that they had just come down from Captain Sutter on special business, and they wanted to see Governor Mason *in person*. I took them in to the colonel, and left them together. After some time the colonel came to his door and called to me.

I went in, and my attention was directed to a series of papers unfolded on his table, in which lay about half an ounce of placer gold.[9] Mason said to

---

[9] Placer gold is the sort found in streams.

me, "What is that?" I touched it and examined one or two of the larger pieces, and asked, "Is it gold?" Mason asked me if I had ever seen native gold. I answered that, in 1844, I was in upper Georgia,[10] and there saw some native gold, but it was much finer than this, and that it was in vials, or in transparent quills; but I said that, if this was gold, it could be easily tested, first, by its malleability, and next by acids.

I took a piece in my teeth, and the metallic luster was perfect. I then called to the clerk, Baden, to bring an axe and hatchet from the backyard. When these were brought, I took the largest piece and beat it out flat, and beyond doubt it was metal, and a pure metal. Still, we attached little importance to the fact, for gold was known to exist at San Fernando, at the south, and yet was not considered of much value.

Colonel Mason then handed me a letter from Captain Sutter, addressed to him, stating that he (Sutter) was engaged in erecting a sawmill at Coloma, about forty miles up the American Fork, above his fort at New Helvetia, for the general benefit of the settlers in that vicinity; that he had incurred considerable expense, and wanted a "preemption" to the quarter-section of land on which the mill was located, embracing the tail-race in which this particular gold had been found. Mason instructed me to prepare a letter in answer for his signature.

I wrote off a letter, reciting that California was yet a Mexican province, simply held by us as a conquest; that no laws of the United States yet applied to it, much less the land laws or preemption laws, which could only apply after a public survey. Therefore it was impossible for the Governor to promise him (Sutter) a title to the land; yet, as there were no settlements within forty miles, he was not likely to be disturbed by trespassers. Colonel Mason signed the letter, handed it to one of the gentlemen who had brought the sample of gold, and they departed.

That gold was the first discovered in the Sierra Nevada, which soon revolutionized the whole country, and actually moved the whole civilized world. . . .

As the spring and summer of 1848 advanced, the reports came faster and faster from the gold mines at Sutter's sawmill. Stories reached us of fabulous discoveries, and spread throughout the land. Everybody was talking of "Gold! gold!" until it assumed the character of a fever. Some of our soldiers began to desert; citizens were fitting out trains of wagons and pack-mules to go to the mines. We heard of men earning fifty, five hundred, and thousands of dollars per day, and for a time it seemed as though somebody would reach solid gold.

Some of this gold began to come to Yerba Buena in trade, and to disturb the value of merchandise, particularly of mules, horses, tin pans, and

---

[10] The previous decade had seen a gold rush in Georgia, which led in part to the expulsion of the Five Civilized Tribes in the Trail of Tears episode.

articles used in mining.[11] I of course could not escape the infection, and at last convinced Colonel Mason that it was our duty to go up and see with our own eyes, that we might report the truth to our government. . . .

Toward the end of June 1848, the gold-fever being at its height, by Colonel Mason's orders I made preparations for his trip to the newly discovered gold mines at Sutter's Fort. I selected four good soldiers, with Aaron, Colonel Mason's black servant, and a good outfit of horses and pack-mules, we started by the usually traveled route for Yerba Buena. . . .

The next day's journey took us to Bodega, where lived a man named Stephen Smith, who had the only steam sawmill in California. He had a Peruvian wife, and employed a number of absolutely naked Indians in making adobes. We spent a day very pleasantly with him, and learned that he had come to California some years before at the personal advice of Daniel Webster, who had informed him that sooner or later the United States would be in possession of California, and that in consequence it would become a great country.

From Bodega we traveled to Sonoma, by way of Petaluma, and spent a day with General Vallejo. . . . From Sonoma we crossed over by way of Napa, Suisun, and Vaca's ranch, to the Puta. In the rainy season, the plain between the Puta and Sacramento Rivers is impassable, but in July the waters dry up; and we passed without trouble, by the trail for Sutter's *embarcadero*, where we encamped at the old slough, or pond, near the fort.

On application, Captain Sutter sent some Indians back into the bushes, who recovered and brought in all our animals. At that time there was not the sign of a habitation there or thereabouts, except the fort, and an old adobe house, east of the fort, known as the hospital. The fort itself was one of adobe walls, about twenty feet high, rectangular in form, with two-story blockhouses at diagonal corners. The entrance was by a large gate, open by day and closed at night, with two iron ship's guns near at hand. Inside there was a large house, with a good shingle roof, used as a storehouse, and all round the walls were ranged rooms, the fort wall being the outer wall of the house. The inner wall was of adobe.

These rooms were used by Captain Sutter himself and by his people. He had a blacksmith's shop, carpenter's shop, etc., and other rooms where the women made blankets. Sutter was monarch of all he surveyed, and had authority to inflict punishment even unto death, a power he did not fail to use. He had horses, cattle, and sheep, and of these he gave liberally and without price to all in need. He caused to be driven into our camp a beef and some sheep, which were slaughtered for our use.

Already the gold mines were beginning to be felt. Many people were

[11] Sherman refers here to the incredible inflation caused by the sudden appearance of large quantities of gold, as prices multiplied overnight—one of many serious economic consequences of the find.

then encamped, some going and some coming, all full of gold stories and each surpassing the other. We found preparations in progress for celebrating the Fourth of July, then close at hand, and we agreed to remain over to assist on the occasion; of course, being the high officials, we were the honored guests. People came from a great distance to attend this celebration of the Fourth of July, and the tables were laid in the large room inside the storehouse of the fort. A man of some note, named Sinclair, presided, and after a substantial meal and a reasonable supply of *aguardiente* we began the toasts. . . .

The next day [namely, July 5, 1848], we resumed our journey toward the mines, and in twenty-five miles of as hot and dusty a ride as possible, we reached Mormon Island. I have heretofore stated that the gold was first found in the tail-race of the sawmill at Coloma, forty miles above Sutter's Fort, or fifteen miles above Mormon Island, in the bed of the American Fork of the Sacramento River. It seems that Sutter had employed an American named Marshall, a sort of millwright, to do this work for him, but Marshall afterward claimed that in the matter of the sawmill they were copartners. At all events, Marshall and a family, in the winter of 1847–48, were living at Coloma, where the pine trees afforded the best material for lumber. He had under him four white men, Mormons, who had been discharged from Cooke's battalion, and some Indians. These were engaged in hewing logs, building a mill dam, and putting up a sawmill. Marshall, as the architect, had made the tub wheel and had set it in motion, and had also furnished some of the rude parts of machinery necessary for an ordinary up-and-down sawmill.

Labor was very scarce, expensive, and had to be economized. The mill was built over a dry channel of the river which was calculated to be the tail-race. After arranging his head-race, dam, and tub wheel, he let on the water to test the goodness of his machinery. It worked very well until it was found that the tail-race did not carry off the water fast enough, so he put his men to work in a rude way to clear out the tail-race. They scratched a kind of ditch down the middle of the dry channel, throwing the coarser stones to one side; then, letting on the water again, it would run with velocity down the channel, washing away the dirt, thus saving labor.

This course of action was repeated several times, acting exactly like the Long Tom afterward resorted to by the miners. As Marshall himself was working in this ditch, he observed particles of yellow metal which he gathered up in his hand, when it seemed to have suddenly flashed across his mind that it was *gold*. After picking up about an ounce, he hurried down to the fort to report to Captain Sutter his discovery.

Captain Sutter himself related to me Marshall's account, saying that, as he sat in his room at the fort one day in February or March, 1848, a knock was heard at his door, and he called out, "Come in." In walked Marshall, who was a half-crazy man at best, but then looked strangely wild. "What is the matter, Marshall?" Marshall inquired if anyone was within hearing, and began to peer about the room, and look under the bed, when Sutter, fearing that some calamity had befallen the party up at the sawmill, and that Marshall was really crazy, began to make his way to the door, demanding of Marshall to explain what was the matter. At last he revealed his discovery, and laid before Captain Sutter the pellicles of gold he had picked up in the ditch.

At first, Sutter attached little or no importance to the discovery, and told Marshall to go back to the mill, and say nothing of what he had seen to his family, or anyone else. Yet, as it might add value to the location, he dispatched to our headquarters at Monterey, as I have already related, the two men with a written application for a preemption to the quarter-section of land at Coloma. Marshall returned to the mill, but could not keep out of his wonderful ditch, and by some means the other men employed there learned his secret. They wanted to gather the gold, and Marshall threatened to shoot them if they attempted it; but these men had sense enough to know that if "placer" gold existed at Coloma, it would also be found farther downstream, and they gradually prospected until they reached Mormon Island, fifteen miles below, where they discovered one of the richest placers on earth. These men revealed the fact to some other Mormons who were employed by Captain Sutter at a grist-mill he was building still lower down the American Fork, and six miles above his fort. . . .

As soon as the fame of the gold discovery spread through California, the Mormons naturally turned to Mormon Island, so that in July 1848, we found about three hundred of them there at work. Sam Brannan was on hand as the high priest, collecting the tithes. . . .

I recall the scene as perfectly today as though it were yesterday. In the midst of a broken country, all parched and dried by the hot sun of July, sparsely wooded with live oaks and straggling pines, lay the valley of the American River, with its bold mountain stream coming out of the Snowy Mountains to the east. In this valley is a flat, or gravel bed, which in high water is an island, or is overflown, but at the time of our visit was simply a level gravel bed of the river. On its edges men were digging, and filling buckets with the finer earth and gravel, which was carried to a machine made like a baby's cradle, open at the foot, and at the head a plate of sheet iron or zinc, punctured full of holes. On this metallic plate was emptied the earth, and water was then poured on it from buckets, while one man shook the cradle with violent rocking by a handle. On the bottom were nailed cleats of wood.

With this rude machine four men could earn from forty to one hundred dollars a day, averaging sixteen dollars, or a gold ounce, per man per day. While the sun blazed down on the heads of the miners with tropical heat, the water was bitter cold, and all hands were either standing in the water or had their clothes wet all the time; yet there were no complaints of rheumatism or cold.

We made our camp on a small knoll, a little below the island, and from it could overlook the busy scene. A few bush huts nearby served as stores, boarding houses, and for sleeping; but all hands slept on the ground, with pine leaves and blankets for bedding. As soon as the word spread that the Government was there, persons came to see us, and volunteered all kinds of information, illustrating it by samples of the gold, which was of a uniform kind, "scale gold," bright and beautiful. A large variety, of every conceivable shape and form, was found in the smaller gulches round about, but the gold in the river bed was uniformly scale gold. . . . That evening we all mingled freely with the miners, and witnessed the process of cleaning up and "panning" out, which is the last process for separating the pure gold from the fine dirt and black sand.

The next day we continued our journey up the valley of the American Fork, stopping at various camps, where mining was in progress; and about noon we reached Coloma, the place where gold had first been discovered. The hills were higher, and the timber of better quality. The river was narrower and bolder, and but few miners were at work there, by reason of Marshall's and Sutter's claims to the site. There stood the sawmill unfinished, the dam and tail-race just as they were left when the Mormons ceased work. Marshall and his family of wife and half a dozen tow-head children were there, guarding their supposed treasure; living in a house made of clapboards. Here also we were shown many specimens of gold, of a coarser grain than that found at Mormon Island.

The next day we crossed the American River to its north side, and visited many small camps of men in what were called the "dry diggings." Little pools of water stood in the beds of the streams, and these were used to wash the dirt; and there the gold was in every conceivable shape and size, some of the specimens weighing several ounces. Some of these diggings were extremely rich, but as a whole they were more precarious in results than at the river. Sometimes a lucky fellow would hit on a "pocket," and collect several thousand dollars in a few days, and then again he would be shifting about from place to place, prospecting, and spending all he had made. Little stores were being opened at every point, where flour, bacon, etc., were sold; everything being a dollar a pound, and a meal usually costing three dollars. Nobody paid for a bed, for he slept on the ground, without fear of cold or rain. We spent nearly a week in that region, and were quite bewildered by the fabulous tales of recent discoveries, which at that time were confined to the several forks of the American and Yuba rivers. . . .

Crossing the Sacramento again by swimming our horses [on the return trip], and ferrying their loads in [a] solitary canoe, we took back track as far as the Napa, and then turned to Benicia, on Carquinez Straits. We found there a solitary adobe house, occupied by Mr. Hastings and his family, embracing Dr. Semple, the proprietor of the ferry. This ferry was a ship's boat, with a latteen sail, which could carry across at one tide six or eight horses.

It took us several days to cross over, and during that time we got well acquainted with the doctor, who was quite a character. He had come to California from Illinois, and was brother to Senator Semple. He was about seven feet high, and very intelligent. When he first reached Monterey, he had a printing press, which belonged to the United States, having been captured at the custom house, and had been used to print custom-house blanks. With this Dr. Semple, as editor, published the *Californian*, a small sheet of news, once a week. . . .

After some time he removed to Yerba Buena with his paper, and it grew up to be the *Alta California* of today. Foreseeing, as he thought, the growth of a great city on the Bay of San Francisco, he selected Carquinez Straits as its location, and obtained from General Vallejo a title to a league of land, on condition of building up a city thereon to bear the name of Vallejo's wife. This was Francisca Benicia; accordingly, the new city was named "Francisca." At this time, the town near the mouth of the bay was known universally as Yerba Buena; but that name was not known abroad, although San Francisco was familiar to the whole civilized world. Now, some of the chief men of Yerba Buena, Folsom, Howard, Leidesdorf, and others, knowing the importance of a name, saw their danger, and by some action of the *ayuntamiento*, or town council, changed the name of Yerba Buena to "San Francisco."

Dr. Semple was outraged at their changing the name to one so like his of *Francisca*, and he in turn changed the name to the other name of Mrs. Vallejo, viz., "Benicia"; and Benicia it has remained to this day. I am convinced that this little circumstance was big with consequences. That Benicia has the best natural site for a commercial city, I am satisfied; and had half the money and half the labor since bestowed upon San Francisco been expended at Benicia, we should have at this day a city of palaces on the Carquinez Straits. The name of "San Francisco," however, fixed the city where it now is; for every ship in 1848–49 which cleared from any part of the world knew the name of San Francisco, but not Yerba Buena or Benicia; and, accordingly, ships consigned to California came pouring in with their contents, and were anchored in front of Yerba Buena, the first town. Captains and crews deserted for the gold mines, and now half the city in front of Montgomery Street is built over the hulks thus abandoned. . . .

On reaching Monterey, we found dispatches from Commodore Shubrick, at Mazatlán, which gave almost positive assurance that the war with Mexico was over; that hostilities had ceased, and commissioners were arranging the terms of peace at Guadalupe Hidalgo. It was well that this news reached California at that critical time; for so contagious had become the gold fever that everybody was bound to go and try his fortune, and the volunteer regiment of Stevenson's would have deserted en masse, had the men not been assured that they would very soon be entitled to honorable discharges.

Many of our regulars did desert, among them the very men who had escorted us faithfully to the mines and back. Our servants also left us, and nothing less than three hundred dollars a month would hire a man in California; Colonel Mason's black boy, Aaron, alone of all our servants proving faithful. We had to resort to all manner of shifts to live. First, we had a mess with a black fellow we called Bustamente as cook; but he got the fever, and had to go. We next took a soldier, but he deserted, and carried off my double-barreled shotgun, which I prized very highly. To meet this condition of facts, Colonel Mason ordered that liberal furloughs should be given to the soldiers, and promises to all in turn, and he allowed all the officers to draw their rations in kind. As the actual value of the ration was very large, this enabled us to live. . . .

Some time in September, 1848, the official news of the treaty of peace reached us, and the Mexican War *was* over. This treaty was signed in May, and came to us all the way by land by a courier from Lower California, sent from La Paz by Lieutenant Colonel Burton. On its receipt, orders were at once made for the muster-out of all of Stevenson's regiment, and our military forces were thus reduced to the single company of dragoons at Los Angeles, and the one company of artillery at Monterey. Nearly all business had ceased, except that connected with gold; and, during that fall, Colonel Mason, Captain Warner, and I made another trip up to Sutter's Fort, going also to the newly discovered mines on the Stanislaus, called "Sonora," from the miners of Sonora, Mexico, who had first discovered them. We found there pretty much the same state of facts as before existed at Mormon Island and Coloma, and we daily received intelligence of the opening of still other mines north and south. . . .

As the winter season approached, Colonel Mason returned to Monterey, and I remained for a time at Sutter's Fort. In order to share somewhat in the riches of the land, we formed a partnership in a store at Coloma, in charge of Norman S. Bestor, who had been Warner's clerk. We supplied the necessary money, fifteen hundred dollars (five hundred dollars each), and Bestor carried on the store at Coloma for his share. Out of this investment, each of us realized a profit of about fifteen hundred dollars.

Warner also got a regular leave of absence, and contracted with Captain Sutter for surveying and locating the town of Sacramento. He received for this sixteen dollars per day for his services as surveyor; and Sutter paid all the hands engaged in the work. The town was laid off mostly up about the fort, but a few streets were staked off along the riverbank, and one or two leading to it. Captain Sutter always contended, however, that no town could possibly exist on the immediate bank of the river, because the spring freshets rose over the bank, and frequently it was necessary to swim a horse to reach the boat landing. Nevertheless, from the very beginning the town began to be built on the very riverbank, viz. First, Second, and Third Streets, with J and K Streets leading back. . . . For several years the site was annually flooded; but the people have persevered in building the levees, and afterward in raising all the streets, so that Sacramento is now a fine city, the capital of the State, and stands where, in 1848, was nothing but a dense mass of bushes, vines, and submerged land. The old fort has disappeared altogether. . . .

The winter of 1848–49 was a period of intense activity throughout California. The rainy season was unfavorable to the operations of gold mining, and was very hard upon the thousands of homeless men and women who dwelt in the mountains, and even in the towns. Most of the natives and old inhabitants had returned to their ranches and houses; yet there were not roofs enough in the country to shelter the thousands who had arrived by sea and by land. The news had gone forth to the whole civilized world that gold in fabulous quantities was to be had for the mere digging, and adventurers came pouring in blindly to seek their fortunes, without a thought of house or food.

———

THE GOLD RUSH revolutionized California, and with it the American West. The amount of the metal found in the mountains was staggering: by 1854, it has been estimated, more than $276,000,000 came out of the California mines. Gold not only attracted hundreds of thousands of settlers,[12] it also provided instant capital for development. Sherman's story aptly describes the economic transformation of the territory. The flow of gold caused tremendous inflation, drawing in merchants and businessmen, large and small. More fortunes were probably made among those (such as Sherman and his partners) who came to buy and sell among the miners rather than from actual prospecting. These flourishing businesses turned to foreign labor for help, especially the thousands of Chinese immigrants, since most locals were more interested in gold. Cities erupted into existence where dusty villages and empty fields had been before.

California's explosion had important consequences for the West. Instead of a steady march of the frontier across the West, the gold rush led to a region weighted at both ends, on the coasts and in the Midwest, but unsettled (by whites) from the Rocky Mountains to the Great Plains. The Great Plains in particular emerged as a transit zone, a path for settlers and

———

[12] In 1849 alone, perhaps 100,000 immigrants flooded into California—more than ten times the white population of Oregon. In 1852, a census set the population at 223,856.

merchants bound for the Pacific. The California experience also led to a series of similar if lesser rushes over the next decade, in places ranging from Nevada to Colorado's Pike's Peak to Idaho, as prospectors hoped for a treasure chest like the one James Marshall had discovered. Countless mining camps burst into existence, only to dry up when deposits (or rumors) ran out.

As for California itself, the gold rush instantly transformed much of it into conquered territory in the war for the West. A large, prosperous population, a booming and well-developed economy, anti-crime vigilante groups, and sweeping, brutal massacres of Indians quickly eradicated local resistance to the advent of American society. In 1850 Congress admitted California as the 31st state, and talk turned to a transcontinental railroad to tie the Pacific coast to the East. In the Northwest, however, settlement proceeded more slowly—and the Indians did not wait to be butchered like the now-forgotten tribes of California.

## 3
# THE NEZ PERCÉ RESISTANCE

Ever since the day that one of Jesse A. Applegate's friends gave an Indian warrior a shove at Fort Walla Walla in 1843, tensions between the Native Americans of the Northwest and the white settlers had grown ever hotter. The first missionaries—Presbyterians Dr. Marcus Whitman and Henry and Eliza Spalding, and Catholic priest John Baptiste Brouillet—created factions among the Oregon tribes, converting some, angering others, and stirring confusion over the different varieties of the white religion. Whitman in particular was inflexible in demanding that the Native Americans adopt white ways. Soon an angry Delaware Indian by the name of Tom Hill appeared among the Cayuses and Nez Percés, spreading tales of how the whites had shattered his own tribe and stolen their lands. Each year, the steady procession of canvas-covered wagons eroded the Indians' patience.

In 1847, this unstable mixture of peoples and beliefs exploded as a train of settlers caused an epidemic of measles that devastated the Cayuse population. Convinced that Dr. Whitman was helping to spread the disease as he tried to treat the sick, Chief Tilokaikt led a Cayuse attack on his mission. The warriors killed more than a dozen (including the doctor and his wife, Narcissa), prompting a counterattack by 550 armed settlers, led by a preacher named Cornelius Gilliam. Gilliam marched his men up the Columbia, attacking Indian villages indiscriminately, until he was finally driven back in defeat. Chief Tilokaikt and four others surrendered to the white authorities, only to be executed for murder.

The settlers had only succeeded in arousing the anger of all the Native Americans of the Oregon Territory. The Cayuse, Palouse, Walla Walla, Umatilla, and Nez Percé tribes now learned to look on the newcomers with greater suspicion and hatred than ever before. In 1850, Congress passed the Oregon Donation Land Law, granting settlers the legal right to occupy any lands in the territory, regardless of what Indians lived there.

Some of the strongest and proudest of these Indians were the Nez Percés, as they were dubbed by the early French explorers. Like most Native American tribes, they were split into various bands, united by a common language and culture rather than a central authority. Missionaries Henry and Eliza Spalding were particularly active among them, leading to the creation of Christian and traditional factions that split many of the bands. But one group, the Wallamwatkin, maintained friendly relations with the Spaldings even as they resisted white intrusions. Led by a man the Spaldings dubbed Chief Joseph, or Old Joseph, the group steadfastly refused to give up any of their traditional lands.

In 1853, the threat to Native American independence was heightened as Congress split Oregon in two, creating the Washington Territory to the north. There an aggressive young army officer named Isaac I. Stevens took charge as governor—bringing with him an ambitious plan to deprive the Indians in his territory of their legal title to their lands (a concept almost inconceivable to the Native Americans). Stevens was matched in his determination by Oregon's Governor George Curry. Governor Stevens pushed into the mountains to the east in the early 1850s, aided by Henry Spalding and an accommodating Nez Percé chief nicknamed Lawyer; with bribery, threats, and lies, he convinced one group of Indians after another to sign treaties depriving them of the legal right to occupy their lands. Old Joseph, however, remained aloof with his Wallamwatkin band.

In 1855, war again broke out in the Northwest. In southwestern Oregon, the Rogue River Indians launched a counterattack against encroaching settlers, only to be defeated by the U.S. Army at the Battle of Big Meadows on May 27, 1856. They found themselves herded onto a cramped reservation, their military power stripped away. To the northeast, tensions raised by Stevens's treaties caused the outbreak of the Yakima War in the Washington Territory. Led by Yakima Chief Kamiakin, the Native American bands of the Columbia Basin rose up against the settlers, leading to a bloody series of skirmishes that petered out inconclusively in 1856.

The war of 1856, however, was only a hint of fighting to come. In May 1858, a band of Indian warriors routed an army column under Lieutenant Colonel Edward J. Steptoe, as he tried to march to the mining camp of Colville. The army, under Colonel George Wright, counterattacked, winning the battles of Spokane Plain and Four Lakes in September 1858. Wright turned east, driving Kamiakin into exile in Canada and imprisoning or executing dozens more Native American leaders. Indian resistance in the Columbia Basin was crushed, and the tribes were driven onto reservations. In 1859 thousands of settlers moved in, marking the final conquest of the area. In that same year, Oregon was admitted to the union as the 33rd state. The Northwest frontier had been conquered once and for all— its meadows and plains converted to farmland, its population absorbed into the mainstream of American society.

Except for one small Oregon valley far to the east. There, Old Joseph (and his son and successor Young Joseph) led the Nez Percés in dogged resistance to white intrusions. Years later, after the final defeat of the Wallamwatkin band, Young Joseph (now better known as Chief Joseph) traveled to Washington, where he delivered an eloquent account of his people's long fight. In the passage that follows, he tells the history of his band's relations with the whites, from the appearance of Lewis and Clark through the Nez Percé treaty of 1863, which was fraudulently applied to his band. It is a moving account of the collision of two irreconcilable cultures, both fighting for the same Wallowa valley—the land of winding water.

## The Struggle of Old Joseph
*by Chief Joseph*

My name is Inmuttooyahlatlat [Thunder Traveling Over the Mountains]. I am chief of the Wallamwatkin band of Chutepalu, or Nez Percés [nose-pierced Indians]. I was born in eastern Oregon, thirty-eight winters ago [1841]. My father was chief before me. When a young man, he was called Joseph by Mr. Spalding, a missionary. He died a few years ago. There was no stain on his hands of the blood of a white man. He left a good name on the earth. He advised me well for my people.

Our fathers gave us many laws, which they had learned from their fathers. These laws were good. They told us to treat all men as they treated us; that we should never be the first to break a bargain; that it was a disgrace to tell a lie; that we should speak only the truth; that it was a shame for one man to take from another his wife, or his property, without paying for it. We were taught to believe that the Great Spirit sees and hears everything, and that he never forgets; that hereafter he will give every man a spirit home according to his deserts. . . .

We did not know there were other people beside the Indian until about a hundred winters ago, when some men with white faces came to our country. They brought many things with them to trade for furs and skins. They brought tobacco, which was new to us. They brought guns with flint stones on them, which frightened our women and children. Our people could not talk with these white-faced men, but they used signs which all people understand. These men were Frenchmen, and they called our people Nez Percés because they wore rings in their noses for ornaments. Although very few of our people wear them now, we are still called by the same name. These French trappers said a great many things to our fathers, which have been planted in our hearts. Some were good for us, but some were bad. Our people were divided in opinion about these men. Some thought they taught more bad than good. An Indian respects a brave man, but he despises a coward. He loves a straight tongue, but he hates a forked tongue. The French trappers told us some truths and some lies.

The first white men of your people who came to our country were named Lewis and Clark. They also brought many things that our people had never seen. They talked straight, and our people gave them a great feast, as a proof that their hearts were friendly. These men were very kind . . . All the Nez Percés made friends with Lewis and Clark, and agreed to let them pass through their country and never to make war on white men.

This promise the Nez Percés have never broken. No white man can accuse them of bad faith, and speak with a straight tongue. It has always been the pride of the Nez Percés that they were the friends of the white men. When my father was a young man there came to our country a white man [the missionary Spalding] who talked spirit law. He won the affections of our people because he spoke good things to them. At first he did not say anything about white men wanting to settle on our lands.

Nothing was said about that until about twenty winters ago [1859], when a number of white people came into our country and built houses and made farms. At first our people made no complaint. They thought there was room enough for all to live in peace, and they were learning many things from the white men that seemed to be good. But we soon found that the white men were growing rich very fast, and were greedy to possess everything the Indian had. My father was the first to see through the schemes of the white men, and he warned his tribe to be careful about trading with them. He had suspicion of men who seemed so anxious to make money. I was a boy then, but I remember well my father's caution. He had a sharper eye than the rest of our people.

Next there came a white officer,[13] who invited all the Nez Percés to a treaty council. After the council was opened he made known his heart. He said there were a great many white people in the country, and many more would come; that he wanted the land marked out, so that the Indians and white men could be separated. If they were to live in peace it was necessary, he said, that the Indians should have a country set apart for them, and in that country they must stay. My father, who represented his band, refused to have anything to do with the council, because he wished to be a free man. He claimed that no man owned any part of the earth, and a man could not sell what he did not own.

Mr. Spalding took hold of my father's arm and said, "Come and sign the treaty." My father pushed him away, and said, "Why do you ask me to sign away my country? It is your business to talk to us about spirit matters, and not to talk to us about parting with our land." Governor Stevens urged my father to sign his treaty, but he refused. "I will not sign your paper," he said. "You can go where you please, so do I. You are not a child, I am no child; I can think for myself. No man can think for me. I have no other home than this. I will not give it up to any man. My people would have no home. Take away your paper. I will not touch it with my hand."

My father left the country. Some of the chiefs of the other bands of the Nez Percés signed the treaty, and then Governor Stevens gave them presents of blankets. My father cautioned his people to take no presents,

---

[13] Isaac I. Stevens, who became governor of the new Washington Territory in 1853. Governor Stevens embarked on a campaign to force the Native Americans onto reservations to encourage white settlement and development.

for "after a while," he said, "they will claim that you have accepted pay for your country." Since that time four bands of the Nez Percés have received annuities from the United States. My father was invited to many councils, and they tried hard to make him sign the treaty, but he was firm as the rock, and would not sign away his home. His refusal caused a difference [division] among the Nez Percés.

Eight years later [1863] was the next treaty council. A chief called Lawyer, because he was a great talker, took the lead in this council, and sold nearly all the Nez Percés' country. My father was not there. He said to me, "When you go into council with the white man, always remember your country. Do not give it away. The white man will cheat you out of your home. I have taken no pay from the United States. I have never sold our land." In this treaty, Lawyer acted without authority from our band. He had no right to sell the Wallowa [Winding Water] country. That had always belonged to my father's own people, and the other bands had never disputed our right to it. No other Indians ever claimed Wallowa.

In order to have all people understand how much land we owned, my father planted poles around it and said, "Inside is the home of my people— the white man may take the land outside. Inside this boundary all our people were born. It circles around the graves of our fathers, and we will never give up the graves to any man."

The United States claimed they had bought all the Nez Percés' country outside of Lapwai Reservation from Lawyer and other chiefs, but we continued to live on this land in peace until eight years ago [1871], when white men began to come inside the bounds my father had set. We warned them that this was a great wrong, but they would not leave our land, and some bad blood was raised. The white men represented that we were going upon the warpath. They reported many things that were false.

The United States Government again asked for a treaty council. My father had become blind and feeble. He could no longer speak for his people. It was then that I took my father's place as chief. In this council I made my first speech to white men. I said to the agent who held the council:

"I did not want to come to this council, but I came hoping that we could save blood. The white man has no right to come here and take our country. We have never accepted any presents from the Government. Neither Lawyer nor any other chief had authority to sell this land. It has always belonged to my people. It came unclouded to them from our fathers, and we will defend this land as long as a drop of Indian blood warms the hearts of men."

The agent said he had orders from the Great White Chief in Washington for us to go upon the Lapwai Reservation, and that if we obeyed he would help us in many ways. "You *must* move to the agency," he said. I answered him, "I will not. I do not need your help; we have plenty, and we are contented and happy if the white man will let us alone. The reservation is too small for so many people with all their stock. You can keep your presents; we can go to your towns and pay for all we need; we have plenty of horses and cattle to sell, and we won't have any help from you. We are free now; we can go where we please. Our fathers were born here. Here they lived, here they died, and here are their graves. We will never leave them." The agent went away, and we had peace for a little while.

Soon after this my father sent for me. I saw he was dying. I took his hand in mine. He said, "My son, my body is returning to my mother earth, and my spirit is going very soon to see the Great Spirit Chief. When I am gone, think of your country. You are the chief of these people. They look to you to guide them. Always remember that your father never sold his country. You must stop your ears whenever you are asked to sign a treaty selling your home. A few years more, and white men will be all around you. They have their eyes on this land. My son, never forget my dying words. This country holds your father's body. Never sell the bones of your father and your mother." I pressed my father's hand and told him I would protect his grave with my life. My father smiled and passed to the spirit land.

I buried him in that beautiful valley of winding rivers. I love that land more than all the rest of the world. A man who would not love his father's grave is worse than a wild animal.

For a short time we lived quietly. But this could not last. White men had found gold in the mountains around the land of winding water [in Idaho]. They stole a great many horses from us, and we could not get them back because we were Indians. The white men told lies for each other. They drove off a great many of our cattle. Some white men branded our young cattle so they could claim them. We had no friend who would plead our cause before the law councils. It seemed to me that some of the white men in Wallowa were doing these things on purpose to get up a war. They knew that we were not strong enough to fight them. I labored hard to avoid trouble and bloodshed. We gave up some of our country to the white men, thinking that then we could have peace. We were mistaken. The white men would not let us alone.

---

YOUNG JOSEPH, NOW Chief Joseph, was right: the white men would never let the Nez Percés alone. His father had been a shrewd observer of the newcomers' ways, but only the remoteness of his valley had kept them at bay; more and more would find their way to this last bastion of resistance. In little more than a decade, Joseph would be forced to flee the land of his fathers and run to the northeast with his people. There, in one of the most celebrated episodes of Indian resistance, the history of the Nez Percés would merge with that of the sprawling land and peoples of the Great Plains.

---

# II

---

# THE BURNING PRAIRIE

## THE GREAT PLAINS
## 1864–1878

| | |
|---|---|
| **1720s** | · The horse widely adopted by Indians of the Great Plains |
| **1750s–70s** | · Sioux driven out of northern Minnesota by the Ojibwa and adapt to the plains |
| **1830** | · Cheyenne split into Northern and Southern branches |
| **1834** | · Fort Laramie founded (originally as Fort William) |
| **1854** | · Kansas-Nebraska Act organizes Kansas and Nebraska Territories; leads to land rush by pro- and anti-slavery partisans |
| **1856** | · Border fighting between Kansas abolitionist "jayhawkers" and Missouri pro-slavery "border ruffians" reaches its height |
| **1858** | · First gold strike in Colorado, at Cherry Creek (within modern Denver) |
| **1859** | · Gold-rush settlers of Colorado organize Jefferson Territory, unrecognized by Congress |
| **1860** | · Gold found in Idaho |
| **1861** | · Abraham Lincoln (Republican) takes office as president; Civil War erupts, forcing pullout of most Regular Army troops from Western posts |
| | · Colorado and Dakota territories organized by Congress; Kansas becomes 34th state |
| **1862** | · Sioux uprising in Minnesota |
| | · Homestead Act |
| | · Legislation passed providing for transcontinental railroad |
| **1863** | · Expeditions against Sioux and Cheyenne tribes by columns under Generals Henry H. Sibley and Alfred Sully |
| | · Construction begins in Omaha on the Union Pacific Railroad, and the Central Pacific begins building east from Sacramento, California |
| | · Idaho Territory organized by Congress |
| | · Confederate bushwhackers from Missouri sack and burn Lawrence, Kansas, murdering more than 150 civilians; Union army retaliates by devastating three and a half counties in western Missouri, dubbed the "Burnt District" |
| **1864** | · Battle of Killdeer Mountain in Dakota Territory |
| | · Sand Creek Massacre in Colorado, followed by Cheyenne retaliation against Julesburg |
| | · Montana Territory organized by Congress |
| | · Bozeman Trail opens |
| **1865** | · Lincoln assassinated; Andrew Johnson (Democrat) takes office as president |
| **1866** | · Ex-Confederate bushwhackers commit first peacetime U.S. bank robbery in Liberty, Missouri; leads to birth of James-Younger Gang |
| **1866–67** | · Red Cloud's War in Wyoming; Oglala leaders Red Cloud and Crazy Horse force the abandonment of the Bozeman Trail and three forts |

| 1867 | · Nebraska becomes 37th state |
|---|---|
| | · First major cattle drive from Texas to Abilene, Kansas |
| 1867–68 | · Two major treaties with Indians: Medicine Lodge (with S. Cheyenne, Arapaho, Comanche, and Kiowa) in 1867, and Fort Laramie (with Sioux and N. Cheyenne) in 1868 |
| 1868 | · Wyoming Territory organized by Congress |
| 1868–69 | · Southern Plains War sees defeat of Southern Cheyenne, Arapaho, Comanche, and Kiowa tribes |
| 1869 | · Ulysses S. Grant (Republican) takes office as president |
| | · Grant names Ely Parker, a Seneca Indian, as his Commissioner of Indian Affairs; declares "Peace Policy" toward Native Americans |
| | · First transcontinental railroad completed at Promontory Point, Utah Territory |
| 1871 | · 600,000 cattle driven from Texas to Kansas, the most for any year |
| 1872 | · Crédit Mobilier scandal exposed, involving embezzlement of millions from construction of the transcontinental railroad |
| 1872–73 | · Modoc War in California |
| 1872–74 | · Peak years for buffalo hunting on southern Great Plains; estimated 4,400,000 bison destroyed by professional hunters |
| 1873 | · Massive financial panic; Northern Pacific Railroad bankrupt |
| | · Ute raids in Colorado led by Chief Ouray |
| 1874 | · Wyoming Stockgrowers' Association organized |
| | · Republican Reconstruction government in Texas falls to resurgent Democrats |
| 1874–75 | · Red River War leads to final defeat of southern Plains tribes |
| | · Texas Rangers reorganized |
| 1875 | · Southern buffalo herd eliminated |

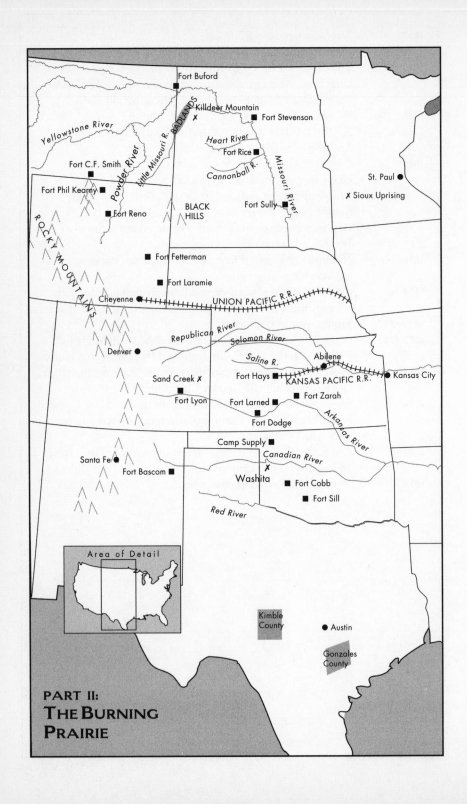

Fort Buford

Yellowstone River

Killdeer Mountain ✗

Fort Stevenson

Heart River

Fort Rice

BADLANDS

Little Missouri R.

Powder River

Cannonball R.

Missouri River

St. Paul ●

✗ Sioux Uprising

Fort C.F. Smith

Fort Phil Kearny ■

Fort Reno

BLACK HILLS

Fort Sully

ROCKY MOUNTAINS

■ Fort Fetterman

■ Fort Laramie

Cheyenne ●━━━━━━━━━━ UNION PACIFIC R.R. ━━━━━━━━

Republican River

Solomon River

Denver ●

Saline R.

Abilene

Sand Creek ✗

Fort Hays

KANSAS PACIFIC R.R.

Kansas City ●

Fort Lyon

Fort Larned

Fort Zarah ■

Fort Dodge

Arkansas River

Santa Fe ●

Camp Supply ■

Canadian River ✗

Fort Bascom ■

Washita

■ Fort Cobb

■ Fort Sill

Red River

Area of Detail

Kimble County

● Austin

Gonzales County

PART II:
### THE BURNING PRAIRIE

# 4

# A TALE OF THE NORTHERN PLAINS

Fanny Kelly was an ordinary nineteenth-century American woman. Tough-minded and intelligent, modest in her morals and particular about her clothing and diet, she was both loyal to her farmer husband and highly capable in her own right. Never famous or powerful, her name rarely appears in books about her era. But this little-known woman found herself swept away by two mighty storms that were transforming American history—the Civil War and the conquest of the Great Plains.

It only took a simple stroke of a pen to unleash these pent-up forces. In May 1854, President Franklin Pierce sat down at his desk in the White House and signed into law the Kansas-Nebraska Act. On the face of it, the bill might not have seemed portentous. All it did was organize the region west of Missouri and Iowa into two new territories: Kansas to the south and Nebraska to the north. But that seemingly straightforward administrative matter brought two great themes in American society to a crisis: the struggle over slavery, and the nation's expansion into the western wilderness. The first would be resolved in four years of intense, bloody fighting in the Civil War; the second would lead to a diverse, widespread conflict over control of the frontier, a war that would flare up and sputter on for the next four decades.

Both of these struggles, in a sense, were about the making of the United States into a single society, with uniform standards, laws, and values. In both the South and on the Western frontier, there lived people with their own cultures and beliefs that came into conflict with the authority of the federal government and the values of the rest of the country. Those beliefs frequently seem distasteful or even evil to us now (especially in the case of slavery), yet large communities believed in such things and fought to preserve them.

The two wars were intertwined from the beginning. In the age of Andrew Jackson, the federal government designated the lands west of the Missouri River as a permanent Indian frontier; the Great Plains were then called the "Great American Desert," considered unfit for habitation by civilized society. But the annexation of the Oregon country and the capture of the Southwest from Mexico changed all that. Now a sizeable population lived on the Pacific Coast, and Americans in fair

51

numbers regularly trekked through the Indians' country on their way farther west. Talk soon spread of building a transcontinental railroad as well—a project that would bring permanent occupation of Native American lands.

The politics of slavery and the transcontinental railroad twisted around each other in the 1850s. Under the Missouri Compromise of 1820, slavery was banned in any territory north and west of Missouri (itself the northwesternmost slave state). As long as the Compromise held sway, Southern congressmen prevented the opening of the Great Plains to white settlement—since, by law, these territories would inevitably become free states. At the same time, states along the western border of the settled East fought over who would get the starting point of the transcontinental railroad—Illinois (Chicago), Missouri (St. Louis), or Louisiana (New Orleans).

Senator Stephen Douglas of Illinois thought he saw a way through the impasse that would also give Chicago a leg up in the competition for the projected railway. He proposed a bill that would organize territories on the central Plains—the region most suitable for a railroad starting in his own state. To get Southern votes, he proposed overturning the slavery ban of the Missouri Compromise with the principle of popular sovereignty— letting settlers in the new territories decide for themselves about the issue. His congressional colleagues from below the Mason-Dixon line agreed, figuring that Kansas, west of Missouri, would naturally become a slave state.

The real result was an organized land rush into Kansas by pro- and antislavery militants. Abolitionists from New England, in particular, formed a well-run effort to move Northern settlers onto the eastern edge of the Great Plains, in east Kansas. Fighting soon broke out between the Yankees and pro-slavery "border ruffians" from Missouri, leading to a period of conflict dubbed "Bleeding Kansas." The settlement of the territory turned into a flashpoint for the outbreak of the Civil War.

The Kansas-Nebraska Act also opened the classic era of the Great Plains frontier. For the first time, white settlers were encouraged to move into the wilderness just west of the Missouri River. Unfortunately, that wilderness was not quite empty. People already lived on the plains, and many of them hardly appreciated the intrusion of the settlers. A new and sweeping conflict was the result—not one between North and South, but between the inhabitants of the West.

According to historian Richard Maxwell Brown, this violent era constituted a full-blown war as first settlers and the U.S. Army, and later lawmen, corporations, and political authorities fought to take over the frontier and remake it in the image of the rest of the country. As Brown writes, westward expansion "resulted in what should at last be recognized as a civil war across the entire expanse of the West—one fought in many places and on many fronts in almost all the Western territories and states from the 1860s and beyond."[1] This "Western Civil War of Incorporation," as he calls it, came in two waves. The first phase was the struggle between white settlers and the original inhabitants of the West—the Native American tribes. The second, described in detail in Brown's introduction and in later chapters of this book, erupted after the Indians had been defeated. At that point frontier communities (including Hispanic settlements in the Southwest) faced the growing control of powerful interests—corporations, wealthy individuals, and government. In the violence that erupted, resisting homesteaders and small ranchers were forced to accept the conservative laws and values that dominated larger American society.

It was the first stage of this war for the West, however, that snatched up the life of young Fanny Kelly. She and her family were among the first Yankee settlers in Kansas, moving there out of a desire for newly opened lands (and perhaps to help set back the cause of slavery). When the Civil War erupted, her husband-to-be loyally went off to fight for the Union, joining the millions of soldiers who battled over the fate of the nation. He returned to his Kansas farm and married Fanny long before the end of the war, only to find that settlers were flowing into the region even faster. In 1862, with Southern Democrats absent from Congress, the Republicans had passed the Homestead Act, which let farmers claim undeveloped frontier land at virtually no cost. They had also passed a law providing for the construction of a transcontinental railroad (along the central route); the act gave loans and land grants for the Union Pacific and Central Pacific railway companies. In addition, gold strikes drew additional flocks of pioneers to the mountains of Colorado and Idaho in the 1850s and 1860s, creating a tide of white settlement that crept onto the Great Plains from the west to match the flow from eastern Kansas and Nebraska. In 1864, Fanny Kelly and her husband decided to leave their spread behind, join the westward tide, and look for new riches in the Idaho mines.

Even as the Kellys debated their family future in their Kansas farmhouse, events far to the north were stirring up a sprawling, alien civilization. Across the Great Plains, the movements of these pioneers were watched uneasily by a series of Native American tribes: the Sioux and the Northern Cheyenne in the north, and the Southern Cheyenne, Kiowa, Arapaho, and Comanche on the central and southern Plains, along with other, less powerful groups such as the Pawnee, Shoshone, and Crow. These tribes had developed a fierce warrior culture, centered around the hunt for

[1] Richard Maxwell Brown, *No Duty to Retreat: Violence and Values in American History and Society* (New York: Oxford University Press, 1991). See also his work in *The Oxford History of the American West* (New York: Oxford University Press, 1994), and, of course, his introduction to this book.

buffalo and the pursuit of glory in fights against their neighbors.[2] Living in small bands, they constantly wandered the Great Plains; each tribe shared a common language and culture, but their leadership was diverse and disunited, each band often going its own way. Even so, the Plains Indians quickly grasped the implications of the growing numbers of settlers and travelers.

A decisive clash was inevitable; Native American and white traditions of land ownership and use could not coexist on the same ground. Though the Indians had fought earlier conflicts with white soldiers (notably against a column under General William S. Harney in the 1850s), these army expeditions had been raids, not true wars of conquest. In 1862, the situation changed drastically. The eastern, or Santee, branch of the Sioux had already been forced onto a reservation on the Minnesota River, where they were driven to near starvation (thanks to the corruption of the government agent assigned to issue their rations). They rose up in revolt and rampaged across southwestern Minnesota. The army threw together locally raised units and put down the rebellion. In 1863, General John Pope (transferred from the East after having been crushed by Robert E. Lee at the Second Battle of Bull Run) decided to march west and punish the relatives of the Santee rebels. With columns under the command of generals Henry H. Sibley and Alfred Sully, Pope launched an offensive against the Yankton, Yanktonai, and distant Lakota branches of the Sioux, all of whom had been uninvolved in the uprising. These attacks sparked more than ten years of almost ceaseless war on the northern Great Plains.

With little knowledge of these events, the Kelly family set out in their covered wagon, thinking only of an easier life in far-off Idaho. One day, as they traveled up the Bozeman Trail[3] (a recently opened route through the Powder River country of Wyoming and Montana), they were surrounded by enraged Sioux warriors, members of the Oglala tribe of the Lakota people. It was the start of a remarkable adventure for Fanny Kelly, who was to witness one of the great turning points in the history of the northern plains. Though steeped in the prejudices of her time, Kelly was later able to write an account of her experiences that is at once vivid and fairly accurate. Interestingly, she found herself capable of sympathizing with the Indians,

[2] Indian-on-Indian warfare often involved struggles over the control of hunting grounds, but in most skirmishes the warriors were intent on taking captives, stealing horses, and seeking personal glory (especially by counting "coups"—touching the live or dead body of an enemy, often with a special coup stick). Pitched, extended battles were rare, but the fighting *was* lethal, and did involve taking scalps. To the very end of the Indian wars, many warriors remained preoccupied with fighting their traditional tribal foes, rather than the army.

[3] The Bozeman Trail ran northwest from Fort Laramie, along a path marked by three forts the army began to build shortly after the events of this chapter: Forts Reno, Phil Kearny, and C.F. Smith (see map for Part II).

doomed as they ultimately were by the white onslaught. Her story is a dramatic glimpse of the clash between two civilizations—a clash brought on as much by settlers such as Kelly herself as by the invading soldiers of General Alfred Sully.

## The Pioneers
*by Fanny Kelly*

The years 1852 to 1856 witnessed, probably, the heaviest immigration the West has ever known in a corresponding length of time. Those who had gone before sent back to their friends such marvelous accounts of the fertility of the soil, the rapid development of the country, and the ease with which fortunes were made, the "Western fever" became almost epidemic. Whole towns in the old, Eastern States were almost depopulated. Old substantial farmers, surrounded apparently by all the comforts that the heart could wish, sacrificed the homes wherein their families had been reared for generations, and, with all their worldly possessions, turned their faces toward the setting sun. And with what high hopes! Alas! how few, comparatively, met their realization.

In 1856, my father, James Wiggins, joined a New York colony bound for Kansas. Being favorably impressed with the country and its people, they located the town of Geneva, and my father returned for his family. Reaching the Missouri River on our way to our new home, my father was attacked with cholera and died. In obedience to his dying instructions, my widowed mother, with her little family, continued on the way to our new home. But, oh! with what saddened hearts we entered into its possession. . . .

Our family remained in this pleasant prairie home, where I was married to Josiah S. Kelly. My husband's health failing, he resolved upon a change of climate. Accordingly, on the 17th of May, 1864, a party of six persons, consisting of Mr. Gardner Wakefield, my husband, myself, our adopted daughter (my sister's child), and two colored servants [named Frank and Andy], started from Geneva, with high-wrought hopes and pleasant anticipations of a romantic and delightful journey across the plains, and a confident expectation of future prosperity among the golden hills of Idaho.

A few days after commencing our journey, we were joined by Mr. Sharp, a Methodist clergyman, from Verdigris River, about thirty miles south of Geneva; and, a few weeks later, we overtook a large train of emigrants, among whom were a family from Allen County with whom we were acquainted—Mr. Larimer, wife, and child, a boy eight years old. Preferring to travel with our small train, they left the larger one and became members of our party. The addition of one of my own sex to our little company was cause of much rejoicing to me, and helped relieve the dullness of our tiresome march. . . .

So passed the first few happy days of our emigration to the land of sunshine and flowers. . . . Upon the beaten road are emigrants wending their way, their household goods packed in long covered wagons, drawn by oxen, mules, or horses; speculators working their way to some new town with women and children; and we meet with half-breed girls, with heavy eyelashes and sunburnt cheeks, jogging along on horseback. I was surprised to see so many women among the emigrants, and to see how easily they adapted themselves to the hardships experienced in a journey across the plains.

As a rule, the emigrants travel without tents, sleeping in and under wagons, without removing their clothing. Cooking among emigrants to the far West is a very primitive operation, a frying pan and perhaps a Dutch oven comprising the major part of the kitchen furniture. The scarcity of timber is a source of great inconvenience and discomfort, "buffalo chips" being the main substitute. At some of the stations,[4] where opportunity offered, Mr. Kelly bought wood by the pound, as I had not yet been long enough inured to plains privations to relish food cooked over a fire made with "chips" of that kind.

We crossed the Platte River by binding four wagon boxes together, then loaded the boat with goods, and were rowed across by about twenty men. We were several days in crossing. Our cattle and horses swam across. The air had been heavy and oppressively hot; now the sky began to darken suddenly, and just as we reached the opposite shore, a gleam of lightning, like a forked tongue of flame, shot out of the black clouds, blinding us by its flash, and followed by a frightful clash of thunder. . . .

All at once it burst upon our unprotected heads in rain. But such rain! Not the gentle droppings of an afternoon shower, nor a commonplace storm, but a sweeping avalanche of water, drenching us completely at the first dash, and continuing to pour, seeming to threaten the earth on which we stood, and tempt the old Platte to rise and claim it as its own. Our wagon covers had been removed in the fording, and we had no time to put up tents for our protection until its fury was exhausted. And so we were forced to brave the elements, with part of our company on the other side of the swollen river, and a wild scene, we could scarcely discern through the pelting rain, surrounded us. One soon becomes heroic in an open-air life, and so we put up what shelter we could when the abating storm gave us the opportunity; and, wringing the water out of our clothes, hair, and eyebrows, we camped in cheerful hope of a bright tomorrow, which did not

---

[4] Small stations were constructed about fifty miles apart on the major stagecoach lines to the far West.

disappoint us and our hundreds of emigrant companions scattered on the way. . . .

## THE ATTACK AND THE CAPTURE

The day on which our doomed family were scattered and killed was the 12th of July, a warm and oppressive day. The burning sun poured forth its hottest rays upon the great Black Hills and the vast plains of Montana, and the great road was strewed with men, women, and children, and flocks of cattle, representing towns of adventurers. . . .

We had no thought of danger or timid misgivings on the subject of savages, for our fears had been all dispersed by constantly received assurances of their friendliness. At the outposts and ranches, we heard nothing but ridicule of their pretensions to warfare, and at Fort Laramie, where information that should have been reliable was given us, we had renewed assurances of the safety of the road and friendliness of Indians. . . . We wended our way peacefully and cheerfully on, without a thought of the danger that was lying like a tiger in ambush in our path.

Without a sound of preparation or a word of warning, the bluffs before us were covered with a party of two hundred and fifty Indians, painted and equipped for war, who uttered the wild war-whoop and fired a signal volley of guns and revolvers into the air. This terrible and unexpected apparition came upon us with such startling swiftness that we had no time to think before the main body halted and sent out a part of their force, which circled us round at regular intervals, but some distance from our wagons. Recovering from the shock, our men instantly resolved on defense and corralled the wagons. My husband was looked upon as leader, as he was principal owner of the train. Without regard to the insignificance of our numbers, Mr. Kelly was ready to stand his ground; but, with all the power I could command, I entreated him to forbear and only attempt conciliation. "If you fire one shot," I said, "I feel sure you will seal our fate, as they seem to outnumber us ten to one, and will at once massacre all of us." . . .

My husband advanced to meet the chief and demand his intentions. The savage leader immediately came toward him, riding forward and uttering the words, "How! How!" which are understood to mean a friendly salutation. His name was Ottowa, and he was a war chief of the Oglala band of the Sioux nation. He struck himself on his breast, saying, "Good Indian, me," and pointing to those around him, he continued, "Heap good Indian, hunt buffalo and deer." He assured us of his utmost friendship for the white people; then he shook hands, and his band followed his example, crowding around our wagons, shaking us all by the hand over and over again, until our arms ached, and grinning and nodding with every demonstration of good will.

Our only policy seemed to be temporizing, in hope of assistance approaching; and, to gain time, we allowed them unopposed to do whatever they fancied. First, they said they would like to change one of their horses for the one Mr. Kelly was riding, a favorite race horse. Very much against his will, he acceded to their request, and gave up to them the noble animal to which he was fondly attached.

My husband came to me with words of cheer and hope, but oh! what a marked look of despair was upon his face, such as I had never seen before.

The Indians asked for flour, and we gave them what they wanted of our provisions. The flour they emptied upon the ground, saving only the sack. They talked to us partly by signs and partly in broken English, with which some of them were quite familiar, and as we were anxious to suit ourselves to their whims and preserve a friendly intercourse as long as possible, we allowed them to take whatever they desired, and offered them many presents besides. . . . They grew bolder and more insolent in their advances. One of them laid hold of my husband's gun, but, being repulsed, desisted.

The chief at last intimated that he desired us to proceed on our way, promising that we should not be molested. We obeyed, without trusting them, and soon the train was again in motion, the Indians insisting on driving our herd, and growing ominously familiar. Soon my husband called a halt. He saw that we were approaching a rocky glen, in whose gloomy depths he anticipated a murderous attack, and from which escape would be utterly impossible. Our enemies urged us still forward, but we resolutely refused to stir, when they requested that we should prepare us supper, which they said they would share with us, and then go to the hills to sleep. The men of our party concluded it best to give them a feast. Mr. Kelly gave orders to our two colored servants to prepare at once to make a feast for the Indians.

Andy said, "I think, if I knows anything about it, they's had their supper"; as they had been eating sugar crackers from our wagons for an hour or more. The two colored men had been slaves among the Cherokees, and knew the Indian character by experience.[5] Their fear and horror of them was unbounded. . . .

Each man was busy preparing supper; Mr. Larimer and Frank were making the fire; Mr. Wakefield was getting provisions out of the wagon; Mr. Taylor was attending to his team; Mr. Kelly and Andy were out some distance gathering wood; Mr. Sharp was distributing sugar among the Indians; supper, that they asked for, was in rapid progress of preparation, when suddenly our terrible enemies threw off their masks and displayed

[5] The Cherokees were one of the "Civilized Tribes" that had been driven out of Georgia and the other southeastern states to the Indian Territory (modern Oklahoma) in the 1830s. Many of them owned slaves and plantations, and fought for the Confederacy.

their truly demonic natures. There was a simultaneous discharge of arms, and when the cloud of smoke cleared away, I could see the retreating form of Mr. Larimer and the slow motion of poor Mr. Wakefield, for he was mortally wounded.

Mr. Kelly and Andy made a miraculous escape with their lives. Mr. Sharp was killed within a few feet of me. Mr. Taylor—I never can forget his face as I saw him shot through the forehead with a rifle ball. He looked at me as he fell backward to the ground a corpse. I was the last object that met his dying gaze. Our poor faithful Frank fell at my feet pierced by many arrows. I recall the scene with a sickening horror. I could not see my husband anywhere, and did not know his fate, but feared and trembled. With a glance at my surroundings, my senses seemed gone for a time, but I could only live and endure.

I had but little time for thought, for the Indians quickly sprang into our wagons, tearing off covers, breaking, crushing, and smashing all hindrances to plunder, breaking open locks, trunks, and boxes, and distributing or destroying our goods with great rapidity, using their tomahawks to pry open boxes, which they split up in savage recklessness.

Oh, what horrible sights met my view! Pen is powerless to portray the scenes occurring around me. They filled the air with the fearful war-whoops and hideous shouts. I endeavored to keep my fears quiet as possible, knowing that an indiscreet act on my part might result in jeopardizing our lives, though I felt certain that we two helpless women would share death by their hands; but with as much of an air of indifference as I could command, I kept still, hoping to prolong our lives, even if but a few moments. I was not allowed this quiet but a moment, when two of the most savage-looking of the party rushed up into my wagon, with tomahawks drawn in their right hands, and with their left seized me by both hands and pulled me violently to the ground, injuring my limbs very severely, almost breaking them, from the effects of which I afterward suffered a great deal. I turned to my little Mary, who, with outstretched hands, was standing in the wagon, took her in my arms and helped her to the ground. I then turned to the chief, put my hand upon his arm, and implored his protection for my fellow prisoner and our children. At first he gave me no hope, but seemed utterly indifferent to my prayers. Partly in words and partly by signs, he ordered me to remain quiet, placing his hand upon his revolver, that hung in a belt at his side, as an argument to enforce obedience. . . .

## BEGINNING OF MY CAPTIVITY

I was led a short distance from the wagon, with Mary, and told to remain quiet, and tried to submit; but oh, what a yearning sprang up in my heart to escape, as I hoped my husband had done! But many watchful eyes were upon me, and enemies on every side, and I realized that any effort then at escape would result in failure, and probably cause the death of all the prisoners.

Mrs. Larimer, with her boy, came to us, trembling with fear, saying, "The men have all escaped, and left us to the mercy of the savages."

In reply, I said, "I do hope they have. What benefit would it be to us, to have them here to suffer this fear and danger with us? They would be killed, and then all hope of rescue for us would be at an end."

Her agitation was extreme. Her grief seemed to have reached its climax when she saw the Indians destroying her property, which consisted principally of such articles as belong to the Daguerrean art [photography]. She had indulged in high hopes of fortune from the prosecution of this art among the mining towns of Idaho. As she saw her chemicals, picture cases, and other property pertaining to her calling being destroyed, she uttered such a wild despairing cry as brought the chief of the band to us, who, with gleaming knife, threatened to end all her further troubles in this world. The moment was a critical one for her. The Indians were flushed with an easy-won victory over a weak party; they had "tasted blood," and it needed but slight provocation for them to shed that even of defenseless women and children.

My own agony could be no less than that of my companion in misfortune. The loss of our worldly possessions, which were not inconsiderable, consisting of a large herd of cattle, and groceries, and goods of particular value in the mining regions, I gave no thought to. The possible fate of my husband; the dark fearful future that loomed before myself and little Mary, for whose possible future I had more apprehension than my own, were the thoughts that flashed through my mind to the exclusion of all mere pecuniary considerations.

But my poor companion was in great danger, and perhaps it was a selfish thought of future loneliness in captivity which induced me to intercede that her life might be spared. I went to the side of the chief, and, assuming a cheerfulness I was very far from feeling, pleaded successfully for her life. I endeavored in every way to propitiate our savage captor, but received no evidences of kindness or relenting that I could then understand. He did present me, however, with a wreath of gay feathers from his own head, which I took, regarding it merely as an ornament, when in reality, as I afterward learned, it was a token of his favor and protection. . . .

[Fanny Kelly was then taken by her captors on a long trek to their main encampment. Along the way, she was separated from Mrs. Larimer. Even worse, Kelly dropped her adopted daughter Mary from her horse to the ground one night, hoping she would escape. Mary's fate was unclear, but the Indians were angered.]

On the 21st of July we left camp early, the day being cool and favorable for traveling. Our route lay over rolling prairie, interspersed with extensive tracts of marsh, which, however, we easily avoided crossing. A few miles brought us to a high, broken ridge, stretching nearly in a north and south direction. As we ascended the ridge we came in sight of a large herd of buffalo, quietly feeding upon the bunch, or buffalo grass, which they prefer to all other kinds. These animals are shortsighted, and scent the approach of an enemy before they can see him, and thus, in their curiosity, often start to meet him, until they approach near enough to ascertain to their satisfaction whether there be danger in a closer acquaintance. In this case they decided in the affirmative, and when they had once fairly made us out, lost no time in increasing the distance between us, starting on a slow, clumsy trot, which was soon quickened to a gait that generally left most pursuers far in the rear.

But the Indians and their horses both are trained buffalo hunters, and soon succeeded in surrounding a number. They ride alongside their victim, and, leveling their guns or arrows, send their aimed shot in the region of the heart, then ride off to a safe distance, to avoid the desperate lunge which a wounded buffalo seldom fails to make, and, shaking his shaggy head, crowned with horns of the most formidable strength, stands at bay with eyes darting, savage and defiant, as he looks at his human foe. Soon the blood begins to spurt from his mouth, and to choke him as it comes. The hunters do not shoot again, but wait patiently until their victim grows weak from loss of blood, and, staggering, falls upon his knees, makes a desperate effort to regain his feet, and get at his slayer, then falling once more, rolls over on his side, dead. . . .

They gave me a knife and motioned me to help myself to the feast. I did not accept, thinking then it would never be possible for me to eat uncooked meat. They remained here overnight, starting early next morning. We were now nearing the village where the Indians belonged. . . .

Ottowa, or Silver Horn, the war chief, was arrayed in full costume. He was very old, over seventy-five, partially blind, and a little below the medium height. He was very ferocious and savage looking, and now, when in costume, looked frightful. His face was red, with stripes of black, and around each eye a circlet of bright yellow. His long, black hair was divided into two braids, with a scalp-lock on top of the head. His ears held great brass wire rings, full six inches in diameter, and chains and bead necklaces were suspended from his neck; armlets and bracelets of brass, together with a string of bears' claws, completed his jewelry. He wore also leggings of deer skin, and a shirt of the same material, beautifully ornamented with beads, and fringed with scalp-locks, that he claimed to have taken from his enemies, both red and white. Over his shoulders hung a great bright-colored quilt, that had been taken from our stores. He wore a crown of eagle feathers on his head; also a plume of feathers depending from the back of the crown.

His horse, a noble-looking animal, was no less gorgeously arrayed. His ears were pierced, like his master's, and his neck was encircled with a wreath of bears' claws, taken from animals that the chief had slain. Some bells and human scalps hung from his mane, forming together, thus arrayed, a museum of the trophies of the old chief's prowess on the war path, and of skill in the chase.

When all was arranged, the chief mounted his horse and rode on in triumph toward the village, highly elated over the possession of his white captive, whom he never looked back at or deigned to notice, except to chastise on account of her slowness, which was unavoidable as I rode a jaded horse and could not keep pace.

The entire Indian village poured forth to meet us, amid song and wild dancing, in the most enthusiastic manner, flourishing flags and weapons of war in frenzied joy as we entered the village, which—stretched for miles along the banks of the stream—resembled a vast military encampment, with the wigwams covered with white skins, like Sibley tents in shape and size, ranged without regard to order, but facing one point of the compass. We penetrated through the irregular settlement for over a mile, accompanied by the enthusiastic escort of men, women, and children.

We rode in the center of a double column of Indians and directly in the rear of the chief, till we reached the door of his lodge, when several of his wives came out to meet him. He had six, but the senior one was absent with the Farmer or Grosventre Indians. Their salutation is very much in the manner of the Mexicans: the women crossed their arms on the chief's breast and smiled. They met me in silence, but with looks of great astonishment.

I got down as directed, and followed the chief into the great lodge or tent, distinguished from the others by its superior ornaments. It was decorated with brilliantly colored porcupine quills and a terrible fringe of human scalp-locks, taken in battle with the Pawnees. On one side was depicted a representation of the Good Spirit, rude in design, and daubed with colors. On the other side was portrayed the figure of the spirit of evil in like manner. . . . The senior wife, who had remained in the lodge, met her husband with the same salutation as the others had done.

I was shown a seat opposite the entrance on a buffalo skin. The chief's spoil was brought in for division by his elderly spouse. As it was spread out before them, the women gathered admiringly around it, and proved their peculiarities of taste. . . .

The chief noticed my fear and shrinking posture, and smiled. Then he rose, and made a speech, which had its effect. The women became quiet. Presently an invitation arrived for the chief to go to a feast, and he rose to comply. I followed his departing figure with regretful glances, for, terrible as he and his men had been, the women seemed still more formidable, and I feared to be left with them, especially with the hot temper and ready knife of the elder squaw.

Great crowds of curious Indians came flocking in to stare at me. The women brought their children. Some of them, whose fair complexion astonished me, I afterward learned were the offspring of fort marriages. One fair little boy, who with his mother had just returned from Fort Laramie, came close to me. Finding the squaw could speak a few words in English, I addressed her, and was told in reply to my questions that she had been the wife of a captain there, but that his white wife arriving from the East, his Indian wife was told to return to her people; she did so, taking her child with her. . . .

Now that the question of property was decided between the women of the chief's family, they seemed kindly disposed toward me, and one of them brought me a dish of meat; many others followed her example, even from the neighboring lodges, and really seemed to pity me, and showed great evidence of compassion, and tried to express their sympathy in signs, because I had been torn from my own people, and compelled to come such a long fatiguing journey, and examined me all over and over again, and all about my dress, hands, and feet particularly. Then, to their great surprise, they discovered my bruised and almost broken limbs that occurred when first taken, also from the fall of the horse the first night of my captivity, and proceeded at once to dress my wounds.

I was just beginning to rejoice in the dawning kindness that seemed to soften their swarthy faces, when a messenger from the war chief arrived, accompanied by a small party of young warriors sent to conduct me to the chief's presence. I did not at first comprehend the summons, and, as every fresh announcement only awakened new fears, I dreaded to comply, yet dared not refuse. Seeing my hesitation, the senior wife allowed a little daughter of the chief's, whose name was Yellow Bird, to accompany me, and I was then conducted to several feasts, at each of which I was received with kindness and promised good will and protection. It was here that the chief himself first condescended to speak kindly to me, and this and the companionship of the child Yellow Bird, who seemed to approach me with a trusting grace and freedom unlike the scared shyness of Indian children generally, inspired hope.

The chief here told me that henceforth I could call Yellow Bird my own, to take the place of my little girl that had been killed. I did not at once comprehend all of his meaning, still it gave me some hope of security.

When at nightfall we returned to the lodge, which, they told me, I must henceforth regard as home, I found the elder women busily pounding a post into the ground, and my fears were at once aroused, being always ready to take alarm, and suggested to me that it betokened some evil. On the contrary, it was simply some household arrangement of her own, for presently, putting on a camp kettle, she built a fire and caused water to boil, and drew a tea, of which she gave me a portion, assuring me that it would cure the tired and weary feeling and secure me a good rest. . . .

I readily adapted myself to my new position. The chief's three sisters shared the lodge with us. The following day commenced my labors, and the chief's wife seemed to feel a protecting interest in me.

The day of the 25th of July was observed by continual feasting in honor of the safe return of the braves. There was a large tent made by putting several together, where all the chiefs, medicine men, and great warriors met for consultation and feasting. I was invited to attend, and was given an elevated seat, while the rest of the company all sat on the ground, and mostly cross-legged, preparatory to the feast being dealt out.

In the center of the circle was erected a flagstaff with many scalps, trophies, and ornaments fastened to it. Near the foot of the flagstaff were planted, in a row on the ground, several large kettles, in which was prepared the feast. Near the kettles on the ground also were a number of wooden bowls, in which the meat was to be served out. And in front, two or three women, who were there placed as waiters to light the pipes for smoking, and also to deal out the food.

In these positions things stood, and all sat with thousands climbing around for a peep at me, as I appeared at the grand feast and council, when at length the chief arose, in a very handsome costume, and addressed the audience, and in his speech often pointed to me. I could understand but little of his meaning. Several others also made speeches that all sounded the same to me. I sat trembling with fear at these strange proceedings, fearing they were deliberating upon a plan of putting me to some cruel death to finish their amusement. It is impossible to describe my feelings on that day, as I sat in the midst of those wild, savage people. Soon a handsome pipe was lit and brought to the chief to smoke. He took it, and after presenting the stem to the north, the south, the east, and the west, and then to the sun that was over his head, uttered a few words, drew a few whiffs, then passed it around through the whole group, who all smoked. This smoking was conducted with the strictest adherences to exact and established form, and the feast throughout was conducted in the most positive silence.

The lids were raised from the kettles, which were all filled with dog's meat alone, it being well cooked and made into a sort of stew. Each guest had a large wooden bowl placed before him, with a quantity of dog's flesh floating in a profusion of soup or rich gravy, with a large spoon resting in the dish, made of buffalo horn.

In this most difficult and painful dilemma I sat, witnessing the solemnity; my dish was given me, and the absolute necessity of eating it was painful to contemplate. I tasted it a few times after much urging, and then resigned my dish, which was taken and passed around with others to every part of the group, who all ate heartily. In this way the feast ended, and all retired silently and gradually, until the ground was left to the waiters, who seemed to have charge of it during the whole occasion.

The women signified to me that I should feel highly honored by being called to feast with chiefs and great warriors; and seeing the spirit in which it was given, I could not but treat it respectfully, and receive it as a very high and marked compliment. . . . As far as I could see and understand, I feel authorized to pronounce the dog feast a truly religious ceremony. . . .

That night was spent in dancing. Wild and furious all seemed to me. I was led into the center of the circle, and assigned the painful duty of holding above my head human scalps fastened to a little pole. The dance was kept up until near morning, when all repaired to their respective lodges. The three kind sisters of the chief were there to convey me to mine.

## PREPARATIONS FOR BATTLE

The next morning the whole village was in motion. The warriors were going to battle against a white enemy, they said, and old men, women, and children were sent out in another direction to a place of safety, as designated by the chief. Everything was soon moving. With the rapidity of custom the tent poles were lowered and the tents rolled up. The cooking utensils were put together, and laid on crossbeams connecting the lower ends of the poles as they trail the ground from the horses' sides, to which they are attached. Dogs, too, are made useful in this exodus, and started off with smaller burdens dragging after them, in the same manner that horses are packed.

The whole village was in commotion, children screaming or laughing; dogs barking or growling under their heavy burdens; squaws running hither and thither, pulling down tepee poles, packing up everything, and leading horses and dogs with huge burdens. . . . The number and utility of these faithful dogs is sometimes astonishing, as they count hundreds, each bearing a portion of the general household goods. . . .

This train was immensely large, nearly the whole Sioux nation having concentrated there for the purposes of war. The chief's sisters brought me a horse saddled, told me to mount, and accompany the already moving column that seemed to be spreading over the hills to the northward. We toiled on all day. Late in the afternoon we arrived at the ground of encampment, and rested for further orders from the warriors, who had gone to battle and would join us there.

I had no means of informing myself at that time with whom the war was raging, but afterward learned that General Sully's army was pursuing the Sioux, and that the engagement was with his men. In three days the Indians returned to camp, and entered on a course of feasting and rejoicing that caused me to believe that they had suffered very little loss in the affray. They passed their day of rest in this sort of entertainment; and here I first saw the scalp dance, which ceremonial did not increase my respect or confidence in the tender mercies of my captors. This performance is only gone through at night and by the light of torches, consequently its terrible characteristics are heightened by the fantastic gleams of the lighted brands. The women, too, took part in the dance, and I was forced to mingle in the fearful festivity, painted and dressed for the occasion, and holding a staff from the top of which hung several scalps. . . .

This country seemed scarred by countless trails where the Indian ponies have dragged lodge poles in their change of habitations or hunting. The antipathy of the Indian to its occupation or invasion by the white man is very intense and bitter. The felling of timber, or killing of buffalo, or traveling of a train, or any signs of permanent possession by the white man excites deadly hostility. It is their last hope; if they yield and give up this, they will have to die or ever after be governed by the white man's laws. Consequently they lose no opportunity to kill or steal from and harass the whites when they can do so. . . .

The Indians felt that the proximity of the troops and their inroads through their best hunting-grounds would prove disastrous to them and their future hopes of prosperity, and soon again they were making preparations for battle; and again, on the 8th of August [probably July 28] the warriors set forth on the warpath, and this time the action seemed to draw ominously near our encampment. . . .

There seemed to be great commotion and great anxiety in the movements of the Indians, and presently I could hear the sound of battle; and the echoes, that came back to me from the reports of the guns in the distant hills, warned me of the near approach of my own people, and my heart became a prey to wildly conflicting emotions, as they hurried on in great desperation, and even forbid me turning my head and looking in the direction of battle. . . . Panting for rescue, yet fearing for its accomplishment, I passed the day. The smoke of action now rose over the hills beyond. The Indians now realized their danger, and hurried on in great consternation.[6]

General Sully's soldiers appeared in close proximity, and I could see them charging on the Indians, who, according to their habits of warfare, skulked behind trees, sending their bullets and arrows vigorously forward into the enemy's ranks. I was kept in advance of the moving column of women and children, who were hurrying on, crying and famishing for water, trying to keep out of the line of firing.

It was late at night before we stopped our pace, when at length we reached the lofty banks of a noble river, but it was some time before they

[6] This was probably the Battle of Killdeer Mountain, July 28, 1864. From her description of these events, it appears she later reconstructed the dates incorrectly. August 8 was the date of another battle in the Little Missouri badlands. The Battle of Killdeer Mountain fits her account quite well.

could find a break in the rocky shores which enabled us to reach the water and enjoy the delicious draught, in which luxury the panting horses gladly participated. We had traveled far and fast all day long, without cessation, through clouds of smoke and dust, parched by a scorching sun. . . .

It was not until next morning that I thought of how they should cross the river, which I suppose to have been the Missouri.[7] It was not very wide, but confined between steep banks; it seemed to be deep and quite rapid; they did not risk swimming at that place, to my joy, but went further down and all plunged in and swam across, leading my horse. I was very much frightened, and cried to Heaven for mercy. On that morning we entered a gorge, a perfect mass of huge fragments which had fallen from the mountains above; they led my horse and followed each other closely, and with as much speed as possible, as we were still pursued by the troops. During the day some two or three warriors were brought in wounded. I was called to see them, and assist in dressing their wounds. This being my first experience of the kind, I was at some loss to know what was best to do; but, seeing it a good opportunity to rise in their estimation, I endeavored to impress them with an air of my superior knowledge of surgery, and as nurse or medicine woman. I felt now, from their motions and meaningful glances, that my life was not safe, since we were so closely pursued over this terrible barren country.

My feelings, all this time, cannot be described, when I could hear the sound of the big guns, as the Indians term cannon. I felt that the soldiers had surely come for me and would overtake us, and my heart bounded with joy at the very thought of deliverance, but sunk proportionately when they came to me, bearing their trophies, reeking scalps, soldiers' uniforms, covered with blood, which told its sad story to my aching heart. One day I might be cheered by some strong hope of approaching relief, then again would have such assurances of my enemies' success as would sink me correspondingly low in despair. . . .

On, and still on, we were forced to fly through a place known among them as the Bad Lands, a section of country so wildly desolate and barren as to induce the belief that its present appearance is the effect of volcanic action. Great boulders of blasted rock are piled scattering round, and hard, dry sand interspersed among the crevices. Everything has a ruined look, as if vegetation and life had formerly existed there, but had been suddenly interrupted by some violent commotion of nature. A terrible blight, like the fulfilling of an ancient curse, darkens the surface of the gloomy landscape, and the desolate, ruinous scene might well represent the entrance to the infernal shades described by classic writers. A choking wind with sand blows continually, and fills the air with dry and blinding dust.

---

[7] This was almost certainly the Little Missouri.

FAR FROM BEING Kelly's salvation, General Sully had provided the most pressing reason for her abduction. His attacks on the Lakota (also known as the Western Sioux or Teton Sioux) actually created the state of war on the northern plains that swallowed up Kelly's wagon train.

As mentioned before, Sully's attack stemmed from the great Sioux uprising of 1862 in southwestern Minnesota. There the Santee (or eastern) Sioux had risen up on their reservation after being driven to starvation by the corrupt government agents, who sold off food and clothing intended for the Indians. General H. H. Sibley suppressed the outbreak with local recruits as General John Pope hurried from the battles of the Civil War to take command. Responding to demands by Minnesota settlers, Pope promptly sent Sibley and Sully on a two-pronged raid into the Dakota Territory in 1863.

None of the generals seemed to grasp the decentralized character of the Sioux people, who were divided into the Lakota (living in modern Montana, Wyoming, and the western Dakota Territory), the central Dakota (east of the Missouri River, in the Dakota Territory), and Santee (or eastern Dakota)—or that each of these groups was subdivided into numerous other tribes. Instead, they acted as if the Sioux were a nation in the sense of the United States—a single political entity to be held responsible for outbreaks of fighting by any of its members. So when the Santee rose up in frustration, Pope, Sibley, and Sully needlessly expanded the war by attacking their Sioux relatives, the Yankton and Yanktonai of the central Dakota and the seven tribes of the Lakota.

This military blundering and provocation continued in 1864, the year Fanny Kelly and her family set out onto the war-torn plains. Generally Sully launched a punishing new campaign, driving north along the western bank of the upper Missouri River. To meet his thrust, the Lakota and some Dakota bands formed a vast village in late July, which included Kelly as well as a man named Sitting Bull, a widely respected war chief and holy man of the Hunkpapa (a Lakota tribe). These Sioux warriors were proud of their long string of victories against their Crow and Assiniboine enemies, and they drastically underestimated Sully's power. On July 28, 1864, at the Battle of Killdeer Mountain (described by Kelly), they learned that their bows and arrows and muzzle-loading muskets were no match for the army's rifles and artillery.

The reports that follow provide the official U.S. view of the 1864 campaign. On one hand, they reveal the army's general ignorance of both the region and the Lakota. They also show the harassing guerrilla tactics adopted by the Indians after their defeat in the massed battle of Killdeer Mountain. War chiefs such as Sitting Bull were forced to confront the fact that they were underarmed, and they switched to hit-and-run attacks.

Sully's report shows how their constant sniping and raiding wore down the army's morale as his column continued its overextended march through the badlands of the Little Missouri River. But as Fanny Kelly's concluding account reveals, the tragic cost of the soldiers' attacks deeply shocked the Lakota people.

---

## The Invaders
*by Generals Henry H. Sibley and Alfred Sully*

REPORT OF GENERAL H. H. SIBLEY,
HEADQUARTERS OF MINNESOTA, DEPARTMENT OF THE NORTHWEST, JULY 3, 1864:

That you may be correctly informed of the state of matters connected with the Indian war on the frontiers of Minnesota, Iowa, and Territory of Dakota, I beg leave to submit, very briefly, the following facts:

First. Shortly after the Sioux outbreak of 1862 on the borders of this State, which was attended with untold horrors, and the massacre of nearly 800 white men, women, and children, I was placed in command of the raw levies hastily thrown forward to check the savages. The battle of Wood Lake, a locality sixty or seventy miles above Fort Ridgely, resulted in the total defeat of the concentrated force of the bands concerned in the outrages. About 2,000 prisoners of Indian men, women, and children were taken, of whom upward of 300 of the former were tried by a military commission appointed by me, found guilty of participation in the murders and other crimes, and condemned to be hung. The President subsequently ordered the execution of thirty-eight of these criminals,[8] who were accordingly hung, and the remainder who have thus far survived the trying effects of close imprisonment are now in military custody at Davenport, Iowa. Some 250 or 300 of the warriors implicated in the outbreak escaped with their families and joined the upper and powerful bands of Sioux or Dakotas, who roam over the great plains between the Upper Missouri and the British boundary line, subsisting on the buffalo almost exclusively.

The Government recognized the necessity of inflicting proper chastisement upon the murderers and those bands who had harbored and protected them, and in pursuance with the orders of Major General Pope, General Sully ascended the Missouri early in 1863 with a column of mounted troops, and another mixed force of infantry and cavalry under my command marched from this direction, it being General Pope's intention

[8] Lincoln actually agonized over the executions, reducing the number to only those found guilty of attacking civilians—the smallest politically acceptable number. They were hung in Mankato, Minnesota, in the largest mass execution in U.S. history.

that the two expeditions should cooperate and finally unite at Devil's Lake. . . .

Since these events occurred the hostile combination has been strengthened by other powerful bands of the Teton Sioux or Dakotas [Lakotas], from the south and west of the Upper Missouri, who avowed their purpose to prosecute the war and put an entire stop to the emigration to Idaho by way of the Upper Missouri River and overland.[9] During the past winter most of the refugee murderers, being entirely destitute the past winter of food and clothing, which they lost during the engagements of the previous season, as before stated, crossed into [Canada]. . . .

These refugees have for the most part since the opening of the spring [of 1864] crossed back into our territories and probably joined the hostile camp, which is said to contain 2,000 lodges, or between 4,000 or 5,000 warriors. General Sully is now advancing upon them with a force of nearly 1,600 cavalry and mounted infantry. . . .

**REPORT OF GENERAL ALFRED SULLY,**
FROM THE HEART RIVER, DAKOTA TERRITORY, JULY 31, 1864:

On the 23rd of this month I reached this point [on the Heart River], having made rapid marches, considering I had a very large emigrant train under my charge. I had started in a direction west, but on the road, receiving information that the Indians were on or near the Knife River, I changed my course in a northerly direction. On my arrival at this point I corralled all my wagons and the emigrant train, leaving it under charge of Captain Tripp, Dakota cavalry, with a sufficient force to guard against danger. . . .

About 3 P.M. of the 26th I succeeded in getting off, and about 10 A.M. of the 28th succeeded in reaching the enemy's camp, about eighty miles' march. All their camp was standing when I reached there, and they prepared for a fight, no doubt with full confidence of whipping me, for they had twenty-four hours' notice of my advance, by a party of my scouts falling in with a war party of theirs not sixteen miles from here. We followed their trail, which led me to the camp. I found the Indians strongly posted on the side of a mountain called Tahkahokuty [Killdeer] Mountain, which is a small chain of very high hills, filled with ravines, thickly timbered and well watered, situated on a branch of the Little Missouri. The prairie in front of the camp is very rolling, and on the left as we approached the high hills. On the top and sides of these hills and on my right, at the base of the mountains, also on the hillocks in front of the prairie, the Indians were

[9] These western bands of the Sioux nation had nothing to do with the Minnesota uprising, but were provoked by Sibley and Sully's invasions of their territory in 1863 and the opening of the Bozeman Trail, which cut through the heart of the Powder River hunting grounds.

posted; there were over 1,600 lodges, at least 5,000 or 6,000 warriors[10] composed of the Hunkpapas, Sans Arcs, Blackfeet, Minneconjous, Yanktonais, and Santee Sioux. . . . The whole of my force numbered on the field about 2,200 men.

Finding it was impossible to charge, owing to the country being intersected by deep ravines filled with timber, I dismounted and deployed six companies of the 6th Iowa on the right and three companies of the 7th Iowa, and on the left six companies of the 8th Minnesota Infantry; placed Pope's battery in the center, supported by two companies of cavalry; the 2nd Cavalry, on the left, drawn up by squadrons, Brackett's Minnesota Battalion on the right in the same order, Jones's battery and four companies of cavalry as a reserve. The few wagons I had closed up, and the rear guard, composed of three companies, followed.

In this order we advanced, driving in the Indians till we reached the plain between the hills and mountain. Here large bodies of Indians flanked me. The 2nd Cavalry drove them from the left. A very large body of Indians collected on my right for a charge. I directed Brackett to charge them. This he did gallantly, driving them in a circle of about three miles to the base of the mountains and beyond my line of skirmishers, killing many of them. The Indians, seeing his position, collected in large numbers on him, but he expelled them, assisted by some well-directed shots from Jones's battery.

About this time a large body of Indians, who we ascertained afterward had been out hunting for me, came up on my rear. I brought a piece of Jones's battery to the rear, and with the rear guard dispersed them. The Indians, seeing that the day would not be favorable for them, had commenced taking down their lodges and sending back their families. I swung the left of my line round to the right and closed on them, sending Pope with his guns and the Dakota cavalry (two companies) forward. The artillery fire soon drove them out of their strong positions in the ravines, and Jones's battery, with Brackett's battalion, moving up on the right, soon put them to flight, the whole of my line advancing at the same time.

By sunset no Indians were on the ground. A body, however, appeared on top of the mountain over which they had retreated. I sent Major Camp, 8th Minnesota, with four companies of the 8th Minnesota, forward. They ascended to the top of the hill, putting the Indians to flight and killing several. The total number of killed, judging from what we saw, was from 100 to 150.[11] I saw them during the fight carry off a great many dead or wounded. The very strong position they held and the advantages they had to retreat over a broken country prevented me from killing more. We slept on the battleground that night.

The next morning before daylight we started to go round the mountain,

[10] Later researchers suggest a figure around 2,000 or fewer.
[11] Later Sioux estimates put the Indian dead at 31.

as I could not get up it with wagons and artillery in front. After six miles' march, I came in sight of the trail on the other side of the mountain, but could not get to it. One sight of the country convinced me there was no use trying to follow up the Indians through such country and find them. . . . I therefore thought the next best thing to do was to destroy their camp. . . .

That afternoon I marched six miles from the battleground and camped. About dark a large body of Indians came on to my pickets and killed two. A command was immediately sent after them, but they fled in all directions. . . .

**REPORT OF GENERAL ALFRED SULLY,**
FROM THE YELLOWSTONE RIVER, AUGUST 13, 1864:

On the fifth day of August we came in sight of the Bad Lands, which extend along the Little Missouri, the valley being about twenty miles across; through the middle of this valley runs the river. When I came in sight of this country from the top of the tableland we were marching on, I became alarmed, and almost despaired of ever being able to cross it, and should have been very much tempted, had I rations enough, to turn back, but on a close examination of my rations, I found I only had rations for six days longer, by some mistake of my commissary, I suppose, for he is not with me to explain, as I left him back at Fort Rice. I therefore had to reduce the bread ration one-third, all the other stores except meat one-half, so as to make it last me to the river. We camped that night with little or no grass, and but a few holes of muddy rain water.

I have not sufficient power of language to describe the country in front of us. It was grand, dismal, and majestic. You can imagine a deep basin, 600 feet deep and twenty-five miles in diameter, filled with a number of stones and oven-shaped knolls of all sizes, from twenty feet to several hundred feet high, sometimes by themselves, sometimes piled up into large heaps on top of one another, in all conceivable shapes and confusion. Most of these hills were of a gray clay, but many of a light brick color, of burnt clay; little or no vegetation. Some of the sides of the hills, however, were covered with a few scrub cedars. Viewed in the distance at sunset it looked exactly like the ruins of an ancient city.

My Indian guide appeared to be confident of success, and trusting to him, I started next morning, and by dint of hard digging, succeeded by night in reaching the banks of the Little Missouri, about twelve miles. I regret very much some gentleman well acquainted with geology and mineralogy did not accompany the expedition, for we marched through a most wonderful and interesting country. . . .

We now reached the river in the middle of the Bad Lands. Having dug our way down to this point it was now necessary to dig our way out. I therefore ordered out a strong working party, with four companies of cavalry, under charge of Lieutenant Colonel Pattee, 7th Iowa Cavalry. I remained in camp to allow the animals to rest and pick up what grass could be found around, there being very little to be found. Some few of the men, however, without orders, took their horses into the timber [along the river] beyond the pickets, leaving their saddles and arms in camp. A small party of the Indians crawled up to them, fired on them, creating a stampede. Most of the men ran away, leaving their horses, and the Indians succeeded in getting a few away, but three or four men having some courage mounted their horses bareback and gave chase, causing the Indians to drop all the horses, which were retaken, save one or two. A company was soon in pursuit, but the Indians escaped through some of the numerous ravines and forests. . . .

By evening the working party under Colonel Pattee returned, having cut three miles of the road. A part of the company, however, by accident had been left behind. They were surrounded by Indians and were near being cut off, but by a hasty retreat they succeeded in getting through the deep gorge, where the road was cut, the Indians firing at them from the tops of the hills. They pursued them to the river and showed themselves on the top of the high bluffs opposite my camp, firing into my camp, but a few shells from Jones's battery soon scattered them, and with the exception of a little picket-firing there was no more trouble that night.[12] I now knew I had come upon the Indians I had fought about a week ago, and in the worst possible section of country I could possibly wish to encounter an enemy.

My road lay through a succession of mountain gorges, down deep ravines, with perpendicular bluffs, so narrow only one wagon could pass at a time, intersected with valleys, down which the Indians could dash onto any point of my train. Stretched out in a single line we were extended from three to four miles. . . .

After marching about three miles we came onto the Indians strongly posted in front and on the flanks of a deep mountain pass. They were dislodged after some little trouble, the shells from Jones's battery doing good execution, and the advance with other troops pushed on, while the pioneer party made the road. The Indians attacked me on the flanks and rear at the same time, but on all occasions they were repulsed with heavy loss by troops nearby, and thus we advanced fighting, hunting a road and digging it out, till we reached a small lake and spring about ten miles from our starting point. . . .

At the spring there was for a short time quite a brisk little skirmish, the Indians trying to keep us from the only water we had that day, and the day

[12] This firing by the picket guards during the night suggests how jittery Sully's men were after these hit-and-run attacks.

was so hot that the animals were suffering very much, having had not much to eat for two days. Part of Colonel McLaren's 2nd Minnesota did most of the work here. One of his companies in advance got separated from the rest and surrounded; they however got into a hollow and defended themselves until relieved by other companies sent out from Colonel Thomas's command. Their loss, however, was slight in comparison to their danger. Unfortunately this day I lost the services of my guide; he was shot, having ventured too far in the advance. He was the only one who knew the country over which we were marching.

The next morning we moved forward. The Indians were in front of us appearing as if they intended to give us battle. . . . We advanced without much trouble, with a little skirmishing in front, and also an attack in rear. The enemy were repulsed on all sides. It was evident, in spite of all their boasting, all fighting was out of them. A few miles brought us to an open country, and the last we saw of the Indians was a cloud of dust some six or eight miles off, running as fast as they could. They were better mounted than we were. . . . It is certain, however, their loss was very heavy. The same Indians I fought before were engaged, besides Cheyennes, Brulés, Minneconjous, and others from the south. . . .

After marching six miles this day, we came to the place where the Indians left about thirty hours before my arrival. From the size of their camp, or rather bivouac, for they had pitched no lodges, I should judge all the Indians in the country had assembled there. The space they occupied was over one mile long and half a mile wide, besides which we discovered camps all over the country, close by this spot. . . . We continued our way across the country to the Yellowstone, which we reached on the 12th of August, over a section of country I never wish to travel again; our animals half dead with hunger; the grass entirely eaten off.

## The Captive
*by Fanny Kelly*

The terrible scarcity of water and grass urged us forward, and General Sully's army in the rear gave us no rest. The following day or two we were driven so far northward, and became so imminently imperiled by the pursuing forces, that they were obliged to leave all their earthly effects behind them, and swim the Yellowstone River for life. By this time the ponies were completely famished for want of food and water, so jaded that it was with great difficulty and hard blows that we could urge them on at all.

When the Indians are pursued closely, they evince a desperate and reckless desire to save themselves, without regard to property or provisions. They throw away everything that will impede flight, and all natural instinct seems lost in fear. We had left, in our compulsory haste, immense quantities of plunder, even lodges standing, which proved immediate help, but in the end a terrible loss.

General Sully with his whole troop stopped to destroy the property, thus giving us an opportunity to escape which saved us from falling into his hands, as otherwise we inevitably would have done. One day was consumed in collecting and burning the Indian lodges, blankets, provisions, etc., and that day was used advantageously in getting beyond his reach. They travel constantly in time of war, ranging over vast tracts of country, and prosecuting their battles or skirmishes with a quiet determination unknown to the whites.

A few days' pursuit after Indians is generally enough to wear and tire out the ardor of the white man, as it is impossible to pursue them through their own country with wagons and supplies for the army, and it is very difficult for American horses to traverse the barren, rugged mountain passes, the Indians having every advantage of their own country, using their own mode of warfare. The weary soldiers return disheartened by often losing dear comrades, and leaving them in a lonely grave on the plain, dissatisfied with only scattering their red foes. . . .

## MOURNING FOR THE SLAIN

As soon as we were safe, and General Sully pursued us no longer, the warriors returned home, and a scene of terrible mourning over the killed ensued among the women. Their cries are terribly wild and distressing on such occasions; and the near relations of the deceased indulge in frantic expressions of grief that cannot be described. Sometimes the practice of cutting the flesh is carried to a horrible and barbarous extent. They inflict gashes on their bodies and limbs an inch in length. Some cut off their hair, blacken their faces, and march through the village in procession, torturing their bodies to add vigor to their lamentations.

Hunger followed on the track of grief; all their food was gone, and there was no game in that portion of the country. In our flight they scattered everything, and the country through which we passed for the following two weeks did not yield enough to arrest starvation. The Indians were terribly enraged, and threatened me with death almost hourly, and in every form.

I had so hoped for liberty when my friends were near; but alas! all my fond hopes were blasted. The Indians told me that the army was going in another direction.

They seemed to have sustained a greater loss than I had been made aware of, which made them feel very revengeful toward me. The next morning I could see that something unusual was about to happen. Notwithstanding the early hour, the sun scarcely appearing above the horizon, the principal chiefs and warriors were assembling in council, where, judging from the grave and reflective expression of their countenances, they were about to discuss some serious question. . . .[13]

Soon they sent an Indian to me, who asked me if I was ready to die—to be burned at the stake. I told him whenever Wakon-Tonka (the Great Spirit) was ready, he would call for me, and then I would be ready and willing to go. He said that he had been sent from the council to warn me, that it had become necessary to put me to death, on account of my white brothers killing so many of their young men recently. He repeated that they were not cruel for the pleasure of being so; necessity is their first law, and he and the wise chiefs, faithful to their hatred for the white race, were in haste to satisfy their thirst for vengeance; and further, that the interest of their nation required it.

As soon as the chiefs were assembled around the council fire, the pipe-carrier entered the circle, holding in his hand the pipe already lighted. Bowing to the four cardinal points, he uttered a short prayer, or invocation, and then presented the pipe to the old chief, Ottowa, but retained the bowl in his hand. When all the chiefs and men had smoked, one after the other, the pipe-bearer emptied the ashes into the fire, saying, "Chiefs of the great Dakota nation, Wakon-Tonka gives you wisdom, so that whatever be your determination, it may be comfortable to justice." Then, after bowing respectfully, he retired.

A moment of silence followed, in which everyone seemed to be meditating seriously upon the words that had just been spoken. At length one of the most aged of the chiefs, whose body was furrowed with the scars of innumerable wounds and who enjoyed among his people a reputation for great wisdom, arose.

Said he, "The pale faces, our eternal persecutors, pursue and harass us without intermission, forcing us to abandon to them, one by one, our best hunting grounds, and we are compelled to seek a refuge in the depths of these Bad Lands, like timid deer. Many of them even dare to come into prairies which belong to us, to trap beaver, and hunt elk and buffalo, which are our property. These faithless creatures, the outcasts of their own people, rob and kill us when they can. Is it just that we should suffer these wrongs without complaining? Shall we allow ourselves to be slaughtered like timid Assiniboines, without seeking to avenge ourselves? Does not the law of the Dakotas say, Justice to our own nation, and death to all pale

---

[13] The incident that follows smacks of literary invention—at the very least, we can wonder whether Kelly really understood what was being said. It has been left in this selection, however, since it certainly reveals her feelings about her captors.

faces? Let my brothers say if that is just," pointing to the stake that was being prepared for me.

"Vengeance is allowable," sententiously remarked Mahpeah (the Sky).

Another old chief, Ottawa, arose and said, "It is the undoubted right of the weak and oppressed; and yet it ought to be proportioned to the injury received. Then why should we put this young, innocent woman to death? Has she not always been kind to us, smiled upon us, and sang for us? Do not all our children love her as a tender sister? Why, then, should we put her to so cruel a death for the crimes of others, if they are of her nation? Why should we punish the innocent for the guilty?"

I looked to Heaven for mercy and protection, offering up those earnest prayers that are never offered in vain; and oh! how thankful I was when I knew their decision was to spare my life. . . .

A terrible time ensued, and many dogs, and horses, even, died of starvation. Their bodies were eaten immediately; and the slow but constant march was daily kept up, in hope of game and better facilities for fish and fruit.

Many days in succession I tasted no food, save what I could gather on my way; a few rose leaves and blossoms was all I could find, except the grass I would gather and chew for nourishment. Fear, fatigue, and long-continued abstinence were wearing heavily on my already shattered frame. Women and children were crying for food; it was a painful sight to witness their sufferings, with no means of alleviating them, and no hope of relief save by travel and hunting. We had no shelter save the canopy of heaven, and no alternative but to travel on, and at night lie down on the cold, damp ground for a resting place. . . .

What exhibitions of their pride and passion I have seen; what ideas of their intelligence and humanity I have been compelled to form; what manifestations of their power and ability to govern had been thrust upon me. . . .

When the [Oglalas] went to obtain their annuities, they transferred me to the Hunkpapas, leaving me in their charge, where there was a young couple and an old Indian who had four wives.[14] He was very brave, it was said, for he had endured the trial which proves the successful warrior. He was one of those who "looked at the sun" without failing in heart or strength.

The custom is as follows: The one who undergoes the operation is nearly

---

[14] According to Robert Utley, Sitting Bull's biographer, the transfer took place *before* the Battle of Killdeer Mountain (again, Kelly appears to have confused the flow of events). The Hunkpapa, influenced by Sitting Bull, refused to accept the government annuities (ordained by treaty) that were distributed at various army posts. The old man described here is very likely to have been Sitting Bull himself, who was renowned for having performed the sun dance many times. Kelly's new captor was a warrior known as Brings Plenty.

naked, and is suspended from the upper end of a pole by a cord, which is tied to some splints which run through the flesh of both breasts. The weight of his body is hung from it, the feet still upon the ground helping to support it very little, and in his left hand he holds his favorite bow, and in his right, with a firm hold, his medicine bag.

A great crowd usually looks on, sympathizing with and encouraging him, but still he continues to hang and "look at the sun," without paying the least attention to anyone about him. The mystery men beat their drums, and shake their rattles, and sing as loud as they can yell, to strengthen his heart to look at the sun from its rising until its setting, at which time, if his heart and strength have not failed him [or the splints torn through his flesh], he is cut down, receives a liberal donation of presents, which are piled before him during the day, and also the name and style of a doctor, or medicine man, which lasts him, and insures him respect, through life. . . .

Savages [the Oglalas] were, and I had longed to be free from them; but now I parted with them with regret and misgiving. Though my new masters, for such I considered them, held out promise of liberty and restoration to my friends, knowing the treacherous nature of the Indians, I doubted them. True, the Oglalas had treated me at times with great harshness and cruelty, yet I had never suffered from any of them the slightest personal or unchaste insult. Let me bear testimony to this redeeming feature in their treatment of me. . . .[15]

I was received with great joy, and even marks of distinction were shown me. That night there was a feast, and everything denoted a time of rejoicing. My life was now changed—instead of waiting upon others, they waited upon me. The day of my arrival in the [Hunkpapa] village was a sad one, indeed, being the first anniversary of my wedding. I met in the village many warriors whom I had seen during the summer, and knew that they had participated in the battles with General Sully. They saw that something had made me sad and thoughtful, and asked what it was. I told them it was my birthday. . . .

One day, I was called to see a man who lay in his tepee in great suffering. His wasted face was darkened by fever, and his brilliantly restless eyes rolled anxiously, as if in search of relief from pain. He was reduced to a skeleton, and had endured tortures from the suppuration of an old wound in the knee. He greeted me with the "How! How!" of Indian politeness, and, in answer to my inquiry why he came to suffer so, replied: "I go to fight the white man. He takes away land, and chases game away; then he takes away

---

[15] This paragraph, and those following up to the story of the fire, have been moved for continuity and historical accuracy. Kelly jumbled the story of her transfer to the Hunkpapa; she seems to have blended it with her transfer to the Blackfeet (another Lakota tribe), which took place in the final days of her captivity.

our squaws. He take away my best squaw." Here his voice choked, and he displayed much emotion.

Pitying his misery, I endeavored to aid him, and rendered him all the assistance in my power, but death was then upon him. The medicine man was with him also, practicing his incantations. The day after the Indian's burial we were again on the move. . . .

## A PRAIRIE ON FIRE

In October, we were overtaken by a prairie fire. At this season of the year the plants and grass, parched by a hot sun, are ready to blaze in a moment if ignited by the least spark, which is often borne on the wind from some of the many campfires.

With frightful rapidity we saw it extend in all directions, but we were allowed time to escape. The Indians ran like wild animals from the flames, uttering yells like demons; and the great walls of fire from the right hand and from the left advanced toward us, hissing, crackling, and threatening to unite and swallow us up in their raging fury. We were amid calcined trees, which fell with a thundering crash, blinding us with clouds of smoke, and were burned by the showers of sparks, which poured upon us from all directions.

The conflagration assumed formidable proportions; the forest shrunk up in the terrible grasp of the flames, and the prairie presented one sheet of fire, in the midst of which the wild animals, driven from their dens and hiding places by this unexpected catastrophe, ran about mad with terror. The sky gleamed with blood-red reflection, and the impetuous wind swept both flames and smoke before it. . . . The earth became hot, while immense troops of buffalo made the ground tremble with their furious tread, and their bellowings of despair would fill with terror the hearts of the bravest men.

Everyone was frightened, running about the camp as if struck by insanity. The fire continued to advance majestically, as it were, swallowing up everything in its way, preceded by countless animals of various kinds that bounded along with howls of fear, pursued by the scourge, which threatened to overtake them at every step. A thick smoke, laden with sparks, was already passing over the camp. Ten minutes more, and all would be over with us, I thought, when I saw the squaws pressing the children to their bosoms. . . .

But, fortunately, the strong breeze which, up to that moment, had lent wings to the conflagration, suddenly subsided, and there was not a breath of air stirring. The progress of the fire slackened. Providence seemed to grant us time. . . .

The Indians, old and young, male and female, began to pull up the grass by the roots all about the camp, then lassoed the horses and hobbled them in the center, and, in a few moments, a large space was cleared, where the herbs and grass had been pulled up with the feverish rapidity which all display in the fear of death.

Some of the Indians went to the extremity of the space, where the grass had been pulled up, and formed a pile of grass and plants with their feet; then, with their flint, set fire to the mass, and thus caused "fire to fight fire," as they call it. This was done in different directions. A curtain of flames rose rapidly around us, and for some time the camp was almost concealed beneath a vault of fire.

It was a moment of intense and awful anxiety. By degrees the flames became less fierce, the air purer; the smoke dispersed; the roaring diminished, and at length we were able to recognize each other in this horrible chaos.

A sigh of relief burst from every heart. Our camp was saved! After the first moments of joy were over, the camp was put in order, and all felt the necessity of repose after the terrible anxieties of the preceding hours; and also to give the ground time enough to cool, so that it might be traveled over by people and horses.

The next day we prepared for departure. Tents were folded and packages were placed upon the ponies, and our caravan was soon pursuing its journey under the direction of the chief, who rode in advance of our band. The appearance of the prairie was much changed since the previous evening. In many places the black and burnt earth was a heap of smoking ashes; scarred and charred trees, still standing, displayed their saddening skeletons. The fire still roared at a distance, and the horizon was still obscured with smoke.

[Kelly won widespread respect among the Hunkpapa, who named her "Real Woman." The army, however, had gained word of her presence among the Hunkpapa, and sent messages asking for her release. Sitting Bull himself—moved by her obvious sadness at her life in captivity— forced her captor, Brings Plenty, to hand her over to the Blackfeet for delivery to Fort Sully.]

Eight chiefs rode in the advance, one leading my horse by the bridle, and the warriors rode in the rear. The cavalcade was imposing. As we neared the fort they raised their war song, loud and wild, on the still, wintry air; and, as if in answer to its notes, the glorious flag of our country was run up. . . .

Then the gate [of Fort Sully] was opened, and Major House appeared, accompanied by several officers and an interpreter, and received the chiefs who rode in advance. . . . As soon as the chiefs who accompanied me entered the gates of the fort, the commandant's voice thundered the order for them to be closed. The [Indians] were shut out, and I was beyond their power to recapture. After a bondage lasting more than five months, during which I had endured every torture, I once more stood free, among people of my own race, all ready to assist me and restore me to my husband's arms.

———

FANNY KELLY ENDURED much suffering during her time in captivity: the destruction of all her worldly possessions, uncertainty about the fate of her husband, the grisly death of her adopted daughter (whose scalp and torn dress she discovered one day), threats to her life, hunger, and exposure. Such trials were even worse for a woman of her background and prejudices. Her writing clearly shows that she believed in white racial superiority; she saw the Indians as savage and barbaric. And yet, even a woman of such deep Victorian values could not help admiring the Lakota for their skillful adaptation to life on the plains, for their courage and determination to survive against heavy odds. The Hunkpapas especially stirred her gratitude, as the people of Sitting Bull treated her warmly before releasing her.

Meanwhile, the military campaign she had witnessed sparked the beginning of an almost continuous war that would rock the Great Plains for another twelve years. From the opening of Nebraska and Kansas to white settlement to the attacks of Sibley and Sully, a virtual race war had begun on the Great Plains between whites and Native Americans. The scene of the fighting soon shifted to the central plains of Colorado and Kansas, where the attack was pressed by hard-bitten frontiersmen—men who sought nothing less than the extermination of the Indians.

———

# 5

# THE CLOSING VISE:
# THE CENTRAL PLAINS, 1864–1868

When Fanny Kelly saw General Alfred Sully's soldiers attack the Lakota at Killdeer Mountain, she witnessed the beginning of the climactic cycle of war against the independent tribes of the Great Plains. The Lakota and Northern Cheyennes could never forgive Sully's unprovoked assault, which was only a prelude to permanent occupation on the northern plains. The general followed up his raid by planting forts in the Dakota Territory along the upper Missouri River (see the map for Part II). Farther west, the Indians took deep offense at the new Bozeman Trail, which took emigrants (such as the Kelly family) right through the heart of the Powder River hunting grounds. The Lakota and Northern Cheyennes responded by sending war pipes to their friends on the central plains, the Arapahos and Southern Cheyennes (who had split from the Northern Cheyennes in an epic migration in 1830), inviting them to share in revenge for the unprovoked white attacks.

Many of the chiefs of these tribes refused to join in the fighting, not wanting to bring on a destructive war—but a large number of young warriors responded with raids on white settlements and travel routes. For the previous several years, they had seen a closing vise of white settlement on the central Great Plains, moving west from Kansas and east from Colorado—where mining towns and travel stops such as Denver formed the basis for expanding settlements along the Rocky Mountain foothills. Bands of young warriors seized the opportunity to strike back to defend their territory.

Those raids, unfortunately, provided the excuse to crank up the pressure from the western tooth of the vise, in Colorado. According to a deceptively wrought treaty of 1861, the Southern Cheyennes and Arapahos were obliged to live in a small reservation in the southeastern corner of the territory. Not surprisingly, the Indians ignored the treaty as they followed the buffalo herds on the Colorado and Kansas prairie. The raids of 1863–64 and the treaty violations provided the excuse for a plan by Colorado Governor John Evans to drive the Indians out.

Evans badly wanted to earn statehood for the Colorado Territory, which had grown rapidly in the previous decade. His political ambitions demanded that he satisfy the region's frightened pioneers, and expand the room for settlement, by driving out the Indians. A good Indian war, Evans figured, would promote the statehood cause—and his own career as well.

Evans's ally in this anti-Indian effort was Colonel John Chivington, who had recently won fame by defeating a Confederate army in the New Mexico Territory. "There was a dark and malevolent side to Chivington," writes historian Alvin Josephy, Jr. "Crude and overbearing, he had grown ruthlessly ambitious, as well as contemptuous of ethical or legal restraints." In 1864, Evans and Chivington boldly plotted a "war of extermination," as Josephy calls it, against the central plains tribes.

Unfortunately for the plotters, important members of the Native American leadership made strenuous efforts to restore peace. As in most Indian societies, the Arapahos and Southern Cheyennes were divided in their approach to the conflict; many warriors held that unstinting resistance was the only course. In 1864, however, the peace faction still carried a great deal of weight in their councils. The main spokesman was Black Kettle, a chief of the Southern Cheyennes. A judicious and far-seeing leader, he understood the changes taking place on the frontier, and sought to ease his people into an accommodation with the expanding white power. Chivington played out the negotiations with Black Kettle until the chief had brought his large band in to establish a winter village near Fort Lyon, on Sand Creek. Black Kettle explicitly asked for, and received, guarantees of government protection. Thus assured, the Southern Cheyenne village prepared for winter in peace. At the end of November, Chivington struck.

William Breakenridge was a young frontiersman who had responded to Evans's declaration of an Indian war by signing up with the Third Colorado Cavalry. Like most of his fellow white Coloradans, he had a special hatred for Indians; to him, they were a racial enemy to be crushed as swiftly as possible. Years later, he wrote freely about his role in Chivington's attack, vividly capturing the cruelty behind one of the most brutal atrocities in U.S. history—an unprovoked assault on a band of Indians who had already surrendered.

## The Sand Creek Massacre
*by William M. Breakenridge*

During the fall and winter of 1863 and the spring and summer of 1864, the Indians had become more and more aggressive, until hardly a day passed that they did not commit some depredation on the isolated ranches, or on emigrants coming into the country. A number of prisoners were taken by the Indians, all of them women and children.

Freight teams were pulled off on account of the raids, and provisions and necessities were getting scarce. Flour was forty-five dollars a sack, and other commodities in proportion. On account of the Civil War the government could not spare any troops to protect the frontier, but the Secretary of War did direct Governor John Evans of Colorado to enlist a regiment of volunteers for the purpose of operating in that country against the Indians. It was a hundred-day regiment, and was known as the Third Colorado Cavalry. . . .

At about the first of September, 1864, Major E.W. Wynkoop, First Colorado Cavalry, in command of Fort Lyon, received a message from Black Kettle, White Antelope, and several other prominent chiefs of the [Southern] Cheyenne and Arapaho tribes, that they wanted to make peace. The chiefs stated that they had some white prisoners, women and children, whom they were willing to give up providing that peace was granted them. . . .

Major Wynkoop went out to the Indian camp at Smoky Hill. . . . They agreed to allow Black Kettle, White Antelope, and Bull Bear of the Cheyennes and two or three Arapaho chiefs to go with him to Denver for the purpose of making peace, and he assured them that he would see them safe back to their camp. Four white prisoners, a woman and three children, were delivered to him by Black Kettle, the head chief of the [Southern] Cheyennes.

General Curtis telegraphed Colonel Chivington[16] that his terms of peace were to require all bad Indians to be given up, all stock stolen by the Indians to be returned, and hostages given by the Indians for their good conduct. The Indians would not comply with these terms. They said they had not received power to make peace on such terms. This ended their talk.[17]

Major Wynkoop on his own authority did allow some of the Indians—a band of about six hundred, together with the chiefs mentioned—to camp at or near Fort Lyon, promised them the protection of our flag, and issued them rations as prisoners of war. Very soon after doing this he was relieved of the command at Fort Lyon, and Major Anthony placed in command at that post. . . .

Major Anthony fed them for about ten days and then told them he would feed them no longer. He returned the few useless arms that they had turned in and drove them from the post. This was about the 12th or 15th of November. . . .

[16] Samuel Curtis was the U.S. military commander for the region; John Chivington commanded the Colorado regiments.

[17] Breakenridge is distorting the record to make it seem as if the Indians, not Chivington and the governor, were being intransigent.

After the Third Colorado was partly mounted and equipped, we were stationed at Bijou Basin, about sixty miles from Denver. . . . [The unit then began a march to the Indian camp near Fort Lyon.]

At Booneville, about twenty miles below Pueblo, Colonel Chivington met us. From that point no one was allowed to pass us in either direction, not even the mail, so that when we reached Fort Lyon we took them by surprise. We arrived there about four o'clock in the afternoon. Old Jim Beckwourth and some of the other scouts had been sent ahead to locate the Indian camp, but they had avoided the fort. At eight o'clock that night the order came to "boot and saddle," and we started northeast for the Indian camp at Sand Creek, about thirty-five or forty miles from Fort Lyon. Colonel Chivington had part of two companies of the First Colorado Cavalry with him, numbering 125 men, and at Fort Lyon we were joined by Major Anthony with two pieces of artillery and 125 men. Our regiment had about 500 men, as, when we got orders to move, a lot of the soldiers were home on leave of absence and were not notified in time to join us.

All the time we were on the road or in camp, the general topic of conversation was that when we got to where the Indians were we were not to take any prisoners; that the only way to put fear into them was to fight them their own way and scalp everyone of them. I had been told that the commanding officer had given orders to take no prisoners. . . .

This was on the 29th of November, 1864. At that season of the year three o'clock in the morning is still dark. When the command came up to where I had left the scouts, I heard Jim Beckwourth tell Colonel Chivington in the presence of the other scouts that the Indians were in camp about six miles from there and that there were 130 lodges of Cheyennes and eight lodges of Arapahos, and that the Arapahos were there on a visit, and were all warriors. This was the same tribe of Indians of which Black Kettle was the head chief. . . .

We had been travelling over a rather level rolling mesa. And as we came to the creek we saw a wide valley with brush and bunch grass growing in it. The Indian camp was on the bank of the creek, which had a small stream of running water in it. A few horses were grazing not far from the camp—not over twenty-five or thirty head, I think—and we saw smoke coming out of the tops of some of the tepees. It is rather hard to express the sensation I felt as we came in sight of the battlefield. While I had been close to several Indian skirmishes I had never been in a real fight with them, but my feelings of antipathy toward the Indians was so strong that I forgot all fear and was only anxious to get into a fight with them. . . .

There were 125 of the First Colorado Cavalry with us, and because they had been in several battles with Indians and Confederates, they were known as "The Bloody First," while our regiment, which had never been in a fight of any kind, was called "The Bloodless Third." We stopped to strip our saddles of blankets, food, and everything else we would not need in the fight, and while we were thus engaged the word came back among our boys that the First should go ahead and clean up the village. This meant that we would not get into it at all, and we would still be known as "The Bloodless Third." So when the order came to charge the camp everybody broke ranks and it was a stampede through the Indian village.

The attack was made about sunrise. The Indians were surprised, but they were better armed than the soldiers and they put up a desperate fight.

The Indians had excavated trenches under the bank of Sand Creek for several miles, and they took shelter in these trenches as soon as the attack came.[18] Although they put up a stubborn resistance and contested every inch of ground, they were slowly driven back from one position to another for about four miles, and finally about two o'clock in the afternoon they dispersed in all directions and were pursued by the troops until night. . . .

In going back to the village I kept down the creek over the ground we had been fighting over, and saw a good many dead Indians, all of them scalped. . . .

The soldiers had been told by Governor Evans's proclamation that they could have for their own use all the property that actually belonged to the Indians that they might capture, and they got quite a lot of buffalo robes and other trophies before the camp was burned.

The scouts and others estimated five persons to a tepee, which would make 650 Cheyennes and forty Arapahos in the village at the time we attacked it, and I cannot see for the life of me how very many of them could have got away, as we were right on top of them all the time. Colonel Chivington in his report stated that he had seven men killed, forty-seven wounded, and one missing; and that he judged that there were five hundred or six hundred Indians killed. . . .

I did not want to scalp an Indian, but I wanted a scalp, so I traded a buffalo robe with one of the boys for two scalps. Shortly after I was mustered out, my sister wrote asking for some of my hair to use in some kind of fancy work she was doing; I answered that I had my hair cut short to prevent being scalped, but that I was sending her two Indian scalps. I guess they did not take very well at home, for I got a letter from mother giving me a good dressing-down for sending such horrible things to my sister.

---

BLACK KETTLE SURVIVED the Sand Creek Massacre, as did Chief Left Hand of the Arapahos. They were stunned by the attack, coming as it did after they had come in to surrender. When word leaked out of the

[18] When the attack began, Black Kettle ran up a U.S. flag to communicate his friendly intentions. It did no good. Nor were there any trenches (though the Indians did run to the sandy banks and dig in to protect themselves during the cavalry's charge).

terrible atrocities, the American people reeled in shock as well. The Colorado cavalrymen had not only scalped their victims, they had mutilated them in the most barbaric fashion, cutting the genitals from dead victims of both sexes. Chivington resigned from the army to escape a court-martial, though little else happened to him. Governor Evans, too, was forced to resign, and his political career ground to a halt.

Meanwhile, the frontier had been set aflame. Black Kettle and Left Hand carried word of the slaughter to the rest of the Plains Indians. A bloody series of raids soon followed—including an assault by a thousand Sioux and Cheyenne warriors on Julesburg, Colorado, on January 7, 1865. General John Pope was now placed in command of the entire region; he promptly launched an ambitious, three-pronged campaign that soon bogged down, accomplishing nothing. The first blow, however, had been struck; before the end of the decade, the Indians would be driven completely off the Colorado prairie.

In the meantime, while Indians raided settlements and evaded the army, the march of commerce advanced unrelenting from the east—forming the second tooth of the vise that was closing in on the central plains. It was the railroad, which began to snake toward California in the early 1860s when Lincoln and the Republican Congress enacted aid for the transcontinental lines. The main thrust came from the Union Pacific, which began moving west out of Omaha in 1863. Farther south, the Kansas Pacific joined the advance, cutting across the Kansas prairie on a path to Denver.

For the expanding white communities on the frontier, the arrival of the railroad wrought a revolution. The slow, dangerous overland routes would be replaced by swift, regularly scheduled trains. The effort required to cross the immense distances would be slashed to a small fraction of what it was before. Even the process of constructing it brought a flow of money onto the frontier, as the railroad bought supplies and paid wages to construction crews.

Native Americans, however, saw the sinister side of the railroad's advance: it was like a spear driving into their traditional hunting grounds, dividing and absorbing their lands. First of all, the railroad vastly increased the flow of white settlers into Indian lands. The easier transportation west, the towns that grew up alongside the tracks, and the vast flow of money and capital into the construction all drew new settlers onto the Great Plains. Second, the railroad companies initiated a hunting program to feed their workers, a program that decimated the buffalo population. Professional hunters were hired to slaughter the bison in massive numbers— striking at the very foundation of Native American civilization.

The most famous of these marksmen was Buffalo Bill Cody,[19] an army scout and an accomplished killer of the great beasts. Through a

[19] His proper name was William F. Cody.

combination of very real prowess on the plains and a true genius for marketing himself, Cody became synonymous with the changes that were transforming the frontier—the slaughter of the buffalo (and what we would today call the transformation of the ecosystem), the expanding railroads, and the war against the Indians. In this passage, Cody lovingly describes his role in stripping the plains of the American bison—in the face of constant attacks by the enraged Indian warriors.

## Railroad Building and Buffalo Killing
*by Buffalo Bill Cody*

The western end of the Kansas Pacific was at this time in the heart of the buffalo country. Twelve hundred men were employed in the construction of the road. The Indians were very troublesome, and it was difficult to obtain fresh meat for the hands. The company therefore concluded to engage expert hunters to kill buffaloes.

Having heard of my experience and success as a buffalo hunter, Goddard Brothers, who had the contract for feeding the men, made me a good offer to become their hunter. They said they would require about twelve buffaloes a day—twenty-four hams and twelve humps, as only the hump and hindquarters of each animal were utilized. The work was dangerous. Indians were riding all over that section of the country, and my duties would require me to journey from five to ten miles from the railroad every day in order to secure the game, accompanied by only one man with a light wagon to haul the meat back to camp. I demanded a large salary, which they could well afford to pay, as the meat itself would cost them nothing. Under the terms of the contract which I signed with them, I was to receive five hundred dollars a month, agreeing on my part to supply them with all the meat they wanted.

I at once began my career as a buffalo hunter for the Kansas Pacific. It was not long before I acquired a considerable reputation, and it was at this time that the title "Buffalo Bill" was conferred upon me by the railroad hands. Of this title, which has stuck to me through life, I have never been ashamed.

During my engagement as hunter for the company, which covered a period of eighteen months, I killed 4,280 buffaloes and had many exciting adventures with the Indians, including a number of hairbreadth escapes, some of which are well worth relating. . . .

[One] adventure which deserves a place in these reminiscences occurred near the Saline River. My companion at the time was Scotty, the butcher who accompanied me on my hunts to cut up the meat and load it on the wagon for hauling to the railroad camp. I had killed fifteen buffaloes, and we were on our way home with a wagonload of meat when we were jumped by a big band of Indians.

I was mounted on a splendid horse belonging to the company, and could easily have made my escape, but Scotty had only the mule team which drew the wagon as a means of flight, and of course I could not leave him.

To think was to act in those days. Scotty and I had often talked of what we would do in case of a sudden attack, and we forthwith proceeded to carry out the plan we had made. Jumping to the ground, we unhitched the mules more quickly than that operation had ever been performed before. The mules and my horse we tied to the wagon. We threw the buffalo hams on the ground and piled them about the wheels so as to form a breastwork. Then, with an extra box of ammunition and three or four extra revolvers which we always carried with us, we crept under the wagon, prepared to give our visitors a reception they would remember.

On came the Indians, but when they got within a hundred yards of us we opened such a sudden and galling fire that they held up and began circling about us. Several times they charged. Their shots killed the two mules and my horse. But we gave it to them right and left, and had the satisfaction of seeing three of them fall to the ground not more than fifty feet away.

When we had been cooped up in our little fort for about an hour we saw the cavalry coming toward us, full gallop, over the prairie.[20] The Indians saw the soldiers almost as soon as we did. Mounting their horses, they disappeared down the canyon of the creek. When the cavalry arrived we had the satisfaction of showing them five Indians who would be "good" for all time. Two hours later we reached the camp with our meat, which we found to be all right, although it had a few bullets and arrows imbedded in it. . . .

Soon after the adventure with Scotty I had my celebrated shooting contest with Billy Comstock, a well-known guide, scout, and interpreter. Comstock, who was chief of scouts at Fort Wallace, had a reputation of being a successful buffalo hunter, and his friends at the fort—the officers in particular—were anxious to back him against me.

It was arranged that I should shoot a match with him, and the preliminaries were easily and satisfactorily arranged. We were to hunt one day of eight hours, beginning at eight o'clock in the morning. The wager was five hundred dollars a side, and the man who should kill the greater number of buffaloes from horseback was to be declared the winner. Incidentally my title of "Buffalo Bill" was at stake.

The hunt took place twenty miles east of Sheridan. . . . Buffaloes were plentiful. It had been agreed that we should go into the herd at the same

[20] Cody mentioned the Tenth Cavalry being stationed in the area; the Tenth was composed of black soldiers.

distance and make our runs, each man killing as many animals as possible.
A referee followed each of us, horseback, and counted the buffaloes killed
by each man. . . .

For the first run we were fortunate in getting good ground. Comstock
was mounted on his favorite horse. I rode old Brigham. I felt confident that
I had the advantage in two things: first, I had the best buffalo horse in the
country; second, I was using what was known at the time as a needle-
gun, a breech-loading Springfield rifle, caliber .50. This was "Lucretia
Borgia" . . . Comstock's Henry rifle, though it could fire more rapidly
than mine, did not, I felt certain, carry powder and lead enough to equal
my weapon in execution.[21]

When the time came to go into the herd, Comstock and I dashed
forward, followed by the referees. The animals separated. Comstock took
the left bunch, I the right. My great forte in killing buffaloes was to get
them circling by riding my horse at the head of the herd and shooting their
leaders. Thus the brutes behind were crowded to the left, so that they were
soon going round and round.

This particular morning the animals were very accommodating. I soon
had them running in a beautiful circle. I dropped them thick and fast till I
had killed thirty-eight, which finished my run.

Comstock began shooting at the rear of the buffaloes he was chasing,
and kept on in a straight line. He succeeded in killing twenty-three, but
they were scattered over a distance of three miles. The animals I had shot
lay close together. . . .

While we were resting we espied another herd approaching. It was a
small drove, but we prepared to make it serve our purpose. The buffaloes were cows and calves, quicker in their movements than the bulls.
We charged in among them, and I got eighteen to Comstock's fourteen. . . .

After a luncheon we resumed the hunt. Three miles distant we saw
another herd. I was so far ahead of my competitor now that I thought I
could afford to give an exhibition of my skill. Leaving my saddle and bridle
behind, I rode, with my competitor, to windward of the buffaloes.

I soon had thirteen down, the last one of which I had driven close to the
wagons, where the ladies were watching the contest. It frightened some of
the tender creatures to see a buffalo coming at full speed directly toward
them, but I dropped him in his tracks before he had got within fifty yards of
the wagon. This finished my run with a score of sixty-nine buffaloes for the
day. Comstock had killed forty-six.

---

[21] Cody's stated preference for this big-caliber, single-shot rifle reflects the prejudice
of buffalo hunters across the West, who felt that smaller-caliber repeaters like the
Henry rifle were underpowered. This sentiment later made some frontiersmen slow to
accept the '73 Winchester, which proved to be the single most important firearm of the
era, due to its reliability and high rate of fire.

It was now late in the afternoon. Comstock and his backers gave up the idea of beating me. The referee declared me the winner of the match, and the champion buffalo hunter of the Plains. . . .

In May, 1868, the Kansas Pacific track was pushed as far as Sheridan. Construction was abandoned for the time, and my services as buffalo hunter were no longer required. A general Indian war was now raging all along the Western borders. General Sheridan had taken up headquarters at Fort Hays, in order to be on the job in person. Scouts and guides were once more in great demand, and I decided to go back to my old calling.

BUFFALO BILL DID his killing well—but he offered only a hint of the massacres to come. Not long after the transcontinental railroad was completed in 1869, someone discovered that buffalo hides made decent leather, and a massive new wave of bison hunting erupted. In the early 1870s, professional hunting parties rode out on the prairies of the Texas panhandle, the Indian Territory, western Kansas, and eastern Colorado to slaughter the big, shaggy animals. General Sheridan condoned the mass hunting, declaring that it would strip the Indians of their material support and prevent them from going to war. The combination of railroad lines, new streams of farmers and ranchers, and intense buffalo hunting would transform the Western landscape.

But first, the Native American warriors of the Great Plains rose up in one more act of resistance—and the Southern Plains War of 1868 erupted in bloody mayhem.

# 6
# WAR FOR THE SOUTHERN PLAINS, 1868–1869

Hero of the dime novel, star of his own Wild West show, Buffalo Bill became such a figure of popular entertainment that it is hard to take him seriously today. But in the late 1860s he served as one of the sharpest weapons the United States ever turned against the Plains Indians. Working for the railroad, he helped spearhead a permanent penetration of their country; slaughtering buffalo, he attacked the very foundation of their civilization. Then, in 1868, he capped it off by joining a climactic war of military conquest—a campaign that finally defeated the Indians of the southern Great Plains and forced them to accept the reservation.

For over a decade, the Southern Cheyenne, Arapaho, Kiowa, and Comanche tribes had faced growing pressure from settlers in Colorado and Kansas; after the Civil War, the railroads joined the westward push. In 1867, an ill-considered military expedition by General W. S. Hancock presented them with a fresh provocation. Soldiers under the field command of General Alfred Sully and General George A. Custer, a dashing and popular hero of the Civil War, chased vainly after the elusive Indians. Increasingly, the peace faction led by Black Kettle lost influence as young warriors bridled with discontent at these encroachments. Now they turned to such men as Tall Bull and Roman Nose, leaders of the militant Dog Soldiers band of the Cheyennes, and Satanta and Lone Wolf, chiefs of the Kiowas.

After Hancock's failure, the government decided to negotiate. The result was the treaty of Medicine Lodge, where chiefs of the Cheyenne, Kiowa, Arapaho, and Comanche tribes agreed to move onto reservations in the Indian Territory (present-day Oklahoma). Tensions, however, had already boiled over. Over Black Kettle's objections, enraged warriors resisted the Medicine Lodge concessions, launching ferocious raids on the westernmost Kansas settlements in the summer of 1868. Open warfare erupted all across the frontier (taking the life of Roman Nose), as the army scrambled to organize a campaign of conquest.

The general in charge of that campaign was Philip H. Sheridan. He knew his task was not an easy one. Manpower shortages loomed: the U.S. Army had only 23,000 men in the West at this time, facing roughly 100,000 hostile Indians—and many of the troops were locked into garrison duty along the Pacific Coast and on the Mexican border. And the same government corruption that starved reservation Indians struck the military as well: commanders often had to cope with rotten food and fodder, and inadequate arms and ammunition. But Sheridan grasped the essential weakness of his Native American enemy: they had families to feed and protect, while the army was supported by a logistics system. If he could strike them when their villages were unable to flee, when they had difficulty hunting buffalo, he had a good chance of defeating them even if he had a smaller force. His solution: a winter campaign, when snow covered the grass and the Indian ponies would be weak and underfed.

In the passage that follows, Sheridan describes the events that led to the war in terms that leave his own harsh opinions perfectly clear. A terse, highly capable, no-nonsense commander, the general believed in force, not negotiations. Ironically, he had been transferred to this command from Louisiana, where he had aroused the anger of President Andrew Johnson essentially for being too fair to the newly freed African Americans, who faced attacks by enraged Southern whites. In the conflict between whites and Indians, his attitude would prove quite different. In Sheridan's eyes, the war for the frontier was a war for civilization itself.

## A Winter Campaign
*by General Philip H. Sheridan*

My new command [as of late 1867] was one of the four military departments that composed the geographical division then commanded by Lieutenant-General Sherman. This division had been formed in 1866, with a view to controlling the Indians west of the Missouri River, they having become very restless and troublesome because of the building of the Pacific railroads through their hunting grounds, and the encroachments of pioneers, who began settling in middle and western Kansas and eastern Colorado immediately after the war.

My department embraced the states of Missouri and Kansas, the Indian Territory, and New Mexico. Part of this section of country—western Kansas particularly—had been frequently disturbed and harassed during two or three years past, the savages now and then massacring an isolated family, boldly attacking the surveying and construction parties of the Kansas Pacific railroad, sweeping down on emigrant trains, plundering and burning stage stations and the like along the Smoky Hill route to Denver and the Arkansas route to New Mexico.

However, when I relieved Hancock, the department was comparatively quiet. Though some military operations had been conducted against the hostile tribes in the early part of the previous summer, all active work was now suspended in the attempt to conclude a permanent peace with the Cheyennes, Arapahos, Kiowas, and Comanches, in compliance with the act of Congress creating what was known as the Indian Peace Commission of 1867 . . .

I did not actually go on duty in the Department of the Missouri till March 1868. On getting back I learned that the negotiations of the Peace Commissioners—held at Medicine Lodge, about seventy miles south of Fort Larned—had resulted in a treaty with the Cheyennes, Arapahos, Kiowas, and Comanches, by which agreement it was supposed all troubles had been settled. The compact, as concluded, contained numerous provisions, the most important to us being one which practically relinquished the country between the Arkansas and Platte rivers for white settlement; another permitted the peaceable construction of the Pacific railroads through the same region; and a third requiring the tribes signing the treaty to retire to reservations allotted them in the Indian Territory.

Although the chiefs and headmen were well-nigh unanimous in ratifying these concessions, it was discovered in the spring of 1868 that many of the young men were bitterly opposed to what had been done. This grumbling was very general in extent, and during the winter found outlet in occasional marauding, so, fearing a renewal of the pillaging and plundering at an early day, to prepare myself for the work evidently ahead the first thing I did on assuming permanent command was to make a trip to Fort Larned and Fort Dodge, near which places the bulk of the Indians had congregated on Pawnee and Walnut Creeks. I wanted to get near enough to the camps to find out for myself the actual state of feeling among the savages, and also to familiarize myself with the characteristics of the Plains Indians, for my previous experience had been mainly with the mountain tribes on the Pacific coast. . . .

It took but a few days at Dodge to discover that great discontent existed about the Medicine Lodge concessions, to see that the young men were chafing and turbulent, and that it would require much tact and good management on the part of the Indian Bureau to persuade the four tribes to go quietly to their reservations, under an agreement which, when entered into, many of them protested had not been fully understood.

A few hours after my arrival a delegation of prominent chiefs called on me and proposed a council, where they might discuss their grievances, and thus bring to the notice of the Government the alleged wrongs done them; but this I refused, because Congress had delegated to the Peace Commission the whole matter of treating with them, and a council might lead only to additional complications. . . .

In July the encampments about Fort Dodge began to break up, each band or tribe moving off to some new location north of the Arkansas, instead of toward its proper reservation south of the river. Then I learned presently that a party of Cheyennes had made a raid on the Kaws—a band of friendly Indians living near Council Grove—and stolen their horses, and also robbed the houses of several white people near Council Grove. This raid was the beginning of the Indian war of 1868. . . .

[Shortly afterward,] a party of warriors had already begun a raid of murder and rapine, which for acts of devilish cruelty perhaps has no parallel in savage warfare. The party consisted of about two hundred Cheyennes and a few Arapahos, with twenty Sioux who had been visiting their friends, the Cheyennes. As near as could be ascertained, they organized and left their camps along Pawnee Creek about the third of August. Traveling northeast, they skirted around Fort Harker, and made their first appearance among the settlers in the Saline Valley, about thirty miles north of that post . . .

Leaving the Saline, this war-party crossed over to the valley of the Solomon, a more thickly settled region, and where the people were in better circumstances, their farms having been started two or three years before. Unaware of the hostile character of the raiders, the people here received them in the friendliest way, providing food, and even giving them ammunition, little dreaming of what was impending. These kindnesses were requited with murder and pillage, and worse, for all the women who fell into their hands were subjected to horrors indescribable by words. Here also the first murders were committed, thirteen men and two women being killed. Then, after burning five houses and stealing all the horses they could find, they turned back toward the Saline, carrying away as prisoners two little girls named Bell, who have never been heard of since.

It was probably their intention to finish, as they marched to the south, the devilish work begun on the Saline, but before they reached that valley on the return, the victims left there originally had fled to Fort Harker, and Captain Benteen[22] was now nearing the little settlement with a troop of cavalry, which he had hurriedly marched from Fort Zarah. The savages were attacking the house of a Mr. Schemerhorn, where a few of the settlers had collected for defense, when Benteen approached. Hearing the firing, the troopers rode toward the sound at a gallop, but when they appeared in view, coming over the hills, the Indians fled in all directions, escaping punishment through their usual tactics of scattering over the Plains, so as to leave no distinctive trail. . . .

Simultaneously with the fiendish atrocities committed on the Saline and Solomon rivers . . . pillaging and murdering began on the Smoky Hill stage route, along the upper Arkansas River and on the headwaters of the Cimarron. That along the Smoky Hill and the north of it was the exclusive work of the Cheyennes, a part of the Arapahos, and the few Sioux allies heretofore mentioned, while the raiding along the Arkansas and Cimarron

---

[22] Captain Frederick Benteen was an officer of the Seventh Cavalry (Custer's regiment), and he proved to be one of Custer's leading critics.

was done principally by the Kiowas under their chief, Satanta, aided by some of the Comanches. . . . The rest of the Comanches and Kiowas escaped from the post [at Larned] and fled south of the Arkansas. They were at once pursued by General Sully with a small force, but by the time he reached the Cimarron the war party had finished its raid on the upper Arkansas, and so many Indians combined against Sully that he was compelled to withdraw to Fort Dodge, which he reached not without considerable difficulty, and after three severe fights.

These, and many minor raids which followed, made it plain that a general outbreak was upon us. The only remedy, therefore, was to subjugate the savages immediately engaged in the forays by forcing the several tribes to settle down on the reservations set apart by the treaty of Medicine Lodge. The principal mischief-makers were the Cheyennes. Next in deviltry were the Kiowas, and then the Arapahos and Comanches. . . . All four tribes together could put on the warpath a formidable force of about 6,000 warriors. The subjugation of this number of savages would be no easy task, so to give the matter my undivided attention I transferred my headquarters from Leavenworth to Fort Hays. . . .

Fort Hays was just beyond the line of the most advanced settlements, and was then the terminus of the Kansas Pacific railroad. For this reason it could be made a depot of supplies, and was a good point from which to supervise matters in the section of country to be operated in, which district is a part of the Great American Plains, extending south from the Platte River in Nebraska to the Red River in the Indian Territory, and westward from the line of frontier settlements to the foothills of the Rocky Mountains, a vast region embracing an area of about 150,000 square miles. With the exception of a half-dozen military posts and a few stations on the two overland emigrant routes—the Smoky Hill to Denver, and the Arkansas to New Mexico—this country was an unsettled waste known only to the Indians and a few trappers. There were neither roads nor well-marked trails, and the only timber to be found—which generally grew only along the streams—was so scraggly and worthless as hardly to deserve the name. Nor was water by any means plentiful. . . .

At the period of which I write, in 1868, the Plains were covered with vast herds of buffalo—the number has been estimated at 3,000,000 head— and with such means of subsistence as this everywhere at hand, the 6,000 hostiles were wholly unhampered by any problem of food supply. The savages were rich, too, according to Indian standards, many a lodge owning from twenty to a hundred ponies; and consciousness of wealth and power, aided by former temporizing [by the U.S. government], had made them confident but defiant. Realizing that their thorough subjugation would be a difficult task, I made up my mind to confine operations during the grazing and hunting season to protect the people of the new settlements and on the overland routes, and then, when winter came, to fall upon the savages relentlessly, for in that season their ponies would be thin, and weak from lack of food, and in the cold and snow, without strong ponies to transport their villages and plunder, their movements would be so much impeded that the troops could overtake them. . . .

To get ready for a winter campaign of six months gave us much to do. The thing most needed was more men, so I asked for additional cavalry, and all that could be spared—seven troops of the Fifth Cavalry—was sent to me. Believing this reinforcement insufficient, to supplement it I applied for a regiment of Kansas volunteers, which request being granted, the organization of the regiment was immediately begun at Topeka. It was necessary also to provide a large amount of transportation and accumulate quantities of stores, since the campaign probably would not end till spring. Another important matter was to secure competent guides for the different columns of troops, for, as I have said, the section of the country to be operated in was comparatively unknown.

In those days the railroad town of Hays City was filled with so-called "Indian scouts," whose common boast was of having slain scores of redskins, but the real scout—that is, a guide and trailer knowing the habits of the Indians—was very scarce, and it was hard to find anybody familiar with the country south of the Arkansas, where the campaign was to be made. Still, about Hays City and the various military posts there was some good material to select from, and we managed to employ several men, who, from their experience on the plains in various capacities, or from natural instinct and aptitude, soon became excellent guides and courageous and valuable scouts, some of them, indeed, gaining much distinction. Mr. William F. Cody ("Buffalo Bill"), whose renown has since become worldwide, was one of the men thus selected. He received his sobriquet from his marked success in killing buffaloes for a contractor, to supply fresh meat to the construction parties of the Kansas Pacific railway. He had given up this business, however, and was now in the employ of the quartermaster's department of the army, and was first brought to my notice by distinguishing himself in bringing me an important despatch from Fort Larned to Fort Hays, a distance of sixty-five miles, through a section infested with Indians. The despatch informed me that the Indians near Larned were preparing to decamp, and this intelligence required that certain orders should be carried to Fort Dodge, ninety-five miles south of Hays. This, too, being a particularly dangerous route—several couriers having been killed on it—it was impossible to get one of the various "Petes," "Jacks," or "Jims" hanging around Hays City to take my communication. Cody, learning of the strait I was in, manfully came to the rescue, and proposed to make the trip to Dodge, though he had just finished his long and perilous ride from Larned. I gratefully accepted his offer, and after four or five hours' rest he mounted a fresh horse and hastened on his journey, halting but once to rest on the way, and then only for an hour, the stop being made at Coon Creek, where he got another mount from a troop of cavalry. At Dodge he took six hours' sleep, and then continued on to his own post—Fort Larned—with more despatches. After resting twelve hours at Larned, he was again in the saddle with tidings for me at Fort Hays, General Hazen sending him, this time, with word that the villages had fled to the south of the Arkansas. Thus, in all, Cody rode about 350 miles in less than sixty hours, and such an exhibition of endurance and courage was more than enough to convince me that his services would be extremely valuable in the campaign, so I retained him at Fort Hays till the battalion of the Fifth Cavalry arrived, and then made him chief of scouts for that regiment.

The information brought me by Cody on his second trip from Larned indicated where the villages would be found in the winter, and I decided to move on them about the first of November. Only the women and children and the decrepit old men were with the villages, however—enough, presumably, to look after the plunder—most of the warriors remaining north of the Arkansas to continue their marauding. Many severe fights occurred between our troops and these marauders, and in these affairs, before November 1, over a hundred Indians were killed, yet from the ease with which the escaping savages would disappear only to fall upon remote settlements with pillage and murder, the results were by no means satisfactory. . . .

The end of October saw completed most of my arrangements for the winter campaign, though the difficulties and hardships to be encountered led several experienced officers of the army, and some frontiersmen like Mr. James Bridger, the famous scout and guide of earlier days, to discourage the project. Mr. Bridger even went so far as to come from St. Louis to dissuade me, but I reasoned that as the soldier was much better fed and clothed than the Indian, I had one great advantage, and that, in short, a successful campaign could be made if the operations of the different columns were energetically conducted. To see to this I decided to go in person with the main column, which was to push down into the western part of the Indian Territory, having for its initial objective the villages which, at the beginning of hostilities, had fled toward the headwaters of the Red River, and those also that had gone to the same remote region after decamping from the neighborhood of Larned at the time that General Hazen sent Buffalo Bill to me with the news.

The column which was expected to do the main work was to be composed of the Nineteenth Kansas Volunteer Cavalry, commanded by Colonel Crawford;[23] eleven troops of the Seventh United States Cavalry,

[23] Samuel J. Crawford had resigned as governor of Kansas to lead the newly raised regiment; as the Republican chief executive, he had been a key figure in handing hundreds of thousands of acres in land grants to the railroads in that state.

under General Custer; and a battalion of infantry under Brevet Major John H. Page. To facilitate matters, General Sully, the district commander, was ordered to rendezvous these troops and establish a supply depot about a hundred miles south of Fort Dodge, as from such a point operations could be more readily conducted. He selected for the depot a most suitable place at the confluence of Beaver and Wolf creeks, and on his arrival there with Custer's and Page's commands, named the place Camp Supply.

In conjunction with the main column, two others were to penetrate the Indian Territory. One of these, which was to march east from New Mexico by way of Fort Bascom, was to be composed of six troops of the Third Cavalry and two companies of infantry, the whole under Colonel A.W. Evans. The other, consisting of seven troops of the Fifth Cavalry, and commanded by Brevet Brigadier-General Eugene A. Carr, was to march southeast from Fort Lyon [Colorado]; the intention being that Evans and Carr should destroy or drive in toward old Fort Cobb any straggling bands that might be prowling through the country west of my own march. The Fort Bascom column, after establishing a depot of supplies at Monument Creek, was to work down the main Canadian, and remain out as long as it could feed itself from New Mexico; Carr, having united with Penrose on the North Canadian, was to operate toward the Antelope Hills and head-waters of the Red River; while I, with the main column, was to move southward to strike the Indians along the Washita, or still farther south on branches of the Red River. . . .

We started from Fort Hays on the fifteenth of November, and the first night out a blizzard struck us and carried away our tents; and as the gale was so violent that they could not be put up again, the rain and snow drenched us to the skin. Shivering from wet and cold, I took refuge under a wagon, and there spent such a miserable night that, when at last morning came, the gloomy predictions of old man Bridger and others rose up before me with greatly increased force. . . .

The evening of November 21 we arrived at the Camp Supply depot, having traveled all day in another snow storm that did not end till twenty-four hours later. General Sully, with Custer's regiment and the infantry battalion, had reached the place several days before, but the Kansas regiment had not yet put in an appearance. All hands were at work trying to shelter the stores and troops, but from the trail seen that morning, believing that an opportunity offered to strike an effective blow, I directed Custer to call in his working parties and prepare to move immediately, without waiting for Crawford's regiment, unaccountably absent. Custer was ready to start by the twenty-third, and he was then instructed to march north to where the trail had been seen near Beaver Creek and follow it on the back track, for, being convinced that the war party had come from the Washita, I felt certain that this plan would lead directly to the villages.

SHERIDAN'S AMBITIOUS PLAN now fell into the hands of George Armstrong Custer, perhaps the most celebrated cavalry commander in the nation. A highly successful boy general in the Civil War, now the self-consciously dashing leader of the Seventh Cavalry Regiment,[24] Custer was already a controversial figure. As Stephen Ambrose has written, he was "a newspaperman's delight," a man who "wallowed in romanticism." The flamboyant commander wore a uniform of his own design (if he wore one at all—in the West he preferred a buckskin outfit), and sported curly locks that led the Indians to name him "Long Hair." He reveled in slam-bang charges that left scores of his men dead. And yet, as Ambrose also notes, "Custer backed his appearance with performance. He embraced the time-honored advice to all combat leaders: never send your men to do something you wouldn't do yourself." Indeed, his personal bravery was legendary. During the Civil War, he launched one foolhardy charge because he knew Sheridan was watching—and he pulled it off, routing the enemy and winning a place as Sheridan's favorite field commander.

But Custer earned controversy for more than his self-congratulating dash. He was harsh on his men, driving them and disciplining them ferociously (he trained his men effectively, but he also sent out a detachment to kill a group of deserters on one occasion). And the young officer was also impetuous, frequently acting without orders. Such tendencies led to his being suspended from duty prior to the Southern Plains War of 1868, but Sheridan called his protege back to field command. Having failed to bring the Indians to battle under Hancock in 1867, having been once suspended, Custer now had to prove himself.

Custer's highly romantic account reaches back to his careful preparations for battle, as he organized his men and trained them to fight. Then his story catches up to where Sheridan left off, providing a riveting description of the cavalry on campaign—and the pivotal (and most tragic) battle of the war, on the banks of the Washita River.

## The Battle of the Washita
*by General George A. Custer*

Before proceeding further in my narrative I will introduce to the reader a personage who is destined to appear at different intervals, and upon interesting occasions, as the campaign proceeds. It is usual on the plains,

[24] Custer was reduced to lieutenant colonel in the smaller post–Civil War regular army. He kept that rank until his death, but he was still referred to as a general by Sheridan and most others—a usage frequently adopted in this book.

and particularly during time of active hostilities, for every detachment of troops to be accompanied by one or more professional scouts or guides. They constitute a most interesting as well as useful and necessary portion of our frontier population. Who they are, whence they come from, or whither they go, their names even, except such as they choose to adopt or which may be given them, are all questions which none but themselves can answer.

When I joined the command I found quite a number of these scouts attached to various portions of the cavalry, but each acting separately. For the purposes of organization it was deemed best to unite them into a separate detachment under command of one of their own number. Being unacquainted personally with the merits or demerits of any of them, the selection of a chief had necessarily to be made somewhat at random. There was one among their number whose appearance would have attracted the notice of any casual observer. He was a man about forty years of age, perhaps older, over six feet in height, and possessing a well-proportioned frame. His head was covered with a luxuriant crop of long, almost black hair, strongly inclined to curl. . . . His face, at least so much of it as was not concealed by the long, waving brown beard and moustache, was full of intelligence and pleasant to look upon. His eye was undoubtedly handsome, black, and lustrous, with an expression of kindness and mildness combined. On his head was generally to be seen, whether asleep or awake, a huge sombrero or black slouch hat. A soldier's overcoat with its large circular cape, a pair of trousers with the legs tucked in the top of his long boots, usually constituted the outside make-up of the man whom I selected as chief scout. He was known by the euphonious title of "California Joe"; no other name seemed ever to have been given him, and no other name ever seemed necessary. His military armament consisted of a long breech-loading Springfield musket, from which he was inseparable, and a revolver and hunting-knife, both the latter being carried in his waist-belt. His mount completed his equipment for the field, being instead of a horse a finely-formed mule, in whose speed and endurance he had every confidence. Scouts usually prefer a good mule to a horse, and wisely, too. . . . The mule will perform a rapid and continuous march without forage, being able to subsist on the grazing to be obtained in nearly all the valleys on the plains during the greater portion of the year. California Joe was an inveterate smoker, and was rarely seen without his stubby, dingy-looking brierwood pipe in full blast. The endurance of his smoking powers was surpassed only by his loquacity. . . . This was the man whom upon a short acquaintance I decided to appoint as chief of scouts. . . .

The Seventh Cavalry, which was to operate in one body during the coming campaign, was a comparatively new regiment, dating its existence as an organization from July, 1866. The officers and companies had not served together before with much over half their full force. A large number of fresh horses were required and obtained; these had to be drilled. All the horses in the command were to be newly shod, and an extra fore and hind shoe fitted to each horse; these, with the necessary nails, were to be carried by each trooper in the saddle pocket.

It had been seen that the men lacked accuracy in the use of their carbines. To correct this, two drills in target practice were ordered each day. . . . The men had been previously informed that out of the eight hundred men composing the command, a picked corps of sharpshooters would be selected, numbering forty men, and made up of the forty best marksmen in the regiment. As an incentive to induce every enlisted man, whether noncommissioned officer or private, to strive for an appointment in the sharpshooters, it was given out from headquarters that the men so chosen would be regarded, as they really would deserve to be, as the elite of the command; not only regarded as such, but treated with corresponding consideration. . . .

It was surprising to observe the marked and rapid improvement in the accuracy of aim attained by the men generally during this period. Two drills at target practice each day, and allowing each man an opportunity at every drill to become familiar with the handling of his carbine, and in judging of the distances of the different targets, worked a most satisfactory improvement in the average accuracy of fire; so that at the end of the period named, by taking the record of each trooper's target practice, I was enabled to select forty marksmen in whose ability to bring down any warrior, whether mounted or not, who might challenge us, as we had often been challenged before, I felt every confidence. They were a superb body of men, and felt the greatest pride in their distinction. . . .

After everything in the way of reorganization and refitting which might be considered as actually necessary had been ordered, another step, bordering on the ornamental perhaps, although in itself useful, was taken. This was what is termed in the cavalry "coloring the horses," which does not imply, as might be inferred from the expression, that we actually changed the color of our horses, but merely classified or arranged them throughout the different squadrons and troops according to color. Hitherto the horses had been distributed to the various companies of the regiment indiscriminately, regardless of color, so that in each company and squadron horses were found of every color. For uniformity of appearance it was decided to devote one afternoon to a general exchange of horses. . . .[25]

Among the other measures adopted for carrying the war to our enemy's doors, and in a manner of "fight the devil with fire," was the employment

---

[25] This was not simply decorative: By giving each unit a distinct set of horses, the commander gained an important tool in identifying his own men in the confusion of battle.

of Indian allies. These were to be procured from the "reservation Indians," tribes who, from engaging in long and devastating wars with the whites and other hostile bands, had become so reduced in power as to be glad to avail themselves of the protection and means of subsistence offered by the reservation plan. These tribes were most generally the objects of hatred in the eyes of their more powerful and independent neighbors of the Plains, and the latter, when making their raids and bloody incursions upon the white settlements of the frontiers, did not hesitate to visit their wrath equally upon whites and reservation Indians. . . . An officer was sent to the village of the Osages to negotiate with the head chiefs, and was successful in his mission, returning with a delegation consisting of the second chief in rank of the Osage tribe, named Little Beaver; Hard Rope, the counsellor or wise man of his people; and eleven warriors, with an interpreter. . . .

Everything being in readiness, the cavalry moved from its camp on the north bank of the Arkansas on the morning of the 12th of November, and after fording the river began its march toward the Indian Territory. That night we encamped on Mulberry creek, where we were joined by the infantry and the supply train. General Sully, commanding the district, here took active command of the combined forces. . . . Nothing occurred giving us any clue to the whereabouts of the Indians until we had been marching several days and were moving down the valley of Beaver creek, when our Indian guides discovered the trail of an Indian war party, numbering, according to their estimate, from one hundred to one hundred and fifty warriors, mounted and moving in a northeasterly direction. The trail was not over twenty-four hours old, and by following it to the point where it crossed Beaver creek, almost the exact numbers and character of the party could be determined from the fresh signs at the crossing. Everything indicated that it was a war party sent from the very tribes we were in search of, and the object, judging from the direction they had been moving, and other circumstances, was to make a raid on the settlements in western Kansas. . . . We shall strike this trail again, but on different ground and different circumstances. . . .[26]

On the sixth day after leaving our camp on the north bank of the Arkansas the expedition arrived at the point which was chosen as our future base, where the infantry were to remain and erect quarters for themselves and storehouses for the military supplies. The point selected—which was then given the name it now bears, Camp Supply—was in the angle formed by Wolf and Beaver creeks, about one mile above the junction of these streams. . . . We of the cavalry knew that our detention at this point would

[26] Custer argued with Sully that he should be allowed to pursue the Indians whose trail they had crossed. Sully refused, desiring to obey Sheridan's orders (and perhaps because he had a healthier respect for the Indians, due to his experiences during the previous summer and in 1864).

be but brief. Within two or three days of our arrival the hearts of the entire command were gladdened by the sudden appearance in our midst of strong reinforcements. These reinforcements consisted of General Sheridan and staff. Hearing of his near approach, I mounted my horse and was soon galloping beyond the limits of camp to meet him. If there were any persons in the command who hitherto had been in doubt as to whether the proposed winter campaign was to be a reality or otherwise, such persons soon would have had cause to dispel all mistrust on this point. Selecting from the train a sufficient number of the best teams and wagons to transport our supplies of rations and forage, enough to subsist the command upon for a period of thirty days, our arrangements were soon completed by which the cavalry, consisting of eleven companies and numbering between eight and nine hundred men, were ready to resume the march. In addition we were to be accompanied by a detachment of scouts, among the number being California Joe; also our Indian allies from the Osage tribe, headed by Little Beaver and Hard Rope. As the country was beyond the limits of the district which constituted the command of General Sully, that officer was relieved from further duty with the troops composing the expedition. . . .

After remaining at Camp Supply six days, nothing was required but the formal order directing the movement to commence. This came in the shape of a brief letter of instructions from Department headquarters. Of course, nothing was known positively as to the exact whereabouts of the Indian villages, [so] the instructions had to be general in terms. In substance, I was to march my command in search of the winter hiding places of the hostile Indians, and wherever found administer such punishment for past depredations as my force was able to. On the evening of November 22nd, orders were issued to be in readiness to move promptly at daylight the following morning. That night, in the midst of other final preparations for a long separation from all means of communication with absent friends, most of us found time to hastily pen a few parting lines, informing them of our proposed expedition, and the uncertainties with which it was surrounded, as none of us knew when or where we should be heard from again once we bade adieu to the bleak hospitalities of Camp Supply. Alas! some of our number were destined never to return.

It began snowing the evening of the 22nd, and continued all night, so that when the shrill notes of the bugle broke the stillness of the morning air at reveille on the 23rd, we awoke at four o'clock to find the ground covered with snow to a depth of over one foot, and the storm still raging in full force. Surely this was anything but an inviting prospect as we stepped from our frail canvas shelters and found ourselves standing in the constantly and rapidly increasing depth of snow which appeared in every direction. "How will this do for a winter campaign?" was the half sarcastic query of the adjutant, as he came trudging back to the tent through a field of snow extending almost to the top of his tall troop boots, after having received the reports of the different companies at reveille. "Just what we want," was the reply. Little grooming did the shivering horses receive from the equally uncomfortable troopers that morning. Breakfast was served and disposed of more as a matter of form and regulation than to satisfy the appetite; for who, I might wonder, could rally much of an appetite at five o'clock in the morning, and when standing around a camp fire almost up to the knees in snow? . . . "Boots and saddles" rang forth, and each trooper grasped his saddle, and the next moment was busily engaged arranging and disposing of the few buckles and straps upon which the safety of his seat and the comfort of his horse depended.

While they were thus employed, my horse being already saddled and held nearby, by the orderly, I improved the time to gallop through the darkness across the narrow plain to the tent of General Sheridan, and say goodbye. I found the headquarter tents wrapped in silence, and first imagined that no one was yet stirring except the sentinel in front of the General's tent, who kept up his lonely tread, apparently indifferent to the beating storm. But I had no sooner given the bridle-rein to my orderly than the familiar tones of the General called out, letting me know that he was awake, and had been an attentive listener to our notes of preparation. His first greeting was to ask what I thought about the snow and the storm. To which I replied that nothing could be more to our purpose. We could move and the Indian villages could not. If the snow only remained on the ground one week, I promised to bring the General satisfactory evidences that my command had met the Indians. With an earnest injunction from my chief to keep him informed, if possible, should anything important occur, and many hearty wishes for a successful issue to the campaign, I bid him adieu. After I had mounted my horse, and had started to rejoin my command, a staff officer of the General, a particular friend, having just been awakened by the conversation, called out, while standing in the door of his tent enveloped in the comfortable folds of a huge buffalo robe, "Goodbye, old fellow; take care of yourself!" and in these brief sentences the usual farewell greetings between brother officers separating for service took place.

By the time I rejoined my men they had saddled their horses and were in readiness for the march. "To horse" was sounded, and each trooper stood at his horse's head. Then followed the commands "Prepare to mount" and "Mount," when nothing but the signal "Advance" was required to put the column in motion. The band took its place at the head of the column, preceded by the guides and scouts, and when the march began it was to the familiar notes of that famous old marching tune, "The girl I left behind me." . . .

The snow continued to descend in almost blinding clouds. Even the appearance of daylight aided us but little in determining the direction of our march. So dense and heavy were the falling lines of snow, that all view of the surface of the surrounding country, upon which the guides depended to enable them to run their course, was cut off. To such an extent was this true that it became unsafe for a person to wander from the column a distance equal to twice the width of Broadway, as in that short space all view of the column was prevented by the storm. None of the command except the Indian guides had ever visited the route we desired to follow, and they were forced to confess that until the storm abated sufficiently to permit them to catch glimpses of the landmarks of the country, they could not undertake to guide the troops to the point where we desired to camp that night. Here was a serious obstacle encountered quite early in the campaign. . . .

There was but one course to pursue now that the guides could no longer conduct us with certainty, and that was to be guided—like the mariner in mid-ocean—by the never-failing compass. There are few cavalry officers but what carry a compass in some more or less simple form. Mine was soon in my hand, and having determined as accurately as practicable, from my knowledge of the map of the country, the direction in which we ought to move in order to strike Wolf creek at the desired camping ground, I became for the time guide to the column, and after marching until about two P.M. reached the valley of Wolf creek, where a resting place for the night was soon determined upon. There was still no sign of abatement on the part of the weather. . . . Our wagons were still far in the rear. While they were coming up every man in the command, officers as well as enlisted men, set briskly to work in gathering a good supply of wood, as our personal comfort in the camp would be largely dependent on the quality and quantity of our firewood. . . . Fires were soon blazing upon the grounds assigned to the different troops, and upon the arrival of the wagons, which occurred soon after, the company cooks were quickly engaged in preparing the troopers' dinner, while the servants of the officers were employed in a similar manner for the benefit of the latter. . . . Tents up at last, dinner was not long in being prepared, and even less time employed in disposing of it. A good cup of coffee went far toward reconciling us to everything that had but a few moments before appeared somewhat uninviting. . . .

If the storm seemed terrible to us, I believed it would prove to be even more terrible to our enemies, the Indians. Promptly at the appointed hour, four o'clock the following morning, camp was bustling and active in response to the bugle notes of reveille. The storm had abated, the snow had ceased falling, but that which had fallen during the previous twenty-four hours now covered the ground to a depth of upward of eighteen inches. The sky was clear, however, to adopt the expressive language of California Joe, "the travellin' was good overhead." . . .

All of the second day we continued to march up the valley of the stream we had chosen as our first camping ground. The second night we encamped under circumstances very similar to those which attended us the first night, except that the storm no longer disturbed us. . . . Resuming the march at daylight on the morning of the third day, our route still kept us in the valley of Wolf creek, on whose banks we were to encamp for the third time. Nothing was particularly worthy of notice during our third day's march, except the immense quantities of game to be seen seeking the weak shelter from the storm offered by the little strips of timber extending along the valleys of Wolf creek and its tributaries. . . .

On that afternoon we again encamped in the same valley up which we had been moving during the past three days. The next morning, following our Indian guides, who had been directed to conduct us to a point on the Canadian river near the Antelope Hills, our course, which so far had been westerly, now bore off almost due south. After ascending gradually for some hours to the crest or divide which sloped on the north down to the valley of the stream we had just left, we reached the highest line and soon began to gradually descend again, indicating that we were approaching a second valley; this the Indians assured us was the valley of the Canadian. Delayed in our progress by the deep snow and the difficulty from the same cause always experienced by our guides in selecting a practicable route, darkness overtook us before the entire command arrived at the point chosen for our camp on the north bank of the Canadian. . . .

If any prowling bands or war parties belonging to either of the tribes with which we were at war were moving across the Canadian in either direction, it was more than probable that their crossing would be made at some point above us, and not more than ten or fifteen miles distant. The season was rather far advanced to expect any of these parties to be absent from the village, but the trail of the war party, discovered by our Indian guides just before the expedition reached Camp Supply, was not forgotten, and the heavy storm of the past few days would be apt to drive them away from the settlements and hasten their return to their village. We had every reason to believe that the latter was located somewhere south of the Canadian. After discussing the matter with Little Beaver and Hard Rope, and listening to the suggestions of California Joe and his confreres, I decided to start a strong force up the valley of the Canadian at daybreak the following morning, to examine the banks and discover, if possible, if Indians had been in the vicinity since the snow had fallen. Three full troops of cavalry under Major Joel H. Elliot, 7th Cavalry, were ordered to move without wagons or *otro impedimento*, each trooper to carry one hundred rounds of ammunition, one day's rations and forage. Their instructions were to proceed up the north bank of the Canadian a distance of fifteen miles. . . .

Major Elliot was a very zealous officer, and daylight found him and his command on the march in the execution of the duty to which they had

been assigned. Those of us who remained behind were soon busily occupied in making preparations to effect a crossing of the Canadian. California
Joe had been engaged since early dawn in searching for a ford which would
be practicable for our wagons; the troopers and horses could cross almost
anywhere. A safe fording place barely practicable was soon reported, and
the cavalry and wagon train began moving over. It was a tedious process;
sometimes the treacherous quicksand would yield beneath the heavily
laden wagons, and double the usual number of mules would be required to
extricate the load. In less than three hours the last wagon and the rear
guard of the cavalry had made a successful crossing. Looming up in our
front like towering battlements were the Antelope Hills. . . .

One by one the huge army wagons, with their immense white covers,
began the long ascent which was necessary to be overcome before attain-
ing the level of the plains. As fast as they reached the high ground the
leading wagons were halted and parked to await the arrival of the last to
cross the river. In the meantime the cavalry had closed up and dismounted,
except the rear guard, which was just then seen approaching from the river,
indicating that everything was closed up.

I was about to direct the chief bugler to sound "To horse," when far in
the distance, on the white surface of the snow, I descried a horseman
approaching us rapidly as his tired steed could carry him. The direction was
that in which Elliot's command was supposed to be, and the horseman
approaching could be none other than a messenger from Elliot. . . . By
means of my field glass I was able to make out the familiar form of Corbin,
one of the scouts. After due waiting, when minutes seemed like hours, the
scout galloped up to where I was waiting, and in a few hurried, almost
breathless words, informed me that Elliot's command, after moving up the
north bank of the Canadian about twelve miles, had discovered the trail of
an Indian party numbering upwards of one hundred and fifty strong; that
the trail was not twenty-four hours old, and the party had crossed the
Canadian and taken a course a little east of south. Elliot had crossed his
command, and at once taken up the pursuit as rapidly as his horses could
travel. Here was news, and of a desirable character. I asked the scout if he
could overtake Elliot if furnished with a fresh horse. He thought he could.
A horse was at once supplied him, and he was told to rejoin Elliot as soon as
possible, with instructions to continue the pursuit with all possible vigor,
and I would move with the main command in such direction as to strike his
trail about dark. . . .

My resolution was formed in a moment, and as quickly put in train of
execution. The bugle summoned all the officers to report at once. There
was no tardiness on their part, for while they had not heard the report
brought in by the scout, they had witnessed his unexpected arrival and his
equally sudden departure—circumstances which told them plainer than
mere words that something unusual was in the air. The moment they were

all assembled about me I acquainted them with the intelligence received from Elliot, and at the same time informed them that we would at once set out to join in the pursuit—a pursuit which could and would only end when we overtook our enemies. And in order that we should not be trammelled in our movements, it was my intention then and there to abandon our train of wagons, taking with us only such supplies as we could carry on our persons and strapped to our saddles. The train would be left under the protection of about eighty men detailed from the different troops, and under the command of one officer, to whom orders would be given to follow us with the train as rapidly as the character of our route would permit. . . .

During all this time Elliot with his three companies of cavalry was following hard and fast upon the trail left by the Indians in the deep snow. By being informed, as we were, of the direction in which the trail was leading, and that direction being favorable to our position, the main command by moving due south would strike the trail of the Indians, and of Elliot also, at some point not far in rear perhaps of Elliot's party. Everything being in readiness to set out at the expiration of the allotted twenty minutes, "The Advance" was sounded and the pursuit on our part began. Our route carried us across the broad, open plains, the snow over a foot in depth, with the surface of course unbroken. This rendered it exceedingly fatiguing to the horses moving in the advance, and changes were frequently rendered necessary. The weather, which during the past few days had been so bitterly cold, moderated on that day sufficiently to melt the upper surface of the snow. After leaving the wagon train, we continued our march rapidly during the remaining hours of the forenoon and until the middle of the afternoon. Still no tidings from Elliot's party nor any sign of a trail. . . . Our scouts and Indian guides were kept far out in front and on the proper flank, to discover, if possible, the trail. At last one of the scouts gave the signal that the trail had been discovered, and in a few moments the command had reached it, and we were now moving with lighter and less anxious hearts. After studying the trail our Osage warriors informed us that the Indians whose trail we were pursuing were undoubtedly a war party, and had certainly passed where we then were during the forenoon. . . .

Selecting a few well-mounted troopers and some of the scouts, I directed them to set out at a moderate gallop to overtake Elliot, with orders to the latter to halt at the first favorable point where wood and water could be obtained, and await our arrival, informing him at the same time that after allowing the men an hour to prepare a cup of coffee and to feed and rest their horses, it was my intention to continue the pursuit during the night—a measure to which I felt urged by the slight thawing of snow that day, which might result in our failure if we permitted the Indians to elude us until the snow had disappeared. Satisfied now that we were on the right course, our anxiety lessened, but our interest increased. . . .

Ten o'clock came and found us in our saddles. Silently the command stretched out its long length as the troopers filed off four abreast. First came two of our Osage scouts on foot; these were to follow the trail and lead the command; they were our guides, and the panther, creeping upon its prey, could not have advanced more cautiously or quietly than did these friendly Indians, as they seemed to glide rather than walk over the snow-clad surface. To prevent the possibility of the command coming precipitately upon our enemies, the two scouts were directed to keep three or four hundred yards in advance of all others; then came, in single file, the remainder of our Osage guides and the white scouts—among the rest California Joe. With these I rode, that I might be as near the advance guard as possible. . . . Orders were given prohibiting even a word uttered above a whisper. No one was permitted to strike a match or light a pipe—the latter a great deprivation to the soldier. In this silent manner we rode mile after mile. Occasionally an officer would ride by my side and whisper some inquiry or suggestion, but aside from this our march was unbroken by sound or deed.

At last we discovered that our two guides in front had halted, and were awaiting my arrival. Word was quietly sent to halt the column until further inquiry in front could be made. Upon coming up with the two Osages we were furnished an example of the wonderful and peculiar powers of the Indian. One of them could speak broken English, and in answer to my question as to "What is the matter?" he replied, "Me don't know, but me smell fire." By this time several of the officers had quietly ridden up, and upon being informed of the Osage's remark, each endeavored, by sniffing the air, to verify or disprove the report. All united in saying that our guide was mistaken. Some said he was probably frightened, but we were unable to shake the confidence of the Osage warrior in his first opinion. I then directed him and his companion to advance even more cautiously than before, and the column, keeping up the interval, resumed its march. After proceeding about half a mile, perhaps further, again our guides halted, and upon coming up with them I was greeted with the remark, uttered in a whisper, "Me told you so"; and sure enough, looking in the direction indicated, were to be seen the embers of a wasted fire, scarcely a handful, yet enough to prove that our guide was right, and to cause us to feel the greater confidence in him. The discovery of these few coals of fire produced almost breathless excitement. . . .

It was almost certain to our minds that the Indians we had been pursuing were the builders of the fire. Were they still there and asleep? We were too near already to attempt to withdraw undiscovered. Our only course was to determine the facts at once, and be prepared for the worst. . . . The matter was soon determined. Our scouts soon arrived at the fire, and discovered it to be deserted. Again the skill and knowledge of our Indian allies came in play. Had they not been with us we should undoubtedly have assumed that the Indians who had occasion to build the fire and those we were pursuing constituted one party. From examining the fire and observing the great number of pony tracks in the snow, the Osages arrived at a different conclusion, and were convinced that we were then on the ground used by the Indians for grazing their herds of ponies. The fire had been kindled by the Indian boys who attend to the herding, to warm themselves by, and in all probability we were then within two or three miles of their village. I will not endeavor to describe the renewed hope and excitement that sprung up. Again we set out, this time more cautiously if possible than before, the command and scouts moving at a greater distance in rear.

In order to judge the situation more correctly, I this time accompanied the two Osages. Silently we advanced, I mounted, they on foot, keeping the head of my horse. Upon nearing the crest of each hill, as is invariably the Indian custom, one of the guides would hasten a few steps in advance and peer cautiously over the hill. Accustomed to this, I was not struck by observing it until once, when the same one who discovered the fire advanced cautiously to the crest and looked carefully into the valley beyond. I saw him place his hand over his eyes as if looking intently at some object, then crouch down and come creeping back to where I waited for him. "What is it?" I inquired as soon as he reached my horse's side. "Heaps Injuns down there," pointing in the direction from which he had just come. Quickly dismounting and giving the reins to the other guide, I accompanied the Osage to the crest, both of us crouching low so as not to be seen in the moonlight against the horizon. Looking in the direction indicated, I could indistinctly recognize the presence of a large body of animals of some kind in the valley below, and at a distance which then seemed not more than half a mile. I looked at them long and anxiously, the guide uttering not a word, but was unable to discover anything in their appearance different from what might be presented by a herd of buffalo under similar circumstances.

Turning to the Osage, I inquired in a low tone why he thought there were Indians there. "Me heard dog bark," was the satisfactory reply. Indians are noted for the large number of dogs always found in their villages, but never accompanying their war parties. I waited quietly to be convinced; I was assured, but I wanted to be doubly so. I was rewarded in a moment by hearing the barking of a dog in the heavy timber off to the right of the herd, and soon after I heard the tinkling of a small bell; this convinced me that it was really the Indian herd I then saw, the bell being worn around the neck of some pony who was probably leader of the herd. I turned to retrace my steps when another sound was borne to my ear through the cold, clear atmosphere of the valley—it was the distant cry of an infant; and savages though they were, and justly outlawed by the number and atrocity of their recent murders and depredations on the helpless settlers of the frontier, I could not but regret that in a war such as we were forced to engage in, the mode and circumstance of battle would possibly prevent discrimination.

Leaving the two Osages to keep a careful lookout, I hastened back until I met the main party of scouts and Osages. They were halted and a message sent back to halt the cavalry, enjoining complete silence, and directing every officer to ride to the point we then occupied. The hour was then past midnight. Soon they came, and after dismounting and collecting in a little circle, I informed them of what I had seen and heard. . . .

The general plan was to employ the hours between then and daylight to completely surround the village, and, at daybreak, or as soon as it was barely light enough for the purpose, to attack the Indians from all sides. The command, numbering, as has been stated, about eight hundred mounted men, was divided into four nearly equal detachments. Two of them set out at once, as they had each to make a circuitous march of several miles in order to arrive at the points assigned them from which to make their attack. The third detachment moved to its position about an hour before day, and until that time remained with the main or fourth column. This last, whose movements I accompanied, was to make the attack from the point from which we had first discovered the herd and village. . . . By this disposition it was hoped to prevent the escape of every inmate of the village. That portion of the command which I proposed to accompany consisted of A, C, D, and K troops, Seventh Cavalry, the Osages and scouts, and Colonel Cook with his forty sharpshooters. Captain Hamilton commanded one of the squadrons, Colonel West the other.

After the first two columns had departed for their posts—it was still four hours before the hour of attack—the men of the other two columns were permitted to dismount, but much intense suffering was unavoidably sustained. The night grew extremely cold towards morning; no fires of course could be permitted, and the men were even ordered to desist from stamping their feet and walking back and forth to keep warm, as the crushing of the snow beneath produced so much noise that it might give the alarm to our wily enemies.

During all these long weary hours of this terribly cold and comfortless night each man sat, stood, or lay on the snow by his horse, holding on to the rein of the latter. The officers, buttoning their huge overcoats closely about them, collected in knots of four or five, and, seated or reclining upon the snow's hard crust, discussed the probabilities of the coming battle— for battle we knew it would be, and we could not hope to conquer or kill the warriors of an entire village without suffering in return more or less injury. Some, wrapping their capes about their heads, spread themselves at full length upon the snow and were apparently soon wrapped in deep slumber. After being satisfied that all necessary arrangements had been made for the attack, I imitated the example of some of my comrades, and gathering the cavalry cape of my greatcoat about my head, lay down and slept soundly for perhaps an hour. At the end of that time I awoke, and on consulting my watch found there remained nearly two hours before we would move to the attack. Walking about among the horses and troopers, I found the latter generally huddled at the feet of the former in squads of three or four, in the endeavor to keep warm. Occasionally I would find a small group engaged in conversation, the muttered tones and voices strangely reminding me of those heard in the death-chamber. . . .

The night passed in quiet. I anxiously watched the opening signs of dawn in order to put the column in motion. We were only a few hundred yards from the point from which we were to attack. The moon disappeared about two hours before dawn, and left us enshrouded in thick and utter darkness, making the time seem to drag even slower than before.

At last faint signs of approaching day were visible, and I proceeded to collect the officers, awakening those who slept. . . .

All were ordered to get ready to advance; not a word to officer or men was spoken above undertone. It began growing lighter in the east, and we moved forward toward the crest of the hill. Up to this time two of the officers and one of the Osages had remained on the hill overlooking the valley beyond, so as to detect any attempt at a movement on the part of the occupants of the village below. These now rejoined the troops. Colonel West's squadron was formed in line on the right, Captain Hamilton's squadron in line on the left, while Colonel Cook with his forty sharpshooters was formed in advance of the left, dismounted. Although the early morning air was freezingly cold, the men were directed to remove their overcoats and haversacks, so as to render them free in their movements. Before advancing beyond the crest of the hill, strict orders were issued prohibiting the firing of a single shot until the signal to attack should be made. The other three detachments had been informed before setting out that the main column would attack promptly at daylight, without waiting to ascertain whether they were in position or not. In fact it would be impracticable to communicate with either of the first two until the attack began.

The plan was for each party to approach as closely to the village as possible without being discovered, and there await the approach of daylight. The regimental band was to move with my detachment, and it was understood that the band should strike up the instant the attack opened. Colonel Myers, commanding the third party, was also directed to move one-half his detachment dismounted. In this order we began to descend the slope leading down to the village. The distance to the timber in the valley proved greater than it had appeared to the eye in the darkness of the night. We soon reached the outskirts of the herd of ponies. The latter seemed to recognize us as hostile and moved quickly away. The light of day was each minute growing stronger, and we feared discovery before we could approach near enough to charge the village. The movement of our horses over the crusted snow produced considerable noise, and would doubtless have led to our detection but for the fact that the Indians, if they heard it at all, presumed it was occasioned by their herd of ponies. I would have given much at that moment to know the whereabouts of the first two columns sent out. Had they reached their assigned positions, or had unseen and unknown obstacles delayed or misled them? These were questions which could not then be answered. We had now reached the level of the valley, and began advancing in line toward the heavy timber in which and close at hand we knew the village was situated.

Immediately in rear of my horse came the band, all mounted, and each with his instrument in readiness to begin playing the moment their leader, who rode at their head, and who kept his cornet to his lips, should receive the signal. I had previously told him to play "Garry Owen" as the opening piece. We had approached near enough to the village now to plainly catch a view here and there of the tall white lodges as they stood in irregular order among the trees. From the openings at the top of some of them we could perceive faint columns of smoke ascending, the occupants no doubt having kept up their feeble fires during the entire night. We had approached so near the village that from the dead silence which reigned I feared the lodges were deserted, the Indians having fled before we advanced. I was about to turn in my saddle and direct the signal for attack to be given—still anxious as to where the other detachments were—when a single rifle shot rang sharp and clear on the far side of the village from where we were. Quickly turning to the band leader, I directed him to give us "Garry Owen."

At once the rollicking notes of that familiar marching and fighting air sounded forth through the valley, and in a moment were reechoed back from the opposite sides by the loud and continued cheers of the men of the other detachments, who, true to their orders, were there and in readiness to pounce upon the Indians the moment the attack began. In this manner the battle of the Washita commenced. The bugles sounded the charge, and the entire command dashed rapidly into the village.

The Indians were caught napping; but realizing at once the dangers of their situation, they quickly overcame their first surprise and in an instant seized their rifles, bows, and arrows, and sprang behind the nearest trees, while some leaped into the stream, nearly waist deep, and using the bank as a rifle pit, began a vigorous and determined defense. Mingled with the exultant cheers of my men could be heard the defiant war-whoop of the warriors, who from the first fought with a desperation and courage which no race of men could surpass. Actual possession of the village and its lodges was ours within a few moments after the charge was made, but this was an empty victory unless we could vanquish the late occupants, who were then pouring in a rapid and well-directed fire from their stations behind trees and banks. At the first onset a considerable number of the Indians rushed from the village in the direction from which Elliot's party had attacked. Some broke through the lines, while others came in contact with the mounted troopers, and were killed and captured.

Before engaging in the fight, orders had been given to prevent the killing of any but the fighting strength of the village; but in a struggle of this character it is impossible at all times to discriminate, particularly when, in a hand-to-hand conflict, such as the one the troops were then engaged in, the squaws are as dangerous adversaries as the warriors, while Indian boys between ten and fifteen years of age were found as expert and determined in the use of the pistol and bow and arrow as the older warriors. . . .

We had gained the center of the village, and were in the midst of the lodges, while on all sides could be heard the sharp crack of the Indian rifles and the heavy responses from the carbines of the troopers. After disposing of the smaller and scattering parties of warriors, who had attempted a movement down the valley, and in which some were successful, there was but little opportunity left for the successful employment of mounted troops. As the Indians by this time had taken cover behind logs and trees, and under the banks of the stream which flowed through the center of the village, from which stronghold it was impracticable to dislodge them by the use of mounted men, a large portion of the command was at once ordered to fight on foot, and the men were instructed to take advantage of the trees and other natural means of cover, and fight the Indians in their own style. Cook's sharpshooters had adopted this method from the first, and with telling effect. Slowly but steadily the Indians were driven from behind the trees, and those who escaped the carbine bullets posted themselves with their companions who were already firing from the banks.

One party of troopers came upon a squaw endeavoring to make her escape, leading by the hand a little white boy, a prisoner in the hands of the Indians, and who doubtless had been captured by some of their war parties during a raid upon the settlements. Who or where his parents were, or whether still alive or murdered by the Indians, will never be known, as the squaw, finding herself and prisoner about to be surrounded by the troops and her escape cut off, determined with savage malignity that the triumph of the latter should not embrace the rescue of the white boy. Casting her eyes quickly in all directions, to convince herself that escape was impossible, she drew from beneath her blanket a huge knife and plunged it into the almost naked body of her captive. The next moment retributive justice reached her in the shape of a well-directed bullet from one of the trooper's carbines. Before the men could reach them life was extinct in the bodies of both the squaw and her unknown captive.

The desperation with which the Indians fought may be inferred from the following: seventeen warriors had posted themselves in a depression in the ground, which enabled them to protect their bodies completely from the fire of our men, and it was only when the Indians raised their heads to fire that the troopers could aim with any prospect of success. All efforts to drive the warriors from this point proved abortive, and resulted in severe loss to our side. They were only vanquished at last by our men securing positions under cover and picking them off by sharpshooting as they exposed themselves to get a shot at the troopers. Finally the last one was despatched in this manner. In a deep ravine near the suburbs of the village the dead bodies of thirty-eight warriors were reported after the fight terminated. . . .

As soon as we had driven the warriors from the village, and the fighting was pushed to the country outside, I directed Romeo, the interpreter, to go around to all the lodges and assure the squaws and children remaining in them that they would be unharmed and kindly cared for; at the same time he was to assemble them in the large lodges designated for that purpose, which were standing near the center of the village. . . .

It was perhaps ten o'clock in the forenoon, and the fight was still raging, when to our surprise we saw a small party of Indians collected on a knoll a little over a mile below the village, and in the direction taken by those Indians who had effected an escape through our lines at the commencement of the attack. My surprise was not so great at first, as I imagined that the Indians we saw were those who had contrived to escape, and having procured their ponies from the herd had mounted them and were then anxious spectators of the fight, which they felt themselves too weak in numbers to participate in. In the meantime, the herds of ponies belonging to the village, on being alarmed by the firing and shouts of the contestants, had, from a sense of imagined security or custom, rushed into the village, where details of troopers were made to receive them.

California Joe, who had been moving about in a promiscuous and independent manner, came galloping into the village, and reported that a large herd of ponies was to be seen nearby, and requested authority and some men to bring them in. The men were otherwise employed just then, but he was authorized to collect and drive in the herd if practicable. He departed on his errand, and I had forgotten all about him and the ponies, when in the course of half an hour I saw a herd of nearly three hundred ponies coming on the gallop toward the village, driven by a couple of squaws, who were mounted, and had been concealed nearby, no doubt; while bringing up the rear was California Joe, riding his favorite mule, and whirling about his head a long lariat, using it as a whip in urging the horses forward. He had captured the squaws while endeavoring to secure the ponies, and very wisely had employed his captives to assist in driving the herd.

By this time the group of Indians already discovered outside our lines had increased until it numbered upwards of a hundred. Examining them through my field glass, I could plainly perceive that they were all mounted warriors; not only that, but they were armed and caparisoned in full war costume, nearly all wearing the bright-colored war-bonnets and floating their lance pennants. Constant accession to their numbers were to be seen arriving from beyond the hill on which they stood. All this seemed inexplicable. . . .

To solve these troublesome questions I sent for Romeo, and taking him with me to one of the lodges occupied by the squaws, I interrogated one of the latter as to who were the Indians to be seen assembling on the hill below the village. She informed me, to a surprise on my part almost equal to that of the Indians at our sudden appearance at daylight, that just below the village we then occupied, and which was a part of the Cheyenne tribe, were located in succession the winter villages of all the hostile tribes of the southern plains with which we were at war, including the Arapahos, Kiowas, the remaining band of Cheyennes, the Comanches; that the nearest village was about two miles distant, and the others stretched along through the timbered valley to the one furthest off, which was not over ten miles.

What was to be done?—for I needed no one to tell me that we were certain to be attacked, and that, too, by greatly superior numbers, just as soon as the Indians below could make their arrangements to do so; and they had probably been busily employed at these arrangements ever since the sound of firing had reached them in the early morning, and been reported from village to village. Fortunately, affairs took a favorable turn in the combat in which we were then engaged, and the firing almost died away. Only here and there where some warrior still maintained his position did the fight continue. Leaving as few men as possible to look out for these, I hastily collected and reformed my command, and posted them in readiness for the attack which we all felt was soon to be made; for already at different points and in more than one direction we could see more than enough warriors to outnumber us, and we knew they were only waiting the arrival of the chiefs and warriors from the lower villages before making any move against us. . . .

Our losses had been severe; indeed we were not then aware how great they had been. Hamilton, who rode at my side as we entered the village, and whose soldierly tones I heard for the last time as he calmly cautioned his squadron, "Now, men, keep cool, fire low, and not too rapidly," was among the first victims of the opening charge, having been shot from his saddle by a bullet from an Indian rifle. He died instantly. . . . Of Major Elliot, the officer second in rank, nothing had been seen since the attack at daylight, when he rode with his detachment into the village. He, too, had evidently been killed, but as yet we knew not where or how he had fallen. . . . On all sides of us the Indians could now be seen in considerable numbers, so that from being the surrounding party, as we had been in the morning, we now found ourselves surrounded and occupying the position of defenders of the village. . . .

The fight soon began generally at all points of the circle. For such in reality had our line of battle become—a continuous and unbroken circle of which the village was about the center. . . . Seeing that they did not intend to press the attack just then, about two hundred of my men were ordered to pull down the lodges in the village and collect the captured property in huge piles preparatory to burning. This was done in the most effectual manner. When everything had been collected the torch was applied, and all that was left of the village were a few heaps of blackened ashes. Whether enraged at the sight of this destruction or from other cause, the attack soon became general along our entire line, and pressed with so much vigor and audacity that every available trooper was required to aid in meeting these assaults.

I now concluded, as the village was off our hands and our wounded had been collected, that offensive measures might be adopted. To this end several of the squadrons were mounted and ordered to advance and attack the enemy wherever sufficient force was exposed to be a proper object of attack, but at the same time to be cautious to avoid ambuscades. . . . The squadrons acting in support of each other, and the men in each being kept well in hand, were soon able to force the line held by the Indians to yield at any point assaulted. . . .

It was now about three o'clock in the afternoon. I knew that the officer left in charge of the train and eighty men would push after us, follow our trail, and endeavor to reach us at the earliest possible moment. From the tops of the highest peaks or round hills in the vicinity of the village I knew the Indians could reconnoiter the country for miles in all directions. I feared if we remained as we were then until the following day, the Indians might in this manner discover the approach of our train and detach a sufficient body of warriors to attack and capture it; and its loss to us, aside from that of its guard, would have proven most serious, leaving us in the heart of the enemy's country, in midwinter, totally out of supplies for both men and horses.

By actual count we had in our possession eight hundred and seventy-five captured ponies, so wild and unused to white men that it was difficult to herd them. . . . The Indians had suffered a telling defeat, involving great losses in life and valuable property. Could they succeed, however, in depriving us of the train and supplies, and in doing this accomplish the killing or capture of the escort, it would go far to offset the damage we had been able to inflict upon them and render our victory an empty one. . . . To guide my command safely out of the difficulties which seemed just then to beset them, I again had recourse to that maxim in war which teaches a commander to do that which his enemy neither expects nor desires him to do. . . .

We did not need the ponies, while the Indians did. If we retained them they might conclude that one object of our expedition against them was to secure plunder, an object thoroughly consistent with the red man's idea of war. Instead, it was our desire to impress upon his uncultured mind that our every act and purpose had been simply to inflict deserved punishment upon him for the many murders and other deprivations committed by him and around the homes of the defenseless settlers on the frontier. Impelled by these motives, I decided neither to attempt to take the ponies with us nor to abandon them to the Indians, but to adopt the only measure left— to kill them. . . .

One of the middle-aged squaws then informed Romeo that she wished to speak on behalf of herself and companions. Assent having been given to this, she began the delivery of an address which for wisdom of sentiment, and easy, natural, but impassioned delivery, might have been heard with intense interest by an audience of cultivated refinement. From her remarks, interpreted by Romeo, I gathered much—in fact, the first reliable information as to what band we had attacked at daylight, which chiefs commanded, and many interesting scraps of information. She began by saying that now she and the women and children about her were in the condition of captivity, which for a long time she had prophesied would be theirs sooner or later. She claimed to speak not as a squaw, but as the sister of the head chief of her band, Black Kettle, who had fallen that morning almost the moment the attack was made. He it was who was the first to hear our advance, and leaping forth from his lodge with rifle in hand, uttered the first war-whoop and fired the first shot as a rally signal to his warriors, and was almost immediately shot down by the opening volley of the cavalry. . . . Not a chief or warrior of the village in her belief survived the battle of the forenoon. And what was to become of all these women and children, bereft of everything and of every friend? . . . Black Kettle, the head chief and the once trusted friend of the white man, had fallen. Little Rock, the chief second in rank in the village, had also met his death while attempting to defend his home against his enemies; others were named in the order of their rank or prowess as warriors, but all had gone the same way. Who was left to care for the women and children who still lived? Only last night, she continued, did the last war party return from the settlements, and it was to rejoice over their achievements that the entire village were engaged until a late hour dancing and singing. This was why their enemies were able to ride almost into their lodges before they were aroused by the noise of the attack. . . . Turning to me she added, "You claim to be a chief. This man" (pointing to Romeo) "says you are the big chief. If this be true and you are what he claims, show that you can act like a great chief and secure for us that treatment which the helpless are entitled to.". . .

At this point Romeo was interrupted by the officer in command of the men detailed to kill the ponies. The firing party was all ready to proceed with its work, and was only waiting until the squaws should secure a sufficient number of ponies to transport all the prisoners on the march. . . .

After driving off the Indians who had attacked us from the outside so as to prevent them from interfering with our operations in the vicinity of the village, parties were sent here and there to look up the dead and wounded of both sides. In spite of the most thorough search, there were still undiscovered Major Elliot and nineteen enlisted men, including the sergeant-major, for whose absence we were unable to satisfactorily account. Officers and men of the various commands were examined, but nothing was elicited from them except that Major Elliott had been seen about daylight charging with his command into the village. . . . It was then evident that when the other bands attempted to reinforce our opponents of the early morning, they had closed their lines about us in such a manner as to cut off Elliott and nineteen of our men. What had been the fate of this party after leaving the main command? This was a question to be answered only in surmises, and few of these were favorable to the escape of our comrades. . . .

The last lodge having been destroyed, and all the ponies except those required for the pursuit having been killed, the command was drawn in and united near the village. Making dispositions to overcome any resistance which might be offered to our advance, by throwing out a strong force of skirmishers, we set out down the valley in the direction where the other villages had been reported, and toward the hills on which were collected the greatest number of Indians. The column moved forward in one body, with colors flying and band playing. . . . They [the Indians] never offered to fire a shot or retard our movements in any manner, but instead assembled their outlying detachments as rapidly as possible, and began a precipitate movement down the valley in advance of us, fully impressed with the idea no doubt that our purpose was to overtake their flying people and herds and administer the same treatment to them that the occupants of the upper village had received. This was exactly the effect I desired. . . .

Facing the command about, it was at once put in motion to reach our train, not only as a measure of safety and protection to the latter, but as a necessary movement to relieve the wants of the command, particularly that portion whose haversacks and overcoats had fallen into the hands of the Indians early in the morning. . . . Great was our joy and satisfaction, about ten o'clock [the next morning], to discover the train safely in camp. The teams were at once harnessed and hitched to wagons, and without halting even to prepare breakfast the march was resumed, I being anxious to encamp at a certain point that night from where I intended sending scouts through with despatches to General Sheridan.

## The Vanquished
*by General Philip H. Sheridan*

I received the first news of Custer's fight on the Washita on the morning of November 29. It was brought to me by one of his white scouts, California Joe, a noted character, who had been experiencing the ups and downs of pioneer life ever since crossing the Plains in 1849. Joe was an invaluable guide and Indian fighter whenever the clause of the statute prohibiting liquors in the Indian country happened to be in full force. At the time in question the restriction was by no means a dead letter, and Joe came through in thirty-six hours, though obliged to keep in hiding during daylight of the twenty-eighth. The tidings brought were joyfully received by everybody at Camp Supply, and they were particularly agreeable to me, for, besides being greatly worried about the safety of the command in the extreme cold and deep snows, I knew the immediate effect of the victory would be to demoralize the rest of the hostiles, which of course would greatly facilitate and expedite our ultimate success. Toward evening the day after Joe arrived the head of Custer's column made its appearance on the distant hills, the friendly Osage scouts and the Indian prisoners in advance. As they drew near, the scouts began a wild and picturesque performance in celebration of the victory, yelling, firing their guns, throwing themselves on the necks and sides of their horses to exhibit their skill in riding, and going through all sorts of barbaric revolutions and gyrations, which were continued till night, when the rejoicings were ended with the hideous scalp dance.

The disappearance of Major Elliot and his party was the only damper upon our pleasure, and the only drawback to the very successful expedition. . . .[27] I was now anxious to follow up Custer's stroke by an immediate move to the south with the entire column. . . .

The expedition, supplied with thirty days' rations, moved out to the south on the seventh of December, under my personal command. We headed for the Wichita Mountains, toward which rough region all the villages along the Washita River had fled after Custer's fight with Black Kettle. My line of march was by way of Custer's battlefield, and thence down the Washita, and if the Indians could not sooner be brought to terms, I intended to follow them into the Wichita Mountains from near old Fort Cobb. The snow was still deep everywhere, and when we started

[27] Custer received bitter criticism for failing to search properly for Elliot; much of the blame came from Captain Frederick Benteen, the most outspoken opponent of Custer within the Seventh Cavalry. The *St. Louis Democrat* published a letter from Benteen on this subject. When Custer read it, he confronted his officers, demanding to know who had written it. Benteen defiantly identified himself, and Custer backed down.

the thermometer was below zero, but the sky being clear and the day very bright, the command was in excellent spirits. The column was made up of ten companies of the Kansas regiment, dismounted; eleven companies of the Seventh Cavalry, Pepoon's scouts, and the Osage scouts. In addition to Pepoon's men and the Osages, there was also California Joe, and one or two other frontiersmen besides, to act as guides and interpreters. Of all these the principal one, the one who best knew the country, was Ben Clark, a young man who had lived with the Cheyennes during much of his boyhood, and who not only had a pretty good knowledge of the country, but also spoke fluently the Cheyenne and Arapaho dialects, and was an adept in the sign language. . . .

We reached the valley of the Washita a little before dark [on the fourth day], and camped some five or six miles above the scene of Custer's fight, where I concluded to remain at least a day, to rest the command and give a chance to refit. In the meantime I visited the battlefield in company with Custer and several other officers, to see if there was a possibility of discovering any traces of Elliot's party. On arriving at the site of the village, and learning from Custer what dispositions had been made in approaching for the attack, the squadron of the escort was deployed and pushed across the river at the point where Elliot had crossed. Moving directly to the south, we had not gone far before we struck his trail, and soon the whole story was made plain by our finding, on an open level space about two miles from the destroyed village, the dead and frozen bodies of the entire party. The poor fellows were all lying within a circle not more than fifteen or twenty paces in diameter, and the little piles of cartridge shells near each body showed plainly that every man had made a brave fight. None were scalped, but most of them were otherwise horribly mutilated. . . . All had been stripped of their clothing, but their comrades in the escort were able to identify the bodies, which being done, we gave them a decent burial. . . .

From the meadow where Elliot was found we rode to the Washita, and then down the river through the sites of the abandoned villages, that had been strung along almost continuously for about twelve miles in the timber skirting the stream. On every hand appeared ample evidence that the Indians had intended to spend the winter here, for the ground was littered with jerked meat, bales of buffalo robes, cooking utensils, and all sorts of plunder usually accumulated in a permanent Indian camp. . . .

At the Kiowa village we found the body of a white woman—a Mrs. Blynn—and also that of her child. These captives had been taken by the Kiowas near Fort Lyon the previous summer, and kept close prisoners until the stampede began, the poor woman being reserved to gratify the brutal lust of the chief, Satanta. . . .

At an early hour on December 12 the command pulled out from its cozy camp and pushed down the valley of the Washita, following immediately on the Indian trail which led in the direction of Fort Cobb. . . . Continuing on this line for three days, we at length came to a point on the Washita where all signs indicated that we were nearing some of the villages. Wishing to strike them as soon as possible, we made a very early start next morning, the seventeenth. A march of four or five miles brought us to a difficult ravine, and while we were making preparations to get over, word was brought that several Indians had appeared in our front bearing a white flag and making signs that they had a communication to deliver. We signaled back that they would be received, when one of the party came forward alone and delivered a letter, which proved to be from General Hazen, at Fort Cobb. The letter showed that Hazen was carrying on negotiations with the Indians. . . .

When I informed the Kiowas that I would respect Hazen's letter, provided they all came into Fort Cobb and gave themselves up, the two chiefs [Satanta and Lone Wolf] promised submission, and, as an evidence of good faith, proposed to accompany the column to Fort Cobb with a large body of warriors, while their villages moved to the same point by easy stages, along the opposite bank of the river—claiming this to be necessary from the poor condition of the ponies. I had some misgivings as to the sincerity of Satanta and Lone Wolf, but as I wanted to get the Kiowas where their surrender would be complete, so that the Cheyennes and Arapahos could then be pursued, I agreed to the proposition, and the column moved on. All went well that day, but the next it was noticed that the warriors were diminishing, and an investigation showed that a number of them had gone off on various pretexts—the main one being to help along the women and children with the villages. With this I suspected that they were playing me false, and my suspicions grew into certainty when Satanta himself tried to make his escape by slipping beyond the flank of the column and putting spurs to his pony. Fortunately, several officers saw him, and quickly giving chase, overhauled him within a few hundred yards. I then arrested both him and Lone Wolf and held them as hostages—a measure that had the effect of bringing back many of the warriors already beyond our reach.

When we arrived at Fort Cobb we found some of the Comanches already there, and soon after the rest of them, excepting one band, came in to the post. The Kiowas, however, were not on hand, and there were no signs to indicate their coming. At the end of two days it was plain enough that they were acting in bad faith, and would continue to unless strong pressure was brought to bear. Indeed, they had already started for the Wichita Mountains, so I put on the screws at once by issuing an order to hang Satanta and Lone Wolf, if their people did not surrender at Fort Cobb within forty-eight hours. The two chiefs promised prompt compliance, but begged for more time, seeking to explain the non-arrival of the women and children through the weak condition of the ponies; but I was tired of their duplicity, and insisted on my ultimatum.

The order for the execution brought quick fruit. Runners were sent out with messages by the two prisoners, appealing to their people to save the lives of their chiefs, and the result was that the whole tribe came in to the post within the specified time. The two manacled wretches thus saved their necks; but it is to be regretted that the execution did not come off, for some years afterward their devilish propensities led them into Texas, where both engaged in the most horrible butcheries.

The Kiowas were now in our hands, and all the Comanches too, except one small band, which, after the Custer fight, had fled toward the head-waters of the Red River. This party was made up of a lot of very bad Indians—outlaws from the main tribe—and we did not hope to subdue them except by a fight, and of this they got their fill; for Evans, moving from Monument Creek toward the western base of the Wichita Mountains on Christmas day, had the good fortune to strike their village. . . .

This sudden appearance of Evans in the Red River region also alarmed the Cheyennes and Arapahos, and their thoughts now began to turn to submission. Food was growing scarce with them, too, as there was but little game to be found either in the Wichita Mountains or on the edge of the Staked Plains,[28] and the march of Carr's column from the Antelope Hills precluded their returning to where the buffalo ranged. Then, too, many of their ponies were dead or dying, most of their tepees and robes had been abandoned, and the women and children, having been kept constantly on the move in the winter's storms, were complaining bitterly of their sufferings.

In view of this state of things they intimated, through their Comanche friends at Fort Cobb, that they would like to make terms. On receiving their messages I entered into negotiations with Little Robe, chief of the Cheyennes, and Yellow Bear, chief of the Arapahos, and despatched envoys to have both tribes understand clearly that they must recognize their subjugation by surrendering at once, and permanently settling on the reservations in the spring. . . .

In due time the entire tribe fulfilled its promise except one small band [the Dog Soldiers] under Tall Bull, but this party received a good drubbing from General Carr on the Republican early in May.[29] After this fight all the Indians of the Southern Plains settled down on their reservations, and I doubt whether the peace would ever again have been broken had they not in after years been driven to hostilities by most unjust treatment.

[28] The Wichita Mountains are located near Fort Cobb. The Staked Plains are an enormous, stunningly flat region centered in the Texas panhandle.

[29] Tall Bull was leading his people north, to the Powder River country, rather than submit to the reservation in the Indian Territory. The final fight took place when Carr launched a surprise attack on Tall Bull's camp at Summit Springs, Colorado, on July 11; the Indian leader died in the fighting. Buffalo Bill Cody took part in this attack as chief scout for Carr's men.

THE SOUTHERN CHEYENNES fulfilled their promise to surrender largely due to another expedition led by Custer. This time, when the long-haired young commander found the enemy village, he refused to attack, negotiating to save the lives of two white women captives. Like Sheridan, Custer took hostages to add force to his negotiations—yet he also saved the captives and secured the peaceful surrender of the remaining Cheyennes. (Interestingly, during the negotiations Cheyenne chief Medicine Arrow laid a curse on the unsuspecting officer as they met in his lodge.) The war was brought to a close in July by Carr's attack on the Dog Soldiers during their trek north, which resulted in the death of Tall Bull and the total defeat of his band.

The tragic irony of Sheridan's victory lies in the key fight of the campaign, the Battle of the Washita. The attack was the decisive blow in driving the Indians into submission, yet it led to the death of Black Kettle; while there was ample evidence that the warriors of his village had taken part in the raids on the Kansas settlements, Black Kettle himself was the leading voice for peace among the Southern Cheyennes.[30] Sheridan wasted no more tears over this death than he did over that of Tall Bull, the most prominent war chief. From his point of view, the brutal winter campaign had been a resounding success. It was also the occasion for his most famous expression. As the warrior Tosawi led his Comanche band to Fort Cobb to join the general surrender, he identified himself to Sheridan: "Tosawi, good Indian." Sheridan replied, "The only good Indians I ever saw were dead."

The army's victory opened the southern Great Plains to sweeping changes. The population of Kansas catapulted from 107,000 in 1860 to well over 364,000 a decade later. Farms, towns, and railroad extensions burst onto the prairie. Meanwhile, professional buffalo hunters began to roam the southern plains, seeking bison hides for the leather factories of the East. Literally millions of buffalo were slaughtered, often left rotting on the plains due to a lack of transportation to the Eastern markets. Within just a few years, the work begun by Buffalo Bill and his early colleagues was complete: the southern herd was essentially eliminated by 1875. It was an effort that Sheridan approved of, saying, "Let them kill, skin, and sell until the buffalo is exterminated, as it is the only way to bring lasting peace and allow civilization to advance."

Not surprisingly, the Indians took offense at the destruction of the physical basis of their culture and independence. In 1874, a group of Comanche warriors, led by chief Quanah Parker, attacked a large buffalo hunting party on the Texas panhandle. The Indians were driven off, but the Red River War of 1874–75 had erupted. Months of relentless chasing

---

[30] As Stephen Ambrose has noted, Custer failed to reconnoiter before his assault—he had no idea whom he was attacking.

by army columns (though few actual battles) forced the Southern Cheyennes, Kiowas, Comanches, and Arapahos into final submission. Never again would they offer armed resistance to the conquest of the plains.

Where the buffalo once roamed, cattle moved in—a species as synonymous with the West in modern minds as the men on horseback who drove them. Coming up from Texas in vast droves, driven by quick-firing, independent-minded cowboys, cattle created a distinctive economy on the newly occupied frontier—as well as a community of small ranchers and cowhands whose resistance to the dictates of the law had to be broken by brute force.

# 7

# KANSAS COWTOWNS AND TEXAS BADMEN: THE OTHER PLAINS WAR

Even before the final defeat of the Native Americans of the southern plains, two legendary gunfighters began to stalk the frontier. They were only two out of many revolver-packing riders out on the Great Plains, but they grew to be folk heroes in their own time. One day, only a couple of years after Custer stormed through Black Kettle's village on the Washita, those two men would meet on the Kansas prairie and only narrowly survive the experience. Their names were Wild Bill Hickok and John Wesley Hardin.

The quick-shooting cowboy, of course, has become a stereotype in American entertainment, prompting many writers to try to debunk the Wild West image by arguing that gunfights were few and far between. But Hickok's and Hardin's wizardry with the six-gun was real, as were their many victims. In fact, the violence that engulfed their lives tells us much about the forces that conquered the frontier anew in the wake of the Indians' defeat.

Wild Bill Hickok and John Wesley Hardin were frontline soldiers in the second phase of the "Western Civil War of Incorporation," as historian Richard Maxwell Brown describes the conquest of the frontier. The first stage of this war on the southern plains we have already seen: in it, U.S. troops (and hired gunmen such as Buffalo Bill) fought to break the military power of the Indian nations, make them accept federal rule, and open their lands to settlers. Close on the heels of this struggle with the Indians came the second stage of this civil war, one far more diffuse and far harder to describe. Like the fight of the Indians, this was a war of resistance waged by heavily armed and fiercely independent communities against the encroaching, conservative power of government, wealthy individuals, and corporations. Only now the resisters were white, Hispanic, and black settlers.

Across the West, the early pioneers moved into areas largely beyond the reach of government, with only rudimentary legal institutions (if any) and with haphazard economic ties to the rest of the country. These rugged frontier dwellers valued independence and self-reliance; violence was a fact of life, and disputes were resolved man-to-man. Egalitarian values were fed by the easy availability of natural resources, while currency was often scarce. But as the early pioneers' numbers and wealth piled up, they attracted the attention of the conservative, established interests of the East. Businessmen followed in their footsteps, bringing manufactured goods, banks, and credit with them; big syndicates and rich men established huge cattle ranches; railroads, with vast land grants, snaked across the country; towns and cities took root. Political rings formed in territorial capitals, as powerful, well-connected men sought to dominate life in their regions, in an age of staggering corruption in public life, when legislators' votes were frequently bought with cash. Meanwhile, the federal government also sought to assert its authority over the wild frontier.

Many of the average settlers prospered as these changes rolled west; in fact, most who flocked to the new towns were eager to establish the law, so they could go about their business without fear. But not a few frontiersmen resisted the new rules. The open country of the West, after all, attracted men and women who flourished in independence; many of them had little regard for the property of big businessmen, cattle barons, and corporations. Often the most insubordinate Westerners hailed from the South, especially Texas, where respect for the federal government hit rock bottom during and after the Civil War. In addition, nineteenth-century America was highly politicized—and nowhere more than in the West. Southerners, small farmers, and independent ranchers were usually Democrats, while town businessmen and territorial authorities were generally Yankees and Republicans. And all the frontiersmen were heavily armed, and accustomed to using their weapons freely. To "incorporate" the West, then—to absorb it and remake it in the image of the East—the growing towns and wealthy businessmen of the frontier hired their own gunmen to force respect for property and the law.

Wild Bill Hickok (whose proper name was James Butler Hickok) was perhaps the most famous of these rough-and-tumble lawmen—or "incorporation gunfighters," as Richard Maxwell Brown calls them. Hickok was a typical warrior for the establishment: a Yankee and a Republican, a veteran of the Union army, he identified with the growing prosperity that came with the gradual integration of the West into American society. At the same time, he was a product of the frontier—tough, steady, quick with a pistol, and ready to enforce the law in a highly personal manner.

Hickok served for a while as a scout for Custer's Seventh Cavalry; he resigned to become the lawman for Hays City. But he won his greatest fame as the town marshal for Abilene, Kansas. As a well-placed stop along the advancing railroad, Abilene became the center for the cattle economy that grew up between central Texas and Kansas. Starting just after the Civil War, hundreds of thousands of cattle were driven up the Chisholm Trail by Texas cowboys for sale in the stockyards of Kansas cowtowns such as Abilene, where they were purchased for shipment to the cities of the East. The system fed a distinctively independent lifestyle on the Texas frontier, where remote communities were home to men who gathered up cattle that wandered through the back country. The businessmen of Abilene were uneasy hosts for these wild cattle drovers; the Texans poured their money into the town's bars and brothels, but they rankled under authority. On the trail, they pulled their pistols on the slightest insult (especially from a hated Yankee or Republican). Hickok's job was to maintain order in the midst of such chaos, imposing the orderly ways of businesslike Kansas on the riders from the Lone Star State. It was a job he carried out well, applying tact, firmness, and brute force.

The deadliest Texan Hickok ever faced was a teenager named John Wesley Hardin. If Hickok was the epitome of the "incorporation gunfighter"—the frontier lawman—then Hardin was the personification of the resister. Already an experienced killer by the time he made his way to Abilene with a herd of cattle, Hardin was the classic "Texas badman." Countless writers from the era tell us of these hard-drinking, hot-tempered gunslingers, who fired their six-shooters without a thought for the law. Coming from isolated rural counties, beyond the reach of formal institutions, they had little respect for the standards of larger society. As Southerners and sympathizers for the lost cause of the Confederacy, they had utter disregard for the authority of government in general. As Democrats, they hated the Republican establishment that held sway after the Civil War, especially the Reconstruction government that ruled Texas until 1874.

The two accounts that follow vividly depict these two men—one who fought to stamp down the wild frontier, and one who resisted. In the first, General George Custer describes Hickok as he knew him in the late 1860s, when he was first a scout for the Seventh Cavalry and later the marshal of Hays City, Kansas. Custer neatly sums up Hickok's character, and provides a vivid description of the violent values and disregard for law that defined life in frontier communities.[31]

In the second account, John Wesley Hardin recalls his adventures in 1871, when he wound up driving a herd of cattle to Hickok's new domain: Abilene. Hardin's account vividly reveals the reality of the Western Civil War of Incorporation as it raged both in Texas and up the trail in Abilene. Like a majority of white Texans, Hardin was a devoted Democrat and Confederate loyalist, and he was outraged that blacks now were not only free but had the right to vote. Hardin—acting on his own and along with armed groups such as the Ku Klux Klan—fought and killed to suppress blacks and to oppose the forces of incorporation. Those forces were gath-

[31] It is interesting to note that during the Civil War Hickok took part in the guerrilla war in Missouri, fighting with Kansas troops to put down Confederate bands of "bushwhackers." He won his nickname "Wild Bill" in Missouri, and after the war he killed ex-Confederate Dave Tutt in the streets of Springfield in the first recorded walkdown. The Missouri bushwhackers turned to banditry after the war, giving birth to the James-Younger gang, among others.

ered in the Republican Party (which had a sizeable white following in Texas), led by Governor Edmund J. Davis, himself a native white Texan. Davis believed in both black suffrage and economic modernization (meaning railroad expansion in particular); to crush the Klan, he organized a new state police force (40% of the troopers were black). The new force moved quickly and effectively to crack down on white violence against the freed people.

As a hotheaded teenager, gun-crazy Hardin inevitably crossed the law in Davis's Texas, and he set out on a flight to Mexico. Along the way, he took refuge amid his large clan of relatives, who took him to Abilene in the greatest year for cattle drives to that city in Western history. His description of the drive offers insight into the life of the cowboy—and into the ways that Democratic Texans carried their political hostilities into Republican Kansas. There Hardin found work as a manhunter, and faced off with Hickok in the street—an encounter with a peculiar outcome. After returning to Texas, he once again confronted the state police in Gonzales County (where the Ku Klux Klan was particularly active). In the passage presented here, "Little Arkansas," as he was nicknamed, reveals the traits of a true badman—loyalty to family and community; a cool head in a scrap; and a violent, racist heart.

## Wild Bill Hickok
*by General George A. Custer*

The most prominent man among [the Great Plains frontiersmen] was "Wild Bill," whose highly varied career was made the subject of an illustrated sketch in one of the popular periodicals a few years ago. Wild Bill was a strange character, just the one which a novelist might gloat over. He was a Plainsman in every sense of the word, yet unlike any other of his class.

In person he was about six feet one in height, straight as the straightest of the warriors whose implacable foe he was; broad shoulders, well-formed chest and limbs, and a face strikingly handsome; a sharp, clear, blue eye, which stared straight in the face when in conversation; a finely-shaped nose, inclined to be aquiline; a well-turned mouth, with lips only partially concealed by a handsome moustache. His hair and complexion were those of the perfect blond. The former was worn in uncut ringlets falling carelessly over his powerfully formed shoulders. Add to this figure a costume blending the immaculate neatness of the dandy with the extravagant taste and style of the frontiersman, and you have Wild Bill, then as now the most famous scout on the Plains. Whether on foot or on horseback, he was one of the most perfect types of physical manhood I ever saw.

Of his courage there could be no question; it had been brought to the test on too many occasions to admit a doubt. His skill in the use of the rifle and pistol was unerring; while his deportment was exactly opposite of what might be expected from a man of his surroundings. It was entirely free from all bluster or bravado. He seldom spoke of himself unless requested to do so. His conversation, strange to say, never bordered either on the vulgar or blasphemous. His influence among the frontiersmen was unbounded, his word was law; and many are the personal quarrels and disturbances which he has checked among his comrades by his simple announcement that "this has gone far enough," if need be followed by the ominous warning that when persisted in or renewed the quarreller "must settle it with me."

Wild Bill is anything but a quarrelsome man; yet no one but himself can enumerate the many conflicts in which he has been engaged, and which have almost invariably resulted in the death of his adversary. I have a personal knowledge of at least half a dozen men whom he has at various times killed, one of these being at the time a member of my command. Others have been severely wounded, yet he always escapes unhurt. On the Plains every man openly carries his belt with its invariable appendages, knife and revolver, often two of the latter. Wild Bill always carried two handsome ivory-handled revolvers of large size; he was never seen without them.

Where this is the common custom, brawls or personal difficulties are seldom if ever settled by blows. The quarrel is not from a word to a blow, but from a word to the revolver, and he who can draw and fire first is the best man. No civil law reaches him; none is applied for. In fact there is no law recognized beyond the frontier but that of "might makes right." Should death result from the quarrel, as it usually does, no coroner's jury is impaneled to learn of the cause of the death, and the survivor is not arrested. But instead of these old-fashioned proceedings, a meeting of citizens takes place, the survivor is *requested* to be present when the circumstances of the homicide are inquired into, and the unfailing verdict of "justifiable," "self-defense," etc., is pronounced, and the law stands vindicated. That justice is often deprived to a victim there is not a doubt. Yet in all the many affairs of this kind in which Wild Bill has performed a part, and which have come to my knowledge, there is not a single instance in which the verdict of twelve fair-minded men would not be pronounced in his favor.[32]

That the even tenor of his way continues to be disturbed by little events of this description may be inferred from an item which has been floating

---

[32] Ironically, Hickok became an officer of the law, and helped establish respect for the law and legal institutions on the frontier he once ruled as a roving scout and Plainsman.

lately through the columns of the press, and which states that "the funeral of Jim Bludso, who was killed the other day by Wild Bill, took place today." It then adds: "The funeral expenses were borne by Wild Bill." What could be more thoughtful than this? Not only to send a fellow mortal out of the world, but to pay the expenses of the transit.

## Up the Chisholm Trail
*by John Wesley Hardin*

I was born in Bonham, Fannin County, Texas, on the 26th of May, 1853. My father, J.G. Hardin, was a methodist preacher and a circuit rider. My mother, Elizabeth Hardin, was a blonde, highly cultured, and charity predominated in her disposition. She made my father a model wife and helpmate. My father continued to travel his circuit as a preacher until 1869, when he moved and located near Moscow, in Polk County, on account of bad health. . . . In the meantime my father was studying law, and in 1861 was admitted to the bar.

The war between the States had broken out at this time. . . . Although I was but 9 years old at this time I had already conceived the idea of running off and going with a cousin to fight Yankees. But my father got on to the little game and put an end to it all by giving me a sound thrashing. Still the principles of the Southern cause loomed up in my mind ever bigger, brighter, and stronger as the months and years rolled by. I had seen Abraham Lincoln burned and shot to pieces in effigy so often that I looked upon him as a very demon incarnate, who was waging a relentless and cruel war on the South to rob her of her most sacred rights. So you can see that the justice of the Southern cause was taught to me in my youth, and if I never relinquished these teachings in after years, surely I was but true to my early training. The way you bend a twig, that is the way it will grow, is an old saying, and a true one. So I grew up a rebel. . . .

In January 1869, I went with my father to Navarro County and engaged in school teaching near Pisga. . . . I had, however, conceived the idea of becoming a cowboy, and as my cousins were in the business I began to drive cattle to shipping points. Of course in this kind of life I soon learned how to play poker, seven-up, and euchre, and it was but a short time until I would banter the best for a game. . . .

In those times if there was anything that could rouse my passion it was seeing impudent negroes lately freed insult or abuse old, wounded Confederates who were decrepit, weak, or old. There were lots of those kind in the country in the sixties, and these negroes bullied both them and even the weaker sex whenever they had the advantage. Frequently I involved myself in almost inextricable difficulties in this way. . . .

[In January 1871, Hardin landed deep in trouble with the law for acting on such feelings, and he began a flight to Mexico. He stopped along the way to see his relatives, the Clements clan.]

These were the Clements: Jim, Manning, Joe, Gip, Mary Jane, and Minerva. The girls were both married, the eldest to Jim Denson, the youngest to Fred Brown. They lived almost directly on my way from Gonzales to Hellena—an old and honored citizen showed me the way to my relatives' home. My guide's name was Jim Cone. I told my relatives I was in trouble and on my way to Mexico. They told me I could go to Kansas with cattle and make some money and at the same time be free from arrest. I therefore concluded to give up my Mexico trip and went to work helping them gather cattle. We gathered mostly for Jake Johnson and Columbus Carol, who were then putting up herds for Kansas. . . .

When we were gathering cattle for the trail, I was in charge of the herd with strict orders to let no one go into the herd. A negro named Bob King came to the herd, rode in, and commenced to cut out cattle without permission. I rode up and asked him by whose permission he was cutting cattle in that herd. He said he did not have to have permission and asked who was the boss.

I said, "I am the man."

"Well," he said, "I have come to cut this herd."

I told him to keep out of it; that Clements would be here directly. He rode right into that herd and cut out a big beef steer. So I rode up to him and struck him over the head with my pistol and told him to get out of my herd. Although he had a six-shooter, he did not do anything, but begged my pardon.

About the last of February we got all our cattle branded and started for Abilene, Kansas, about the 1st of March. Jim Clements and I were to take these 1200 head of cattle up to Abilene and Manning, Gip, and Joe Clements were to follow with a herd belonging to Doc Burnett. Jim and I were getting $150 a month.

Nothing of importance happened until we got to Williamson County, where all the hands caught the measles except Jim and myself. We camped about two miles south of Corn Hill and there we rested up and recruited. I spent the time doctoring my sick companions, cooking, and branding cattle. . . .

After resting there about ten days, all the hands recovered from the measles; and the cattle and horses having improved so much in flesh, we started again north.

After several weeks of travel we crossed the Red River at a point called Red River Station, or Bluff, north of Montague County. We were now in the Indian country [the Indian Territory] and two white men had been killed by Indians about two weeks before we arrived at the town. Of course, all the talk was Indians and everybody dreaded them. We were now on what is called the Chisholm Trail and game of all kinds abounded: buffalo, antelope, and other wild animals too numerous to mention. There were a great many cattle driven that year from Texas. The day we crossed Red River about fifteen herds had crossed and of course we intended to keep close together going through the Nation for our mutual protection. The trail was thus one line of cattle and you were never out of sight of a herd. I was just about as much afraid of an Indian as I was of a coon. In fact, I was anxious to meet some on the warpath. . . .

One morning on the South Canadian River I went out turkey hunting and killed as fine a gobbler as I ever saw. I went over to where he fell, picked him up, and started for my pony. It was just about daylight, and when I got close to my pony I saw he was snorting and uneasy. I looked in the direction that he seemed afraid of, and about twenty yards off I saw an Indian in the very act of letting fly an arrow at me, and quick as thought, I drew my pistol and fired at him. The ball hit him squarely in the forehead and he fell dead without a groan. I got away from there with my turkey as quickly as I could, went to camp, and we all went to see a dead Indian. . . . We got a spade and an axe and dug a grave and buried the Indian with his bow and arrows, covering the grave with leaves to hide the spot from other Indians.

These Indians had established a custom of taxing every herd that went through the Nation 10 cents per head. Several other herds joined with us in refusing to pay this, and we never did, though many times it looked like war. . . .

When we had crossed into Kansas we felt better and safer. On reaching a place called Cow House, about twenty miles on this side of Wichita, a party of men interested in changing the trail from Wichita came out to the herd and induced us to go to the left of Wichita and cross the river about twelve miles above. They wished us to open this trail, as they were interested in building up a new town on the north bank of the Arkansas River. We followed a plough furrow on this new trail and these men furnished a guide. When we had crossed the river a delegation from the new town came out to meet us and invite all those that could leave the cattle to enjoy the hospitalities of the new town.

About sixty cowboys went to that town and it is needless to say filled up on wine, whiskey, etc., some getting rather full. We all came back to the herd in a little while and started out again for Abilene.

We were now on the Newton prairie, and my herd was right in front of a herd driven by Mexicans.[33] This Mexican herd kept crowding us so closely that at last it took two or three hands to keep the Mexican cattle from getting into my herd. The boss Mexican got mad at me for holding, as he

---

[33] These men were very likely Hispanic Americans—often referred to as "Mexicans" by English-speaking Americans.

said, his cattle back. I told him to turn to the outside of the trail, as he did not have to follow me. This made him all the madder. He fell back from the front of his herd and quit leading the cattle. The result of this was that, no one being in front of them, they rushed right into my herd, so I turned them off to the left. The boss Mexican rode back up to where I was and cursed me in Mexican. He said he would kill me with a sharpshooter as quick as he could get it from the wagon. In about five minutes I saw him coming back with a gun. He rode up to within about 100 yards of me, got down off his horse, took deliberate aim at me and fired. The ball grazed my head, going through my hat and knocking it off. He tried to shoot again, but something got wrong with his gun and he changed it to his left hand and pulled his pistol with his right. He began to advance on me, shooting at the same time. He called up his crowd of six or seven Mexicans. In the meanwhile Jim Clements, hearing that I was in a row, had come to my assistance.

I was riding a fiery gray horse and the pistol I had was an old cap and ball, which I had worn out shooting on the trail.[34] There was so much play between the cylinder and the barrel that it would not burst a cap and fire unless I held the cylinder with one hand and pulled the trigger with the other. I made several unsuccessful attempts to shoot the advancing Mexican from my horse but failed. I then got down and tried to shoot and hold my horse, but failed in that, too. Jim Clements shouted at me to "turn that horse loose and hold the cylinder." I did so and fired at the Mexican, who was only ten paces from me. I hit him in the thigh and stunned him a little. I tried to fire again, but snapped. The Mexican had evidently fired his last load, so we both rushed together in a hand-to-hand fight.

The other Mexicans had by this time come close up and were trying to shoot me every chance they got. Jim Clements, seeing I had no show to win, rushed between me and the other Mexicans and told them not to shoot, but to separate us as we were both drunk and did not know what we were doing. Another Mexican who had not been there at the beginning of the fight then rode up and fired two shots at me, but missed. We covered him with our pistols and he stopped. It was then agreed to stop the fight for a time, so the Mexicans went back to their herd. . . .

Jim and I went straight back to camp and loaded two of the best pistols there. While we were doing this a message came from the Mexicans that time was up and they were coming. We of course sent the messenger back

---

[34] This was probably the Civil War–era .36 caliber Colt Navy revolver. Unlike more recent makes, which took all-in-one metal cartridges, this model fired a paper round (containing ball and powder) which required an external percussion cap. The lightweight, well-balanced Navy was a popular sidearm during the Civil War, and was produced in enormous quantities by both sides. In 1871 the pistol was still common, if a little out of date.

and told the Mexicans to keep off our herd and not to come around; that we did not want any more trouble.

Seven of them gathered on the west side of the herd and seemed to talk matters over. Presently the boss, José, my old foe, with three men, came around to the east side where we were. I had changed horses, so I rode to meet him. He fired at me when about seventy-five yards away, but missed me. I concluded to charge him and turn my horse loose at him, firing as I rode. The first ball did the work. I shot him through the heart and he fell over the horn of his saddle, pistol in hand and one in the scabbard, the blood pouring from his mouth. In an instant I had his horse by the reins and Jim Clements relieved him of his pistols and José fell dead to the ground.

The other Mexicans kept shooting at us, but did not charge. They were in two parties, one about seventy-five yards to the south, the other about 150 yards to the west. We charged the first party and held our fire until we got close to them. They never weakened, but kept shooting at us all the time. When we got right on them and opened up, they turned their horses, but we were in the middle of them, dosing them with lead. They wheeled and made a brave stand. We were too quick for them, however, in every way, and they could not go our gait. A few more bullets quickly and rightly placed silenced the party forever.

The other party was now advancing on us and shooting as they came. We, therefore, determined to stampede the herd, which we did in short order by shooting a steer in the nose. This seemed to demoralize them for a while and they all broke to the cattle except one, who stood still and continued to use his pistol. We cross-fired on him and I ended his existence by putting a ball through his temples. We then took after the rest, who now appeared to be hunting protection from other herders. We caught up with two of them, and Jim Clements covered and held them while I rounded in two more. These latter two said they had nothing to do with the fight and that their companions must have been drunk. We let these two go to the cattle.

A crowd of cowmen from all around had now gathered. I suppose there were twenty-five of them around these two Mexicans we had first rounded up. We thus had good interpreters and once we thought the matter was settled with them, when suddenly the Mexicans, believing they "had the drop," pulled their pistols and both fired point blank at me. I don't know how they missed me. In an instant I fired first at one, then at the other. The first I shot through the heart and he dropped dead. The second I shot through the lungs and Jim shot him too. He fell off his horse and I was going to shoot him again when he begged and held up both his hands. I could not shoot a man, not even a treacherous Mexican, begging and down. Besides, I knew he would die anyway. In comparing notes after the fight, we agreed that I had killed five out of the six dead Mexicans.

Nothing of interest happened until we reached North Cottonwood, where we went into camp to deliver our cattle. We were now about thirty-five miles from Abilene, Kansas, and it was about the 1st of June that we all got word to come into Abilene, draw our pay, and be discharged.

I have seen many fast towns, but I think Abilene beat them all. The town was filled with sporting men and women, gamblers, cowboys, desperadoes, and the like. It was well supplied with bar rooms, hotels, barber shops, and gambling houses, and everything was open.

Before I got to Abilene, I had heard much talk of Wild Bill, who was then marshal of Abilene. He had a reputation as a killer. I knew Ben Thompson and Phil Coe were there and had met both these men in Texas. Besides these, I learned that there were many other Texans there and so, although there was a reward offered for me, I concluded to stay some time there as I knew that Carol and Johnson, the owners of my herd, "squared" me with the officials. When we went to town and settled up, Jim Clements insisted on going home, although they offered him $140 per month to stay. I continued in their employ to look after their stray cattle at $150 per month. Thus we settled our business and proceeded to take in the town. . . .

Jim Clements took the train and went back to Texas. Phil Coe and Ben Thompson at that time were running the Bull's Head saloon and gambling hall. They had a big bull painted outside the saloon as a sign, and the city council objected to this for some special reason.[35] Wild Bill, the marshal, notified Ben Thompson and Phil Coe to take the sign down or change it somewhat. Phil Coe thought the ordinance all right, but it made Thompson mad. Wild Bill, however, sent up some painters and materially changed the offending bovine.

For a long time everybody expected trouble between Thompson and Wild Bill, and I soon found out that they were deadly enemies. Thompson tried to prejudice me every way he could against Bill, and told me how Bill, being a Yankee, always picked out Southern men to kill, and especially Texans. I told him: "I am not doing anybody's fighting just now except my own, but I know how to stick to a friend. If Bill needs killing why don't you kill him yourself?"

He said: "I would rather get someone else to do it."

I told him then that he had struck the wrong man. I had not yet met Bill Hickok, but really wished for a chance to have a set-to with him just to try my luck.

One night in a wine room he was drinking with some friends of mine when he remarked that he would like to have an introduction with me. George Johnson introduced us, and we had several glasses of wine together. He asked me all about the fight on the Newton prairie and showed me a proclamation from Texas offering a reward for my arrest.

He said: "Young man, I am favorably impressed with you, but don't let

---

[35] Hardin here is being disingenuous; the sign graphically depicted a bull with an erect member.

Ben Thompson influence you. You are in enough trouble now, and if I can do you a favor, I will do it." I was charmed with his liberal views, and told him so. We parted friends.

I spent most of my time in Abilene in the saloons and gambling houses, playing poker, faro, and seven-up. One day I was rolling ten pins and my best horse was hitched outside in front of the saloon. I had two six-shooters on and of course I knew the saloon people would raise a row if I did not pull them off. Several Texans were there rolling ten pins and drinking. I suppose we were pretty noisy. Wild Bill came in and said we were making too much noise and told me to pull off my pistols until I got ready to go out of town. I told him I was ready to go now, but did not propose to put up my pistols, go or no go. He went out and I followed him. I started up the street when someone behind me shouted out: "Set up. All down but nine."[36]

Wild Bill whirled around and met me. He said: "What are you howling about, and what are you doing with those pistols on?"

I said: "I am just taking in the town."

He pulled his pistol and said: "Take those pistols off. I arrest you."

I said all right and pulled them out of the scabbards, but while he was reaching for them I reversed them and whirled them over on him with the muzzles in his face, springing back at the same time. I told him to put his pistol up, which he did. I cursed him for a long-haired scoundrel that would shoot a boy with his back to him (as I had been told he intended to do me). He said, "Little Arkansas, you have been wrongly informed."

By this time a big crowd had gathered with pistols and arms. They kept urging me to kill him. Down the street a squad of policemen were coming, but Wild Bill motioned them to go back and at the same time asked me not to let the mob shoot him.

I shouted: "This is my fight and I'll kill the first man that fires a gun."

Bill said: "You are the gamest and quickest boy I ever saw. Let us compromise this matter and I will be your friend. Let us go in here and take a drink, as I want to talk to you and give you some advice."

At first I thought he might be trying to get the drop on me, but he finally convinced me of his good intentions and we went in and took a drink. We went into a private room and I had a long talk with him and we came out friends.

I had been drinking pretty freely that day and towards night went into a restaurant to get something to eat. A man named Pain was with me, a Texan who had just come up the trail. While we were in the restaurant several drunken men came in and began to curse Texans. I said to the nearest one: "I'm a Texan."

---

[36] The cry must have come from inside the saloon, where (as Hardin indicates) customers were bowling.

He began to curse me and threatened to slap me over. To his surprise I pulled my pistol and he promptly pulled his. At the first fire he jumped behind my friend Pain, who received the ball in his only arm. He fired one shot and ran, but I shot at him as he started, the ball hitting him in the mouth, knocking out several teeth and coming out behind his left ear. I rushed outside, pistol in hand, and jumped over my late antagonist, who was lying in the doorway. I met a policeman on the sidewalk, but I threw my pistol in his face and told him to "hands up." He did it.

I made my way to my horse and went north to Cottonwood, about thirty-five miles, to await results. While I was there a Mexican named Bideno shot and killed Billy Coran, a cowman who had come up the trail with me. He was bossing a herd then, holding it nearby Abilene for the market. His murder by this Mexican was a most foul and treacherous one, and although squad after squad tried to arrest this Mexican, they never succeeded in either killing or arresting him.

Many prominent cowmen came to me and urged me to follow the murderer. I consented if they would go to Abilene and get a warrant for him. They did so and I was appointed a deputy sheriff and was given letters of introduction to cattlemen whom I should meet. About sunrise on the 27th of June, 1871, I left the North Cottonwood with Jim Rodgers to follow Bideno. . . . We hoped to catch up with him before he got to the Nation [Indian Territory], and specially before he got to Texas. Off we went in a lope and got to Newton, about fifty miles away, by 4 P.M. I had learned of a herd there bossed by a brother of the dead Billy Coran and I sent a messenger to him, telling him (the messenger) not to spare the horseflesh. Coran came and one Anderson with him. I told him of his brother's death, and we were soon on the trail with fresh horses and four instead of two in our party. . . .

We reached Wichita about eleven o'clock that night, having traveled 100 miles since starting. We concluded to rest until morning and then go on the south side of the river and make inquiry. I knew there were several Mexican herds near the river which Bideno might have gone to for a change of horses. We went next morning to these herds, going from one to the other, hunting for information. Finally we struck a Mexican who said that just such a man had stayed at his camp about ten o'clock last night and had traded horses with one of his men early in the morning. He said the horse he had traded for was the best in the camp. We were convinced that this must have been Bideno, so changing horses and flushed with hope, we hit the trail again about 7 A.M. in a long lope.

We saw a herder about eight o'clock who told us that two hours before he had seen a Mexican wearing a broad-brimmed hat and going south in a lope, keeping about 200 yards from the trail. We were now satisfied we were on the right track and pulled out again, expecting horses at Cow House creek, about fifteen miles further on. We met a man near Cow House who told us that he had seen a Mexican wearing a broad-brimmed hat going south in a lope. When we got to Cow House we changed our horses at once and found that Bideno had done likewise an hour before. . . .

After going about twenty miles we again changed horses, so that if we ran up on him our horses would be fresh. When we got to within two miles of Bluff Creek the road forked. Anderson and I went through the city, while Rodgers and Coran took the other fork; all agreeing to meet in the Indian Nation on the other side of the creek.

Anderson and I, before going far, got direct information that Bideno had just unsaddled his horse and had gone up town inquiring for a restaurant. We fired off our pistols and by this means got Coran and Rodgers to hear us and come back.

We soon got to Bluff, which was a town of about fifty houses. There were some bar rooms and restaurants in a line; and we agreed to ride up like cowboys, hitch our horses, and divide into two parties, each going into different places. Anderson and I went into a restaurant, but before we reached it we had to go into a saloon. I called for the drinks and took in the situation. I asked if we could get dinner and if a Mexican herder was eating dinner back there. They said there was; so I told my partner to get out his gun and follow me. We stepped into the entrance, and I recognized Bideno. With my pistol by my side I said: "Bideno, I am after you; surrender; I do not wish to hurt you and you shall not be hurt while you are in my hands."

He was sitting at the table eating and shook his head and frowned. He then dropped his knife and fork and grabbed his pistol. As he did it I told him to throw up his hands. When he got his pistol out, I fired at him across the table and he fell over a dead man, the ball hitting him squarely in the center of the forehead. . . .

In the meantime the waiter was jumping up and down, begging us not to kill him; that he was a friend of cowboys, etc. I quieted him by telling him if he did not get out he might, perhaps, get shot accidentally, and he promptly acted on my suggestion. . . .

Quite a crowd had collected by this time and they all wanted to know what the shooting was about. I got outside the saloon and told the crowd how this Mexican had murdered a prominent cow man on the 26th at North Cottonwood. . . . They all commended our actions and I gave those people $20 to bury him.

[Hardin went back to Abilene to be paid for killing Bideno, but he was soon in more trouble: bothered by the snoring of a man in an adjacent room, he fired through the wall, killing the noisy sleeper. Hardin returned to Texas to evade Wild Bill's wrath, arriving at the house of Manning Clement with his cousin Gip on August 7, 1871.]

E.J. Davis was governor then [in Reconstruction-era Texas] and his State Police were composed of carpetbaggers, scalawags from the North, with ignorant negroes frequently on the force. . . . We all knew that many members of this State Police outfit were members of some secret vigilante band, especially in DeWitt and Gonzales counties. We were all opposed to mob law and so soon became enemies. The consequence was that a lot of negro police made a raid on me without lawful authority. . . .[37]

They found me at a small grocery store in the southern portion of Gonzales County. I really did not know they were there until I heard someone say: "Throw up your hands or die!"

I said "all right," and turning around saw a big black negro with his pistol cocked and presented. I said: "Look out, you will let that pistol go off, and I don't want to be killed accidentally."

He said: "Give me those pistols."

I said "all right," and handed him the pistols, handle foremost. One of the pistols turned a somersault in my hand and went off. Down came the negro, with his pistol cocked, and as I looked outside I saw another negro on a white mule firing into the house at me. I told him to hold up, but he kept on, so I turned my Colt's .45[38] on him and knocked him off his mule with my first shot. I turned around then to see what became of No. 1 and saw him sprawling on the floor with a bullet through his head, quivering in blood. I walked out of the back door to get my horse, and when I got back to take in the situation the big negro on the white mule was making for the bottom at a 2:40 gait. . . .

The negro I killed was named Green Paramoor and the one on the white mule was a blacksmith from Gonzales named John Lackey—in fact they were both from that town. News of this of course spread like fire, and myself and friends declared openly against negro or Yankee mob rule and misrule in general. In the meantime the negroes of Gonzales and adjoining counties had begun to congregate at Gonzales and were threatening to come out to the Sandies and with torch and knife depopulate the entire county. We at once got together about twenty-five men good and true and sent these negroes word to come along, that we would not leave enough of them to tell the tale. They had actually started, but some old men from Gonzales talked to them and made them return to their homes. From that time on we had no negro police in Gonzales. This happened in September, 1871.

[37] Edmund J. Davis, like most Texas Republicans, was not a carpetbagger from the North but a native Texan (Hardin here confuses his insults—"scalawag" referred to Southern Republicans, not Northern immigrants). At this time, the Ku Klux Klan was very active in terrorizing black voters; the state police was formed to combat it. The racist and extremely deadly Hardin was a natural target for arrest. His description of the state police and a "secret vigilante band" of blacks is pure propaganda.

[38] Westerners in the nineteenth century universally referred to weapons produced by the Colt's Patent Firearms Manufacturing Company as "Colts." This particular pistol was most likely the famed single-action Peacemaker revolver.

HARDIN'S VICIOUS RACISM speaks for itself, as does his deadly way with a revolver. But his killings and his hatreds bring to life the forces that created a civil war on the Great Plains. As a typical resistance gunfighter, Hardin was driven by his Southern loyalties and violent nature to battle Yankees, Republicans, the law, and newly freed blacks. His case is particularly revealing because, like so many badmen, he was not a thief or a robber—politics and prejudice mattered more than personal gain when he drew his gun. Hardin simply had no respect for society and its rules when he was in full fury (which was often). And his description of the violence in Gonzales County—which stemmed from both racism and suspicion of the Union-minded government—reveals that his entire community shared his hard-bitten values.

But the political and racial battles continued to rage on, despite Hardin's killings. Historian Eric Foner writes that Governor Davis's state police were extremely effective in quashing Klan violence, arresting more than 6,000 men between 1870 and 1872. Ironically, Texas—the source of many of the resistance gunfighters in battles all across the West—became one of the few Southern states where former slaves were adequately protected.

Given the fluid nature of the unsettled frontier, of course, the Civil War of Incorporation was not always so straightforward. Hardin's own account reveals how Wild Bill Hickok—deadly as he was—had to mix discretion with gunplay to maintain order. And "Little Arkansas" himself sometimes lifted his pistol against Hispanics and Indians (two groups who also resisted America's westward expansion); he even found work as a bounty hunter in his pursuit of Bideno. But the old hostilities carried on: in Abilene, for example, Hickok's feud with Texans Ben Thompson and Phil Coe came to a head when (after Thompson had already left town) Wild Bill faced off with Coe in the street. Marching toward each other until they were eight feet apart, the two men blazed away, and only Hickok remained standing.

Back in the Lone Star State, meanwhile, the struggle to control the frontier counties fell on the shoulders of the famed Texas Rangers. In the election of 1873, the Democrats were able to defeat the Republican Governor Davis thanks to heavy white immigration from Southern states and a blatantly racist campaign. After taking office in 1874, they immediately dismantled the state police. But Texas was a hotbed of social conflict: individual families fell into the savage feuds that plagued the hill country, and whites continued to battle blacks and Hispanics. And despite the Democratic victory, the process of incorporation continued. Within a few years, the independent cowboys and small ranchers on the frontier began to skirmish with a new foe: railroads, corporations, wealthy men, and syndicates, which established vast ranches in the late 1870s and early 1880s. To cope with the violence along this vast, sparsely settled front, the new Democratic government revived the famous Texas Rangers.

One of these rugged lawmen was young J.B. Gillett, who signed up when he was still a teenager. Out of his six years of service, the time he spent cleaning up Kimble County, in the central Texas hill country, provides a fascinating glimpse of the incorporation process described by Richard Maxwell Brown. In Kimble County, the outlaws were not the antisocial loners seen in the movies; they belonged to the local community, and shared a common set of violent values and disregard for law, the rights of property, and legal authority.

Of course, these men were hardly heroes—many killed and thieved out of anger and greed. But they lived under the protection of their neighbors, moving in and out of a gray area of crime and violence that was accepted by their friends and relatives. Out in Kimble County, everyone took it for granted that a man stood up for himself, that the stage companies and cattle barons could afford to lose a little by way of robberies and rustling. There wasn't even a single jail in the county. The "curbstone talk," as one of Gillett's victims put it, was universally disrespectful of the law. So when the Texas Rangers came in, they had to plant a whole new set of rules with deadly force—in fact, they swept up virtually the entire male population.

Here Gillett quickly sums up the Rangers' organization and equipment, then moves on to his assignment in Kimble County, where he repeatedly tangled with the criminally prolific Dublin family. But first, he had an appointment to witness the end of the road for one John Wesley Hardin.

---

## The Rangers Clean Up Kimble County
*by J.B. Gillett*

In 1874 conditions along the frontier had become so acute that the need for an organized mounted police for the protection of settlers against the continued Indian raids became apparent. As in the past, the state looked again to her rangers. Early in 1874, during the administration of Richard Coke, the first Democratic governor since secession, the legislature appropriated $300,000 for frontier defense, thus authorizing the formation of the Texas Rangers as now constituted. The governor immediately issued a call for four hundred and fifty volunteers. These were formed into six companies of seventy-five men each. Each of these was officered by a captain and a first and second lieutenant. The companies were designated A, B, C, D, E, and F, and received the official name of the Frontier Battalion of the Texas Rangers. . . .

Though formed into military units and officered as a soldier, the ranger is not a military man, for scant attention is paid to military law and precedent. The state furnishes food for the men, forage for their horses, ammunition, and medical attendance. The ranger himself must furnish his horse, his accoutrements, and his arms. There is, then, no uniformity in the matter of dress, for each ranger is free to dress as he pleases and in the garb experience has taught him most convenient for utility and comfort. A ranger, as any other frontiersman or cowboy, usually wears heavy woolen clothes of any color that strikes his fancy. Some are partial to corduroy suits, while others prefer buckskin. A felt hat of any make and color completes his outfit. While riding, a ranger always wears spurs and very high-heeled boots to prevent his foot from slipping through the stirrup, for both the ranger and the cowboy ride with the stirrup in the middle of the foot. For arms, the ranger after 1877 carried a Winchester rifle or carbine, a Colt's .45 revolver, and a bowie knife. Two cartridge belts, one for Winchester and one for revolver ammunition, completed his equipment, and thus armed he was ready to mount and ride. . . .

The fame of the rangers had, of course, become common knowledge among all Texans. Their deeds of adventure and their open, attractive life along the frontier appealed to me, and I had conceived the desire to enlist in the battalion. . . .

[After two years of service with the Rangers, Gillett was selected for Company E, a hand-picked unit under Lieutenant "Mage" Reynolds.]

On September 1, 1877, the company was sworn in. The new command was the most formidable body of men I had ever seen. Our commander, Lieutenant Reynolds, was over six feet tall and weighed probably one hundred and seventy-five pounds. He was a very handsome man, a perfect blond, with steel-blue eyes and a long, light moustache. At that time he was about thirty years of age, vigorous in mind and body, and had a massive determination to succeed as a ranger. His mind was original, bold, profound, and quick, with a will that no obstacle could daunt. He was the best ranger in the world—there was never another like him. . . .

In the summer of 1877, Lieutenant Armstrong of Captain Hall's company, assisted by Detective Jack Duncan of Dallas, Texas, captured the notorious John Wesley Hardin. It has been said by some wag that Texas, the largest state in the Union, has never produced a real world's champion at anything. Surely this critic overlooked Hardin, the champion desperado of the world. His life is too well known in Texas for me to go into detail, but, according to his own story, which I have before me, he killed no fewer than twenty-seven men, the last being Charley Webb, deputy sheriff of Brown County, Texas. So notorious had Hardin become that the state of Texas offered a $4,000 reward for his capture. Hardin had left Texas and at the time of his capture was in Florida. His captors arrested and overpowered him while he was sitting in a passenger coach.

In September, 1877, Sheriff Wilson of Comanche County, in whose jurisdiction Hardin had killed Webb, came to Austin to convey the prisoner to Comanche for trial. Wilson requested the governor for an escort of rangers. Lieutenant Reynolds's company, being in Austin at the time, was ordered to accompany Wilson and protect Hardin from mob violence. This was the first work assigned to Company E under its new commander.

The day we left Austin between one and two thousand people gathered about the Travis County jail to see this notorious desperado. The rangers were drawn up just outside the jail, and Henry Thomas and myself were ordered to enter the prison and escort Hardin out. Heavily shackled and handcuffed, the prisoner walked very slowly between us. . . .

At his trial Hardin was convicted, and sentenced to twenty-five years in the penitentiary. . . . Hardin served seventeen years of his sentence, and while in prison studied law. Governor Hogg pardoned him in 1894 and restored him to full citizenship.

Despite all the kind advice given him by eminent lawyers and citizens, Hardin was unequal to the task of becoming a useful man. He practiced law for a time in Gonzales, then drifted away to El Paso, where he began drinking and gambling. On August 19, 1895, he was standing at a bar shaking dice when John Selman, constable of Precinct No. 1, approached him from behind and with a pistol blew his brains out. Though posing as an officer, Selman was himself an outlaw and a murderer of the worst kind. He killed Hardin for the notoriety it would bring him and nothing more.

After delivering Hardin to the sheriff of Comanche County in 1877, Lieutenant Reynolds was ordered to Kimble County for duty. Of all the counties in Texas at that time Kimble was the most popular with outlaws and criminals, for it was situated south of Menard County on the North and South Llano rivers, with cedar, pecan, and mesquite timber in which to hide, while the streams and mountains furnished fish, game, and wild cattle in abundance for subsistence.

On the South Llano lived old Jimmie Dublin. He had a large family of children, most of them grown. The eldest of his boys, Richard, or Dick, as he was known, and a friend, Ace Lankford, killed two men in a country store in Lankford's Cove, Coryell County, Texas. The state offered $500 for the arrest of Dublin and the county of Coryell offered an additional $200. To escape capture Dick and his companion fled west into Kimble County. While I was working as cowboy with Joe Franks in the fall of 1873 I became acquainted with the two murderers, for they attached themselves to our outfit. They were always armed and constantly on the watch for fear of arrest. Dublin was a large man, stout and of dark complexion, who looked more like the bully of a prize ring than the cowman he was. I often heard him say he would never surrender. While cowhunting with us he discovered that the brushy and tangled region of Kimble County offered shelter for such as he, and persuaded his father to move out into that country.

Dublin had not lived long in Kimble County before another son, Dell Dublin, killed Jim Williams, a neighbor. Thus two of the Dublin boys were fugitives charged with murder. They were supposed to be hiding near their father's home. Bill Allison, Starke Reynolds, and a number of bandits, horse and cattle thieves, and murderers were known to be in Kimble County, so Lieutenant Reynolds was sent with his company to clean them up.

It was late in October, 1877, when the company reached its destination and camped on the North Llano River below the mouth of Bear Creek. As soon as our horses were rested and camp was fully established for the winter we began scouting. Several men wanted on minor charges were captured. We then raided Luke Stone's ranch, which was about ten miles from our camp, and captured Dell Dublin. He was fearfully angry when he found escape impossible. He tore his shirt bosom open and dared the rangers to shoot him. While he was being disarmed his elder brother, Dick, rode out of the brush and came within gunshot of the ranch before he discovered the presence of the rangers. He turned his horse quickly and made his escape, though the rangers pursued him some distance and fired many shots at him. When Dick learned that the Banister boys and myself were with Lieutenant Reynolds's company and hot on his trail, remembering us as beardless boys with Joe Franks's cow outfit, he declared he would whip us with a quirt as a man would whip a dog if he ever came upon us. However, he never attempted to make good his threat, but took very good care to keep out of our way until the fatal January 18, 1878.

A few days afterward the sheriff of Tom Green County, following the trail of a bunch of stolen cattle, came into our camp. Lieutenant Reynolds sent Sergeant Nevill and a scout of rangers with the sheriff. The trail led over to the South Llano, where the cattle were recovered. While scouting around the herd, Sergeant Nevill discovered a man riding down the trail toward him. He and his men secreted themselves and awaited the stranger's approach. It was getting quite dark, and when the newcomer had risen almost over the concealed rangers without noticing their presence they rose up, presented their guns, and ordered him to halt.

"Yes—like hell!" he exclaimed, and, turning his horse, dived into a cedar brake. A shower of bullets followed, but failed to strike the fugitive. It was the notorious Dick Dublin with a $700 reward on his head.

Sergeant Nevill returned to camp with about fifty head of cattle on which the brand had been defaced with a hot iron, but he had let the most notorious criminal in the county escape. Lieutenant Reynolds was disappointed at this, and said he did not understand how four crack rangers could let a man ride right over them and then get away. He declared his negro cook could have killed Dublin had he been in their place. This mortified the boys a great deal.

The latter part of 1877, Lieutenant Reynolds sent a scout out on Little Saline, Menard County. On Christmas day this detail had a running fight with four men. John Collins, the man who stole a yoke of oxen at Fredericksburg and drove them up to within two miles of our camp, was captured, as was also John Gray, wanted for murder in one of the eastern counties. Jim Pope Mason, charged with the murder of Rance Moore, was in this skirmish, but escaped.

One cold morning about the middle of January Corporal Gillett [the author], with privates John and Will Banister, Tom Gillespie, Dave Ligon, and Ben Carter, were ordered on five days' scout. We saddled our horses and packed two mules. When all was ready I walked over to Lieutenant Reynolds. He was sitting on a camp stool before his tent and seemed in deep study. I saluted and asked for orders.

"Well, Corporal," he said, after a moment's hesitation, "it is a scout after Dick Dublin again. That man seems to be a regular Jonah to this company. He lives only ten miles from here and I have been awfully disappointed at not being able to effect his capture. It is a reflection on all of Company E. There is one thing sure, if I can't capture him I will make life miserable for him. I will keep a scout in the field after him constantly."

I then asked if he had any instructions as to the route I should travel.

"No, no," he replied. "I rely too much on your judgment to hamper you with orders. After you are once out of sight of camp you know these mountains and trails better than I do. Just go and do your best. If you come in contact with him don't let him get away."

After riding half a mile from camp the boys began inquiring where we were going and who we were after. I told them Dick Dublin. We quit the road and traveled south from our camp over to the head of Pack Saddle Creek. Here we turned down the creek and rounded up the Potter ranch, but no one was at home, so we passed on into the cedar brake without having been seen.

On the extreme headwaters of South Llano River some cattlemen had built a large stock pen and were using it to confine wild cattle. This was far out beyond any settlement and probably fifty or sixty miles from our camp. I thought it possible that Dick Dublin might be hanging around the place, so we traveled through the wood most of the way to it. Here I found that the cattlemen had moved.

The scout had now been out two days, so we began our return journey. We traveled probably twenty-five miles on the third day. On the fourth day I timed myself to reach the Potter ranch about night. Old man Potter, a friend and neighbor of Dublin's, lived here with two grown sons. It was known that Dublin frequented the place, and I hoped to catch him here unawares. About sundown we were within a mile of the ranch. Here we unsaddled our horses and prepared to round up the house. If we met with no success we were to camp there for the night. I left John Banister and Ligon to guard camp while Gillespie, Will Banister, and Ben Carter, with myself, approached the ranch on foot. If I found no one there I intended to return to our camp unseen and round up the ranch again the following morning.

We had not traveled far before we discovered a man riding slowly down the trail to the Potter ranch. We remained hidden and were able to approach within fifty yards of the house without being seen. We now halted in the bed of a creek, squatting down in the shallow water, for a short consultation. The one-room cabin had only a single door, and before it was a small wagon. The Potters cooked out of doors between the house and the wagon. We could see a horse tied to the south side of the vehicle, but could not see the campfire for the wagon and the horse. To our right, and about twenty-five steps away, old man Potter and one of his sons were unloading some hogs from a wagon into a pen.

We knew the moment we left the creek bed we would be in full view of the Potters and the ranch house. We decided, then, that we would advance on the house as fast as we could run and so be in good position to capture the man who had ridden into the camp. We rose from the creek running. Old man Potter discovered us as we came into view and yelled, "Run, Dick, run! Here come the rangers!"

We then knew the man we wanted was at the camp. We were so close upon Dublin that he had no time to mount his horse or get his gun, so he made a run for the brush. I was within twenty-five yards of him when he came from behind the wagon, running as fast as a big man could. I ordered him to halt and surrender, but he had heard that call too many times and kept going. Holding my Winchester carbine in my right hand I fired a shot directly at him as I ran. In a moment he was out of sight.

I hurried to the place where he was last seen and spied him running up a little ravine. I stopped, drew a bead on him, and again ordered him to halt. As he ran, Dublin threw his hand back under his coat as though he were attempting to draw a pistol. I fired. My bullet struck the fugitive in the small of the back just over the right hip bone and passed out near his left collar bone. It killed him instantly. He was bending over as he ran, and this caused the unusual course of my ball. . . .

In the month of February, 1878, Lieutenant Reynolds started to Austin with five prisoners we had captured in Kimble and Menard counties. They were chained together in pairs, John Stephens, the old man, being shackled by himself. As guard for these prisoners Reynolds had detailed Will and John Banister, Dave Ligon, Ben Carter, Dick Ware, and myself.

On the Junction City and Mason road, some ten miles east of our camp, was the small ranch of Starke Reynolds, a fugitive from justice, charged with horse-stealing and assault to kill. . . .

We passed the Starke Reynolds home about ten o'clock in the morning, and Lieutenant Reynolds remarked that it was hardly worth while to round up the house as he had done so many times in the past without result, but that he would surely like to capture the fellow. We had not ridden more than half a mile beyond the ranch when we came face to face with Starke Reynolds himself. He was a small man and riding an exceedingly good brown pony. We were about four hundred yards apart and discovered each other at the same instant. The outlaw was carrying a small sack of flour in front of him. He immediately threw this down, turned his horse quickly, and made a lightning dash for the Llano bottoms, some three miles away.

At that point the Junction City and Mason road winds along a range of high mountains with the country sloping downward to the Llano River. This grade was studded with scrubby live oak and mesquite brush not thick enough to hide a man but sufficiently dense to retard somewhat his flight through it. We gave chase at once and for a mile and half it was the fastest race I ever saw the rangers run. We were closely bunched the entire distance, with Lieutenant Reynolds, who was riding a fast race horse, always slightly in the lead. He finally got close enough to the fugitive to demand his surrender. Starke only waved his gun defiantly and redoubled his speed. Lieutenant Reynolds then drew his six-shooter and began firing at the outlaw. After emptying this he began using his Winchester.

The Llano bottoms were now looming up in front of us. The race had been fast enough to run every horse into a big limber [state of exhaustion], and Carter, Ware, and Ligon now dropped out. Up to this time I had contented myself with trying to keep up with Lieutenant Reynolds, for it is always easier to follow a man through the brush than to run in the lead. I had a good grip on my bridle reins and was trying to steady my pony as best I could. I now saw that the outlaw was beginning to gain on us. I ran up beside the lieutenant and said: "He is getting away from us. May I go after him?"

Lieutenant Reynolds turned to me with the wildest look on his face I have ever seen. His hat was gone, his face was badly scratched by the brush, and the blood was running down over his white shirt bosom.

"Yes, God damn him! Stop him or kill him!"

I changed the bridle reins to my left hand, drew my gun with my right and, digging my spurs deep into my pony's side, I was out of sight of the lieutenant in three hundred yards. The fugitive saw that I was alone and that I was going to overhaul him. He suddenly brought his pony to a standstill, jumped down, took shelter behind the animal, and drew a bead on me with his gun.

"God damn you, stop, or I'll kill you!" he cried.

I tried to obey his order, but my pony was running down hill and ran straight at him for twenty-five yards more before I could stop. I jumped down from my horse and made ready to fight, but Starke broke for the thicket on foot. As soon as he ran out from behind his pony I fired at him. The bullet must have come rather close to him, for he turned quickly and took shelter behind his mount again. As he peeped over his saddle at me I attempted to draw a bead on his head, but I was tired, nervous, and unsteady. Before I could shoot, Dave Ligon galloped up to the outlaw and ordered him to surrender and drop his gun, which Starke did at once. The boys had heard me shoot and in five minutes were all on the scene.

The captive was searched and ordered to remount his pony. With one of the boys leading it, we started back to the wagon, nearly three miles away. As soon as the outlaw was a prisoner and knew he could not be harmed no matter what he said, he began a tirade against the rangers. He declared the whole battalion was a set of damned murderers, especially Company E, and said it was curbstone talk in Menard, Mason, and Kimble counties that Lieutenant Reynolds's men would kill a man and then yell for him to throw up his hands. . . .

As we rode along, one of the boys remarked that my pony was limping badly. "I wish his leg would come right off up to his shoulder," declared Starke in disgust. "If it hadn't been for him I would have made it to the bottoms and escaped."

On approaching the wagon the prisoner Stephens, a man of some intelligence and humor, stood up and called out to Starke, "By God, old man, they got you! They rode too many corn-fed horses and carried too many guns for you. I don't know who you are, but I'm sorry for you. While they were chasing you I got down on my knees here in this wagon and with my face turned up to the skies I prayed to the Almighty God that you might get away." . . .

[One year later, the remaining Dublin brother, Role, and Mack Potter were also arrested. They were arraigned together with Dell Dublin.]

During their trial the mystery of the Peg Leg stage robberies was finally cleared up. The Dublin boys were the guiding spirits in the holdups and worked with great cleverness. Old man Jimmie Dublin's ranch on the South Llano was their headquarters. From the ranch to Peg Leg station on the San Saba it was about sixty miles across a rough, mountainous country. As there were no wire fences in those days the robbers would ride over to the station, rob the stage, and in one night's ride regain their home. Traveling at night, they were never observed. Dick Dublin, whose death while resisting capture has already been described, was the leader of the bandit gang. . . .

The arrest and convictions of the Dublins, together with the other men Lieutenant Reynolds had captured or killed, completely cleaned out the stage robbers, cattle and horse thieves, and murderers who made Kimble County their rendezvous. Today, this is one of the most prosperous and picturesque counties in the state.

# III

---

# THE CONFLAGRATION

## THE CONQUEST OF THE
## NORTHERN PLAINS
## 1875–1886

| 1866-67 | · Red Cloud's War; Oglala leaders Red Cloud and Crazy Horse defeat army detachments on the Bozeman Trail |
|---|---|
| 1868 | · Fort Laramie Treaty creates Great Sioux Reservation in Dakota Territory and sets aside large area in Nebraska, Wyoming, and Montana as Unceded Indian Territory; Bozeman Trail and three forts guarding it are abandoned |
| 1869 | · Ulysses S. Grant (Republican) takes office as president; declares a "peace policy" toward Indians and appoints Ely Parker, a Seneca, as Commissioner of Indian Affairs (forced to resign in 1871) |
| 1873 | · Sitting Bull and other Hunkpapa leaders skirmish with Northern Pacific surveying parties, escorted by George Custer, on the Yellowstone River |
| 1874 | · Custer's expedition into the Black Hills discovers gold and sparks massive rush of prospectors |
| | · Introduction of Turkey Red winter wheat transforms Plains farming |
| 1875 | · Silver and (in 1880) copper found in Butte, Montana |
| 1876 | · Colorado becomes 38th state |
| | · Great Sioux War; Indian victories at the Rosebud and Little Bighorn |
| | · Wild Bill Hickok murdered in Deadwood, Dakota Territory; James-Younger gang annihilated in Northfield, Minnesota |
| 1877 | · Rutherford B. Hayes (Republican) takes office as president |
| | · Crazy Horse and most Sioux and Cheyenne Indians surrender; Sitting Bull flees to Canada; Crazy Horse is killed in captivity |
| | · Chief Joseph's Nez Percé band flees Oregon for Canada, and is stopped by General Nelson Miles at Bearpaw Mountain in Montana |
| 1879 | · Ute Rebellion in Colorado |
| 1880 | · Kansas outlaws alcohol |
| 1881 | · James Garfield (Republican) takes office as president; succeeded by Chester Arthur after being assassinated |
| | · Jesse James assassinated by last two gang members in St. Joseph, Missouri |
| | · Sitting Bull returns from Canada and surrenders |
| 1883 | · Northern Pacific, Southern Pacific, and Santa Fe railroads completed, making a total of four transcontinental railway lines |
| 1885 | · Grover Cleveland (Democrat) takes office as president |
| 1880s | · Cattle boom in Montana and Wyoming |

- Granville Stuart sweeps opposition to big ranchers out of Montana with a death squad known as "Stuart's Stranglers"
- Wyoming Stockgrowers' Association hires gunmen to force out small ranchers

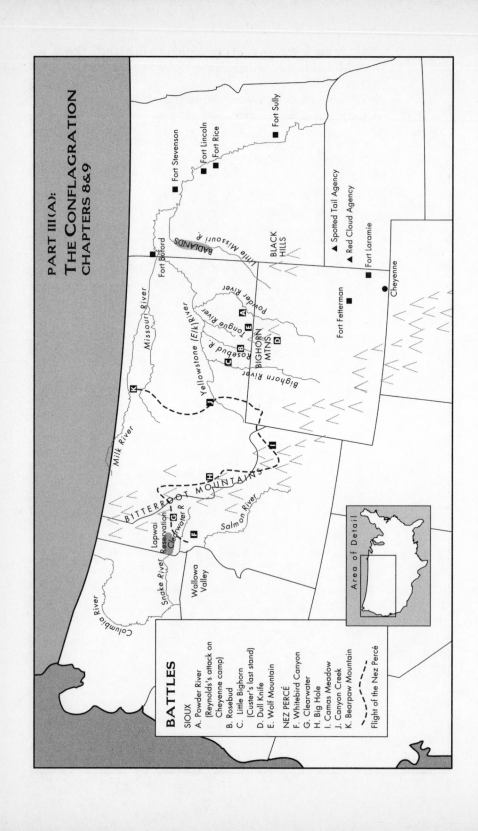

PART III(A):
THE CONFLAGRATION
CHAPTERS 8&9

**BATTLES**

SIOUX
A. Powder River
   (Reynolds's attack on
   Cheyenne camp)
B. Rosebud
C. Little Bighorn
   (Custer's last stand)
D. Dull Knife
E. Wolf Mountain

NEZ PERCÉ
F. Whitebird Canyon
G. Clearwater
H. Big Hole
I. Camas Meadow
J. Canyon Creek
K. Bearpaw Mountain

--- Flight of the Nez Percé

Area of Detail

Columbia River
Snake River
Wallowa Valley
Lapwai Reservation
Clearwater R.
Salmon River
BITTERROOT MOUNTAINS
Milk River
Missouri River
Yellowstone (Elk) River
Bighorn River
Rosebud R.
Tongue River
Powder River
BIGHORN MTNS.
Little Missouri R.
BADLANDS
BLACK HILLS

Fort Buford
Fort Stevenson
Fort Lincoln
Fort Rice
Fort Sully
Spotted Tail Agency
Red Cloud Agency
Fort Laramie
Cheyenne
Fort Fetterman

# 8

# WAR FOR THE BLACK HILLS:
# THE GREAT SIOUX WAR OF 1876

In July 1876, the United States announced to the world that it had come of age as a great power. In Philadelphia, leaders from across the globe arrived to pay their respects on the 100th anniversary of the nation's independence at the spectacular Centennial Exhibition, where Americans proudly displayed their technological marvels and industrial might. It was a splendid show by a nation reveling in its strength. But on July 5, the celebrations were shattered by a telegraph dispatch from the distant wilderness of the Great Plains: the pride of the army, General George Armstrong Custer, and more than two hundred men of the Seventh Cavalry had been annihilated by a band of nomadic, pre-industrial tribesmen.

The impact of that stunning news has echoed down to this day. Almost immediately, Custer's Last Stand transformed into a mythical event with little air of reality. But the battle,[1] and the war that swirled around it, were real indeed; in fact, the Great Sioux War of 1876, as it has been dubbed, was a pivotal event in the conquest of the West. By the mid-1870s, the Lakota and Northern Cheyennes were about the last Native Americans left undefeated. Most of the Indian wars of the 1870s were revolts—acts of resistance by tribes that had already been driven onto reservations: the Modoc War in California in 1872–73, the Red River War in Texas and the Indian Territory in 1874–75, the Bannock rebellion in the Pacific Northwest in 1878, the Ute revolt in Colorado in 1879. In the Southwest, the Navajos had been crushed in the 1860s, and the Apaches were driven onto reservations by General George Crook's campaign of the early 1870s. The Lakota and the Northern Cheyennes were the most important exception—one that the Great Sioux War of 1876 was meant to rectify.

For the background to this epic war, we must return to the aftermath of General Alfred Sully's invasion of the northern plains in 1864 (described in Chapter 4). Sully's attacks had been the first blow in the decades-long war to incorporate this vast region into the rest of the United States. White

---

[1] Formally called the Battle of the Little Bighorn (after the river that ran through the site of the conflict).

settlers came late to this part of the Great Plains, but the army was anxious to protect travelers (such as Fanny Kelly) passing through to the Rocky Mountains, and to assert federal authority over the Plains tribes. General Sully, therefore, followed up his offensive of 1863–64 by establishing forts along the upper Missouri River, while construction began on three other forts along the Bozeman Trail (Forts C. F. Smith, Phil Kearny, and Reno— see the map for Part II), in the Powder River country of southeastern Montana and northern Wyoming. All were deep in Lakota and Northern Cheyenne hunting grounds. The Indians responded with a two-pronged offensive against the forts.

That counterattack reflected a key fact about Native American society, one missed by most whites: unlike the United States itself, the Indian tribes were extremely decentralized, without central leadership. The Lakota, for example, shared a common language and culture, but were divided into no less than seven tribes, each of which was split into separate bands—which themselves often lacked firm leadership.

The Indian offensives of the late 1860s, then, had no direct connection to each other. The first was led by a man who would eventually become the most famous—and notorious—Native American in the country: Sitting Bull. As a tremendously respected war chief and *Wichasha Wakan* (holy man) of the Hunkpapa tribe of the Lakota, he organized a siege and repeated raids on the bastions that Sully had planted on the upper Missouri. His attacks ultimately failed. The other offensive, against the Bozeman Trail forts, was pushed by the Oglala tribe under the strategic guidance of Red Cloud and the tactical inspiration of a mystical war leader named Crazy Horse. In what became known as Red Cloud's War, Crazy Horse won notable victories—including the annihilation of a column of almost one hundred troops under Captain William Fetterman. This campaign succeeded, and the U.S. agreed to abandon the trail and its three posts (C. F. Smith, Phil Kearny, and Reno) in a treaty signed at Fort Laramie in 1868.[2]

Red Cloud and Crazy Horse's success reinforced the misconception in white minds that the hostile Indians were led by all-powerful chiefs who orchestrated elaborate strategies. In fact, despite skillful planning and brave personal leadership by both Sitting Bull and Crazy Horse, their warriors largely followed their own whims, in keeping with their traditions. War was a matter of winning loot, revenge, and new hunting grounds— and it offered a chance to win prestige with acts of personal bravery. Young men might follow their chiefs into battle, but they usually acted on their own once they got there. Red Cloud's success in simply keeping together a

[2] Stephen Ambrose has demonstrated that the army's failure on the Bozeman Trail was ultimately due to General Sherman's refusal to believe that the Lakota would take the offensive against the forts. Red Cloud's men, as a result, were actually better supplied (though not better armed) than their white opponents.

coalition to besiege the Bozeman Trail forts was an almost unparalleled feat. Crazy Horse only managed to trap Captain Fetterman's column after repeated failures.

Ironically, the 1868 treaty that sealed Red Cloud's victory led to a profound split in the already diffuse Lakota leadership and society. Under the treaty, the government established agencies to distribute goods to the Indians, seeking to keep them peaceful and to lure them into abandoning the buffalo chase and onto reservations in the Dakota territory. In addition, Washington recognized that many bands had not signed the treaty, and a vast area was designated "Unceded Indian Territory"—with the idea that the Native Americans would one day settle into farming. The wild plains, government negotiators foresaw, would eventually be integrated into the rest of the country.

Red Cloud immediately transformed from an intransigent defender of the hunting life to leader of the "agency Indians"—those who settled around the government agency posts and on the reservations. His turn of mind was not as dramatic as might be thought; he remained a vocal defender of Lakota culture and autonomy. But his acceptance of agency life caused a split with Crazy Horse—and a division between the bands of the Lakota. Now they were divided into the hunting bands (led by men such as Crazy Horse and Sitting Bull), who followed the buffalo full-time; agency Indians (led by Red Cloud and Spotted Tail), who settled down and accepted the government's supplies; and those who moved back and forth, living on the agency in the winter and hunting in the summer.

In 1870, these internal tensions—along with the ongoing conflict with the whites—led the Sioux hunting bands to declare Sitting Bull the head chief of all the Lakota. Such a position (as Sitting Bull's biographer Robert Utley notes), was unprecedented, wholly outside their traditions, and ultimately powerless in itself. But it symbolized the hardening of resistance among the non-agency Indians to white encroachments, and the growing national unity among the diverse Lakota. Sitting Bull never gave orders in the sense of a white general, but his tremendous stature as a war leader, diplomat, and *Wichasha Wakan* made him a rallying point for the Sioux who still resisted the reservation.

Together with his Oglala ally Crazy Horse, the Hunkpapa leader decided to avoid contact with whites if possible, but to fiercely resist intrusions into their lands. Meanwhile, the wandering Lakota bands pursued their traditional ways: hunting buffalo and warring with their Crow enemies, whom they had driven west not many years before. What Red Cloud had accepted—the inexorable advance of the whites—Sitting Bull tried to ignore.

White intrusions, however—in the triple thrust of roving settlers, business expansion, and government power—built to a climax in the 1870s. First came the Northern Pacific Railroad, an attempt to build a transcontinental line like the one that had cut through the central plains in the late

1860s. Surveying parties started up the Yellowstone River in 1871 (escorted by soldiers under the command of Custer, among others), unaware that the river was sacred to the Lakota, who called it the Elk River. The furious Sioux fought back with inconclusive hit-and-run attacks—hampered, as always, by their individualistic fighting style. The work, and the battles, stopped when the railroad company collapsed in the financial panic of 1873.

Tensions continued to rise. White settlers pushed onto the edges of the unceded territory, leading to scourging raids by Lakota and Northern Cheyenne warriors. In the summer of 1874, the Sioux expanded their age-old war on the Crows by assaulting the agency post for the Crow reservation. Another clash came in 1875, when Fellows D. Pease tried to establish a trading post on the Yellowstone. His small establishment came under fierce attack and a prolonged siege. Pease abandoned it after a cavalry detachment came to the rescue.

The gravest insult of all, however, came in 1874. It was delivered not by settlers, Crows, or traders, but by General George Custer—the man the Lakota called "Long Hair." In the face of persistent rumors of gold in the Black Hills, the romantic young officer set out on a mission to probe the secrets of that mysterious land. The expedition was in clear violation of both the 1868 treaty and Lakota sensibilities. To many Sioux, the *Paha Sapa* were a holy land, a place to go for visions (as noted by Francis Parkman). To others, like Sitting Bull, they were an invaluable resource, where the poor could always find food, even in a brutal winter. And apart from their cultural importance, the Black Hills were Lakota territory by federal law. The economic depression set off by the 1873 panic, however, fueled the gold-hunting urge. And so "Long Hair" marched forth with a mass of soldiers, geologists, and (self-dramatizing as always) reporters. Before long he sent word that there was gold in the Black Hills "from the grass roots down."

Almost immediately, the Grant administration was thrown onto the horns of a legal and political dilemma. Once Custer publicized his findings, tens of thousands of whites flooded the *Paha Sapa*, easily evading half-hearted army patrols. But the dilemma came less from the Indians (who, divided as always, made only scattered resistance to the invasion) than from U.S. law. By treaty, the Black Hills clearly belonged to the Lakota—and most of their chiefs laughed at requests that they sell the land (while others squabbled about the price). On the other hand, the administration simply would not order whites out of that gold-rich country. Pressed on two sides, the Grant administration decided to eliminate the legal basis of Lakota ownership by provoking a war.

On December 3, 1875, the Department of the Interior set the stage for war by peremptorily ordering all Indians of the northern plains—hunting bands included—to report to the agencies by January 31, 1876. The deadline, of course, was meaningless to the wandering Lakota and Cheyennes. When they failed to come in, the administration decided it was justified in declaring war. On February 7, 1876, President Grant authorized General Sheridan, commander of the Military District of the Missouri, to conduct operations against "hostile Indians."

Sheridan planned an operation similar to his winter campaign of 1868. Three columns were to lance into the unceded territory in the heart of winter, driving the Indians to exhaustion or extinction. One was to move north from Fort Fetterman under General George Crook. The other two were to move down the Yellowstone River, under General Alfred Terry, who was to personally lead Custer's Seventh Cavalry while placing the other column under Colonel John Gibbon.

In March 1876, General George Crook began his march north from Fort Fetterman, searching for the unsuspecting Indians. His was the only force to move—Terry was stuck until spring, when the thaw would allow supply trains to run again. As Crook's men marched out through deep snow and subzero weather, his cavalry probed ahead, under the command of Colonel Joseph J. Reynolds. On March 17, 1876, Reynolds found an Indian camp on the Powder River and launched an attack, firing the first shots of the Great Sioux War.

In that camp was a tall, strong young warrior named Wooden Leg, together with a band of Northern Cheyennes. Only a teenager, Wooden Leg still occasionally heard people call him by his childhood name, Eats From His Hand; in the days ahead, however, he would win new respect, and the old name would disappear forever (his adult name signified his tremendous endurance). In later years, he told an interpreter a remarkable personal history of those tense days: the rumors of an impending, inexplicable invasion by white soldiers, the sudden onset and retreat of the cavalrymen, and the flight of the Northern Cheyennes to join up with the stalwart bands of Lakota under Crazy Horse and Sitting Bull. Here Wooden Leg eloquently describes the conflict from the Native American point of view, vividly capturing the outrage and alienation caused by the theft of the Black Hills. His story carries the history of the war (which went into a lull when Crook retreated following Reynolds's attack) through to the spring, when all three army columns moved out to renew the attack on the hunting bands.

## Out of the Black Hills
*by Wooden Leg (Translated by Thomas B. Marquis)*

After we had been driven from the Black Hills and that country was given to the white people, my father would not stay on any reservation. He said it was no use trying to make farms as the white people did. In the first place, that was not the Indian way of living. All of our teachings and beliefs were that land was not made to be owned in separate pieces by persons and that the plowing up and destruction of vegetation placed by the Great Spirit and the planting of other vegetation according to the ideas of men was an interference with the plans of the Above. In the second place, it seemed that if the white people could take away from us the Black Hills after that country had been given to us and accepted by us as ours forever, they might take away from us any other lands we should occupy whenever they might want these other lands. In the third place, the last great treaty had allowed us to use all of the country between the Black Hills and the Bighorn River and mountains as hunting grounds so long as we did not resist the traveling of white people through it on their way to or from their lands beyond its borders. My father decided to act upon this agreement to us. He decided we should spend all of our time in the hunting region. We could do this, gaining our own living in this way, or we could be supported by rations given to us at the agency. He chose to stay away from all white people. His family all agreed with him. So, for more than a year before the great battle of the Little Bighorn, we were all the time in the hunting lands. . . .

Last Bull, leading chief of the Fox warriors,[3] came to us with his family at the end of the winter [February 1876]. He was the first to disturb our peace of mind with the announcement: "Soldiers are coming to fight you."

He said that the whites would fight all Cheyennes and Sioux who were off the reservation. He did not know from what forts the soldiers would come. He had not heard who would be their chiefs. But this did not matter. He and his family stayed with us. Other Cheyennes came. We did not believe Last Bull's report. We thought someone had told him what was not true. The treaty allowed us to hunt here as we might wish, so long as we did not make war upon the whites. We were not making war upon them. . . . We were trying to stay away from all white people, and we wanted them to stay away from us. . . .

Lots of buffalo were feeding on the grass at the upper Tongue and Powder rivers, on all of their branches and on the other lands in this whole region. Lots of elk, deer, and antelope could be found almost anywhere the hunter might go to seek them. Lots of colts were being born in our horse herds this spring. We were rich, contented, at peace with the whites so far as we knew. Why should soldiers come out to seek for us and fight us? No, the report seemingly was a mistake.

Spotted Wolf, Medicine Wolf, and Twin, three Cheyenne chiefs, came to us as we camped on Powder River. They advised us to go to our agency.

---

[3] The Fox were one of a number of warrior societies within Northern Cheyenne culture. Two Moons, who appears later, was a minor chief of the Fox society.

"Soldiers will come to fight you," they assured us. We now believed this to be true. The chiefs in our band had a council. The next day they had another council. "No, we shall stay here," they decided. "If the soldiers come we shall steal their horses. Then they cannot fight us."

Forty lodges of Cheyennes now were in camp on the west side of the Powder River, forty or fifty miles above where Little Powder flows into it. The report brought by the three chiefs aroused us into watchful activity. Every hunting party was on the lookout for white soldiers or for their trails. The women and old people in the camp kept themselves ever ready for immediate flight. . . .

The council of old men decided we should keep away from the soldiers, not try to fight them. They sent out an old man herald to proclaim: "Soldiers have been seen. We think they are looking for us. Today we move camp far down the river."

Our hunters and scouts kept a lookout for the soldiers. Our camp was moved to a point just above where Little Powder River flows into Powder River and on the west side of the larger stream. The soldiers went over the hills to the headwaters of Hanging Woman Creek. They followed this stream down to the Tongue River. We felt safe then. Many of our people thought they were not seeking us at all.

But one day some Cheyennes hunting antelope at the head of Otter Creek, just over the hills west from our camp, saw the soldiers camped there. The hunters urged their horses back to warn us. . . . A herald notified the people. All was excitement. The council of old men appointed ten young men to go out that night and watch the movements of the soldiers. Others were out scouting or were awake and watching, but these ten had the special duty. Most of the people slept, feeling secure under the protection of the appointed outer sentinels. Early in the morning an old man arose and went to the top of a nearby knoll to observe or to pray, as old men were in the habit of doing. He had been there only a few moments when he began shouting toward the camp: "The soldiers are right here! The soldiers are right here!"[4]

Already the attacking white men were between the horse herd and the camp. The ten scouts during the hours of darkness and storm had missed meeting the soldiers. They found a trail, this trail going up the creek valley. They turned their horses and whipped them in the effort to get ahead of the invaders. But the tired horses played out. They did not catch up with the soldiers until these had arrived at the camp, or afterward.

Women screamed. Children cried for their mothers. Old people tottered and hobbled away to get out of reach of the bullets singing among the

---

[4] This attack on the Cheyenne village is noted on the map as the Powder River battle. The army, believing mistakenly that they had struck an Oglala camp, designated it the Crazy Horse Village battle.

lodges. Braves seized whatever weapons they had and tried to meet the attack. I owned a muzzle-loading rifle, but I had not bullets for it. I owned also a cap-and-ball six-shooter, but I had loaned it to Star, a cousin who was one of the ten special scouts of the night before. In turn, he had let me have the bow and arrows he had borrowed from Puffed Cheek. My armament then consisted of this bow and arrows belonging to Puffed Cheek.[5]

I skirted around afoot to get at our horse herd. I looped my lariat rope over the neck of the first convenient one. It belonged to Old Bear, the old man chief of our band. But just now it became my war pony. I quickly made a lariat bridle and mounted the recovered animal. A few other Cheyennes did the same as I had done. But most of them remained afoot. I shot arrows at the soldiers. Our people had not much else to shoot. Only a few had guns and also ammunition for them.

All the soldiers who first appeared had white horses.[6] Another band of those who charged soon afterward from another direction had only bay horses. I started back to try to get to my home lodge. I wanted my shield, my other medicine objects, and whatever else I might be able to carry away. Women were struggling along burdened with packs of precious belongings. Some were dragging or carrying their children. All were shrieking in fright. I came upon one woman who had a pack on her back, one little girl under an arm, and an older girl clinging to her free right hand. She was crying, both of the girls were crying, and all three of them were almost exhausted. They had just dived into a thicket for a rest when I rode up to them. It was Last Bull's wife and their two daughters.

"Let me take one of the children," I proposed. The older girl, aged about ten years, was lifted behind me. A little further on I picked up also an eight-year-old boy who was trudging along behind his mother carrying on her back a baby and under her arms two other children. The girl behind me clasped her arms about my waist. I wrapped an arm about the boy in front of me. With my free arm and hand I guided my horse as best I could. The animal too was excited by the tumult. It shied and plunged. But I got the two children out of danger. Then I went back to help in the fight.

Two Moons, Bear Walks on a Ridge, and myself were together. We centered an attack upon one certain soldier. Two Moons had a repeating

---

[5] Wooden Leg's limited arsenal was typical: firearms were hard to come by, and up-to-date weapons such as repeating rifles (especially the Winchester) were quite rare. Robert Utley writes that lack of ammunition was a real problem for the Indians; they often tried to reuse old, spent cartridges by refilling them with powder and lead, which led to jammed weapons and misfires.

[6] Each troop of a U.S. cavalry regiment usually rode horses of the same color, for easy recognition in the field (see Custer's account of "coloring the horses").

rifle.[7] As we stood in concealment he stood it upon end in front of him and passed his hands up and down the barrel, not touching it, while making medicine. Then he said: "My medicine is good; watch me kill that soldier." He fired, but his bullet missed. Bear Walks on a Ridge then fired his muzzle-loading rifle. His bullet hit the soldier in the back of the head. We rushed up on the man and beat and stabbed him to death. Another Cheyenne joined us to help in the killing. He took the soldier's rifle. I stripped off the blue coat and kept it. Two Moons and Bear Walks on a Ridge took whatever else he had they wanted.

One Cheyenne was killed by the soldiers. Another had his forearm badly shattered. Braided Locks had the skin of one cheek furrowed by a bullet. The Cheyennes were beaten away from the camp. From a distance we saw the destruction of our village. Our tepees were burned, with everything in them except what the soldiers may have taken. Extra flares at times showed the explosion of powder, and there was the occasional pop of a cartridge from the fires. The Cheyennes were rendered very poor. I had nothing left but the clothing I had on, with the soldier coat added. My eagle wing bone flute, my medicine pipe, my rifle, everything else of mine, were gone.

This was in the last part of the winter [March 17, 1876]. Melted snow water was running everywhere. We waded across the Powder River and set off to the eastward. All of the people except some of the warriors were afoot. The few young men on horseback stayed behind to guard the other people as they got away. One old woman, a blind person, was missing. All others were present except the Cheyenne who had been killed.

The soldiers did not follow us. That night we who had horses went back to see what had become of them. At the destroyed camp we saw one lodge still standing. We went to it. There was the missing old blind woman. Her tepee and herself had been left entirely unharmed. We talked about this matter, all agreeing that the act showed the soldiers had good hearts.

We found their soldier camp. We found also our horses they had taken. We crept toward the herd, out a little distance from the camp. One Cheyenne would whisper, "I see my horse." Another would say, "This is mine." Some could not see their own, but they took whichever ones they could get. I got my own favorite animal. We made some effort then to steal some of the horses of the white men. But they shot at us, so we went away with the part of our own herd that we could manage. When we returned with them and caught up with our people we let the women and some of the old people ride. I gave then to Chief Old Bear his horse I had captured when the soldiers first attacked us. He said, "Thank you, my friend," and he gave the horse to his woman while he kept on afoot.

We kept going eastward and northward. We forded the Little Powder

---

[7] Possibly a Winchester, which held twelve to fifteen rounds. As mentioned earlier, these rapid-firing rifles were highly prized.

River and went upon the benches beyond. Three nights we slept out. Only a few had robes. There was but little food, only a few women having little chunks of dry meat in their small packs. There was hard freezing at night and there was mud and water by day. But nobody appeared to become ill from the exposure. Early on the fourth day we arrived at where we had aimed, a camp of the Oglala Sioux far up a creek east of Powder River. Three or four Oglala lodges had been beside our Cheyenne camp when the soldiers came. These people traveling with us led us to their main camp.

The Oglalas received us hospitably, as we knew they would do. Crazy Horse was their principal chief. Heads of lodges all about the camp were calling out to us: "Cheyennes, come and eat here." They fed us to fullness and gave us temporary shelter and robes. At night a council was held by the chiefs of the two bands. At the council our people told about the soldier attack. It was decided that the Oglalas and the Cheyennes should go together to the Hunkpapa Sioux, located northeastward from us. The next forenoon all of us set out in that direction. Horses were loaned to the Cheyennes by the Oglalas, so none of us had to walk.

Buffalo Bull Sitting Down, known to the white people as Sitting Bull, was the principal chief of the Hunkpapas in that camp. There were more of them than of Cheyennes and Oglalas combined. When we arrived there they set up at once two big special lodges in the center of their camp circle. Our men were placed in one of these lodges, our women in the other. In each lodge set a circle of Cheyennes about the inner wall. Hunkpapa women had set their pots to boiling when first we had been seen. Now they came with meat. They kept on coming, coming with more and more meat. We were filled up, and we had plenty of extra to keep for another day. A Hunkpapa herald went riding about the camp and calling out: "The Cheyennes are very poor. All who have blankets or robes or tepees to spare should give to them."

Crowds of women and girls came with gifts. A ten-year-old Hunkpapa girl put a buffalo robe in front of me and left it there. . . . Oh, what good hearts they had! I never can forget the generosity of Sitting Bull's Hunkpapa Sioux on that day. . . .

This triple camp was fifty or more miles east of Powder River, on east from a big and tall white stone which the white people call Chalk Butte. . . .

A band of Minneconjou Sioux arrived at the Hunkpapa camp either just before or just after we got there. They had not been troubled by the soldiers, but they wanted to keep out of trouble. Lame Deer was their principal chief. The Cheyennes were well acquainted with the Minneconjou. . . . We never had associated closely with the Hunkpapas. They were almost strangers to us. We knew of them only by hearsay from the Oglalas and the Minneconjou.

The movement to the Hunkpapas was because they had a much larger band in the hunting grounds than had any of the other tribes. Some of them, with Sitting Bull as their leader, had been out all of the time for several years. At this first assembling, the Oglala band was in number next to the Hunkpapas. The Minneconjou had not quite as many as had the Oglalas. The Cheyenne band was the smallest. During past times, when the Cheyennes and the Oglalas and the Burned Thighs (Brulé Sioux) had fought the white soldiers many times in the country farther southward, not many of the Hunkpapas had been with them. These people kept mostly at peace by staying away from all white settlements. Now it was becoming generally believed among Indians that this was the best plan.

Sitting Bull had come into notice as the most consistent advocate of the idea of living out of all touch with white people. He would not go to the reservation nor would he accept any rations or other gifts coming from the white man government. He rarely went to the trading posts. Himself and his followers were wealthy in food and clothing and lodges, in everything needful to an Indian. . . . He had now come into admiration by all Indians as a man whose medicine was good—that is, as a man having a kind heart and good judgment as to the best course of conduct. He was considered as being altogether brave, but peaceable. He was strong in religion—the Indian religion. He made medicine many times. He prayed and fasted and whipped his flesh into submission to the will of the Great Spirit.

So, in attaching ourselves to the Hunkpapas, we other tribes were not moved by a desire to fight. They had not invited us. They simply welcomed us. We supposed that the combined camps would frighten off the soldiers. We hoped thus to be freed from their annoyance. Then we could separate again into the tribal bands and resume our quiet wandering and hunting.

The four camps could not remain long together in any one location. The food game would become scarce there and the feed for our horses would be eaten away. We had to move on. A council of the tribal chiefs decided we should go northward to the head of the next stream flowing into the east side of the Powder River. The next morning after the decision was made, the four different bands set off in procession toward the appointed place.

The Cheyennes were in the lead. The Oglalas came next. Following them were the Minneconjou. The Hunkpapas were last. The order of movement was the result of an agreed plan. The Cheyennes and the Hunkpapas had the specially dangerous positions. I do not know on just what grounds this was the arrangement, but I know that this was the intention. The Cheyennes kept scouts out in front looking forward from high points. The Hunkpapas had always some of their young men staying back to observe if any enemies were following. The Oglalas and the Minneconjou sent guardians off to the hill points at the sides. . . .

[Over the next several weeks, the great village moved about in search of buffalo and other game. In the meantime, they were joined by other Sioux bands, including Sans Arcs and Blackfeet, along with more bands of Cheyennes coming off the reservation.]

Councils of the chiefs of the six tribes assembled together were held at each place of camping. They talked of whatever might be of general interest. Particularly, a council settled where we should go next, at each move. We had not set out to go into any special region. The moves depended upon reports of the hunting parties or scouts. They learned and reported where was most of such game as we were seeking.

Many young men were anxious to go for fighting the soldiers. But the chiefs and old men all urged us to keep away from the white men. They said that fighting wasted energy that ought to be applied in looking only for food and clothing, trying only to feed and make comfortable ourselves and our families. Our combination of camps was simply for defense. . . .

At [a camp on the Rosebud], the Hunkpapas had a great medicine dance [sun dance]. No other Indians took part in it, but great throngs of people from the other camp circles assembled to look on. The medicine lodge was pitched just north from the Hunkpapa camp circle. . . .[8] I was not there. I was then traveling up the Tongue River valley, with ten other Cheyenne buffalo hunters. . . .

We did not find any big herd of buffalo. We had killed only four by the time we arrived at Hanging Woman Creek. We decided then to go on over to the Powder River. We followed Powder River almost up to the mouth of Lodgepole Creek . . .

One of our men named Lame Sioux went out to a hill for a look over the country. Pretty soon he began to signal. He had seen a camp of soldiers.[9] All of us got out to look. Yes, this was a soldier camp. We dropped back into hiding. Ourselves and our horses were put into concealment until darkness came. Then we dressed ourselves, painted ourselves, and went on a night scout for a closer view. We saw the camp fires burning. We worked our way carefully toward them. It was after the middle of the night when we arrived at a point where we could see the entire scene. But all of the soldiers then were gone. . . .

The trail led us northwestward over the divide and down Crow Creek. Near where Crow Creek empties into Tongue River we saw the soldier camp. The time was late in the afternoon. . . . We hid ourselves among the trees [across the stream] and slept until morning.

From a cliff the next morning we saw first a band of about twenty Indians riding away from the soldier camp. Were they Crows? Were they Shoshones? We exchanged guesses, but we did not know. We talked among ourselves about making an attack upon them. There was some talk of

[8] At this dance Sitting Bull experienced a profound, widely noted vision of numerous white soldiers falling right into the Indian camp.

[9] This was the camp of General Crook's column, which finally renewed its attack north with the coming of spring. All of the soldiers described by Wooden Leg here were Crook's men.

trying to steal soldier horses. We were anxious to do something warlike, to get horses or to count coups. But the general agreement was that it was too risky. We considered it most important that we return and notify our people on the Rosebud. . . .[10]

Before the sun was up [the next day] we were several miles down the Rosebud valley. We did not know just where our people were, but we knew they were somewhere on this stream. We found them strung along [the valley]. We wolf-howled and aroused the people. Cheyennes flocked to learn why we had given the alarm. We went on into camp and reported to an old man. Some Sioux were there, and they carried the news to their people. Soon all of the camp circles were in a fever of excitement. Heralds in all of them were riding and shouting: "Soldiers have been seen. They are coming in this direction. Indians are with them."

Councils were called. Lots of young men wanted to go out and fight the soldiers, but the chiefs would not allow this. Our chiefs appointed Little Hawk, Crooked Nose, and two or three others to go scouting and find out about the further movements of the white men. . . .

The Indians all moved camp, going on up the valley about ten miles. . . . The next morning, we went down the slopes to what we called Great Medicine Dance Creek, but known now to the white people as Reno Creek. . . .

Little Hawk and the other scouts returned to us here. They reported the soldiers as being on the upper branches of the Rosebud. The Sioux were told of this report, or they may have had information from scouts of their own. Heralds in all six of the camps rode about and told the people. The news created an unusual stir. Women packed up all articles except such as were needed for immediate use. Some of them took down their tepees and got them ready for hurrying away if necessary. Additional watchers were put among the horse herds. Young men wanted to go out and meet the soldiers to fight them. The chiefs of all camps met in one big council. After a while they sent heralds to call out: "Young men, leave the soldiers alone unless they attack us."

But as darkness came we slipped away. Many bands of Cheyennes and Sioux young men, with some older ones, rode out up the south fork toward the head of Rosebud creek. Warriors came from every camp circle. We had our weapons, war clothing, paints, and medicines. I had my six-shooter. We traveled all night. We found the soldiers about seven or eight o'clock in the morning.

---

BEFORE THE END of the day, on June 17, 1876, Wooden Leg and his fellow Sioux and Cheyenne warriors would leap into one of the greatest

[10] It seems that some of the Cheyennes who remained behind to watch the camp, or possibly some Lakota scouts, did open fire—see Finerty, next selection.

fights in Western history, the Battle of the Rosebud. For the Indians, it would prove to be a climactic event, surpassed only by the Battle of the Little Bighorn just a few days later.

For the soldiers on the other side of the hill, however, the march to the Rosebud was an exercise in frustration. More than a thousand strong, they were under the command of General George Crook. After Reynolds's botched attack on Wooden Leg's village in March, Crook had fallen back to base to wait for spring. In May, both he and General Terry finally moved to carry out General Sheridan's three-column plan of attack—and Crook's men trudged north once again.

Along for the trip was John Finerty, an adventurous young immigrant from Ireland. A correspondent for a Chicago newspaper, he eagerly absorbed the details of the massive campaign—and took part with gusto. Finerty was disappointed that he wasn't allowed to go with General Custer's column, but he soon had good reasons to be satisfied with his assignment. The officers and men under Crook, Finerty found, were anxious to strike the enemy quickly; the more experienced soldiers knew how exasperating an Indian campaign could be, since the highly mobile tribesmen always seemed to scatter whenever the army finally found them. Hit-and-run attacks, not stand-up fights, characterized Indian warfare.

The old hands, however, were in for a surprise: their thrust would be met not by retreat, but by the masses of confident warriors described by Wooden Leg, who charged forth and fought them toe-to-toe in the valley of Rosebud.

---

## Battle of the Rosebud
*by John F. Finerty*

In the beginning of May 1876, I was attached to the city department of the Chicago *Times*. One day, Mr. Clinton Snowden, the city editor, said to me, "Mr. Storey wants a man to go out with the Big Horn and Yellowstone expedition, which is organizing under Generals Crook and Terry, in the departments of the Platte and Dakota. There is apt to be warm work out there with the Indians, so if you don't care to go, you needn't see Mr. Storey."

"I care to go, and I'll see Mr. Storey," was my answer.

The famous editor of the Chicago *Times* [Storey] was a tall, well-built, white-haired, white-bearded, gray-eyed, exceedingly handsome man of sixty, or thereabout, with a courteous, but somewhat cynical, manner.

"You are the young man Mr. Snowden mentioned for the Plains?" he asked, as soon as I made my presence known. . . . I replied in the affirmative. "Well, how soon can you be ready?" he inquired.

"At any time it may please you to name," was my prompt reply.

"You should have your outfit first. Better get some of it here—perhaps all. You are going with Crook's column," said Mr. Storey, with his customary decisiveness and rapidity.

"I understood I was to go with Custer," I rejoined. "I know General Custer, but am not acquainted with General Crook."

"That will make no difference, whatever," said he. "Terry commands over Custer, and Crook, who knows more about the Indians, is likely to do the hard work. Custer is a brave soldier—none braver—but he has been out there some years already, and has not succeeded in bringing the Sioux to a decisive engagement. Crook did well in Arizona. However, it is settled that you go with Crook. Go to Mr. Patterson (the manager) and get what funds you may need for your outfit and expenses. . . ."

I left Chicago to join General Crook's command on Saturday morning, May 6, 1876. The rain fell in torrents, and the wind shrieked fiercely, as the train on the Northwest road, well-freighted with passengers, steamed out of the depot, bound for Omaha. I reached the latter city on Sunday morning, and found General Crook at his headquarters, busily engaged in reading reports from officers stationed on the Indian frontier. He was then a spare but athletic man of about forty, with fair hair, clipped close, and a blonde beard which seemed to part naturally at the point of his chin. His nose was long and aquiline, and his blue-gray eyes were bright and piercing. He looked, in fact, every inch a soldier, except that he wore no uniform.

The General saluted me curtly, and I handed him the letter of introduction which I had procured in Chicago from General Sheridan, who then commanded the Military Division of the Missouri. Having read it, Crook smiled and said, "You had better go to Fort Sidney or Fort Russell, where the expedition is now being formed. You will need an animal, and can purchase one, perhaps, at Cheyenne. Can you ride and shoot fairly well?"

"I can ride fairly, General. As for shooting, I don't know; I'd engage, however, to hit a haystack at two hundred yards."

He laughed and said, "Very well. We'll have some tough times, I think. I am going with my aide, Mr. Bourke, to the agencies to get some friendly Indians to go with us. I fear we'll have to rely upon the Crows and Snakes [Shoshone], because the Sioux, Cheyennes, and Arapahos are disaffected, and all may join the hostiles. However, I'll be at Fort Fetterman about the middle of the month. . . ."

[After a long train ride, Finerty arrived in the town of Cheyenne, Wyoming.] The railroad platform was crowded with soldiers and citizens, many of the latter prospectors driven from the southern passes of the Black Hills of Dakota by the hostile Indians. I put up at an inviting hotel, and was greatly interested in the conversation around me. All spoke of "the Hills," of the Indian hostilities, and of the probable results of the contemplated military expedition.

As I was well acquainted in Cheyenne, I had little difficulty in making myself at home. Nobody seemed to know when the expedition would start, but all felt confident that there would be "music in the air" before the June roses came into bloom. At a bookstore, with the proprietor of which I was on friendly terms, I was introduced to Col. Guy V. Henry, of the 3rd Cavalry. He was, then, a very fine-looking, although slight and somewhat pale, officer, and what was still better, he was well up in all things concerning the projected Indian campaign.

"We will march from this railroad in two columns," said he. "One will form at Medicine Bow, ninety miles or so westward, and will cross the North Platte River at Fort Fetterman. The other will march from Fort Russell to Fort Laramie, cross the North Platte there, and march by the left bank, so as to join the other column in front of Fetterman. This I have heard not officially, but on sufficiently good authority. From Fetterman we will march north until we strike the Indians. That is about the program." . . .

The next day I called upon the commandant of [Fort Russell], Gen. J.J. Reynolds, colonel of the 3rd Cavalry, who received me with that courteous bearing so characteristic of the American regular officer. He spoke pleasantly of the approaching campaign, but he regretted that he personally could have no part in it. He did not say why, but I understood perfectly that he and the department commander, General Crook, were not on good terms, owing to a disagreement relative to Reynolds's action during the short Crazy Horse village campaign of the preceding March.[11] Reynolds stormed the village, but was unable to retain it, and, in his retreat, the Indians attacked his rear guard and stampeded the pony herd of 800 horses he had captured. General Crook held that General Reynolds ought to have shot the ponies rather than allow them to fall again into the hands of their savage owners. A court martial grew out of the controversy. . . .

As I was taking my leave, General Reynolds said: "As you have not been out after Indians previously, allow an old soldier to give you this piece of advice—Never stray far from the main column, and never trust a horse or an Indian."

I promised to follow the General's advice as closely as possible, and made my adieux. Orders had reached the Fort that the troops were to move to Fort Laramie on the morning of the 17th [of May], and all felt grateful that the period of inaction was almost at an end. Before giving my account of the famous campaign, I must briefly relate the causes of the great Indian War of 1876.

---

[11] This was the attack on the Cheyenne village described by Wooden Leg; the army mistakenly believed it was Crazy Horse's camp of Oglala Sioux.

## THE BLACK HILLS FEVER

There had raged for many years a war between the Sioux Nation, com-posed of about a dozen different tribes of the same race under various designations, and nearly all other Indian tribes of the Northwest. The Northern Cheyennes were generally confederated with the Sioux in the field, and the common enemy would seem to have been the Crow, or Absorake, Nation. . . . Nearly all of Dakota, northern Nebraska, northern Wyoming, northern and eastern Montana lay at the mercy of the savages, who, since the completion of the treaty of 1868 . . . had been mainly successful in excluding all white men from the immense region, which may be roughly described as bounded on the east by the 104th meridian; on the west by the Big Horn mountains; on the south by the North Platte; and on the north by the Yellowstone River. In fact, the northern boundary, in Montana, extended practically to the frontier of the British possessions [Canada]. About 240,000 square miles were comprised in the lands ceded, or virtually surrendered, by the government to the Indians. . . . All this magnificent territory was turned over and guaranteed to the savages by solemn treaty with the United States government.

The latter made the treaty with what may be termed undignified haste. The country, at the time, was sick of war [known as Red Cloud's War]. Colonel [Captain] Fetterman, with his command of nearly one hundred men and three officers, had been overwhelmed and massacred by the Sioux near Fort Phil Kearny in December, 1866. Other small detachments of the army had been slaughtered here and there throughout the savage re-gion. . . . The government weakly agreed to dismantle the military forts established along the Montana emigrant trail. . . .

The white man's government might make what treaties it pleased with the Indians, but it was quite a different matter to get the white man himself to respect the official parchment. Three-fourths of the Black Hills region, and all of the Big Horn, were barred by the Great Father and Sitting Bull against the enterprise of the daring, restless, and acquisitive Caucasian race. . . . The expedition of General Custer, which entered the Black Hills proper—those of Dakota—in 1874, confirmed the reports of gold finds, and, thereafter, a wall of fire, not to mention a wall of Indians, could not stop the encroachments of that terrible white race. . . .

In vain did the government issue its proclamations; in vain were our vet-eran regiments of cavalry and infantry, commanded by warriors true and tried, drawn up across the path of the daring invaders. . . . They laughed at the proclamations, evaded the soldiers, broke jail, did without wagons or outfit of any kind, and, undaunted by the fierce war whoops of the exasper-ated Sioux, rushed on to the fight for gold with burning hearts and naked hands! Our soldiers, whom no foe, white, red, or black, could make recreant to their flag upon the field of honor, overcome by the moral epidemic, deserted by the squad to join the grand army of indomitable adventurers. . . .

Thickly as mushrooms grow in the summer nights on the herbage-robbed sheep range, rose "cities" innumerable, along the Spearfish and the Deadwood and Rapid creeks. Placer and quartz mines developed with marvelous rapidity, and, following the first, and boldest, adventurers, the eager but timid and ease-loving capitalists came in swarms. Rough board shanties and hospital tents were the chief architectural features of the new "cities," which swarmed with gamblers, harlots, and thieves, as well as with honest miners. By the fall of 1875, the northern segment of the irregular, warty geological formation, known as the Black Hills, was prospected, staked, and in fairly good proportion, settled, after the rough, frontier fashion. . . .

All the passes leading into the Hills swarmed with hostile Indians. . . . The rocks of Buffalo Gap and Red Canyon rang with rifle shots of the savages, and the return fire of the hardy immigrants, many of whom paid with their lives the penalty of their ambition. . . . But enough historical retrospection. I will now resume my narrative of the long and weary march. . . .


## THE MARCH

The final order to move out on the expedition reached Fort Russell on May 16th. I met there Mr. T.C. McMillan, who was going out as correspondent for another Chicago newspaper. He was fortunate in making messing arrangements with Captain Sutorious [of the 3rd Cavalry], who was the soul of hospitality. . . .

Captain Sutorious welcomed us warmly, and introduced us to the two officers of the 2nd Cavalry, Captain Wells and Lieutenant Sibley. The former was a veteran of the Civil War, covered with honorable scars, bluff, stern, and heroic. Lieutenant Sibley . . . was a young West Pointer, who had distinguished himself under General Reynolds in the attack upon, and capture of, Crazy Horse's village on March 17th of that eventful year. He was about the middle height, well but slightly built, and with a handsome, expressive face. . . .

The conversation turned chiefly on the campaign upon which we were entering. Captain Wells said that the Indians were in stronger force than most people imagined, and that General Crook, accustomed mostly to the southern Indians, hardly estimated at its real strength the powerful array of the savages. He joked, in rough soldierly fashion, McMillan and myself on having had our hair cropped, as, he said, it would be a pity to cheat the Sioux out of our scalps. . . .

[The command then marched on to Fort Fetterman, the campaign base, where Crook joined the expedition.]

General Crook, impatient for action, hardly gave us time to have our soiled clothing properly washed and dried, when, everything being ready, he marched us northward at noon on the 29th of May. . . .

[During the long march that followed,] the absence of Indians surprised the men who had been over the road previously. Around the campfires, both officers and rank and file asked, "Where are the Sioux?" This interrogation was addressed by Sutorious to Captain Wells, at a bivouac fire of the 3rd Cavalry.

"Don't be alarmed," said Wells, in his grim, abrupt way, "if they want to find us, we will hear from them when we least expect. If they don't want to find us, we won't hear from them at all, but I think they will." . . .

"By the way," said Lieutenant Reynolds, "you all remember how on the night Bourke's tent was fired into at Crazy Woman, a soldier got out of his tent, and in the frosty air of midnight, shouted loudly enough for all the command to hear him, 'I want to go ho-o-o-ome!' "

A roar of laughter rewarded the Lieutenant's anecdote, and we all, soon afterward, turned in for the night. . . .

Than the morning of Sunday, June 3, 1876, a lovelier never dawned in any clime. It was six o'clock when our entire command—no company or troop being detached—struck their tents and prepared for their day's march. An hour later we had turned our backs on Powder River. . . .

Our column, including cavalry, infantry, wagon train, pack train, and ambulances, stretched out a distance of, perhaps, four miles. The infantry generally accompanied the wagon train, and acted as a most efficient escort. On June 3rd, the ten companies of the 3rd Cavalry, under Major Evans, formed the van of the horse brigade, while five companies of the 2nd Cavalry, under Major Noyes, formed the rear. Crook, with his staff, was away in advance of everything, as was his custom. . . . Were I to live in the age of the biblical patriarchs, I can never forget the beauty of that scene. A friend and myself allowed the soldiers to file somewhat ahead, in order that we might enjoy a complete view. The cavalry rode by twos, the intervals between the companies, except those which formed the rear guard behind the pack mules, being just sufficient to define the respective commands. The wagons, 120 in all, with their white awnings and massive wheels, covered the rising ground in advance of the horsemen, while the dark column of infantry was dimly discernible in the van, because Crook always marched out his foot, for obvious reasons, an hour or two ahead of his horse. . . . Our course lay over a gently swelling or billowy plain, nearly bare of trees, but sufficiently carpeted with young grass to render it fresh and vernally verdant. . . . Fifty miles in our front—we were marching almost due westward—rose the mighty wall of the Big Horn mountains. . . .

On the morning of the 9th some cavalry soldiers, who had been out hunting buffalo, reported having found a fresh Indian trail, and during the night Captain Dewees's company of the 2nd Cavalry had been disturbed by something, and the firing of their pickets had aroused the whole camp, so that expectation and excitement began to run pretty high. Some of the veterans swore that a recruit had been alarmed by the swaying of a bunch of sage brush in the night breeze, and it remained for the Indians in the flesh to appear, before many of them would believe that there were any hostiles in the country.

At about 6:30 o'clock, on the evening of the 9th, just as the soldiers were currying their horses on the picket line, a shot was heard on the right of the camp, and it was quickly followed by a volley which appeared to come from the commanding bluff beyond the river. This opinion was soon confirmed by the whistling and singing of bullets around our ears, and some of us did lively jumping around to get our arms. The Indians had come at last, and were ventilating our tents, by riddling the canvas, in a masterly manner. We were taken by surprise, and the men stood by their horses waiting for orders.

Meanwhile Sheol appeared to have broken loose down by the river and all around the north line of our camp. If the casualties had borne any proportion to the sound of the firing, the mortality must have been immense. On our extreme left, the pickets of the 2nd Cavalry kept up an incessant fire, which was very spiritedly responded to by the Sioux. The higher bluff, which commanded the entire camp, situated almost directly north, seemed alive with redskins, judging by the number of shots, although only two Indians, mounted on fleet ponies, were visible on the crest. They rode up and down in front of us, repeatedly, and appeared to act in the double capacity of chiefs and lookouts. Although a great number of soldiers fired upon them, they appeared to bear charmed lives. But the savages were rapidly getting the range of our camp, and making things uncomfortably warm. Crook's headquarters and the infantry lines were immediately below them, while our tents, on the southern slope, offered a very attractive target. . . . All at once a young staff-officer, excited and breathless, rode into the camp of the 1st Battalion of the 3rd Cavalry.

"Colonel Mills! Colonel Mills!" he shouted.

"Here, sir," replied the commander of the battalion.

"General Crook desires that you mount your men instantly, Colonel, cross the river and clear those bluffs of the Indians."

"All right," said Col. Mills, and he gave the order. . . .

"Forward!" shouted the colonel, and forward we went. A company of the 2nd Cavalry was extended among the timber on our left, to cover the attack on the bluffs. In a minute our charging companies were half wading, half swimming, through Tongue River, which is swift and broad at that point. The musketry continued to rattle and the balls to whiz as we crossed. Partially screened by cottonwood trees in the bottom-land, we escaped unhurt. In another minute we had gained the base of the bluffs, when we were ordered to halt and dismount, every eighth man holding the horses of the rest. Then we commenced to climb the rocks, under a scattering fire from our friends, the Sioux. The bluffs were steep and slippery, and took quite a time to surmount. . . .

We could see our late assailants scampering like deer, their fleet ponies carrying them as fast as the wind up the first ascent, where they turned and fired. Our whole line replied, and the boys rushed forward with a yell. The Sioux gave us another salute, the balls going about 100 feet above our heads, and skedaddled to the bluff further back. There, nothing less than a long-range cannon could reach them, and we could pursue them no farther, as the place was all rocks and ravines, in which the advantage lay with the red warriors. The latter showed themselves, at a safe distance, on the east of the ridge, and appeared to take delight in displaying their equestrian accomplishments. . . . To say the truth, they did not seem very badly scared, although they got out of the way with much celerity when they saw us coming in force.

Our firing having completely ceased, we could hear other firing on the south side of the river, far to the left, where the 2nd Cavalry had their pickets. This, we subsequently learned, was caused by a daring attempt by the Indians to cross a ford at that point and take the camp in rear, with the object of driving off the herd. They failed signally, and lost one man killed and some wounded. Whether our party killed any of the Sioux I don't know. . . . Our casualties were comparatively few, owing to the prompt action of Mills's battalion, but quite sufficient to cure skeptics of the idea that there were no hostiles in the neighborhood. After the Indians retired, Mills's men were withdrawn to the camp, and the bluff was garrisoned by Captain Rawolle's company of the 2nd Cavalry. . . .

### INDIANS IN WAR PAINT

[A few days later,] just as we began to give up all hope of ever again seeing our scouts or hearing from our Indian allies, Frank Grouard[12] and Louis Richard, accompanied by a gigantic Crow chief, came into camp at noon on the 14th, and amid the cheers of the soldiers, rode direct to the General's headquarters. . . . Louis Richard, the Indian scout, and Major Burt went back for the Crows. We waited impatiently for their arrival. At six o'clock a picket galloped into camp to notify Crook that his allies were in sight.

[12] Grouard, who was of mixed white and Polynesian ancestry, had once been adopted by Sitting Bull as a brother; he had since left the Hunkpapa, however, and now was an army scout.

Then we saw a grove of spears and a crowd of ponies upon the northern heights, and there broke up on the air a fierce, savage whoop. The Crows had come in sight of our camp, and this was their mode of announcing their satisfaction. We went down to the creek to meet them, and a picturesque tribe they were. . . . "How! How!" the Crows shouted to us, one by one, as they filed past. When near enough, they extended their hands and gave ours a hearty shaking. Most of them were young men, many of whom were handsomer than some white people I have met. . . .

The head sachems were Old Crow, Medicine Crow, Feather Head, and Good Heart, all deadly enemies of the Sioux. Each man wore a gaily colored mantle, handsome leggings, eagle feathers, and elaborately worked moccasins. In addition to their carbines and spears, they carried the primeval bow and arrow. Their hair was long, but gracefully tied up and gorgeously plumed. . . . Quick as lightning they gained the center of our camp, dismounted, watered and lariated their ponies, constructed their "tepees" or lodges, and like magic the Indian village arose in our midst. . . .

That night an immense fire was kindled near Crook's tents, and there all the chiefs of both tribes [Crow and Snake], together with our commanding officers, held "a big talk." Louis Richard acted as interpreter, and had a hard time of it, having to translate in three or four languages. . . . The Indians were quite jolly, and laughed heartily whenever the interpreter made any kind of blunder. The Snakes retired from the council first. They said very little.

Old Crow, the greatest chief of the Crow nation, made the only consecutive speech of the night, and it was a short one. Translated, it was as follows: "The great white chief will hear his Indian brother. These are our lands by inheritance. The Great Spirit gave them to our fathers, but the Sioux steal them from us. They hunt upon our mountains. They fish in our streams. They have stolen our horses. They have murdered our squaws, our children. What white man has done these things to us? The face of the Sioux is red, but his heart is black. But the heart of the pale face has ever been red to the Crow. (Ugh! Ugh! Hey!) The scalp of no white man hangs in our lodges. They are thick as grass in the wigwams of the Sioux. (Ugh!) The great white chief will lead us against the other tribe of red men. Our war is with the Sioux and only with them. We want back our lands. We want their women for our slaves—to work for us as our women have had to work for them. We want their horses for our young men, and their mules for our squaws. We shall spit upon their scalps. (Ugh! Hey! and terrific yelling.) The great white chief sees that my young men have come to fight. No Sioux shall see their backs. Where the white warrior goes there shall we be also. It is good. Is my brother content?" The chief and Crook shook hands amid a storm of "Ughs" and yells. . . .

Crook was bristling for a fight. The Sioux were said to be encamped on the Rosebud, near the Yellowstone River, holding Gibbon at bay. "They are numerous as grass," was the definite Crow manner of stating the strength of the enemies. . . .

All day of the 15th was devoted to active preparation for the approaching movement against the hostiles. Arms were cleaned, horses re-shod, haversacks and saddlebags filled, and ammunition stowed wherever it could be carried. The General determined to move out on the following morning with his pack train only. The wagons were to be left behind under the command of Major and Quartermaster John V. Furey, with one hundred men to guard them, beside the mule-drivers. . . .

The great mass of the soldiers were young men, careless, courageous, and eminently light-hearted. The rank and file, as a majority, were of either Irish or German birth or parentage, but there was also a fair-sized contingent of what may be called Anglo Americans, particularly among the noncommissioned officers. Taken as a whole, Crook's command was a fine organization, and its officers, four-fifths of whom were native [white] Americans and West Pointers, were fully in sympathy with the ardor of their men. . . .

The sun was low when we approached the Rosebud valley, but still, in the distance, right, left, and in front, we could hear the rapid crackling of the Indian [Crow] guns, as they literally strewed the plain with the carcasses of unfortunate bisons. Quiet reigned only when the sun had set, and we went into camp in an amphitheatrical valley, commanded on all sides by steep, but not lofty, bluffs. Pickets were posted along the elevations, and the command proceeded to bivouac in a great circle. . . .

The whole command sank early to repose, except those whose duty it was to watch over our slumbers, and the boastful, howling Indians [the allied Crows and Snakes], who kept up their war songs throughout most of the night. Captain Sutorious, lying on the ground next to me, with saddle for pillow, and wrapped in his blanket, said, "We will have a fight tomorrow, mark my words—I feel it in the air." These were the last words I heard as I sank to sleep. . . .

## BATTLE OF THE ROSEBUD

Dawn had not yet begun to tinge the horizon above the eastern bluffs, when every man of the expedition was astir. How it came about, I do not know, but, I suppose, each company commander was quietly notified by the headquarters' orderlies to get under arms. . . .

Presently we saw the infantry move out on their mules, and, within a few minutes, the several cavalry battalions were properly marshaled, and all were moving down the valley, in the gray dawn, with the regularity of a machine, complicated, but under perfect control. . . . At about eight o'clock, we halted in a valley, very similar in formation to the one in which we had pitched our camp the preceding night. Rosebud stream, indicated by the thick growth of wild roses, or sweet brier, from which its name is derived, flowed sluggishly through it, dividing it from south to north in two almost equal parts. The hills seemed to rise on every side, and we were within easy musket shot of those most remote. . . .

The sun became intensely hot in that close valley, so I threw myself upon the ground, resting my head upon my saddle. Captain Sutorious, with Lieutenant Von Leutwitz, who had been transferred to Company E, sat near me smoking. At 8:30 o'clock, without any warning, we heard a few shots from behind the bluffs to the north. "They are shooting buffalo over there," said the Captain. Very soon we began to know, by the alternate rise and fall of the reports, that the shots were not all fired in one direction. Hardly had we reached this conclusion, when a score or two of our Indian scouts appeared upon the northern crest, and rode down the slopes with incredible speed. "Saddle up, there, saddle up, there, quick!" shouted Colonel Mills, and immediately all the cavalry within sight, without waiting for formal orders, were mounted and ready for action.

General Crook, who appreciated the situation, had already ordered the companies of the 4th and 9th Infantry, posted at the foot of the northern slopes, to deploy as skirmishers, leaving their mules with the holders. Hardly had this precaution been taken, when the flying Crow and Snake scouts, utterly panic stricken, came into camp shouting at the top of their voices, "Heap Sioux! Heap Sioux!" gesticulating wildly in the direction of the bluffs which they had abandoned in such haste. All looked in that direction, and there, sure enough, were the Sioux in goodly numbers, and in loose but formidable array. The singing of the bullets above our heads speedily convinced us that they had called on business. . . . Up, meanwhile, bound on bound, his gallant horse covered with foam, came Lemley.

"The commanding officer's compliments, Colonel Mills!" he yelled. "Your battalion will charge those bluffs on the center."

Mills immediately swung his fine battalion, consisting of Troops A, E, I, and M, by the right into line, and, rising in his stirrups, shouted "Charge!" Forward we went at our best pace, to reach the crest occupied by the enemy who, meanwhile, were not idle, for men and horses rolled over pretty rapidly as we began the ascent. Many horses, owing to the rugged nature of the ground, fell upon their riders without receiving a wound. We went like a storm, and the Indians waited for us until we were within fifty paces. We were going too rapidly to use our carbines, but several of the men fired their revolvers, with what effect I could neither then nor afterward determine, for all passed "like a flash of lightning, or a dream." I remember, though, that our men broke into a mad cheer as the Sioux, unable to face that impetuous line of the warriors of the superior race, broke and fled, with what white men would consider undignified speed. . . .

We got that line of heights, and were immediately dismounted and formed in open order, as skirmishers, along the rocky crest. While Mills's battalion was executing the movement described, Colonel Crook ordered the 2nd Battalion of the 3rd Cavalry, under Col. Guy V. Henry . . . to charge the right of the Sioux array, which was hotly pressing our steady infantry. Henry executed the order with characteristic dash and promptitude, and the Indians were compelled to fall back in great confusion all along the line.

General Crook kept the five troops of the 2nd Cavalry, under Noyes, in reserve, and ordered Troops C and G of the 3rd Cavalry, under Captain Van Vliet and Lieutenant Crawford, to occupy the bluffs on our left rear, so as to check any movement that might be made by the wily enemy from that direction. . . .

General Crook divined that the Indian force before him was a strong body—not less perhaps than 2,500 warriors—sent out to make a rear guard fight, so as to cover the retreat of their village, which was situated at the other end of the canyon. He detached Troop I of the 3rd Cavalry . . . from Mills to Henry, after the former had taken the first line of heights. He reinforced our line with the friendly Indians, who seemed to be partially stampeded, and brought up the whole of the 2nd Cavalry within supporting distance.

The Sioux, having rallied on the second line of heights, became bold and impudent again. They rode up and down rapidly, sometimes wheeling in circles, slapping an indelicate portion of their persons at us, and beckoned us to come on. One chief, probably the late lamented Crazy Horse, directed their movements by signals made with a pocket mirror or some other reflector.

Under Crook's orders, our whole line remounted, and, after another rapid charge, we became masters of the second crest. When we got there, another just like it rose on the other side of the valley. There, too, were the savages, as fresh apparently as ever. We dismounted accordingly, and the firing began again. It was now evident that the weight of the fighting was shifting from our front, of which Major Evans had general command, to our left where Royall and Henry cheered on their men.

Still the enemy were thick enough on the third crest, and Colonel Mills, who had active charge of our operations, wished to dislodge them. The volume of fire, rapid and ever increasing, came from our left. The wind freshened from the west, and we could hear the uproar distinctly. Soon, however, the reckless foe came back upon us, apparently reinforced. He [the enemy] made a vigorous push for our center down some rocky ravines, which gave him good cover. Just then a tremendous yell arose behind us, and along through the intervals of our battalions, came the tumultuous array of the Crow and Shoshone Indians, rallied and led back into action by Major George M. Randall and Lieutenant John G. Bourke, of General Crook's staff. . . .

The two bodies of savages, all stripped to the breechcloth, moccasins, and war bonnet, came together in the trough of the valley, the Sioux having descended to meet our allies with right good will. All . . . were mounted. The wild foemen, covering themselves with their horses, while going at full speed, blazed away rapidly. Our regulars did not fire because it would have been sure death to some of the friendly Indians, who were barely distinguishable by a red badge they carried. Horses fell dead by the score—they were heaped there when the fight closed—but, strange to relate, the casualties among the warriors, on both sides, did not certainly exceed five and twenty. . . . The absence of very heavy losses in this combat goes far to prove the wisdom of the Indian method of fighting.

Finally the Sioux on the right, hearing the yelping and firing of the rival tribes, came up in great numbers, and our Indians, carefully picking up their wounded, and making their uninjured horses carry double, began to draw off in good order. . . .

In order to check the insolence of the Sioux, we were compelled to drive them from the third ridge. Our ground was more favorable for quick movements than that occupied by Royall, who found much difficulty in forcing the savages from his front—mostly the flower of the brave Cheyenne tribe—to retire. One portion of his line, under Captain Vroom, pushed out beyond its supports, deceived by the rugged character of the ground, and suffered quite severely. In fact, the Indians got between it and the main body, and nothing but the coolness of its commander and the skillful management of Colonels Royall and Henry saved Troop L of the 3rd Cavalry from annihilation on that day. . . . In repelling the audacious charge of the Cheyennes upon his battalion, Colonel Henry, one of the most accomplished officers in the army, was struck by a bullet, which passed through both cheek bones, broke the bridge of his nose, and destroyed the optic nerve in one eye. His orderly, in attempting to assist him, was also wounded, but, temporarily blinded as he was, and throwing blood from his mouth by the handful, Henry sat on his horse for several minutes in front of the enemy. He finally fell to the ground, and, as that portion of our line, discouraged by the fall of so brave a chief, gave ground a little, the Sioux charged over his prostrate body, but were speedily repelled, and he was happily rescued by some soldiers of his command. . . .[13]

As the day advanced, General Crook became tired of the indecisiveness of the action, and resolved to bring matters to a crisis. He rode up to where the officers of Mills's battalion were standing, or sitting, behind their men, who were prone on the skirmish line, and said, in effect, "It is time to stop this skirmishing, Colonel. You must take your battalion and go for their village away down the canyon."

---

[13] Crook's Indian allies played a critical role repelling the Lakota and Cheyenne charge, here and elsewhere during the battle.

"All right, sir," replied Mills, and the order to retire and remount was given. The Indians, thinking we were retreating, became audacious, and fairly hailed bullets after us, wounding several soldiers. . . . Troops A, E, and M of Mills's battalion, having remounted, guided by the scout Grouard, plunged immediately into what is called, on what authority I know not, the Dead Canyon of the Rosebud valley. . . .

The bluffs, on both sides of the ravine, were thickly covered with rocks and fir trees, thus affording ample protection to an enemy, and making it impossible for our cavalry to act as flankers. . . . We began to think of our force as rather weak for so venturous an enterprise, but Lieutenant Bourke informed the Colonel that the five troops of the 2nd Cavalry, under Major Noyes, were marching behind us. . . .

The day had become absolutely perfect, and we all felt elated, exhilarated as we were by our morning's experience. Nevertheless, some of the more thoughtful officers had their misgivings, because the canyon was certainly a most dangerous defile, where all the advantage would be on the side of the savages. General Custer, although not marching in a position so dangerous, and with a force nearly equal to ours, suffered annihilation at the hands of the same enemy, about eighteen miles further westward, only eight days afterward.

Noyes, marching his battalion rapidly, soon overtook our rear guard and the whole column increased its pace. Fresh signs of Indians began to appear in all directions, and we began to feel that the sighting of their village must be only a question of a few miles further on. We came to a halt in a kind of cross canyon, which had an opening toward the west, and there tightened up our horse girths and got ready for what we believed must be a desperate fight. The keen-eared Grouard pointed toward the occident [west], and said to Colonel Mills, "I hear firing in that direction, sir." Just then there was a sound of fierce galloping behind us, and a horseman dressed in buckskin and wearing a long beard, originally black but turned temporarily gray by the dust, shot by the halted command, and dashed up to where Colonel Mills and the other officers were standing.

It was Major A.H. Nickerson of the General's staff. . . . "Mills," he said, "Royall is hard pressed, and must be relieved. Henry is badly wounded, and Vroom's troop is all cut up. The General orders that you and Noyes defile by your left flank out of this canyon and fall on the rear of the Indians who are pressing Royall." This, then, was the firing that Grouard had heard. Crook's order was instantly obeyed, and we were fortunate enough to find a comparatively easy way out of the elongated trap into which duty had led us. We defiled, as nearly as possible, by the heads of companies, in parallel columns, so as to carry out the order with greater celerity. We were soon clear of Dead Canyon, although we had to lead our horses carefully over and among the boulders and fallen timber. The crest of the side of the ravine proved to be a sort of plateau, and there we could hear quite plainly the noise of the attack on Royall's front. . . .

"Prepare to mount—mount!" shouted the officers, and we were again in the saddle. Then we urged our animals to their best pace, and speedily came in view of the contending parties. The Indians had their ponies, guarded mostly by mere boys, in rear of the low, rocky crest which they occupied. The position held by Royall rose somewhat higher, and both lines could be seen at a glance. There was very heavy firing, and the Sioux were evidently preparing to make an attack in force, as they were riding in by the score, especially from the point abandoned by Mills's battalion in its movement down the canyon. . . .

Suddenly the Sioux lookouts observed our unexpected approach, and gave the alarm to their friends. We dashed forward at a wild gallop, cheering as we went, and I am sure we were all anxious at that moment to avenge our comrades of Henry's battalion. But the cunning savages did not wait for us. They picked up their wounded, all but thirteen of their dead, and broke away to the northwest on their fleet ponies, leaving us only the thirteen scalps, 150 dead horses and ponies, and a few old blankets and war bonnets as trophies of the fray. Our losses, including the friendly Indians, amounted to about fifty, most of the casualties being in the 3rd Cavalry, which bore the brunt of the fight on the Rosebud. Thus ended the engagement which was the prelude to the great tragedy that occurred eight days later in the neighboring valley of the Little Big Horn.

The General was dissatisfied with the result of the encounter, because the Indians had clearly accomplished the main object of their offensive movement—the safe retreat of their village[14] . . . We had driven the Indians about five miles from the point where the fight began, and the General decided to return there, in order that we might be nearer water. . . .

General Crook decided that evening to retire on his base of supplies—the wagon train—with his wounded, in view of the fact that his rations were almost used up, and that his ammunition had run pretty low. . . . We learned during the [next] night that the General had determined to send the wagon train, escorted by most of the infantry, to Fort Fetterman for supplies, and that the wounded would be sent to that post at the same time. He had sent a request for more infantry, as well as cavalry, and did not intend to do more than occasionally reconnoiter the Sioux until reinforcements arrived. . . .

[While awaiting reinforcements, several days later] General Crook was . . . up in the mountains over our camp, on another hunt. Colonel Royall, who had heard further reports of a massacre of our cavalry by Indians, . . . sent a few companies of the 3rd after the General. . . . Crook

[14] The Indian village was nowhere near the scene of the battle. Crook had endangered his entire force by sending Mills on this wild goose chase.

received all the news with his customary placidity, and then set about cleaning himself up after his long turn in the mountains. He felt morally certain, however, that some dire disaster had befallen a portion of Terry's command, and he feared the impetuous Custer was the victim. His fears were sadly realized on Monday morning, July 10th, when Louis Richard . . . came in from Fetterman with the official account of the catastrophe. With it came a characteristic despatch from General Sheridan to Crook, in which the former said, referring to the Rosebud fight, "Hit them again, and hit them harder!" Crook smiled grimly when he read the telegram, and remarked, "I wish Sheridan would come out here himself and show us how to do it."

---

THE BATTLE OF the Rosebud was a devastating defeat for General Crook. As Robert Utley writes, "the true victory, both tactical and strategic, lay with the Indians. They had attacked a force twice as large as or larger than their own, kept it off balance and largely reactive all day, inflicted serious casualties, and sent it in stunned retreat back to the security of the base camp." The Lakota and Cheyenne warriors had fought fiercely, charging in among the soldiers in hand-to-hand combat, and had seemed on the verge of overwhelming the main force while Colonel Mills was away on the wild goose chase down the valley. Crook was so shaken that he reeled back, basically withdrawing from the campaign for the next two months.

Meanwhile, the other two columns of Sheridan's planned triple attack worked their way toward the Native American camp. On June 21, General Terry, Colonel Gibbon, and Custer met on the steamboat *Far West* on the Yellowstone River to plan their attack. Terry correctly suspected the location of the Indian village; he assigned Custer to drive up the Rosebud with his Seventh Cavalry regiment and attack as soon as he found the enemy. Gibbon, with a slower-moving infantry force, would move to the mouth of the Little Bighorn to cut off the Indians' retreat. Custer moved out the next day, and on June 25 he found Sitting Bull's camp.

When word came of Custer's annihilation, General Sheridan told the *New York Times* that the flamboyant commander had been "rashly impudent to attack such a large number of Indians." But General Terry had planned for "Long Hair" to make the attack on his own; indeed, neither he nor Custer realized the size of the hostile village, now swollen in numbers by Indians who had left their agencies after the Lakota and Cheyenne victory on the Rosebud. Custer *was* impetuous; but his impetuosity had won him many battles before against less confident enemies. He had complete assurance in himself and his men in the face of a foe they considered racially inferior. "Long Hair" was far more worried about the Indians scattering than fighting back.

On locating the vast camp, Custer planned to wait a day to rest his men—but a passing party of Indians made him fear that his presence had been discovered. Pushing the attack on the same day, he divided his command as he had at the Washita in 1868. Captain Frederick W. Benteen was ordered to scout to the south; the pack train and an escort lagged behind with orders to follow as soon as possible. Then Major Marcus A. Reno led a battalion of 175 troopers across the Little Bighorn in a direct attack on the south side of the village. Custer himself took 210 men on a wide swing to strike the enemy from the north.

Northern Cheyenne warrior Two Moons was in the northern end of the camp when word came of Reno's attack. He was a minor chief of the Fox warrior society, and Wooden Leg tells us that the Fox men were serving as "camp policemen" that day. Here he briefly recounts the events already told by Wooden Leg, then vividly describes the panic in the village, his efforts to carry out his duties by calming and organizing his people, and his ride to join the repulse of Reno, whose attack fell on the Hunkpapa camp at the rear of the great Indian village. Two Moons then joined the sudden shift to meet Custer's threat from the north, and he tells of the swirling battle that brought the flamboyant "Long Hair" to his sudden, unexpected demise in the valley of the Little Bighorn—or Greasy Grass to the Indians.

Two Moons's account is immediately followed by Wooden Leg's story of the Indians' wanderings after the victory, when the various tribes decided to split up to feed themselves more easily.

---

## Custer's Last Stand
*by Two Moons (as told to Hamlin Garland)*

That spring [March 1876], I was camped on Powder River with fifty lodges of my people—Cheyennes. The place is near what is now Fort McKenney. One morning soldiers charged my camp. They were in command of Three Fingers.[15] We were surprised and scattered, leaving our ponies. The soldiers ran all our horses off. That night the soldiers slept, leaving the horses on one side; so we crept up and stole them back again, and then we went away.

We traveled far, and one day we met a big camp of Sioux at Charcoal Butte. We camped with the Sioux, and had a good time, plenty grass, plenty game, good water. Crazy Horse was head chief of the camp. Sitting Bull was camped a little ways below, on the Little Missouri River. Crazy Horse said to me, "I'm glad you are come. We are going to fight the white man again."

The camp was already full of wounded men, women, and children. I said

[15] "Three Fingers" was the Indian name for Col. Ranald Mackenzie, but the attack was actually led by J.J. Reynolds (described in detail earlier by Wooden Leg).

to Crazy Horse, "All right, I am ready to fight. I have fought already. My people have been killed, my horses stolen. I am satisfied to fight." I believed at that time the Great Spirits had made Sioux, put them there (he drew a circle to the right) and white men and Cheyennes here (indicating two places to the left) expecting them to fight. The Great Spirits I thought liked to see them fight; it was to them all the same like playing. So I thought then about fighting.

About May, when the grass was tall and the horses strong, we broke camp and started across the country to the mouth of the Tongue River. Then Sitting Bull and Crazy Horse and all went up the Rosebud. There we had a big fight with General Crook, and whipped him. Many soldiers were killed—few Indians. It was a great fight, much smoke and dust.[16]

From there we all went over the divide, and camped in the valley of the Little Bighorn. Everybody thought, "Now we are out of the white man's country. He can live there, we will live here." After a few days, one morning when I was in camp north of Sitting Bull, a Sioux messenger rode up and said, "Let everybody paint up, cook, and get ready for a big dance."

Cheyennes then went to work to cook, cut up tobacco, and get ready. We all thought to dance all day. We were very glad to think we were far away from the white man. I went to water my horses at the creek, and washed them off with cool water, then took a swim myself. I came back to the camp afoot. When I got near my lodge, I looked up the Little Bighorn towards Sitting Bull's camp. I saw a great dust rising. It looked like a whirlwind. Soon a Sioux horseman came rushing into camp shouting, "Soldiers come! Plenty white soldiers!"

I ran into my lodge, and said to my brother-in-law, "Get your horses; the white man is coming. Everybody run for horses." Outside, far up the valley, I heard a battle cry, *Hay-ay, hay-ay!* I heard shooting, too, this way (clapping his hands very fast). I couldn't see any Indians. Everybody was getting horses and saddles. After I had caught my horse, a Sioux warrior came again and said, "Many soldiers are coming." Then he said to the women, "Get out of the way, we are going to have a hard fight."

I said, "All right, I am ready." I got on my horse, and rode out into my camp. I called out to the people all running about, "I am Two Moons, your chief. Don't run away. Stay here and fight. You must stay and fight the white soldiers. I shall stay even if I am to be killed."

I rode swiftly toward Sitting Bull's camp. There I saw white soldiers fighting in a line.[17] Indians covered the flat. They began to drive the

[16] This rapid summary brings events up through the battle of the Rosebud, the fight described here.

[17] This was Reno's detachment, which made a direct assault on the southern end of the Indian village (the Hunkpapa camp) as Custer swung around to the north. When Two Moons arrived, Reno's men were still arrayed in an organized line of battle—though, as he describes, they were soon routed by the Lakota counterattack.

soldiers all mixed up—Sioux, then soldiers, then more Sioux, and all shooting. The air was full of smoke and dust. I saw the soldiers fall back and drop into the riverbed like buffalo fleeing. They had no time to look for a crossing. The Sioux chased them up the hill, where they met more soldiers in wagons,[18] and then messengers came saying more soldiers were going to kill the women, and the Sioux turned back. Chief Gall[19] was there fighting. Crazy Horse also.

I then rode toward my camp, and stopped squaws from carrying off lodges. When I was sitting on my horse I saw flags come up over the hill to the east like that (he raised his fingertips). Then the soldiers rose all at once, all on horses, like this (he put his fingers behind each other to indicate that Custer appeared marching in columns of fours). They formed into three bunches with a little ways between. Then a bugle sounded, and they all got off horses, and some soldiers led the horses back over the hill.

Then the Sioux rode up the ridge on all sides, riding very fast. The Cheyennes went up the left way. Then the shooting was quick, quick. Pop-pop-pop, very fast. Some of the soldiers were down on their knees, some standing. Officers all in front. The smoke was like a great cloud, and everywhere the Sioux went the dust rose like smoke. We circled all round him—swirling like water round a stone. We shoot, we ride fast, we shoot again. Soldiers drop, and horses fall on them. Soldiers in line drop, but one man rides up and down the line—all the time shouting. He rode a sorrel horse with white face and white forelegs. I don't know who he was. He was a brave man.

Indians kept swirling round and round, and the soldiers killed only a few. Many soldiers fell. At last all horses killed but five. Once in a while some man would break out and run toward the river, but he would fall. At last about a hundred men and five horsemen stood on the hill all bunched together. All along the bugler kept blowing his commands. He was very brave, too. Then a chief was killed. I hear it was Long Hair, I don't know; and then the five horsemen and the bunch of men, maybe forty, started toward the river. The man on the sorrel horse [possibly a civilian scout] led them, shouting all the time. He wore a buckskin shirt, and had long black hair and mustache. He fought hard with a big knife. His men were all

[18] These late-arriving troops belonged to Benteen's detachment and the supply train (which had pack mules, not wagons). In the panic of the retreat across the Little Bighorn, Reno lost forty dead and thirteen wounded; Wooden Leg clubbed two men into the raging current. Reno and Benteen's men dug in at the top of the hill.

[19] Gall was a prominent Hunkpapa warrior, one of Sitting Bull's closest friends and allies. As an aging chief, Sitting Bull was not expected to fight; but since Reno's attack fell on the Hunkpapa part of the village, endangering women and children, he picked up a Winchester and helped turn back the assault. Then he stayed with the Hunkpapa camp, and did not join the fight against Custer himself.

covered with white dust. I couldn't tell whether they were officers or not. One man all alone ran far down toward the river, then round up over the hill. I thought he was going to escape, but a Sioux fired and hit him in the head. He was the last man. He wore braid on his arms [suggesting a sergeant].

All the soldiers were now killed, and the bodies were stripped. After that no one could tell which were the officers. The bodies were left where they fell. We had no dance that night.[20] We were sorrowful.

The next day, four Sioux chiefs and two Cheyennes and I, Two Moons, went up on the battlefield to count the dead. One man carried a little bundle of sticks. When we came to dead men, we took a little stick and gave it to another man, so we counted the dead. There were 388.[21] There were thirty-nine Sioux and seven Cheyennes killed, and about a hundred wounded. Some white soldiers were cut with knives to make sure they were dead; and the war women mangled some. Most of them were left just where they fell. We came to the man with the big mustache; he lay down the hills toward the river. The Indians did not take his buckskin shirt. The Sioux said, "That is a big chief. That is Long Hair." . . .

That day as the sun was getting low our young men came up the Little Bighorn riding hard. Many white soldiers were coming in a big boat, and when we looked we could see the smoke rising. I called my people together, and we hurried up the Little Bighorn, into Greasy Grass Valley. We camped there three days, and then rode swiftly back over our old trail to the east. Sitting Bull went back into the Rosebud and down the Yellowstone, and away to the north. I did not see him again.[22]

## After the Victory
*by Wooden Leg*

The Cheyenne warriors had a dance at the Greasy Grass camp. Charcoal Bear, our medicine chief, brought the buffalo skin from the sacred tepee and put it upon the top of a pole in the center of our camp circle. We danced around this pole. No women took part in the dancing. Many of

[20] Wooden Leg, in the next selection, contradicts Two Moons, saying the Northern Cheyenne did have a dance, though the Hunkpapa did not. Two Moons may have forgotten, or may have been edgy about telling a white reporter that he celebrated after killing Custer and his men.

[21] This figure is about a hundred too many. Custer had about 225 men with him; in addition, forty men were killed out of Reno's detachment. Reno and Benteen eventually escaped, after further fighting.

[22] In this last paragraph, Two Moons has condensed events that actually lasted much longer than he describes, as seen in Wooden Leg's account next.

them had sore legs from the mourning cuts.[23] Our dance was not carried very far into the night. It was mostly a short telling of experiences, a counting of coups. My father told, in a few words, what his two sons had done. When he had ended the telling of my warrior acts, he said: "The name of this son of mine is Wooden Leg." Up to this time some people still used my boyhood name, Eats From His Hand. But now this old name was entirely gone.

Some of the Sioux people had little dances here, the same as the Cheyennes were having. But not all of them did this. The Hunkpapas did not dance. They said it was not time, that we ought to mourn yet a while. Some of them came to look on quietly at our gathering.

Only one sleep we stayed at the Greasy Grass location. The great band of Indians trailed from there on top of the Little Bighorn valley. . . . We turned eastward and went over the hills to the extreme upper Rosebud. One sleep at this place. We moved on down, going past the ground where we fought the soldiers on this creek. We camped a few miles below where this fight had taken place. One sleep here. The movement was kept up down this valley. . . .

I was not with the camps at all of these stopping places. Like many others, I was out a part of the time looking for meat. I took it to my people when I could get any. Buffalo were scarce along the line of travel, so most of the game killed was elk, deer, or antelope. Many people among the Indians were hungry for more food. Partly because of the fast traveling and partly because the hunters were not going far on account of soldiers in the country, the food demands of the people could not be supplied to their full satisfaction. . . .

[After more traveling,] we were now in the same region where all of the tribes had come together three months before this time. In coming back to the gathering place all of the Indians traveled together, as we had done in going westward from it. The Cheyennes still were moving in the advance. The Hunkpapas still were following last and camping last. On the return we hurried from place to place. There was no stopping for special hunting. I believe we remained only one sleep at each of the camps. . . .

The Indians were hungry. Our meat was all gone. The horses had been traveling hard every day and were tired. The fat and sleek soldier horses we had were more tired than the Indian ponies. It was said this was because they were not used to living on grass alone, as the Indian ponies were. . . .

Every day, the chiefs met in council. Finally, they decided on a separation of the tribes. It seemed there was no danger just now from soldiers.[24] By

---

[23] See Fanny Kelly's account, in "The Captive," for a description of how Sioux and Cheyenne women would cut themselves in mourning.

[24] In fact, both Crook and Terry *had* fallen back after their sharp defeats, both out of shock and to refit for a new attack.

traveling separately, or in small bands, more meat and skins could be taken by each tribe or band. The horses all could get more grass when scattered. Everybody agreed it was best to separate. I think this was the intention of the chiefs all the time, but we were staying together for yet a few days of final visiting in a quiet camp before the separation.

The Cheyennes went first down the Powder River. We followed it to where it flows into Elk [Yellowstone] River. . . . We saw a steamboat on Elk River. Soldiers were on the boat. As they passed along, some of the Cheyennes shot at them. I do not know whether or not any soldiers shot at them. They did not shoot back at us. The boat did not stop. . . .

All during the remainder of the summer the Cheyennes traveled and hunted. We kept mostly in the upper parts of the valleys. Not many of our people went to the reservation. But some more came out and joined us. Dull Knife, the old man chief, was with us soon after the separation of the tribes. All four of the old men chiefs now were here. Charcoal Bear kept our tribal medicine lodge set up at every place of camping. When the leaves began to fall we were on Powder River. We camped and hunted along up its valley. As the snows of winter began to fall we moved farther up.

---

AS THE GREAT Indian camp broke up into smaller bands, the United States reeled with the news of the annihilation of Custer and his men. For many whites—especially those who lived along the frontier, exposed to Native American attacks—the battle on the Little Bighorn was a catastrophe of the first order. There were others, mainly in the East, who saw a measure of poetic justice in the disaster. It was Custer, after all, who had personally led the fateful expedition into the Black Hills and publicized the discovery of gold—leading inexorably to the outbreak of this tragic war. As the *New York Times* commented, "The invasion of the Black Hills has been condemned over and over by the peace party, and there are very many who can truthfully say, 'I told you so.' From that unwarranted invasion the present difficulties have gradually sprung up."

Of course, as attractive as it may be to see the bombastic, self-promoting Custer as the villain in this story, the truth is far more complex. The clash of whites and Indians on the frontier was the nearly inevitable result of the inexorable expansion of the United States. The outbreak of war as the different civilizations fought for the same land and resources was almost unavoidable, and no individual can bear the blame. In fact, frontier settlers glorified Custer for protecting their families from Indian raids—or at least for hunting Indian raiders.

Meanwhile, the Indians' spectacular victories over Crook and Custer sparked a massive response by the U.S. Army. The war born out of land theft was now driven by wounded pride. Sheridan was utterly determined to defeat Sitting Bull, Crazy Horse, and their allies. The expanded campaign was joined by General (then Colonel) Nelson Miles—like Custer, a boy general of the Civil War who had stayed on in the postwar army at reduced rank. Miles and Custer had been good friends, and were similar in many respects: both loved publicity, promoted themselves relentlessly, and were usually very effective in combat.

In the pages that follow, Miles describes how he talked himself into the campaign, and his key role in hounding the Lakota and Cheyennes into submission. As Miles relates, his most effective work came after the summer ended, when the demoralized columns under Terry and Crook had retreated to base for the winter. Miles and his hardy infantry stayed in the field, chasing the wandering bands under Sitting Bull, Crazy Horse, Dull Knife, and others. He killed few enemy warriors, but his constant pursuit made it almost impossible for them to secure the buffalo they needed to feed and clothe their people.

## Chasing Sitting Bull
*by General Nelson A. Miles*

The announcement of the annihilation of Custer and this large body of men . . . shocked the entire country, and was telegraphed around the world as a great disaster. I remember reading on the morning of July 5, at Fort Leavenworth, Kansas, the headline of a newspaper, printed in the largest kind of type and running across the entire page the single word: HORRIBLE. It shocked our little community there perhaps more than it did any other part of the country, as General Custer was well known among us. He and his regiment were most popular throughout all that region, and the disaster seemed to their friends most appalling. It seemed to magnify in the public mind the power and terrors of the Sioux Nation, and immediate orders were sent to different parts of the country directing that detachments of troops be ordered to the seat of war.

Six companies of my regiment were ordered to move from Fort Leavenworth under Lieutenant-Colonel Whistler, but as six companies were more than half of the regiment, I claimed that by right it was a colonel's command and requested to be ordered with it myself, which request was at once granted. Subsequently the remainder of the regiment was ordered to follow. . . .

As we passed through the towns and villages it reminded me of the time when the troops were going to war for the Union in the days of 1861 and '62. Many of the public buildings and private houses were draped in mourning, and frequently the national colors were displayed in token of sympathy for the dead and encouragement of the living. The command was cheered wherever it passed a gathering of citizens, and finally went on board a large river steamer at Yankton. . . .

For ten days the great steamer plowed its way up the Missouri. . . . We then moved on up the Yellowstone. . . . We continued our journey up to the Rosebud and I reported my command to Brigadier-General Terry. We formed part of his forces during the two months following, and moved up the Rosebud, where General Terry's troops joined those under Brigadier-General Crook. This brought the two department commanders together with one of the largest bodies of troops ever marshalled in that country.

The combined forces were then moved east across the Tongue River to the mouth of the Powder River. There the commands separated again, General Crook crossing the tributaries of the Yellowstone and Little Missouri, then going southeast, crossing the Belle Fourche, and going into camp near the Black Hills. His command suffered very much for want of food and many of his animals perished on this march. He sent some troops on in advance, under the command of Captain Anson Mills, to obtain supplies. This gallant and skillful officer surprised a band of Indians near Slim Buttes and captured their camp, containing a large amount of supplies which proved of great benefit to his detachment and also to the troops of General Crook when they came up. . . .[25]

From the mouth of the Powder River the remaining portion of the command, under General Terry, moved north to the Big Dry, thence east, then south again, and ultimately to Glendive, on the Yellowstone. There it embarked in steamers and returned to the various stations, leaving my command, the 5th Infantry, with six companies of the 22nd Infantry, in the field to occupy that country during the approaching winter. It was contemplated that my troops should build a cantonment, but it was not supposed that they would do much more than occupy that much of the country until next spring. . . .

It was my purpose when I found I had been designated to remain in that country not to occupy it peaceably—in conjunction with the large bodies of Indians that were then in the field, and which practically included the entire hostile force of the five Indian tribes, namely: the Hunkpapas under Sitting Bull, the Oglalas under Crazy Horse, the Northern Cheyennes under Two Moons, and the Minneconjou and Sans Arcs under their trusted leaders. Judging from our experience of winter campaigning in the southwest [the Red River War of 1874–75], I was satisfied that the winter was the best time for subjugating these Indians. . . . I remarked to General Terry that if given proper supplies and a reasonable force, I would clear the Indians out of that country before spring. He remarked that it was impossi-

---

[25] While acclaimed by many as an army victory, this fight was essentially a draw. Mills (with Finerty along for the ride) battled Sitting Bull and the Hunkpapas, Crazy Horse's Oglalas, and others; after capturing their camp, he withdrew under heavy fire. Some Indians in the group planned to surrender but changed their minds after this attack.

ble to campaign in the winter, and that I could not contend against the elements. . . .

My command moved from Glendive to the junction of the Tongue River with the Yellowstone, where ground had already been selected for our cantonment by Lieutenant-Colonel J.N.G. Whistler. . . . We were abundantly supplied with food and clothing, and every precaution was taken to protect both men and animals against the severity of this intense cold. Every effort was also made to keep the train and riding animals in full flesh. They were fed abundance of corn to give as much heat to their systems as possible, and plenty of hay whenever it could be obtained. . . .

The number of troops originally ordered by General Sheridan, commanding the army, to winter on the Yellowstone under my command was fifteen hundred, but owing to various circumstances and causes the force had been reduced until only about one-third of that number were placed at my disposal. I learned through spies and other means of the design of Sitting Bull to move to the mouth of Powder River, and other particulars of his intended movements. The fact of a party of warriors under Chief Gall making an attack on my train confirmed the reports I had received through other sources, and on October 17, 1876, I moved across the Yellowstone at the mouth of the Tongue River, proceeding thence northeast in order that I might, if possible, intercept the march of the hostiles.

On the 21st my command was brought into contact with the hostile tribes of Minneconjou, Sans Arcs, and Hunkpapas under the command of Sitting Bull, Low Neck, Gall, Pretty Bear, and other chiefs. At the time there were two friendly Indians from the agency in their camp and for some reason they sent out by these two men a flag of truce, and desired to have a talk. As we were approaching their camp, although at that point we did not know its exact locality, I agreed to meet Sitting Bull between the lines with six men—one officer and five men—while he was to have the same number of warriors with him. His force consisted of about a thousand warriors, and I had three hundred and ninety-four riflemen with one piece of artillery.

We met, and after some conversation he desired to know what the troops were remaining in that country for, and why they did not go back to their posts or into winter quarters. He was informed that we were out to bring him and his Indians in, and that we did not wish to continue the war against them, but that if they forced the war it would end, as all Indian wars had ended and must end, by their putting themselves under the authorities in Washington. He was told that he could not be allowed to roam over the country, sending out parties to devastate the settlements.

He claimed that the country belonged to the Indians and not to the white men, and declared that he had nothing to do with the white men and wanted them to leave that country entirely to the Indians. He said that the white man never lived who loved an Indian, and that no true Indian ever lived that did not hate the white man. He declared that God Almighty made him an Indian, and did not make him an agency Indian either, and he did not intend to be one. After much talk, and after using all the powers of persuasion of which I was master, I was convinced that something more than talk would be required.

On first meeting Sitting Bull I naturally studied his appearance and character. He was a strong, hardy, sturdy looking man of about five feet eleven inches in height, well-built, with strongly marked features, high cheek bones, prominent nose, straight, thin lips, and strong underjaw, indicating determination and force. He had a wide, large, well-developed head and low forehead. He was a man of few words and cautious in his expressions, evidently thinking twice before speaking. He was very deliberate in his movements and somewhat reserved in his manner. At first he was courteous, but evidently void of any genuine respect for the white race. . . . I found that it was useless to endeavor to persuade him to accept peaceable terms, and made an excuse for discontinuing the talk. I then moved with my men back in the direction from which we had come.

The next morning I moved soon after daylight in the direction in which I believed their main camp to be located, and discovered it after a march of ten miles. Sitting Bull again came forward with a flag of truce and desired another talk, which was granted, but it resulted as fruitlessly as the first. The only condition of peace which he would consent to was the abandonment of the entire country, including military posts, lines of travel, settlements; in fact everything but a few trading posts which might be left to furnish them with ammunition and supplies in exchange for their buffalo robes and whatever they had to sell. . . . He was told that no advantage of his being under the flag of truce would be taken, and he would be allowed to return to his camp, but that in fifteen minutes, if he did not accept the terms offered, we would open fire and hostilities would commence.

He and the men who accompanied him then returned with all speed toward their lines, calling out to the Indians to prepare for battle, and the scene was, for the next few minutes, one of the wildest excitement. The prairies were covered with savage warriors dashing hither and thither making ready for battle. At the end of the time mentioned, I ordered an advance of the entire body of troops, and immediately the Indians commenced setting fire to the dry prairie grass around the command, together with other acts of hostility. An engagement immediately followed in which the Indians were driven out of their camp for several miles, and in the two days following were pursued for a distance of more than forty miles. The Indians lost a few of their warriors and a large amount of property both in their camp and on their retreat, including their horses, mules, and ponies, which fell into our hands. . . .

The energy of the attack and the persistence of the pursuit created such consternation in their camp that, after a pursuit of forty-two miles, the

Indians sent out another flag of truce and again requested an interview. During this interview two thousand of them agreed to go to their agencies and surrender. They gave up five of their principal chiefs as hostages for the faithful execution of this agreement. . . . But Sitting Bull, Pretty Bear, and several other chiefs, with nearly four hundred people, broke away from the main camp and retreated north toward the Missouri.

The command on returning to the cantonment at the mouth of the Tongue River was immediately reorganized, and with a force of 434 men of the 5th Infantry, again moved north in pursuit of Sitting Bull and the chiefs mentioned. Striking the trail on a tributary of the Big Dry, we followed it for some distance, and until it was obliterated by a severe snowstorm. . . .

No one can realize the condition and circumstances, or the responsibility attendant upon moving a command in that country in midwinter. The condition of a ship in northern latitudes in a dense dry fog in the track of icebergs would be in a somewhat similar situation with what our command in that severe climate in a country, which as General Sheridan described it in his reports, was practically "unknown." Indeed it was unknown. So tenaciously had those bands of warriors held it that it had been impossible for white men to explore it. . . .

On returning to the cantonment on the Yellowstone I again reorganized the command for a movement against Crazy Horse and the Cheyennes and Oglalas, who, I had been informed, were near the headwaters of the Tongue River, some seventy-five or eighty miles from our cantonment. They had committed many depredations in the vicinity of our cantonment, stealing a good part of what few horses we had, and nearly all the beef belonging to the contractor. . . .

The snow was then a foot deep on a level, and in many places it proved to be much deeper. The wagon trains and troops marched over the ice in the valley of the Tongue River, and after considerable delay reached the vicinity of the Indian camp, having a few skirmishes on the way, and being somewhat annoyed by the presence of parties of the enemy. We lost two of our men who were surprised and killed by a small band of Indians. The camp was found to be located on the Tongue River, extending along that stream a distance of three miles above Otter Creek, and as the command approached them, the Indians moved farther up the stream toward the Big Horn mountains to what they supposed to be a safe distance.

On January 7, following, the advance guard captured a small party of Indians, including one young warrior, four women, and three children. This event afterward proved of considerable importance, as they were relatives of some of the most prominent men in the hostile camp. That evening an attempt was made by a band of about three hundred warriors to recapture them, which resulted in a sharp skirmish and the repulse of the Indians.

On the morning of the 8th the command deployed to meet and attack the main body of warriors, led by Crazy Horse, Little Big Man, White Bull, Big Crow, Two Moons, Hump, and other prominent chiefs of the Cheyennes and Oglalas.[26] The country was very rough—mountainous in fact; and as the Indians moved down the valley to encounter the troops they evidently had every confidence of making it another massacre. They outnumbered the troops more than two to one, and must have had at least a thousand warriors on the field. From the heights overlooking the valley where they had stationed themselves they called out to the troops, "You have had your last breakfast," and similar expressions. . . . Some of our scouts, particularly Yellowstone Kelly, who understood Sioux and could reply to them in their own language, responded with equal defiance, challenging them to the encounter, and shouting back to them that they were all "women."

As the fight opened the canvas covers were stripped off the pieces of artillery, and the two Napoleon guns exploded shells within their lines, creating great consternation; and the re-echoing of the guns through the valley, while it gave the troops much confidence, undoubtedly multiplied the number of our guns in the estimates of the Indians themselves. At one time they had completely surrounded the command, but the key of the position was a high bluff to the left of the line of troops, and the sharpest fighting was for the possession of this ground.

The Indians who held it were led by Big Crow, a medicine man who had worked himself up to such a frenzy that he had made the Indians believe that his medicine was so strong that the white men could not harm him. He rushed out in front of the warriors, attired in the most gorgeous Indian battle costume of the brightest colors, and with a headdress made of waving plumes of the eagle falling down his back, jumped up and down, ran in a circle and whooped and yelled. Our men turned their guns upon him, but for several minutes he was unharmed, notwithstanding their efforts to reach him with their rifles.[27]

Then a charge was made by troops under Majors Casey and Butler, and Captains McDonald and Baldwin. It was done with splendid courage, vim, and determination, although the men were so encumbered with their heavy winter clothing, and the snow was so deep, that it was impossible to move faster than a slow walk. Captain Baldwin was conspicuous in this charge for his boldness and excellent judgment. In the very midst of his daring acts of bravado, Big Crow fell, pierced by a rifle shot, and his loss, together with the success of the charge that had been made and the

[26] This fight is known as the Battle of Wolf Mountain.

[27] This "running the daring line" was part of the Lakota and Cheyenne emphasis on performing feats of individual bravery for their own sake. In the next selection Wooden Leg reveals that Big Crow was not actually in command—another case of cross-cultural misinterpretation of Native American behavior.

important ground gained, seemed to cause a panic among the Indians, and they immediately fled in utter rout up the valley down which they had come a few hours before with such confidence.

The latter part of the engagement occurred during a snowstorm, which added an inexpressible weirdness to the scene. I think every officer realized the desperate nature of this encounter, the command being then between three and four hundred miles from any railroad or settlement. If they had met with disaster it would have been many weeks before relieving command could have reached the ground from the nearest possible source of aid. . . . While the engagement was not of such a serious character as to cause a great loss of life on either side, yet it demonstrated the fact that we could move in any part of the country in the midst of winter, and hunt the enemy down in their camps wherever they might take refuge.

---

IT WAS THE Northern Cheyennes, as much as any other band, that felt the pain of Miles's blows. But Miles was not the only commander still in the field. On November 26, 1876, Wooden Leg and several other young men were out hunting when Crook's cavalry commander, Ranald McKenzie, smashed into the Northern Cheyenne village on the eastern base of the Big Horn mountains (in a fight known as the Dull Knife Battle, after the Cheyenne chief). The warrior returned to find his people destitute—their goods, lodges, and clothing destroyed in McKenzie's sudden attack. In the passage that follows, he describes how he and the hunting party discovered their stricken people, and the search for their friends and allies, the Oglalas under Crazy Horse. The young warrior then provides an Indian view of the Battle of Wolf Mountain (described at the end of Miles's account above). As Wooden Leg vividly tells, it was a harrowing winter for the Northern Cheyennes and Oglala Sioux—one that could only lead to surrender and defeat.

---

### Last Days of the Northern Cheyennes
*by Wooden Leg*

[At the end of November, Wooden Leg had set out with a big hunting party, when they came across the survivors of what was called the Dull Knife battle.]

Somewhere below the mouth of Hanging Woman Creek our scouts caught sight of Indians coming down the valley. All of us got to where we might see. Most of the Indians were afoot. Only a few had horses. We watched and wondered. Who were these people?

The band of walking Indians were our Cheyennes, the whole tribe. They had but little food. Many of them had no blankets or robes. They had no lodges. Only here and there was one wearing moccasins. The others had their feet wrapped in loose pieces of skin or of cloth. Women, children, and old people were straggling along over the snow-covered trail down the valley. The Cheyennes were very poor.

Our people told us of soldiers and Pawnee Indians having come to the camp far up Powder River where we had left them. The Cheyennes had to run away with only a few small packs, as our small band had done on lower Powder River during the late winter before this time [Reynolds's attack in March 1876]. The same as we had done, they had to see all of their lodges burned and most of their horses taken. Many of our men, women, and children had been killed. Others had died of wounds or had starved and frozen to death on the journey through the mountain snow to Tongue River. Three Cheyenne women and a boy had been captured by the Pawnees.

The tribe was hunting now for the Oglala Sioux, where Crazy Horse was the principal chief. These Sioux were somewhere in this region. We crossed to the east side of the Tongue River. . . . Eleven sleeps the tribe had journeyed when we arrived at the place on Beaver Creek. . . . Here we found the Oglalas.

The Oglala Sioux received us hospitably. They had not been disturbed by soldiers, so they had good lodges and plenty of meat and robes. They first assembled in a great body and fed us all we wanted to eat. To all of the women who needed other food they gave a supply. They gave us robes and blankets. They shared with us their tobacco. Gift horses came to us. Every married woman got skins enough to make some kind of lodge for her household. Oh, how generous were the Oglalas! Not any Cheyenne was allowed to go to sleep hungry or cold that night.

We had traveled and hunted much during past times with these Sioux people. At all times there was some one or more families of them with us or some of our Cheyennes with them. Of our friendly intermarrying, there was more connection with the Oglalas than with any other tribe. . . . From them we learned that the big chief of the soldiers [at Little Bighorn] was Long Hair, the same man who several years before this time had fought the Southern Cheyennes.

After we had rested with the Oglalas a few days the chiefs counciled together and decided that the tribes should join in movement up the Tongue River. . . . At Hanging Woman Creek it was decided the two tribes would separate. . . . Just as the tribes were about to separate, some scouts brought in the report: "Soldiers are coming!"

The two bands of Indians began to come again together. The warriors mingled themselves as being of one tribe. The women and children and older men of both sets of people moved together up the Tongue River.

The young men put themselves behind their fleeing people. Somebody said to me: "They have captured some women. Your sister is one of them."[28]

My heart jumped when this news came to me. I lashed my horse into a run toward where it was said they had been captured. There I saw tracks of soldier horses. The trail led to the river ice. On the opposite side of the river, the west side, were soldiers. They began shooting at me. I had to get away. I did not see any of the women, so I supposed they had been killed. My heart then became bitter toward these white men.

I hid my horse in the brush at the foot of a ridge where some warriors were on its top. I walked up there. Many Indians were hidden behind rocks and were shooting toward the soldiers. I chose for myself a hiding place and did the same. I had my soldier rifle [a Springfield carbine captured at the Little Bighorn] and plenty of cartridges. Many soldiers were coming across the ice to fight us. But we had the advantage of them because of our position on the high and rocky ridge.

Big Crow, a Cheyenne, kept walking back and forth along the ridge on the side toward the soldiers. He was wearing a war bonnet. He had a gun taken from the soldiers at the Little Bighorn battle. He used up his cartridges and came back to us hidden behind the rocks to ask for more. Cheyennes and Sioux here and there each gave him one or two or three. He soon got enough to fill his belt. He went out again to walk along the ridge, to shoot at the soldiers and to defy them in their efforts to hit him with a bullet. All of us others kept behind the rocks, only peeping around at times to shoot. Crazy Horse, the Oglala chief, was near me. Bullets glanced off the shielding rocks, but none hit us. One came close to me; it whizzed through the folds of my blanket at my side.

Big Crow finally dropped down. He lay there alive, but apparently in great distress. A Sioux went with me to crawl down to where he was and bring him into shelter. Another Sioux came after us. When we got to the wounded man I took hold of his feet and the two Sioux grasped his hands. The three of us crawled and dragged him along on the snow. Bullets began to shower around us. We let loose our holds and dodged behind rocks. When the firing quieted, we crept out again and got him. My brother just then called out to me: "Wooden Leg, come, we are going away from here." I let loose again and went to my brother. The two Sioux continued to drag Big Crow.[29]

The Indians moved back and forth, down and up, fighting the soldiers at different times all day. After darkness came, the fighting stopped. The group where I was built a little fire, so we might warm ourselves. As soon as the light of it showed, the bullets began to sing over our heads. We quickly

[28] See Miles's description of this fight, the Battle of Wolf Mountain.
[29] This retreat from the ridge is also described by Miles.

threw snow upon the fire. Then we moved to another place. All of the Indians left there during the night. . . .

We did not know where these soldiers had come from. We did not know either how far they might follow us. But our scouts remaining behind saw them go back down Tongue River. At the camp, Big Crow's relatives went about inquiring for him. . . . [He] was our one man lost in the battle. Two Sioux were killed. . . .

The Cheyennes and the few Oglalas now with us traveled far up the Tongue River. We found plenty of buffalo there. We went on west to the Little Bighorn. . . . Most of the last part of the winter was spent in camp on this valley. All of the time during the next few months we had good hunting. Soldiers did not trouble us nor did we trouble them. . . .

Just before the grass began to show itself in the early part of the spring, two visitors arrived at our camp on the Little Bighorn. One of these was our captured old woman, Sweet Woman [captured by Miles at Wolf Mountain]. The other was a half-breed Sioux we called White [Bruyere, a scout for Miles]. . . . The visitors said they had been sent out from the soldier fort at the mouth of the Tongue River, to invite us to come there and surrender peaceably. They brought a promise from Bear Coat [Miles], the soldier chief there, that we should not be harmed and we should be given plenty of food. Sweet Woman told us all of the captives were well.

———

MILES'S EMISSARIES DID their work well. The Northern Cheyennes were tired of constantly running and fighting; Miles's dogged pursuit, in the dead of winter, had badly hurt their morale, even if he had caused few casualties. After much discussion, the people of Wooden Leg and Two Moons agreed to surrender.

Meanwhile, General Crook had been active as well. It was his cavalry commander, Ranald McKenzie, who had struck the Cheyenne village on November 25, 1876 (which led to the destitution so vividly described by Wooden Leg). Much to Miles's irritation, Crook had followed up with his own diplomatic offensive, carried out by Indian messengers selected from the agencies. On May 7, 1877, these negotiations bore fruit as a thousand Indians, led by Crazy Horse, rode onto the Red Cloud reservation and surrendered. It was the culmination of a cataclysmic spring for the Lakota and Cheyennes; one by one, the resisting bands had given up.

For Sitting Bull, there was only one course left. In early May, he led about a thousand beleaguered, destitute followers across the border into Canada—"the Grandmother's [Queen Victoria's] country," as the Sioux called it. There, for the first time, he found white officials (the Northwest Mounted Police) who treated him honestly and fairly. For the moment, his band was able to live in peace, hunting still-ample buffalo on the Canadian plains.

The future for the Lakota, however, was bleak. A new era had dawned on the northern Great Plains, symbolically marked by the killing of Crazy Horse in September 1877. Resentful at the confinement of reservation life, he died while struggling with soldiers sent to arrest him—a symbolic reflection of the fate of his people as a whole. From now on, the Indians sat on the reservations and collected government rations as white settlers rushed onto their old hunting grounds.

Sitting Bull remained the one last hope of the tribes seeking to resist the reservation. Far to the west, in the Wallowa valley of eastern Oregon, a band of Nez Percés had long refused to sign the white man's treaties; when they found themselves being forced to accept a reservation in 1877, they looked to the great Hunkpapa leader in exile for refuge. The result was an epic trek for freedom that would end only a few miles from the Canadian border.

# 9

# REFUGEES OF CONQUEST

For decades after the first whites set foot in Oregon, the lush Wallowa valley remained the home of a proud, independent band of the Nez Percés. While other members of the tribe, led by an eloquent spokesman called "Lawyer," signed a treaty in 1863 and accepted life on reservations, the people of the aging Chief Old Joseph refused to give up their Wallowa homeland. Relatively few white settlers moved to the region, located in far northeastern Oregon, and Old Joseph was able to persist in his resistance; in 1873, President Grant actually confirmed the rights of his band to the valley.

Within just a few short years, however, the advance of white settlement brought the conflict to a crisis. Under pressure from white ranchers who envied the grassy Wallowa, Grant opened it to settlement in 1875. General Oliver O. Howard was assigned to the region's military command, with specific instructions to move the resisting Nez Percés onto reservations.

Howard was a respected veteran of the Civil War and the former head of the Freedmen's Bureau who had a reputation as an openhearted humanitarian. Deeply religious, Howard saw himself as an emissary to the nonwhite races. After founding all-black Howard University in Washington, D.C., he immersed himself in Indian affairs. In 1872, he won a notable success in persuading Cochise to bring his Apache followers onto a reservation in Arizona (see Part IV). He had every reason to expect success with the Native Americans of the Northwest.

Instead of glory, however, Howard found only frustration and humiliation as he lost patience in the face of the Nez Percés' dignified opposition. In November 1876 and May 1877, he had two unsuccessful meetings with the Indian leaders—Toohoolhoolzote, Looking Glass, White Bird, Eagle from the Light, and Young Joseph, who had succeeded his widely respected father after Old Joseph's death in 1871. Flustered by eloquent Native American speeches that justified their resistance, he ordered them to move onto the reservation in thirty days or face an armed attack. Reluctantly, the chiefs complied.

In the following passage, Chief Joseph describes the rapid tumble of events that followed. After the chiefs agreed to go to the reservation, young warriors promptly undermined them by killing some white settlers. Faced with retaliatory attacks by the army, the chiefs decided to flee to the "buffalo country"—the Great Plains—and then on to Canada, where they might find refuge with the legendary exile Sitting Bull and his people. In June 1877, the Nez Percés set off on their epic trek over the mountains and through the plains. As General Howard pursued the Indians from behind, colonels Gibbon, Sturgis, and Miles turned from their recently completed war against the Sioux to lash out at the fleeing tribe from the east. With skill and determination, the refugees outmaneuvered and out-fought their pursuers over hundreds of miles—until they were finally intercepted by Miles just a short distance from the Canadian border.

## The Great Trek of the Nez Percés
*by Chief Joseph*

Through all the years since the white men came to Wallowa we have been threatened and taunted by them and the treaty Nez Percés. They have given us no rest. We have had a few good friends among white men, and they have always advised my people to bear these taunts without fighting. Our young men were quick-tempered, and I have had great trouble in keeping them from doing rash things. I have carried a heavy load on my back ever since I was a boy. I learned then that we were but few, while the white men were many, and that we could not hold our own with them. We were like deer. They were like grizzly bears. We had a small country. Their country was large. We were contented to let things remain as the Great Spirit Chief made them. They were not; and would change the rivers and mountains if they did not suit them.

Year after year we have been threatened, but no war was made upon my people until General Howard came to our country two years ago [November 1876] and told us that he was the white war chief of all that country. He said: "I have a great many soldiers at my back. I am going to bring them up here, and then I will talk to you again. I will not let white men laugh at me the next time I come. The country belongs to the government, and I intend to make you go upon the reservation."

I remonstrated with him against bringing more soldiers to the Nez Percés' country. He had one house full of troops all the time at Fort Lapwai.

The next spring the agent at Umatilla agency sent an Indian runner to tell me to meet General Howard at Walla Walla. I could not go myself, but I sent my brother and five other headmen to meet him, and they had a long talk.

General Howard said: "You have talked straight, and it is all right. You can stay in Wallowa." He insisted that my brother and his company should go to Fort Lapwai. When the party arrived there General Howard sent out runners and called all the Indians to a grand council. I was in that council. I said to General Howard, "We are ready to listen." He answered that he could not talk then, but would hold a council the next day, when he would talk plainly. I said to General Howard: "I am ready to talk today. I have been in a great many councils, but I am no wiser. We are all sprung from a woman, although we are unlike in many things. We cannot be made over again. You are as you were made, and as you were made you can remain. We are just as we were made by the Great Spirit, and you cannot change us; then why should children of one mother and one father quarrel—why should one try to cheat the other? I do not believe that the Great Spirit Chief gave one kind of men the right to tell another kind of men what they must do."

General Howard replied: "You deny my authority, do you? You want to dictate to me, do you?"

Then one of my chiefs—Toohoolhoolzote—rose in the council and said to General Howard: "The Great Spirit Chief made the world as it is, and as he wanted it, and he made a part of it for us to live upon. I do not see where you get the authority to say that we shall not live where he has placed us."

General Howard lost his temper and said: "Shut up! I don't want to hear any more such talk. The law says you shall go upon the reservation to live, and I want you to do so, but you persist in disobeying the law. If you do not move, I will take the matter into my own hand, and make you suffer for your disobedience."

Toohoolhoolzote answered: "Who are you, that you ask us to talk, and then tell me I shall not talk? Are you the Great Spirit? Did you make the world? Did you make the sun? Did you make the rivers to run for us to drink? Did you make the grass to grow? Did you make all these things, that you talk to us as though we were boys? If you did, then you have the right to talk as you do."

General Howard replied, "You are an impudent fellow, and I will put you in the guard house," and then ordered a soldier to arrest him.

Toohoolhoolzote made no resistance. He asked General Howard: "Is that your order? I don't care. I have expressed my heart to you. I have nothing to take back. I have spoken for my country. You can arrest me, but you cannot change me or make me take back what I have said." The soldiers came forward and seized my friend and took him to the guard house. My men whispered among themselves whether they should let this thing be done.

I counseled them to submit. I knew if we resisted that all the white men present, including General Howard, would be killed in a moment, and we would be blamed. If I had said nothing, General Howard would never have given another unjust order against my men. I saw the danger, and while they dragged Toohoolhoolzote to prison, I arose and said: *"I am not going to talk now.* I don't care whether you arrest me or not." I turned to my people and said: "The arrest of Toohoolhoolzote was wrong, but we will not resent the insult. We were invited to this council to express our hearts, and we have done so." Toohoolhoolzote was prisoner for five days before he was released.

The council broke up for that day. On the next morning General Howard came to my lodge, and invited me to go with him and White Bird and Looking Glass, to look for land for my people. As we rode along we came to some good land that was already occupied by Indians and white people. General Howard, pointing to this land, said: "If you will come onto the reservation, I will give you these lands and move these people off."

I replied: "No. It would be wrong to disturb these people. I have no right to take their homes. I have never taken what did not belong to me. I will not now."

We rode all day upon the reservation, and found no good land unoccupied. I have been informed by men who do not lie that General Howard sent a letter that night, telling the soldiers at Walla Walla to go to Wallowa Valley, and drive us out upon our return home.

In the council, next day, General Howard informed me, in a haughty spirit, that he would give my people *thirty days* to go back home, collect all their stock, and move onto the reservation, saying, "If you are not there in that time, I shall consider that you want to fight, and will send my soldiers to drive you on."

I said: "War can be avoided, and it ought to be avoided. I want no war. My people have always been the friends of the white man. Why are you in such a hurry? I cannot get ready to move in thirty days. Our stock is scattered, and Snake River is very high. Let us wait until fall, then the river will be low. We want time to hunt up our stock and gather supplies for winter."

General Howard replied: "If you let the time run over one day, the soldiers will be there to drive you onto the reservation, and all your cattle and horses outside of the reservation at that time will fall into the hands of the white men."

I knew I had never sold my country, and that I had no land in Lapwai; but I did not want bloodshed. I did not want my people killed. I did not want anybody killed. Some of my people had been murdered by white men, and the white murderers were never punished for it. I told General Howard about this, and again said I wanted no war. I wanted the people who lived upon the lands I was to occupy at Lapwai to have time to gather their harvest.

I said in my heart that, rather than have war, I would give up my country. I would give up my father's grave. I would give up everything rather than have the blood of white men upon the hands of my people.

General Howard refused to allow me more than thirty days to move my people and their stock. I am sure that he began to prepare for war at once. When I returned to Wallowa I found my people very much excited upon discovering that the soldiers were already in the Wallowa Valley. We held a council, and decided to move immediately, to avoid bloodshed.

Toohoolhoolzote, who felt outraged by his imprisonment, talked for war, and made many of my young men willing to fight rather than be driven like dogs from the land where they were born. He declared that blood alone would wash out the disgrace General Howard had put upon him. It required a strong heart to stand up against such talk, but I urged my people to be quiet, and not to begin a war.

We gathered all the stock we could find, and made an attempt to move. We left many of our horses and cattle in Wallowa, and we lost several hundred in crossing the river. All of my people succeeded in getting across in safety. Many of the Nez Percés came together in Rocky Canyon to hold a grand council. I went with all my people. This council lasted ten days. There was a great deal of war talk, and a great deal of excitement. There was a young brave present whose father had been killed five years before. This man's blood was bad against white men, and he left the council calling for revenge.

Again I counseled peace, and I thought the danger was past. We had not complied with General Howard's order because we could not, but we intended to do so as soon as possible. I was leaving the council to kill beef for my family, when news came that the young man whose father had been killed had gone out with several other hot-blooded young braves and killed four white men. He rode up to the council and shouted: "Why do you sit there like women? The war has begun already."

I was deeply grieved. All the lodges were moved except my brother's and my own. I saw clearly that the war was upon us when I learned that my young men had been secretly buying ammunition. I heard then that Toohoolhoolzote had been successful in organizing a war party. I knew that their acts would involve all my people. I saw that the war could not then be prevented. The time had passed. . . . We hoped the white settlers would not join the soldiers. Before the war commenced we had discussed this matter all over, and many of my people were in favor of warning them that if they took no part against us they would not be molested in the event of war being begun by General Howard. This plan was voted down in the war council.

There were bad men among my people who had quarreled with white men, and they talked of their wrongs until they roused all the bad hearts in the council. Still I could not believe that they would begin the war. I know that my young men did a great wrong, but I ask, Who was first to blame? They had been insulted a thousand times; their fathers and brothers had been killed; their mothers and wives had been disgraced; they had been driven to madness by whisky sold to them by white men; they had been told by General Howard that all their horses and cattle which they had been unable to drive out of Wallowa were to fall into the hands of white men; and, added to this, they were homeless and desperate. . . .

I could see no other way to avoid a war. We moved over to White Bird

Creek, sixteen miles away, and there encamped, intending to collect our stock before leaving; but the soldiers attacked us, and the first battle was fought.[30] We numbered in that battle sixty men, and the soldiers a hundred. The fight lasted but a few minutes, when the soldiers retreated before us for twelve miles. They lost thirty-three killed, and had seven wounded. When an Indian fights, he only shoots to kill; but soldiers shoot at random. None of the soldiers were scalped. We do not believe in scalping, nor in killing wounded men. Soldiers do not kill many Indians unless they are wounded and left upon the battlefield. Then they kill Indians.

Seven days after the first battle, General Howard arrived in the Nez Percés' country, bringing seven hundred more soldiers. It was now war in earnest. We crossed over Salmon River, hoping General Howard would follow. We were not disappointed. He did follow us, and we got back between him and his supplies, and cut him off for three days. He sent two companies to open the way. We attacked them, killing one officer, two guides, and ten men.

We withdrew, hoping the soldiers would follow, but they had got fighting enough that day. They entrenched themselves, and next day we attacked them again. The battle lasted all day, and was renewed next morning. We killed four and wounded seven or eight. About this time General Howard found that we were in his rear. Five days later he attacked us with three hundred and fifty soldiers and settlers. We had two hundred and fifty warriors. The fight lasted twenty-seven hours.[31] We lost four killed and several wounded. General Howard's loss was twenty-nine men killed and sixty wounded.

The following day the soldiers charged upon us, and we retreated with our families and stock a few miles, leaving eighty lodges to fall into General Howard's hands. Finding that we were outnumbered, we retreated to Bitter Root Valley. Here another body of soldiers came upon us and demanded our surrender. We refused. They said, "You cannot get by us." We answered, "We are going by you without fighting if you will let us, but we are going by you anyhow." We then made a treaty with these soldiers. We agreed not to molest anyone, and they agreed that we might pass through the Bitter Root country in peace. We bought provisions and traded stock with white men there.

We understood that there was to be no more war. We intended to go peaceably to the buffalo country, and leave the question of returning to our country to be settled afterward. With this understanding we traveled

[30] This clash became known as the Battle of White Bird Canyon, fought on June 17, 1877. Chief Joseph provides accurate figures for the men involved and the casualties; the Indian refugees soon totaled 300 men and 500 women and children.

[31] This fight, known as the Battle of Clearwater (after the nearby river), was fought on July 11 and 12 and ended in the retreat of the Nez Percés, as described here. General Howard, however, was slow in his pursuit, allowing Chief Joseph's people to escape.

on for four days, and, thinking that the trouble was all over, we stopped and prepared tent poles to take with us. We started again, and at the end of two days we saw three white men passing our camp. Thinking that peace had been made, we did not molest them. We could have killed or taken them prisoners, but we did not suspect them of being spies, which they were.

That night the soldiers surrounded our camp.[32] About daybreak one of my men went out to look after his horses. The soldiers saw him and shot him down like a coyote. I have since learned that these soldiers were not those we had left behind. They had come upon us from another direction. The new white war chief's name was Gibbon. He charged upon us while some of my people were still asleep. We had a hard fight. Some of my men crept around and attacked the soldiers from the rear. In this battle we lost nearly all our lodges, but we finally drove Colonel Gibbon back.

Finding that he was not able to capture us, he sent to his camp a few miles away for his big guns, but my men had captured them and all the ammunition. We damaged the big guns all we could, and carried away the powder and lead. In the fight with General Gibbon we lost fifty women and children and thirty fighting men. We remained long enough to bury our dead. The Nez Percés never make war on women and children; we could have killed a great many women and children while the war lasted, but we would feel ashamed to do so cowardly an act.[33]

We retreated as rapidly as we could toward the buffalo country. After six days General Howard came close to us, and we went out and attacked him, and captured nearly all his horses and mules (about 250 head). We then marched on to Yellowstone Basin. . . .

Nine days' march brought us to the mouth of Clarke's Fork of the Yellowstone. We did not know what had become of General Howard, but we supposed that he had sent for more horses and mules. He did not come up, but another new war chief [Colonel Samuel D. Sturgis and the Seventh Cavalry] attacked us. We held him in check while we moved our women and children and stock out of danger, leaving a few men to cover our retreat.[34]

[32] These troops (about 200 infantrymen) were under the command of Colonel John Gibbon, who had operated with Custer under General Terry's command in the recently concluded war against the Lakota and Northern Cheyennes. Gibbon was able to catch up to the refugees because Looking Glass, a Nez Percé chief, had talked the other chiefs into stopping on the Big Hole River. Gibbon attacked the morning of August 9.

[33] Defeated and driven into retreat by the Indian counterattack, Gibbon's force suffered seventy-one casualties at the Battle of Big Hole. The colonel himself was wounded in the fighting, and his artillery was captured and disabled.

[34] During this period, the Nez Percé band slipped past Sturgis by making a feint to the south, then marching through the newly designated Yellowstone National Park on their way to the plains (they very nearly ran into a party of visitors that included General William T. Sherman). At the Battle of Canyon Creek, on September 13, 1877, they halted Sturgis's pursuit. They also discovered, to their dismay, that the local Crow Indians had been serving as scouts for the Seventh Cavalry.

Several days passed, and we heard nothing of General Howard, or Gibbon, or Sturgis. We had repulsed each in turn, and began to feel secure, when another army, under General Miles, struck us. This was the fourth army, each of which outnumbered our fighting force, that we had encountered within sixty days.[35]

We had no knowledge of General Miles's army until a short time before he made a charge upon us, cutting our camp in two and capturing nearly all our horses. About seventy men, myself among them, were cut off. My little daughter, twelve years of age, was with me. I gave her a rope, and told her to catch a horse and join the others who were cut off from the camp. I have not seen her since, but I have learned that she is alive and well.[36]

I thought of my wife and children, who were now surrounded by soldiers, and I resolved to go to them or die. With a prayer in my mouth to the Great Spirit Chief who rules above, I dashed unarmed through the line of soldiers. It seemed to me that there were guns on every side, before and behind me. My clothes were cut to pieces and my horse was wounded, but I was not hurt. As I reached the door of my lodge, my wife handed me my rifle, saying: "Here's your gun. Fight!"

The soldiers kept up a continuous fire. Six of my men were killed in one spot near me. Ten or twelve soldiers charged into our camp and got possession of two lodges, killing three Nez Percés and losing three of their men, who fell inside our lines. I called my men to drive them back. We fought at close range, not more than twenty steps apart, and drove the soldiers back upon their main line, leaving their dead in our hands. We secured their arms and ammunition. We lost, the first day and night, eighteen men and three women. General Miles lost twenty-six killed and forty wounded. The following day General Miles sent a messenger into my camp under protection of a white flag. I sent my friend Yellow Bull to meet him.

Yellow Bull understood the messenger to say that General Miles wished me to consider the situation; that he did not want to kill my people unnecessarily. Yellow Bull understood this to be a demand for me to surrender and save blood. Upon reporting this message to me, Yellow Bull said he wondered whether General Miles was in earnest. I sent him back with my answer, that I had not made up my mind, but would think about it and send word soon. A little later he sent some Cheyenne scouts with another mes-

[35] Colonel Nelson Miles's force of 400 men struck the Nez Percé camp on September 30, beside Snake Creek. He had marched west from Fort Keogh, which he had occupied since the end of the Sioux war. The week-long battle that followed his arrival at Snake Creek is known as the Battle of Bearpaw Mountain.

[36] The raid on the pony herd was conducted by a squadron of the Second Cavalry; the Seventh Cavalry launched a frontal charge and lost sixty men, including six officers and seven sergeants (the Indians knew to aim for the commanders). Frederick Benteen, the old critic of Custer and a survivor of the Little Bighorn, was promoted to brevet brigadier general for his role in the fighting. The battle turned into a siege.

sage. I went out to meet them. They said they believed that General Miles was sincere and really wanted peace. I walked on to General Miles's tent. He met me and we shook hands. He said, "Come, let us sit down by the fire and talk this matter over." I remained with him all night; next morning Yellow Bull came over to see if I was alive, and why I did not return.

General Miles would not let me leave to see my friend alone. Yellow Bull said to me: "They have got you in their power, and I am afraid they will never let you go again. I have an officer in our camp, and I will hold him until they let you go free."

I said: "I do not know what they mean to do with me, but if they kill me you must not kill the officer. It will do us no good to avenge my death by killing him."

Yellow Bull returned to my camp. I did not make any agreement that day with General Miles. The battle was renewed while I was with him. I was very anxious about my people. I knew that we were near Sitting Bull's camp in King George's land [Canada], and I thought maybe the Nez Percés who had escaped would return with assistance. No great damage was done to either party during the night.

On the following morning I returned to my camp by agreement, meeting the officer who had been held a prisoner in my camp at the flag of truce. My people were divided about surrendering.[37] We could have escaped from Bear Paw Mountain if we had left our wounded, old women, and children behind. We were unwilling to do this. We had never heard of a wounded Indian recovering while in the hands of white men.

On the evening of the fourth day General Howard came in with a small escort, together with my friend Chapman. We could now talk understandingly. General Miles said to me in plain words, "If you will come out and give up your arms, I will spare your lives and send you to your reservation." I do not know what had passed between General Miles and General Howard.

I could not bear to see my wounded men and women suffer any longer; we had lost enough already. General Miles had promised that we might return to our own country with what stock we had left. I thought we could start again. I believed General Miles, or *I would never have surrendered*. I have heard that he has been censured for making the promise to return us to Lapwai. He could have not made any other terms with me at that time. I would have held him in check until my friends came to my assistance, and then neither of the generals nor their soldiers would have ever left Bear Paw Mountain alive.

On the fifth day I went to General Miles and gave up my gun, and said, "From where the sun now stands I will fight no more." My people needed rest—we wanted peace.

[37] One group of 300 under White Bird actually did break off and escape to Canada.

I was told we could go with General Miles to Tongue River and stay there until spring, when we would be sent back to our country. Finally it was decided that we were to be taken to Tongue River. We had nothing to say about it. After our arrival at Tongue River, General Miles received orders to take us to Bismarck. The reason given was that subsistence would be cheaper there. General Miles was opposed to this order. He said: "You must not blame me. I have endeavored to keep my word, but the chief who is over me has given the order, and I must obey it or resign. That would do you no good. Some other officer would carry out the order." . . .

General Miles turned my people over to another soldier, and we were taken to Bismarck. Captain Johnson, who now had charge of us, received an order to take us to Fort Leavenworth. . . . We were moved to the Indian Territory, and set down without our lodges. We had but little medicine, and we were nearly all sick. Seventy of my people have died since we moved there. . . . It is not a healthy land. There are no mountains or rivers. The water is warm. It is not a good country for stock. I do not believe my people can live there. I am afraid they will all die. . . .

I cannot understand how the government sends a man out to fight us, as it did with General Miles, and then breaks his word. Such a government has something wrong about it. . . .

Let me be a free man—free to travel, free to stop, free to work, free to trade where I choose, free to choose my own teachers, free to follow the religion of my fathers, free to think and talk and act for myself—and I will obey every law, or submit to the penalty.

Whenever the white man treats the Indian as they treat each other, then we will have no more wars. We shall all be alike—brothers of one father and one mother, with one sky above us and one country around us, and one government for all. Then the Great Spirit Chief who rules above will smile upon this land, and send rain to wash the bloody spots made by brothers' hands from the face of the earth. For this time the Indian race are waiting and praying. I hope that no more groans of wounded men and women will ever go to the ear of the Great Spirit Chief above, and that all people may be one people.

Inmuttooyahlatlat has spoken for his people.

---

PERHAPS THE MOST tragic element in the flight of the Nez Percés was that, ultimately, there would have been no escape in Canada. The Canadian authorities were sympathetic to the Indians' plight, but the presence of Sioux refugees was already causing trouble in their relations with the United States. Furthermore, the buffalo herds dwindled rapidly after 1877; Sitting Bull and his people found themselves competing against hostile Canadian tribes for ever fewer of the precious animals—and he inevitably crossed the border during the hunts. These border crossings led the American government to protest to the British and Canadians, heightening international tensions. Indeed, Chief Joseph was mistaken to think that he would get help from the Indians in Canada during his fight with Miles—Sitting Bull, though tempted to go to the rescue, could not afford to give up his precarious refuge. The Nez Percé flight was doomed from the beginning. Now, instead of being sent to a crowded reservation in the Pacific Northwest, they were shipped off to the Indian Territory, where they were treated as prisoners of war.

Sitting Bull himself did not have much time left in Canada. Facing pressure from the Canadian authorities (whom he greatly respected), near starvation, and defections among many of his followers, Sitting Bull crossed the border to surrender at Fort Buford on July 19, 1881. "I wish it to be remembered," he announced, "that I was the last man of my tribe to surrender my rifle." Indeed he was. From that moment on, the life of Sitting Bull was wrapped up in the struggle of the Lakota to adapt to reservation life, under the firm control of the U.S. government.

The 1870s, then, brought to a climax the first stage in the war for the frontier—the struggle between the white and Native American civilizations. At the end of the decade, the whites had clearly won. Apart from Sitting Bull's band of exiles, Chief Joseph's band of Nez Percés had been the last sizeable tribe to fight against being confined to a reservation. Now the struggle for the frontier was between citizens of the victorious nation—between cattlemen and horse thieves, men of property and men of prey.

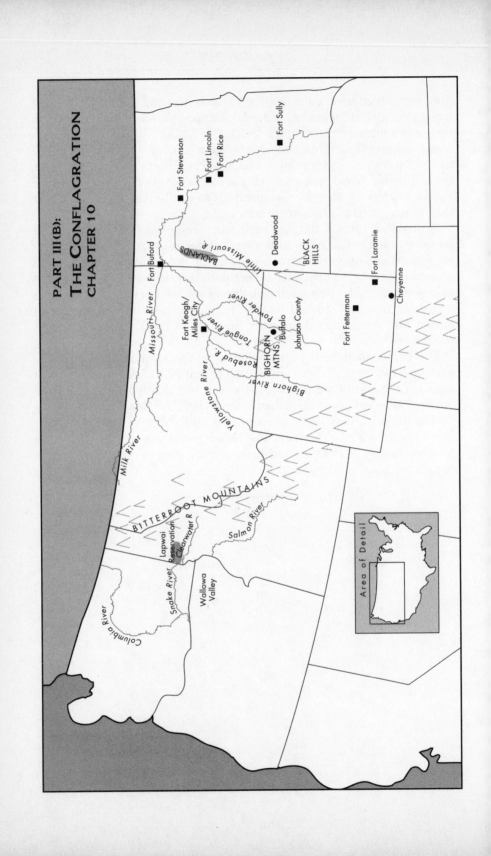

PART III (B):

# THE CONFLAGRATION
## CHAPTER 10

Fort Sully

Fort Stevenson

Fort Lincoln

Fort Rice

Fort Buford

BADLANDS

Little Missouri R.

Deadwood

BLACK HILLS

Fort Laramie

Cheyenne

Fort Fetterman

Johnson County

Buffalo

BIGHORN MTNS.

Fort Keogh/ Miles City

Tongue River

Powder River

Rosebud R.

Bighorn River

Missouri River

Yellowstone River

Milk River

BITTERROOT MOUNTAINS

Salmon River

Clearwater R.

Lapwai

Reservation

Snake River

Wallowa Valley

Columbia River

Area of Detail

# 10

# CATTLE BARONS AND HORSE THIEVES

When Sitting Bull returned to the plains of the upper Missouri to surrender in 1881, it was already a different land from that he had defended only four years before. The buffalo were gone: professional hunters had done their work, far too well. Sitting Bull's people had been disarmed, stripped of their horses, and herded onto reservations. And into the void now flowed a river of men and cattle.

An economic boom swept the lands that had so recently been Lakota and Cheyenne hunting grounds. With the Indians out of the way, the Black Hills gold rush roared ahead, and people of all stripes saw the chance to make a profit off the hungry markets in the mining towns. Merchants moved in to set up shop; immigrants from Scandinavia and northern Europe came directly to the Dakota Territory to farm the prairie; and the Northern Pacific began to build again. And a new breed of cattle baron arose, covering the northern Great Plains with herds to supply the Black Hills and the cities of the East.

One of the men who staked out the newly opened country of the upper Missouri was Theodore Roosevelt, who arrived from New York in the early 1880s. Roosevelt set up a ranch in the badlands of the Little Missouri River—the same country that General Sully chased the Sioux through in 1864, when the region was virtually unknown to white explorers. The son of an established, wealthy family, he quickly identified with the conservative cattle barons who were taking over the northern plains: men such as Granville Stuart, an early Montana pioneer and one of the biggest ranchers, who helped organize the Montana Stockgrowers' Association during those years.

This newly opened country also attracted an entirely different breed— horse thieves, rustlers, drifting killers, homesteaders, and small ranchers with little respect for the property of the new cattle kings. Like the Texas badmen on the southern plains (many of them were, in fact, Texans), they formed their own scattered communities in places such as Hole-in-the-Wall, Wyoming, and the upper Missouri River in the Montana and Dakota territories. Most drifted in and out of crime: the law was too weak, local values too easygoing, and the opportunities too great for men to resist a little rustling and horse theft now and then, and few felt any inhibitions against taking a man's life. Furthermore, they resented the growing power of the great stock-raising entrepreneurs, who crowded them off the open range. It was against this threat that the big cattlemen organized the Montana Stockgrowers' Association.

In 1888, after Roosevelt had returned to the East to begin his political career, he wrote about the life being staked out by the conquering new Americans on what had so recently been Native American lands—lands that now belonged to the federal government but were grazed for private gain. In the passage that follows, he describes the process of occupation—the movement of the big herds of cattle, the building of ranches, the people who flourished there. He also describes the second wave of conquest that shook the plains: the blow struck by the big cattlemen against the outlaws and shadowy, independent types who thrived on the open frontier. As Roosevelt writes, the same environment that fostered outlawry led to raids by vigilante gangs—death squads, in fact—who hunted men down indiscriminately, leaving trails of bodies behind them.

## The Making of the Cattle Country
*by Theodore Roosevelt*

The great grazing lands of the West lie in what is known as the arid belt, which stretches from British America [Canada] on the north to Mexico on the south, through the middle of the United States. . . . In this arid belt, and in this arid belt only—save only a few similar tracks on the Pacific slope—stock-raising is almost the sole industry, except in the mountain districts where there is mining. The whole region is one vast stretch of grazing country, with only here and there spots of farmland, in most places there being nothing more like agriculture than is implied in the cutting of some tons of wild hay or the planting of a garden patch for home use.

This is especially true for the northern portion of the region, which comprises the basin of the Upper Missouri, and with which alone I am familiar. Here there are no fences to speak of, and all the land north of the Black Hills and the Big Horn Mountains and between the Rockies and the Dakota wheatfields might be spoken of as one gigantic, unbroken pasture, where cowboys and branding-irons take the place of fences. . . .

The high plains of the Upper Missouri and its tributary rivers were first opened, and are still held, by the stockmen, and the whole civilization of the region has received the stamp of their marked and individual characteristics. They were from the South, not from the East, although many men from the latter region came out along the great transcontinental railway lines and joined them in their northern migration.

They were not dwellers in towns, and from the nature of their industry lived as far apart from each other as possible. In choosing new ranges, old cowhands, who are also seasoned plainsmen, are invariably sent ahead, perhaps a year in advance, to spy out the land and pick the best places. One of these may go by himself, or more often, especially if they have to penetrate little known or entirely unknown tracts, two or three will go together, the owner or manager of the herd himself being one of them. Perhaps their herds may already be on the border of the wild and uninhabited country: in that case they may have to take but a few days' journey before finding the stretches of sheltered, long-grass land they seek.

For instance, when I wished to move my own elkhorn steer brand on to a new ranch I had to spend barely a week in traveling north among the Little Missouri badlands before finding what was then untrodden ground far outside the range of any of my neighbors' cattle. But if a large outfit is going to shift its quarters it must go much farther; and both the necessity and the chance for long wanderings were especially great when the final overthrow of the northern horse Indians opened the whole upper Missouri basin at one sweep to the stockmen. Then the advance-guards or explorers, each on one horse and leading another with food and bedding, were often absent months at a time, threading their way through the trackless wastes of plain, plateau, and riverbottom. . . .

These lookouts or forerunners having returned, the herds are set in motion as early in the spring as may be, so as to get on the ground in time to let the travel-worn beasts rest and gain flesh before winter sets in. Each herd is accompanied by a dozen, or a score, or a couple of score of cowboys, according to its size, and beside it rumble and jolt the heavy four-horse wagons that hold the food and bedding of the men and the few implements they will need at the end of their journey. As long as possible they follow the trails made by the herds that have already traveled in the same direction, and when these end they strike out for themselves. In the upper Missouri basin, the pioneer herds soon had to scatter out and each find its own way among the great dreary solitudes, creeping carefully along so that the cattle might not be overdriven and might have water at the halting places. An outfit might thus be months on its lonely journey, slowly making its way over melancholy, pathless plains, or down the valleys of lonely rivers. It was a tedious, harassing work, as the weary cattle had to be driven carefully and quietly during the day and strictly guarded at night, with a perpetual watch kept for Indians or white horse-thieves. Often they would skirt the edges of the streams for days at a time, seeking for a ford or a good swimming crossing, and if the water was up and the quicksand deep the danger to the riders was serious and the risk of loss among the cattle very great.

At last, after days of excitement and danger and after months of dreary, monotonous toil, the chosen ground is reached and the final camp pitched.

The footsore animals are turned loose to shift for themselves, outlying camps of two or three men being established to hem them in. Meanwhile the primitive ranch-house, out-buildings, and corrals are built, the unhewn cottonwood logs being chinked with moss and mud, while the roofs are of branches covered with dirt, spades and axes being the only tools needed for the work. Bunks, chairs, and tables are all homemade, and as rough as the houses they are in. The supplies of coarse, rude food are carried perhaps two or three hundred miles from the nearest town, either in the ranch-wagons or else by some regular freighting outfit, whose huge canvas-topped prairie schooners are each drawn by several yoke of oxen, or perhaps by six or eight mules. . . .

The small outlying camps are often tents, or mere dugouts in the ground. But at the main ranch there will be a cluster of log buildings, including a separate cabin for the foreman or ranchman; often another in which to cook and eat; a long house for the men to sleep in; stables, sheds, a blacksmith's shop, etc.—the whole group forming quite a little settlement, with the corrals, the stacks of natural hay, and the patches of fenced land for gardens or horse pastures. This little settlement might be situated right out in the treeless, nearly level open, but much more often is placed in the partly wooded bottom of a creek or river, sheltered by the usual background of somber brown hills.

When the northern plains began to be settled, such a ranch would at first be absolutely alone in the wilderness, but others of the same sort were sure soon to be established within twenty or thirty miles on one side or the other. The lives of the men in such places were strangely cut off from the outside world, and, indeed, the same is true to a hardly less extent at the present day [1888]. Sometimes the wagons are sent for provisions, and the beef-steers are at stated times driven off for shipment. Parties of hunters and trappers call now and then. More rarely small bands of emigrants go by in search of new homes. . . . But this is all. Civilization seems as remote as if we were living in an age long past. The whole existence is patriarchal in character: it is the life of men who live in the open, who tend their herds on horseback, who go armed and ready to guard their lives by their own prowess, whose wants are very simple, and who call no man master. . . .[38]

All cattle are branded,[39] usually on the hip, shoulder, and side, or on any one of them, with letters, numbers, or figures, in every combination, the outfit being known by its brand. Near me, for instance, are the Three Sevens, the Thistle, the Bellows, the OX, the VI. . . . All brands are registered, and thus protected against imitators, any man tampering with them

[38] Most of the Western states and territories were disproportionately populated by men, a matter of some concern to the male residents. In 1869, the Wyoming Territory led the nation in granting the vote to women, perhaps partially out of a desire to attract more women to the area.

[39] This paragraph and the next have been moved for narrative continuity.

being punished as severely as possible. Unbranded animals are called *mavericks*, and when found on the round-up are either branded by the owner of the range on which they are, or else are sold for the benefit of the [stockmen's] association. At every shipping point, as well as where the beef cattle are received, there are stock inspectors who jealously examine all the brands on the live animals or on the hides of the slaughtered ones, so as to determine any foul play, which is immediately reported to the association. It becomes second nature with a cowboy to inspect and note the brands of every bunch of animals he comes across. . . .

The ranching industry itself was copied from the Mexicans, of whose land and herds the Southwestern frontiersmen of Texas took forcible possession; and the traveler in the Northwest will see at a glance that the terms and practices of our business are largely of Spanish origin. The cruel curb-bit and heavy stock-saddle, with its high horn and cantle, prove that we have adopted Spanish-American horse-gear; and the broad hat, huge blunt spurs, and leather *chaperajos* of the rider, as well as the corral in which the stock are penned, all alike show the same ancestry. Throughout the cattle country east of the Rocky Mountains, from the Rio Grande to the Saskatchewan, the same terms are in use and the same system is followed. . . .

A true "cow town" is worth seeing—such a one as Miles City, for instance, especially at the time of the annual meeting of the great Montana Stock-raisers' Association. Then the whole place is full to overflowing, the importance of the meeting and the fun of the attendant frolics, especially the horse races, drawing from the surrounding ranch country many hundreds of men of every degree, from the rich stockowner worth his millions to the ordinary cowboy who works for forty dollars a month. It would be impossible to imagine a more typically American assemblage, for although there are always a certain number of foreigners, usually English, Irish, or German, yet they have become completely Americanized; and on the whole it would be difficult to gather a finer body of men in spite of their numerous shortcomings.

The ranchowners differ more from each other than do the cowboys; and the former certainly compare very favorably with similar classes of capitalists in the East. Anything more foolish than the demagogic outcry against "cattle kings" it would be difficult to imagine. Indeed, there are very few businesses so absolutely legitimate as stock-raising and so beneficial to the nation at large. . . . Stockmen in the West are the pioneers of civilization, and their daring and adventurousness make the after settlement of the region possible. The whole country owes them a great debt. . . . Stockmen are learning more and more to act together; and certainly the meetings of their associations are conducted with a dignity and good sense that would do credit to any parliamentary body. . . .

But the cowboys resemble one another much more and outsiders much less than is the case even with their employers, the ranchmen. A town in the cattle country, when for some cause it is thronged with men from the neighborhood about, always presents a picturesque sight on the wooden sidewalks of the broad, dusty streets. The men who ply the various industries known only to frontier existence jostle one another as they saunter to and fro or lounge lazily in front of the straggling, cheap-looking board houses. . . . If the town is on the borders of the mountain country, there will also be sinewy lumbermen, rough-looking miners, and packers, whose business it is to guide the long mule trains that go where wagons cannot and whose work in packing needs special and peculiar skill. And mingled with and drawn from all these classes are desperadoes of every grade, from the gambler up through the horse-thief to the murderous professional bully, or, as he is locally called, "bad man"—now, however, a much less conspicuous object than formerly.

But everywhere among these plainsmen and mountainmen, and more important than any, are the cowboys—the men who follow the calling that has brought such towns into being. Singly, or in twos or threes, they gallop their wiry little horses down the street. . . . When drunk on the villainous whisky of the frontier towns, they cut mad antics, riding their horses into the saloons, firing their pistols right and left, from boisterous light-heartedness rather than from any viciousness, and indulging too often in deadly shooting affrays, brought on either by the accidental contact of the moment or on account of some long-standing grudge, or perhaps because of bad blood between two ranches or localities; but except while on such sprees they are quiet, rather self-contained men, perfectly frank and simple. . . .

The bulk of the cowboys themselves are Southwesterners; but there are also many from the Eastern and Northern states, who if they begin young do quite as well as the Southerner. The best hands are fairly bred to the work and follow it from their youth up. Nothing can be more foolish than for an Easterner to think he can become a cowboy in a few months' time. . . .

Some of the cowboys are Mexicans, who generally do the actual work well enough, but are not trustworthy; moreover, they are always regarded with extreme disfavor by the Texans in an outfit, among whom the intolerant caste spirit is very strong. Southern-born whites will never work under them, and look down upon all colored or half-caste races. One spring I had with my wagon a Pueblo Indian, an excellent rider and roper, but a drunken, worthless, lazy devil; and in the summer of 1886 there were with us a Sioux half-breed, a quiet, hard-working, faithful fellow, and mulatto, who was one of the best cowhands in the whole round-up. . . .

As a rule the cowboys are known to each other only by their first names, with, perhaps, as a prefix, the title of the brand for which they are working. Thus I remember once overhearing a casual remark to the effect that "Bar

Y Harry" had married "the seven Open A girl," the latter being the daughter of a neighboring ranchman. Often they receive nicknames, as, for instance, Dutch Wannigan, Windy Jack, and Kid Williams, all of whom are on the list of my personal acquaintances.

No man traveling through or living in the country need fear molestation from the cowboys unless he himself accompanies them on their drinking bouts, or in other ways plays the fool, for they are, with us at any rate, very good fellows, and the most determined and effective foes of real law-breakers, such as horse and cattle thieves, murderers, etc. Few of the outrages quoted in Eastern papers as their handiwork are such in reality, the average Easterner apparently considering every individual who wears a broad hat and carries a six-shooter a cowboy. These outrages are, as a rule, the work of the roughs and criminals who always gather on the outskirts of civilization and who infest every frontier town until the decent citizens become sufficiently murderous and determined to take the law into their own hands and drive them out.

The old buffalo-hunters, who formed a distinct class, became powerful forces for evil once they had destroyed the vast herds of mighty beasts whose pursuit had been their means of livelihood. They were absolutely shiftless and improvident; they had no settled habits; they were inured to peril and hardship but entirely unaccustomed to steady work; and so they afforded just the materials from which to make the bolder and more desperate kinds of criminals. When the game was gone they hung round the settlements for some little time, and then many of them naturally took to horse-stealing, cattle-killing, and highway robbery, although others, of course, went into honest pursuits. They were men who died off rapidly, however; for it is curious to see how many of these plainsmen, in spite of their iron nerves and thews, have their constitutions completely undermined, as much by the terrible hardships they have endured as by the fits of prolonged and bestial revelry with which they have varied them.

The "bad men," or professional fighters and man-killers, are of a different stamp, quite a number of them being, according to their light, perfectly honest. These are the men who do most of the killing in frontier communities; yet it is a noteworthy fact that the men who are killed generally deserve their fate. These men are, of course, used to brawling, and are not only sure shots, but, what is equally important, able to "draw" their weapons with marvelous quickness. They think nothing whatever of murder, and are the dread and terror of their associates; yet they are very chary of taking the life of a man of good standing, and will often weaken and back down at once if confronted fearlessly. With many of them their courage arises from confidence in their own powers and knowledge of the fear in which they are held; and men of this type often show the white feather when they get in a tight place. Others, however, will face any odds without flinching. On the other hand, I have known of these men fighting, when mortally wounded, with a cool, ferocious despair that was terrible. As elsewhere, so here, very quiet men are often those who in an emergency show themselves as best able to hold their own.

These desperadoes always try to "get the drop" on a foe—that is, to take him at a disadvantage before he can use his own weapon. I have known more men killed in this way, when the affair was wholly one-sided, than I have known to be shot in fair fights; and I have known fully as many who were shot by accident. It is wonderful, in the event of a streetfight, how few bullets seem to hit the men they are aimed at.

During the last two or three years the stockmen have united to put down all these dangerous characters, often by the most summary exercise of lynch law. Notorious bullies and murderers have been taken out and hung, while the bands of horse and cattle thieves have been regularly hunted down and destroyed in pitched fights by parties of armed cowboys; and as a consequence most of our territory is now perfectly law-abiding. One such fight occurred on the banks of the Missouri; two of their number were slain, and the others were driven on the ice, which broke, and two more were drowned. A few months previously another gang, whose headquarters were near the Canadian line, were surprised in their hut; two or three were shot down by the cowboys as they tried to come out, while the rest barricaded themselves in and fought until the great log-hut was set on fire, when they broke forth in a body, and nearly all were killed at once, only one or two making their escape. A little over a year ago one committee of vigilantes in eastern Montana shot or hung nearly sixty—not, however, with the best judgment in all cases.

———

"THE PIONEERS OF civilization," Roosevelt calls them—yet these same cattle kings organized the brutal war against the outlaws, drifters, and small ranchers of the upper Missouri described above. It was Roosevelt's wealthy friend from Montana, Granville Stuart, who organized the "committee of vigilantes" (who called themselves "Stuart's Stranglers") that failed to show "the best judgment in all cases" as they summarily executed between sixty and a hundred men. The future president heartily approved of these vigilante raids: they scored a significant victory in the struggle to make the newly conquered territory safe for the wealthy, conservative stockmen who, as Roosevelt believed, rivaled the Eastern capitalists.

Of course, many of the men murdered by Stuart's Stranglers and other bands probably *were* outlaws (though most were responsible for no worse a crime than horse stealing). But these events were pivotal battles in the Western Civil War of Incorporation. The frontier was defined by the absence of civil institutions and legal norms more than the mere absence of settlers; in this environment, criminal activity flourished, and was even winked at by the local population. But the same conditions allowed wealthy men to ignore the almost nonexistent law by hiring gunmen to enforce their will—a first step toward establishing both social stability and their own influence and power.

In 1880, a young gunman by the name of Frank Canton arrived to take a hand in this rough-and-tumble fight. No angel himself,[40] he soon found work on the side of the new frontier establishment. As a gunslinger rather than a wealthy man like Roosevelt, Canton provides his own perspective on the war unleashed by Granville Stuart and other cattle kings. About the time of these events, Canton moved to the still-unconquered country of Wyoming, where widespread outlawry (with such centers as the Hole-in-the-Wall in the Big Horn Mountains) lingered longer than in almost any other part of the West. First as an armed detective for the Wyoming Stockgrowers' Association, then as sheriff of huge Johnson County, he eagerly worked to impose the authority of the big ranchers on an unwilling territory—at the point of a Winchester and six-gun.

---

## The Sheriff of Johnson County
*by Frank M. Canton*

At that time the terminus of the Northern Pacific Railroad was at Miles City [Montana] and the only means of travel west of there was by saddle horse or stagecoach. This railroad company had furnished free transportation from the East to all laborers who wanted to go West. The loose criminal element in New York, Chicago, and other cities took advantage of this opportunity to leave the Eastern states. The result was that the country west of Miles City, Montana, was soon overrun with the most desperate gang of cutthroats that ever went unhung. . . .

Stolen cattle was driven into railroad camps and sold to contractors at half their value. Horses were stolen in broad daylight. It was not an unusual sight to see floating down the river the body of some railroad laborer, with his throat cut or a bullet through him, who had been robbed and murdered after receiving his week's pay. Sheriff Irvin and his deputies worked day and night. . . . The officers were brave and determined, and did their duty, but there were not enough of them. The actual residents in Montana then took a hand in the game. The miners and ranchers organized vigilance committees in many different localities. The thieves would be given fair warning to leave the country or take their medicine, but they never received a second warning. If the first warning was not obeyed, you would find several dead bodies hanging from telegraph poles. The vigilantes soon ran the crooks out of town.

[40] Canton, whose original name was Joe Horner, had been a cowboy and outlaw in Texas before heading north.

Then Granville Stuart, president of the Montana Stock Association, at the head of fifty cowboys, commenced a war of extermination against the criminals on the range, along the Yellowstone and Musselshell and the Missouri rivers. Early Montana history has recorded what Granville Stuart and his cowboys did that made it possible for an honest man to live in Montana and enjoy the fruits of his labor. The criminals who were fortunate enough to get out of Montana alive all came south into Wyoming and Idaho. They knew if they went north and crossed the Missouri River they would be in Canada and have the Northwest Mounted Police to deal with, which was not much encouragement to a horse thief.[41]

I moved from Miles City in 1880 and settled at Buffalo, in Johnson County, Wyoming, but I was still in the employ of the Wyoming Stock Association.[42] I secured four hundred and eighty acres of land twelve miles southwest of Buffalo at the foot of the Big Horn Mountains and commenced farming and stock raising. At the time Johnson County, Wyoming, covered an immense area of land. The eastern boundary was south Dakota, the nothern line was Montana, and the southern line was Albany County on the North Platte River. West of Buffalo it had taken in all of the Big Horn and Wind River Mountains out to the line of Idaho. The mountains were full of big game, elk, bear, and mountain sheep and black-tailed deer; while the valleys were covered with antelope and some buffalo. It was the best rendezvous for outlaws that I have ever seen, and they were there, plenty of them.

I was elected sheriff of Johnson County in 1882. At that time our nearest railroad point was Rock Creek, Wyoming, two hundred and fifty miles south of Buffalo on the Union Pacific Railroad. This trip was made over a stage line. Later on, when the Northern Pacific Railroad was completed, we traveled to Custer Station, Montana, one hundred and fifty miles north of Buffalo. We had no penitentiary at that time and the territorial authorities made a contract with the State of Illinois to keep our convicts at Joliet.

I appointed John McDermott my undersheriff, to take charge of the office work. He was an excellent clerical man and a brave and loyal officer. I selected eighteen picked men for field deputies, who knew the country and were especially fitted for such work. I had but little time to stay in my office for the next two years, for I was in charge of the field work myself, and in the saddle most of the time. District court convened at Buffalo once a year.

---

[41] Canton was an employee of the big cattlemen, so his account is obviously highly biased. The armed sweeps by vigilante gangs led by Granville Stuart and others struck at anyone (criminals or not) who made it difficult for the wealthy ranchers to enforce their will.

[42] The Wyoming Stockgrowers' Association was a group of the most powerful ranchers in the territory; many were absentee English landowners, who hired local men to manage their spreads. Canton refers to its opponents as "outlaws," when many were (as in Montana) small, independent ranchers and homesteaders.

We always had a large bunch of convicts after court to take over the long trip by stagecoach to the railroad, then to Joliet. It would sometimes take two stagecoaches for the prisoners and guards.

In 1885 I married Annie Wilkerson, the daughter of W.H. Wilkerson, who moved out from Illinois with his family and settled near the little town of Big Horn, Wyoming. My wife liked the country and we were very happy in our new home.

During those days the worst criminals we had to deal with were the stage robbers, or road agents, as they were called in that country. The Wells Fargo treasure was carried by stagecoach through the mountains from Rock Creek, Wyoming, to Custer Station, Montana—a distance of four hundred and fifty miles. While the United States Government had offered a standing reward of one thousand dollars for the arrest and conviction of each stage robber, hardly a week passed but that the stage was robbed somewhere along the line, and the driver generally shot down from ambush. Several United States paymasters were robbed and large amounts taken, until finally Big-Nosed George, leader of the gang, was shot down and killed and three of his men captured and sentenced for life. Shortly after the death of Big-Nosed George, I captured the notorious stage robber, Bill Brown, and his partner on Pinney Creek, north of Buffalo. These two outlaws were both tried in federal court in Cheyenne, Wyoming, and sentenced for life. T. Jeff Carr, one of the best-known officers in that part of the country, helped me get the evidence to convict these two men. This put a damper on stage robbing in the northwest.

The Black Hills gold excitement had brought many people into south Dakota. The mines were paying well, and this made a good market for work horses and mules. The country in Idaho, Utah, Oregon, and Nevada was overstocked with ranch horses and no market for them whatever. There was a notorious outlaw who had a rendezvous with his gang in Jackson's Hole, and in the Teton Mountains. He was called Teton Jackson. This man had run a pack train for General Crook during the Sioux War. He was placed in the guard house for stealing government mules. He killed two soldiers and escaped to the Teton Mountains.

He was a Mormon and was a member of a gang of Mormon outlaws whom they called the Destroying Angels. John D. Lee, who was executed for the Mountain Meadows massacre, was his uncle. Jackson was a most dangerous and vicious character. He had killed several Deputy United States Marshals in Utah and Idaho, who had followed him into the mountains. The Territory of Utah had offered three thousand five hundred dollars for his capture, dead or alive, but as he could always get assistance from one of the Mormons in any of their settlements along the borders of Idaho and Utah, it was almost impossible to get an even break with him. He had about a dozen hard men with him.

When he found that they could sell horses in the Black Hills for a good price, they began stealing horses from the ranchers in the adjoining territories. The system this band adopted was to steal ten or fifteen head from each herd on the range scattered over a large area of country, and drive them into Jackson's Hole, which was a basin of country covering several square miles, and was almost walled in by the mountains; this was the most talked-of outlaw rendezvous in the world. The owners would probably not miss their stock for months, and even then would think the little bunch had strayed off.

When the thieves had secured eight hundred or a thousand head, they would then doctor the brands and as soon as the new brands healed over they would put the herd on the trail and drive them over through Johnson County, Wyoming, to Deadwood and other mining towns in the Black Hills where they would find a good market for them. This systematic stealing continued for several years. One day I received a telegram from Billy Hosford, an officer whom I knew at Blackfoot, Idaho, saying that Teton Jackson had recently stolen about fifty head of fine horses from two ranchmen by the names of High and Stout, and that he was seen by two Snake Indians heading toward the Big Horn mountains.

There was an old trapper and hunter by the name of Lucas, who had a cabin at the mouth of Paint Rock Creek Canyon in the Basin, whom I suspected of being in league with this band of horse thieves. His cabin was forty miles from Buffalo over the Big Horn Mountains. I selected Chris Gross and Ed Loyd, two of my best deputies, and left Buffalo about dark, and by hard riding through pine timber and windfalls, reached the cabin about two hours before daylight. We tied our horses to some trees and got positions in good shooting distance of the cabin, which had only one door and one window. Of course, we did not know that Teton was there and only suspected that he was in the cabin. But I did not intend to take any more chances than I would have done had I been sure that he was there.

Just before daybreak a candle was lighted in the cabin and in a few minutes sparks began to come out of the chimney. We then approached nearer the cabin. I gave my Winchester to Gross and Loyd and gave orders for them to watch the window and door and stop anyone who might try to escape. I then drew my six-shooter and stepped quickly into the cabin. I recognized Teton Jackson instantly by the description I had of him. He was squatting down in front of the fireplace trying to light his pipe with a splinter. He was only half dressed and had not yet buckled on his six-shooter, although it was lying within his reach with a belt full of cartridges. I covered him at once with my revolver, and ordered him to throw up his hands, and at the same time called for my deputies to come in and handcuff him. Lucas was slicing up venison for breakfast. . . . After we had breakfast I sent Lucas out with my two deputies and told him that if he did not round up and bring in every horse that Teton had driven into the canyon I would arrest him too and take him to Buffalo. . . .

After they left I was in the cabin alone with Teton. He was not a pleasant companion. I have never seen a man of his description before or since. He was about forty-five, over six feet in height, weighed a hundred and ninety, stubby beard, raw-boned, coarse features, flaming red hair, red face, and eyes that were black as a snake's. . . . I had taken a seat about six feet from him with my revolver in my hand. He began to complain that the hand-cuffs were so tight that the blood could not circulate and that he was in great pain, and that if I would take them off he would keep quiet and promise not to hurt me. I told him that I was not the least bit uneasy about his hurting me, and that I had no objection to granting his request, but that he was the one taking all the chances, for if he made the slightest move I would kill him. He said he understood the situation. I then threw the keys over to him, and he unlocked the handcuffs and pitched the keys and cuffs back to me.

After he had removed the cuffs he began rubbing his wrists and said that I would never take him to Buffalo and that he wanted to serve notice on me right there and then that he was a better man than I was, even without a six-shooter. He began to talk very abusive. I told him that I would take him to Buffalo and that he was worth as much to me dead as alive. I told him I would prefer to take his dead body as it would be less trouble to handle than a live one. I then threw the open handcuffs on the floor at his feet and told him that if he did not snap them on his wrists in ten seconds, he could take his medicine. I think he put them on in less time than I had given him.

My deputies returned in about an hour with the stolen horses, which proved to be the property of High and Stout. We put Teton on one of the horses, tied his feet together under the horse's body, and landed him in jail in Buffalo that night. . . .

With Teton Jackson out of the way, the backbone of the band was broken. Red Anderson and Black Tom, two members of the band, were shot and killed near the Yellowstone Park. George Stevens, alias Big George, was shot and killed on the Big Horn Mountains by Chris Gross, who also captured Frank Lamb. The rest of the gang left the Teton Mountains and most of them were picked up by officers in adjoining territories and sent to the penitentiary. Up to this time we had convicted many horse thieves and had succeeded in breaking up one of the best-organized gangs of stage robbers in the Northwest.

---

FRANK CANTON, OF course, did not end crime on the northern frontier. He did, however, play a small but key role in the battle to erase the violent resistance of independent frontiersmen. Lawman though he was, Canton was not simply a disinterested agent of law and order. He also worked as a hired gun for the Wyoming Stockgrowers' Association—the organization of cattle barons who ruled, or sought to rule, the open range in the same way the Montana association did in the "conquered territory" (to use Richard Maxwell Brown's phrase) to the north.

Wyoming was not quite conquered yet. It would remain one of the last true frontier regions, shaken by violent confrontations between independent small-timers and men of power. And crime, of course, would always continue. But by the mid-1880s, the West had turned a corner: the institutions of government, big business, the market economy, and law enforcement—carried forward by naked force—had begun to change the rules of life for good.

# IV

# THE MOUNTAINS AND THE DESERT

BATTLES OF THE SOUTHWEST
1861–1884

| 1609 | · Santa Fe founded by the Spanish |
|---|---|
| 1821 | · Mexico independent from Spain |
| | · Santa Fe Trail opens, beginning overland trade with the United States |
| 1835–36 | · Texas revolution leads to independence from Mexico |
| 1845 | · Texas annexed by the United States |
| 1846–48 | · Mexican War; New Mexico swiftly conquered by Stephen Kearny |
| 1848 | · Treaty of Guadalupe Hidalgo cedes area of California, Arizona, New Mexico, Nevada, Utah, and parts of Colorado to United States |
| 1850 | · New Mexico Territory (including Arizona) organized by Congress |
| 1853 | · Gadsden Purchase confers southern New Mexico to United States |
| 1861 | · Apache war breaks out when Lieutenant George Bascom takes Chiricahua chief Cochise hostage; Cochise escapes and leads warriors in a counterattack |
| | · Civil War erupts; regular army units withdrawn from the Southwest; Apache and Navajo raids scourge the region |
| 1862 | · Confederate army under General H.H. Sibley invades New Mexico and is defeated by Western volunteers under Colonel John Chivington |
| 1863 | · Arizona organized by Congress as a separate territory |
| | · Apache chief Mangas Colorado murdered in captivity by U.S. soldiers |
| 1863–64 | · Colonel Kit Carson, under command of General James Carleton, leads fight against Apaches and Navajos; Navajos defeated and forced onto Bosque Redondo reservation; thousands die of exposure and malnutrition |
| 1868 | · Navajos allowed to return to ancestral homeland, Canyon de Chelly, Arizona; enter into prosperous, peaceful era as sheepherders |
| 1871 | · Tucson townspeople massacre peaceful Aravaipa Apaches at Camp Grant; twenty-seven surviving children sold into slavery in Mexico |
| 1871–73 | · General George Crook takes command in Southwest; launches fierce attacks on resisting Apaches |
| 1872 | · Cochise meets with General Oliver O. Howard and agrees to live on a reservation at Apache Pass; peace until Cochise's death in 1874 |
| 1870s | · Silver and copper mining begins to flourish in Arizona; cattle ranching booms in New Mexico |

|  |  |
|---|---|
|  | · Maxwell Land Grant Company defeats local gunfighters in the Colfax County War, New Mexico |
| 1877 | · Desert Land Act passed, providing free arid land to settlers who would develop it; rich silver lode found in Tombstone, Arizona |
| 1878 | · Lincoln County War ravages southeastern New Mexico |
| 1878–81 | · Cochise County War, Arizona; the Earp brothers help Tombstone businessmen defeat gunfighting rural cowboys |
| 1879–80 | · Victorio leads Warm Springs Apaches on an epic raiding campaign |
| 1880–81 | · Billy the Kid becomes bandit and folk hero; killed by Pat Garrett |
| 1883 | · Santa Fe, Southern Pacific, and Northern Pacific railroads completed |

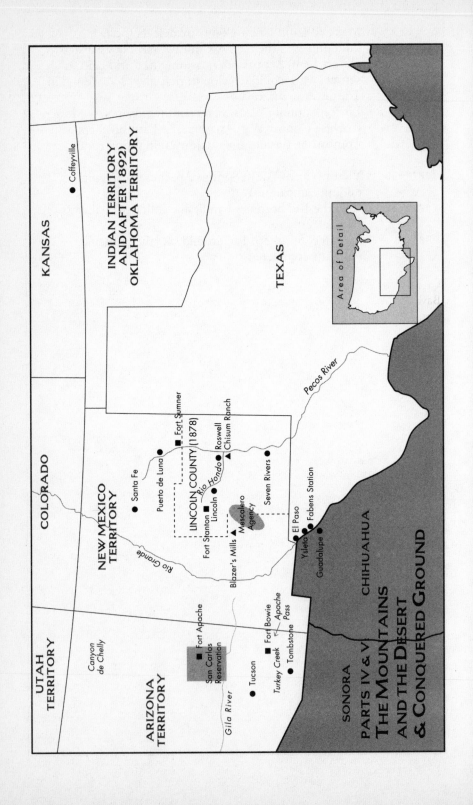

UTAH
TERRITORY

COLORADO

KANSAS

• Coffeyville

INDIAN TERRITORY
AND (AFTER 1892)
OKLAHOMA TERRITORY

NEW MEXICO
TERRITORY

• Santa Fe

• Puerto de Luna

■ Fort Sumner

LINCOLN COUNTY (1878)

Rio Hondo

Roswell
Chisum Ranch

Pecos River

Fort Stanton ■
Lincoln ■

▲ Mescalero
Agency

• Seven Rivers

TEXAS

Blazer's Mills ▲

El Paso •

Ysleta •
Guadalupe •
• Fabens Station

Rio Grande

Canyon
de Chelly

ARIZONA
TERRITORY

Fort Apache ■

San Carlos
Reservation ■

Fort Bowie ■

Apache
Pass

Tucson •

Turkey Creek •

Tombstone •

Gila River

Area of Detail

SONORA

CHIHUAHUA

PARTS IV & VI
THE MOUNTAINS
AND THE DESERT
& CONQUERED GROUND

## 11

# THE LONG FIGHT OF THE APACHES

In 1879, Texas Ranger J.B. Gillett left the hill country behind and transferred to Company C of the Frontier Battalion, stationed in El Paso County. In recognition of his able service, the ranger command elevated Gillett to first sergeant, second in command under Lieutenant John Walker Baylor—a tall, forty-seven-year-old veteran of the Confederate army and numerous Indian fights. Baylor was a literate and well-educated officer, with the offhand racism of most white Texans; he was also unstintingly courageous. "I have not the power of language to describe Lieutenant Baylor's bravery," Gillett wrote, "because he was as brave as it is possible for man to be. He thought everyone else should be the same, and he did not see how a white man could be a coward."

Gillett's new assignment would soon test his own courage. In September 1879, he arrived at his post at Ysleta, El Paso County, where the point of Texas's western arrowhead joined the borders of both old and New Mexico. It was a fascinating crossing-ground of the Western frontier, inhabited by Hispanics, Native Americans, whites, and blacks (many current or former soldiers of the U.S. cavalry). Languages and people mingled in this sparsely populated land, crossing freely over the Rio Grande and the New Mexico line. But mingling did not mean liking: the area simmered with feuds, outlawry, and racial tension.

It was here, in this wild, multilingual, multicultural frontier, that the young veteran met his deadliest enemy: the Apaches. He had heard about them from the talkative Baylor—stories of their daring raids, their innate toughness, their legendary fighting skill. But Gillett remained skeptical; he had seen plenty of action against the Indian warriors of the Great Plains, and he wondered if the tales about the Apaches might not be a bit exaggerated. His first battle with them would prove quite an education.

Less than a month after Gillett's arrival on the Rio Grande, a young Latino boy brought word of an Apache raid. The confident ranger sergeant eagerly organized his company for the chase, confident in the capabilities of himself and his men. That chase would become a fascinating ride through the Hispanic culture of the Southwest frontier—and a sharp lesson in Apache prowess on the warpath.

## Our First Fight with the Apaches
*by J.B. Gillett*

On October 3, 1879, at midnight, Pablo Mejia brought Lieutenant Baylor a note from Captain Gregorio Garcia of San Elizario [a nearby town], stating that a band of Apaches had charged a camp of five Mexicans[1] who were engaged in cutting hay for the stage company fourteen miles north of La Quadra stage station and had killed them. As first sergeant I was ordered to make a detail of ten men and issue them five days' rations. I detailed Second Sergeant Tom Swilling, Privates Gus Small, George Lloyd, John Thomas, George Harold, Doc Shivers, Richard Head, Bill Rutherford, and Juan Garcia for the scout, and myself made the tenth man. It required an hour to arouse the men, issue the rations and ammunition, and pack the two mules, so it was one o'clock in the morning when we finally left Ysleta.

By daylight we reached Hawkins Station, near where Fabens now is. Here we were told we would find the survivor of the terrible massacre. Riding up to the door of the stage house, we had to thump some time before we had evidence that anyone was alive on the premises. Finally, the door was opened very cautiously about an inch and a Mexican peeped out. Lieutenant Baylor asked him if he had been one of the *grameros*, or hay cutters.

"*Sí, señor*," replied the sleepy Mexican.

Asked for an account of the massacre, the native said it was nearly dark when the Indians, numbering from twenty-five to thirty, charged the camp uttering such horrible yells that everyone took to his heels and was soon in the chaparral. The speaker saw his *pobrecito papa* (poor papa) running, with the Indians about to lance him, and knew that he and the remainder of the party were killed. Only he himself escaped. As he mentioned the tragic death of his beloved parent the tears rolled down his cheeks. Lieutenant Baylor comforted the weeper as best he could and asked him if he would not guide the rangers to the raided camp; he declined with thanks, saying he must stay to help the station keeper take care of the stage mules, but he directed us to the ranch where some of the dead men's families lived and where a guide could be obtained.

When we arrived at the ranch below Hawkins Station it was sunrise and we halted for breakfast after a night ride of forty miles. The people at the ranch were very uneasy when we rode up, but rejoiced when they realized we were rangers. On learning our mission they showed us every attention.

[1] Gillett, like most English-speaking Texans, commonly referred to Hispanic Americans as Mexicans, regardless of citizenship.

Among the first to come out to us was an old Mexican who had been in the hay camp when it was attacked. He gave a lurid account of the onset. His son had been one of the *grameros*, and when he mentioned him the tears began to flow.

"*Ah, hijo de mi cara Juan*. I shall never see him again," he lamented. "All were killed and I alone escaped!"

Lieutenant Baylor then explained to the weeping father that his son was very much alive and that we had seen him that very night bewailing the death of the father he thought killed. It now developed that all the dead men were alive. When the camp was attacked all the Mexicans had scattered, and the Apaches had been too busy looting the stores to follow the fugitives. Moreover, those ranchers would fight and the Indians did not care to follow them into the brush.

A bright young Mexican went with us to the hay camp, which was about six miles toward Comales. The Apaches had made a mess of things in camp sure enough. They had broken all the cups and plates, poured salt into the sugar, this combination into the flour and beans, and the conglomeration of the whole upon the ground, as the sacks were all they wanted. They had smashed the coffee pot, the frying pan, the skillet, and the water barrels with an ax. Then, taking all the blankets, they had started eastward as though they intended to go to the Sierra Prieta, but after going a mile the trail turned south. We found the redskins had come from the north by way of Las Cornudas and were probably from Fort Stanton, New Mexico, on a raid into Mexico. They were in dry country and making for the Rio Grande, fourteen miles to the south. When they discovered the hay camp on their route they charged it and fired on the hay cutters. The Mexicans scattered and made their escape in the darkness, each thinking himself the sole survivor and so reporting on reaching his home, though as a matter of fact not a single life was lost.

Our guide went back to give the alarm to the ranches below and we followed the trail down the mesa until opposite the Mexican town of Guadalupe. There we crossed the overland stage route near the present Rio Grande station and found our guide waiting for us. He had discovered the trail, and fearing the Indians might ambush the road below, had stopped and awaited our arrival. The trail made straight for the Rio Grande, crossing about one mile west of Guadalupe. From the pony and mule tracks Lieutenant Baylor judged there were fifteen to twenty Indians in the band. We had some trouble following the trail after we got to the river bottom, where loose horses and cattle ran, but a few of us dismounted and worked the trail out, crossed the river, and struck camp for dinner.

Lieutenant Baylor sent Pablo Mejia into town to inform the president of Guadalupe that we had followed a fresh Apache trail to the Rio Grande going south into Mexico, and asked permission to follow the Indians into his country. The scout soon returned and reported that the president was not only pleased that we had pursued the redskins, but would willingly join us himself with all the men he could muster. . . .

After leaving Guadalupe the trail went south, following closely the stage road from Juarez to Chihuahua. Not long after leaving town we met a courier coming to Guadalupe from Don Ramon Arranda's ranch, San Marcos de Cantarica, twenty-one miles distant, who informed us that the Apaches had killed a herder on that ranch and had taken four horses and sixteen mules belonging to the stage company. We hurried onward and reached Cantarica at sunset, having traveled seventy-eight miles since one o'clock that morning. Both men and horses were rather tired.

All was confusion at the ranch. The Mexican herder had been shrouded and laid out with a cross at his head and several little lighted candles near the body. Many women were sitting around the room with black shawls pulled up over their heads. The Apaches, numbering sixteen well-armed and well-mounted warriors, had slain their victim and captured the stock near the ranch about noon. Mexican volunteers from Guadalupe and San Ignacio began to ride in until our combined force numbered twenty-five or twenty-six men. Everyone was excited at the thought of a brush with the redskins responsible for the murder.

Accompanied by our volunteer allies we left the ranch at daylight next morning and picked up the trail at once. It led off south along the base of the Armagora or Sierra Bentano mountains. As the Mexicans were familiar with the country they took the lead and followed the trail rapidly. About eleven o'clock the trailers halted at the mouth of the Canyon del Marranos, an ugly black hole cut in the mountains, looking grim and defiant enough without the aid of Apache warriors. When we had joined the Mexicans—we were traveling some half a mile behind them—Lieutenant Baylor and Captain Garcia held a short conference. The lieutenant turned to me and said that Captain Garcia declared the Indians were in the canyon among the rocks, and ordered me to detail two men to guard our horses while we scaled the mountain on foot and investigated it. I could not bring myself to believe that a band of Indians that had killed a man and driven off all the stage stock six days before had gone only thirty miles and were now lying in wait for us.

"You don't know the Apaches," Lieutenant Baylor declared, when I voiced my thoughts. "They are very different from the plains Indians, the kind you have been used to following. These Apaches delight to get into the rocks and lay for their enemies."

At the conference the Mexicans suggested that Lieutenant Baylor should take nine of his men and ten of their volunteers and follow the trail up the canyon, but the lieutenant declared that this would never do, as the Apaches had no doubt anticipated such a move and hidden themselves in the cliffs where they could kill their attackers without exposing themselves in the least. He proposed scaling the mountains and following them down on top of the ridge in the Indians' rear, and this was the strategy finally adopted.

The Mexicans dismounted and started up the mountainside about one hundred yards to our left. Lieutenant Baylor and his eight rangers marched straight forward from our horses and began the ascent. As we went along, the lieutenant pulled some bunch grass and stuck it all around under his hatband so his head would look like a clump of grass and conceal his head and body if he should have to flatten himself on the ground. He counseled us to follow his example. I had taken some Mexican cheese out of my saddle pockets and was eating it as we marched carelessly up the mountain.

Honestly, I did not believe there was an Indian within a hundred miles of us, but it was not long before I changed my mind. Suddenly there came a loud report of a gun and then another. I looked up to where the Mexicans had taken position behind a ledge of rocks and saw where a bullet had struck the stones a foot above their heads. I did not want any more cheese. I threw down what I had in my hand and spat out what I had in my mouth.

The Apache warriors, high in the cliffs above us, then turned their attention to our little band of rangers and fired twenty-five or thirty shots right into our midst. One of these big caliber bullets whizzed so close to my head that it made a noise like a wild duck flying downstream at fifty to sixty miles an hour. Lieutenant Baylor ordered us to charge at once.

In running up the mountain I was somewhat in advance of the boys. We came to a rock ledge three or four feet high. I quickly scaled this, but before I could straighten up an Indian rose from behind a rock about fifteen to twenty yards ahead and fired pointblank at me. The bullet struck a small soap-weed three feet in front of me and knocked the leaves into my mouth and face. I felt as if I had been hit, but it was leaves and not blood that I wiped out of my mouth with my left hand. I turned my head and called to the boys to look out, but the warning was unnecessary—they had already taken shelter under the ledge of rock.

Just as I turned my head a second shot from the Apache carried away the entire front part of my hat brim. I saw the warrior throw another cartridge into his gun and brought my Winchester quickly to bear upon him. When he saw that I was about to shoot he shifted his position and turned sideways to me. We both fired at the same instant. My bullet hit the redskin just above his hip and, passing straight through his body, broke the small of his back and killed him almost instantly. He was a big man, probably six feet tall, with his face painted in red and blue paint. He used an old octagon-barrel Winchester rifle and he had with him an old shirtsleeve, tied at one end, in which there were two hundred and fifty Winchester cartridges.

Some Indians fifty yards up the mountain now began to shell our position, so I took shelter behind the ledge of rock. Fifteen or twenty feet to our left and a little higher up the mountain, Lieutenant Baylor was sheltered behind some boulders. He raised his head slightly above the parapet for a peep at the Indians and those keen-sighted warriors saw him;

a well-directed shot cut part of the grass out of his hat. Had the bullet been six inches lower it would have struck him full in the face.

"Darn that old Indian," exclaimed Baylor, ducking his head. "If I had a shotgun I would run up and jump right on top of him."

The lieutenant was mad now, and ordered a charge. The boys hesitated, and George Harold, an old scout, said, "Lieutenant, if we leave this shelter and start up the mountain the Indians hidden behind those rocks seventy-five yards above will kill us all."

"Yes, I suppose you are right; they would be hard to dislodge," replied Baylor.

The Apaches evidently had plenty of ammunition, for they kept up a desultory fire all day. Seeing we were not going to fall into their trap, they turned their attention to our horses. Although the animals were four or five hundred yards from the foot of the mountain they killed Sergeant Swilling's horse, the bullet passing entirely through the body just behind the shoulders. When it staggered and tumbled over, Swilling began to mourn, for he had the horror of walking all Western men have. John Thomas, however, got the laugh on him by saying, "Sergeant, you had better wait and see if you are going back to camp." We could see the Indians' bullets knocking up dust all around the horses and the guard replying to the fire. Lieutenant Baylor now sent a man to the guard with an order to move the horses out of range.

During the afternoon the Apaches moved up higher toward the crest of the mountain, and in doing so one of the Indians exposed himself. The Mexicans to our left spotted him and killed him with a well-directed shot. The warrior fell in open ground where he was literally shot to pieces.

We had been without water all day, and when night came Lieutenant Baylor and Captain Garcia decided it was useless to continue the fight any longer, so we withdrew toward our horses. After reaching the animals we could still hear the Indians firing on our positions. . . .

We reached our headquarters at Ysleta after being out five days and traveling two hundred and twenty-two miles, sustaining no other damage than a few bruises from scaling the mountain and the loss of Sergeant Swilling's horse. This first brush with the Apaches, however, was but a prelude to other expeditions after this tribe.

---

WHO WERE THESE warriors, who sent off the formidable Texas Rangers empty-handed and minus a horse? For Gillett, this sharp little fight was a harrowing personal introduction to the Apaches. But this small Indian victory reflected a larger truth: by October 1879, the time of this skirmish, the Apaches were almost the last Native Americans left who consistently offered armed resistance to the military might of the United States.

As detailed in earlier chapters, the 1870s witnessed the near-final victory of the United States Army over the independent power of the Native Americans, from the Great Plains to the Rocky Mountains to the Pacific Northwest. In the Southwest the process of conquest and confinement on reservations was largely complete by the early part of the decade. Resistance had centered on the Navajos and the Apaches, two of the most warlike of the many Indian nations in the region. After fierce fighting, the Navajos were defeated during the early 1860s by soldiers led by the legendary figure of Kit Carson, under the overall command of General James Carleton. The tribe then endured a harrowing exile to the barren Bosque Redondo reservation. After much suffering, they were eventually allowed to return to their homeland of Arizona's Canyon de Chelly, where they lived in peace thereafter.

The Apaches, however, fought on. They had been fighting for centuries, in fact, by the time the whites arrived. Arizona and New Mexico were settled in the sixteenth and seventeenth centuries by the Spanish, who were met with raids by the fierce tribe. After Mexico's independence, the Santa Fe Trail opened commerce with the United States—but few Americans settled in the area. Even after the U.S. conquest in the 1840s, daily life remained much the same; as Gillett's story suggests, both Hispanics and Indians maintained their old ways.

Those old ways included mutual hatred. The Apaches developed a kind of symbiosis with the Mexican settlements, alternately trading and raiding; these raids came to play an important role in their tribal economy and warrior culture. Mexico's state governments responded by offering a reward for each Apache scalp—whether it was from a man, woman, or child—feeding the bitter violence. But the Mexicans and Apaches were both relatively poor and few in number, and the age-old conflict simmered along without coming to a head. The situation would change drastically, however, when settlers and soldiers from the United States arrived in quantity in the 1860s and '70s. Neither the pioneers nor their government would tolerate the Apache raids the way the Mexican villagers had for so many generations. A climactic war loomed on the horizon.

One of the most famous Apache warriors to come of age during this final era of Apache independence was a man named Goyakla—better known as Geronimo, a name given to him by the Mexicans. Geronimo was born into one of the smaller of the many Apache bands, though he eventually became a part of the Chiricahua (the people of another noted warrior-chief, Cochise).[2] He was not a hereditary chief, but emerged as a prominent war leader, thanks to his considerable military prowess.

[2] The Apaches, like most Native American nations, were divided into a number of tribes, including the White Mountain, Chiricahua, Coyotero, Warm Springs, and others; some hated each other. And to make matters more confusing, many tribes went by multiple names, in English, Spanish, and the Apache language.

How he came to achieve that prowess is a chilling story of murder and revenge. Geronimo suffered the loss of his father when he was still young; perhaps, as he grew to manhood, it left him with an extra sense of responsibility, or a feeling that he had to prove himself. Or perhaps he was a typical young warrior, eager to win recognition for his bravery. His passion for battle and the hunt, however, was almost overshadowed by his feelings for Alope, a woman he took as his spouse early in life. Much later, Geronimo recounted his life story to an interpreter named S.M. Barrett; he fondly recalled his days with Alope, as the pair created a family in their small Apache community.

His contentment would soon disappear into the vortex of Apache–Mexican hatred. On a bloodstained mountaintop far inside Mexico, years before he ever fought with a white American, Geronimo's life was transformed into a never-ending search for vengeance and death.

## The Making of a Warrior
*by Geronimo (as told to S.M. Barrett)*

I was born in Nodoyohn Canyon, Arizona, June, 1829. In that country which lies around the headwaters of the Gila River I was reared. This range was our fatherland; among these mountains our wigwams were hidden; the scattered valleys contained our fields; the boundless prairies, stretching away on every side, were our pastures; the rocky caverns were our burying places.

I was fourth in a family of eight children—four boys and four girls.[3] . . . When a child my mother taught me the legends of our people; taught me of the sun and sky, the moon and stars, the clouds and storms. She also taught me to kneel and pray to Usen for strength, health, wisdom, and protection. We never prayed against any person, but if we had aught against any individual we ourselves took vengeance. We were taught that Usen does not care for the petty quarrels of men. My father had often told me of the brave deeds of our warriors, of the pleasures of the chase, and the glories of the warpath. . . .

When we were old enough to be of real service we went to the field with our parents; not to play, but to toil. When the crops were to be planted we broke the ground with wooden hoes. We planted the corn in straight rows, the beans among the corn, and the melons and pumpkins in irregular order over the field. We cultivated these crops as there was need. . . .

Besides grinding the corn (by hand with stone mortars and pestles) for bread, we sometimes crushed it and soaked it, and after it had fermented made from this juice tiswin, which had the power of intoxication, and was

[3] Four was a holy number in Apache culture.

very highly prized by the Indians. This work was done by the squaws and children. When berries or nuts were to be gathered the small children and the squaws would go in parties to hunt them, and sometimes stay all day. . . .

The Indians knew what herbs to use for medicine, and how to prepare them, and how to give the medicine. This they had been taught by Usen in the beginning, and each succeeding generation had men who were skilled in the art of healing. In gathering the herbs, in preparing them, and in administering the medicine, as much faith was held in prayer as in the actual effect of the medicine. Usually about eight persons worked together in making medicine, and there were forms of prayer and incantations to attend each stage of the process. Four attended to the incantations and four to the preparation of the herbs.

Some of the Indians were skilled in cutting out bullets, arrow heads, and other missiles with which warriors were wounded. I myself have done much of this, using a common dirk or butcher knife. . . .

To celebrate each noted event a feast or dance would be given. Perhaps only our own people, perhaps neighboring tribes would be invited. These festivities usually lasted for about four days. By day we feasted, by night under the direction of some chief we danced. The music for our dance was singing led by the warriors, and accompanied by beating the *esadadedne* (buckskin-on-a-hoop). No words were sung—only the tones. When the feasting and dancing were over we would have horse races, foot races, wrestling, jumping, and all sorts of games. . . .

When I was about eight or ten years old I began to follow the chase, and to me this was never work. Out on the prairies, which ran up to our mountain homes, wandered herds of deer, antelope, elk, and buffalo, to be slaughtered when we needed them. Usually we hunted buffalo on horseback, killing them with arrows and spears. Their skins were used to make tepees and bedding; their flesh, to eat.

It required more skill to hunt the deer than any other animal. We never tried to approach a deer except against the wind. Frequently we would spend hours in stealing upon grazing deer. If they were in the open we would crawl long distances on the ground, keeping a weed or brush before us, so that our approach would not be noticed. Often we could kill several out of one herd before the others would run away. Their flesh was dried and packed in vessels, and would keep in this condition for many months. The hide of the deer was soaked in water and ashes and the hair removed, and then the process of tanning continued until the buckskin was soft and pliable. Perhaps no other animal was more valuable to us than the deer. . . .

The Apache Indians are divided into six sub-tribes. To one of these, the Bedonkohe, I belong.[4] Our tribe inhabited that region of mountainous

---

[4] The passage describing the Apache sub-tribes has been inserted here for continuity.

country which lies west from the east line of Arizona, and south from the headwaters of the Gila River.

East of us lived the Chihenne (Ojo Caliente or Warm Springs) Apaches. Our tribe never had any difficulty with them. Victorio, their chief, was always a friend to me. He always helped our tribe when we asked him for help. He lost his life in the defense of the rights of his people. He was a good man and a brave warrior. . . .

North of us lived the White Mountain Apaches. They were not always on the best of terms with our tribe, yet we seldom had any war with them. . . . Their range was next to that of the Navajo Indians, who were not of the same blood as the Apaches. We held councils with all Apache tribes, but never with the Navajo Indians. However, we traded with them and sometimes visited them.

To the west of our country ranged the Chieahen Apaches. They had two chiefs within my time, Cosito and Codahooyah. They were friendly, but not intimate with our tribe.

South of us lived the Chokonen [Chiricahua] Apaches, whose chief in the old days was Cochise, and later his son, Naiche [also known as Natchez]. This tribe was always on the most friendly terms with us. We were often in camp and on the trail together. Naiche, who was my companion in arms, is now my companion in bondage.

To the south and west of us lived the Nedni Apaches. Their chief was Ju, called by the Mexicans Captain Ju.[5] They were our firm friends. The land of this tribe lies partly in Old Mexico and partly in Arizona. Ju and I often camped and fought side by side as brothers. My enemies were his enemies, my friends his friends. . . .

During my minority we had never seen a missionary or a priest. We had never seen a white man. Thus quietly lived the Bedonkohe Apaches. . . .

In 1846, being seventeen years of age, I was admitted to the council of the warriors. Then I was very happy, for I could go wherever I wanted and do whatever I liked. I had not been under the control of any individual, but the customs of our tribe prohibited me from sharing the glories of the warpath until the council admitted me. When the opportunity offered, after this, I could go on the warpath with my tribe. This would be glorious. I hoped soon to serve my people in battle. I had long desired to fight with our warriors.

Perhaps the greatest joy to me was that now I could marry the fair Alope, daughter of Noposo. She was a slender, delicate girl, but we had been lovers for a long time. So, as soon as the council granted me these privileges I went to see her father concerning our marriage. Perhaps our love was of no interest to him; perhaps he wanted to keep Alope with him, for she was a dutiful daughter; at any rate he asked for many ponies for her. I made no

---

[5] "Ju" is pronounced "whoa."

reply, but in a few days appeared before his wigwam with the herd of ponies and took with me Alope. This was all the marriage ceremony necessary in our tribe.

Not far from my mother's tepee I had made for us a new home. The tepee was made of buffalo hides and in it were many bear robes, lion hides, and other trophies of the chase, as well as my spears, bows, and arrows. Alope had made many little decorations of beads and drawn work on buckskin, which she placed in our tepee. . . . Three children came to us— children that played, loitered, and worked as I had done.

## THE MASSACRE

In the summer of 1858, being at peace with the Mexican towns as well as with all the neighboring Indian tribes, we went south into Old Mexico to trade. Our whole tribe (Bedonkohe Apaches) went through Sonora toward Casa Grande, our destination, but just before reaching that place we stopped at another Mexican town called by the Indians Kaskiyeh. Here we stayed for several days, camping just outside the city. Every day we would go into town to trade, leaving our camp under the protection of a small guard so that our arms, supplies, and women and children would not be disturbed during our absence.

Late one afternoon when returning from town we were met by a few women and children who told us that Mexican troops from some other town had attacked our camp, killed all the warriors of the guard, captured all our ponies, secured our arms, destroyed our supplies, and killed many of our women and children. Quickly we separated, concealing ourselves as best we could until nightfall, when we assembled at our place of rendezvous—a thicket by the river.[6] Silently we stole in one by one; sentinels were placed, and, when all were counted, I found that my aged mother, my young wife, and my three small children were among the slain. There were no lights in camp, so without being noticed I silently turned away and stood by the river. How long I stood there I do not know, but when I saw the warriors arranging for a council I took my place.

That night I did not give my vote for or against any measure; but it was decided that as there were only eighty warriors left, and as we were without arms or supplies, and were furthermore surrounded by Mexicans far inside their own territory, we could not hope to fight successfully. So our chief, Mangas Colorado, gave the orders to start at once in perfect silence for our homes in Arizona, leaving the dead upon the field.

I stood until all had passed, hardly knowing what I would do—I had no

[6] The Apaches customarily designated a site some distance from their camps as a rendezvous; if attacked, they would scatter and later reassemble at the appointed place.

weapon, nor did I hardly wish to fight, neither did I contemplate recovering the bodies of my loved ones, for that was forbidden. I did not pray, nor did I resolve to do anything in particular, for I had no purpose left. I finally followed the tribe silently, keeping just within hearing distance of the soft noise of the feet of the retreating Apaches. . . .

Within a few days we arrived at our own settlement. There were the decorations that Alope had made—and there were the playthings of our little ones. I burned them all, even our tepee. I also burned my mother's tepee and destroyed all her property.

I was never again contented in our quiet home. True, I could visit my father's grave, but I had vowed vengeance upon the Mexican troopers who had wronged me, and whenever I came near his grave or saw anything to remind me of former happy days my heart would ache for revenge upon Mexico.

## REVENGE

As soon as we had again collected some arms and supplies Mangas Colorado, our chief, called a council and found that all our warriors were willing to take the warpath against Mexico. I was appointed to solicit the aid of other tribes in this war.

When I went to the Chokonen [Chiricahua] Apaches, Cochise, their chief, called a council at early dawn. Silently the warriors assembled at an open place in a mountain dell and took their seats on the ground, arranged in rows according to their ranks. Silently they sat smoking. At a signal from the chief I arose and presented my cause as follows:

"Kinsmen, you have heard what the Mexicans have recently done without cause. You are my relatives—uncles, cousins, brothers. We are men the same as the Mexicans are—we can do to them what they have done to us. Let us go forward and trail them—I will lead you to their city—we will attack them in their homes. I will fight in the front of the battle—I only ask you to follow me to avenge this wrong done by these Mexicans—will you come? It is well—you will all come.". . .

I returned to my own settlement, reported this success to my chieftain, and immediately departed to the southward into the land of the Nedni Apaches. Their chief, Ju, heard me without comment, but he immediately issued orders for a council, and when all were ready gave a sign that I might speak. I addressed them as I had addressed the Chokonen tribe, and they also promised to help us.

It was in the summer of 1859, almost a year from the date of the massacre of Kaskiyeh, that these three tribes were assembled on the Mexican border to go upon the warpath. Their faces were painted, the war bands fastened upon their brows, their long scalp-locks ready for the hand

and the knife of the warrior who could overcome them. Their families had been hidden away in a mountain rendezvous near the Mexican border. With these families a guard was posted, and a number of places of rendezvous designated in case the camp should be disturbed.

When all was ready the chieftains gave the command to go forward. None of us were mounted and each warrior wore moccasins and also a cloth wrapped about his loins. This cloth could be spread over him when he slept, and when on the march would be ample protection as clothing. In battle, if the fight was hard, we did not wish much clothing. Each warrior carried three days' rations, but as we often killed game while on the march, we seldom were without food.

We traveled in three divisions: the Bedonkohe Apaches led by Mangas Colorado, the Chokonen Apaches by Cochise, and the Nedni Apaches by Ju; however, there was no regular order inside the separate tribes. We usually marched about fourteen hours per day, making three stops for meals, and traveling forty to forty-five miles a day.

I acted as guide into Mexico, and we followed the river courses and mountain ranges because we could better keep our movements concealed. We entered Sonora and went southward past Quitaco, Nocozari, and many smaller settlements.

When we were almost at Arispe we camped, and eight men rode out from the city to parley with us. These we captured, killed, and scalped. This was to draw the troops from the city, and the next day they came. The skirmishing lasted all day without a general engagement, but just at night we captured their supply train, so we had plenty of provisions and some more guns.

That night we posted sentinels and did not move our camp, but rested quietly all night, for we expected heavy work the next day. Early the next morning the warriors were assembled to pray—not for help, but that they might have health and avoid ambush or deceptions by the enemy.

As we had anticipated, about ten o'clock in the morning the whole Mexican force came out. There were two companies of cavalry and two of infantry. I recognized the cavalry as the soldiers who had killed my people at Kaskiyeh. This I told to the chieftains, and they said I might direct the battle.

I was no chief and never had been, but because I had been more deeply wronged than others, this honor was conferred upon me, and I resolved to prove worthy of the trust. I arranged the Indians in a hollow circle near the river, and the Mexicans drew their infantry up in two lines, with the cavalry in reserve. We were in the timber, and they advanced until within about four hundred yards, when they halted and opened fire. Soon I led a charge against them, at the same time sending braves to attack their rear. In all the battle I thought of my murdered mother, wife, and babies—of my father's grave and my vow of vengeance—and I fought with fury. Many fell by my hand, and constantly I led the advance. Many braves were killed. The battle lasted about two hours.

At the last four Indians were alone in the center of the field—myself and three other warriors. Our arrows were all gone, our spears broken off in the bodies of dead enemies. We had only our hands and knives with which to fight, but all who had stood against us were dead. Then two armed soldiers came up on us from another part of the field. They shot down two of our men and we, the remaining two, fled toward our own warriors. My companion was struck down by a saber, but I reached our warriors, seized a spear, and turned. The one who pursued me missed his aim and fell by my spear. With his saber I met the trooper who had killed my companion and we grappled and fell. I killed him with my knife and quickly rose over his body, brandishing his saber, seeking other troopers to kill. There were none. But the Apaches had seen. Over the bloody field, covered with the bodies of Mexicans, rang the fierce Apache war-whoop.

Still covered with the blood of my enemies, still holding my conquering weapon, still hot with the joy of battle, victory, and vengeance, I was surrounded by the Apache braves and made war chief of all the Apaches. Then I gave orders for scalping the slain.

I could not call back my loved ones, I could not bring back the dead Apaches, but I could rejoice this revenge. The Apaches had avenged the massacre of Kaskiyeh. All other Apaches were satisfied after the battle of Kaskiyeh, but I still desired more revenge.

[Geronimo then embarked on a series of bloody raids into Mexico over the next several years, seeking plunder for his people and revenge for himself. A pair of examples follow.]

In the summer of 1862 I took eight men and invaded Mexican territory. We went south on the west side of the Sierra Madre mountains for five days; then in the night crossed over to the southern part of the Sierra de Sahuaripa range. Here we again camped to watch for pack trains. About ten o'clock next morning four drivers came past our camp with a pack-mule train. As soon as they saw us they rode for their lives, leaving us the booty. This was a long train, and packed with blankets, calico, saddles, tinware, and loaf sugar. We hurried home as fast as we could with these provisions, and on our return while passing through a canyon in the Santa Catalina range of mountains in Arizona, met a white man driving a mule pack train. When we first saw him he had already seen us, and was riding at full tilt up the canyon. We examined his train and found that his mules were all loaded with cheese. We put them in with the other train, and resumed our journey. We did not attempt to trail the driver and I am sure he did not try to follow us.

In two days we arrived at home. Then Mangas Colorado, our chief, assembled the tribe. We gave a feast, divided the spoils, and danced all night. Some of the pack mules were killed and eaten.[7]

---

[7] Apaches generally favored horses for riding, and frequently butchered and ate the mules they captured.

This time after our return we kept out scouts so that we would know if Mexican troops should attempt to follow us. On the third day our scouts came into camp and reported Mexican cavalry dismounted and approaching our settlement. All our warriors were in camp. Mangas Colorado took command of one division and I of the other. We hoped to get possession of their horses, then surround the troops in the mountains, and destroy the whole company. This we were unable to do, for they, too, had scouts. However, within four hours after we started we had killed ten troopers with the loss of only one man, and the Mexican cavalry was in full retreat, followed by thirty armed Apaches, who gave them no rest until they were far inside the Mexican country. No more troops came that winter.

Another summer [1863] I selected three warriors and went on a raid into Mexico. We went south into Sonora, camping in the Sierra de Sahuaripa mountains. About forty miles west of Casa Grande is a small village in the mountains, called by the Indians Crassanas. We camped near this place and concluded to make an attack. We had noticed that just at midday no one seemed to be stirring; so we planned our attack at the noon hour. The next day we stole into the town at noon. We had no guns, but were armed with spears and bows and arrows. When the war-whoop was given to open the attack the Mexicans fled in every direction; not one of them made any attempt to fight us. We shot some arrows at the retreating Mexicans, but killed only one. Soon all was silent in the town and no Mexicans could be seen.

When we discovered that all the Mexicans were gone we looked through their homes and saw many curious things. These Mexicans kept many more kinds of property than the Apaches did. Many of the things we saw in the houses we could not understand, but in the stores we saw much that we wanted; so we drove in a herd of horses and mules, and packed as much provisions and supplies as we could on them. Then we formed these animals into a pack train and returned safely to Arizona. The Mexicans did not even trail us.

When we arrived in camp we called the tribe together and feasted all day. We gave presents to everyone. That night the dance began, and it did not cease until noon the next day. This was perhaps the most successful raid ever made by us into Mexican territory. . . . We had supplies enough to last our whole tribe a year or more. . . .

During my many wars with the Mexicans I received eight wounds, as follows: shot in the right leg above the knee, and still carry the bullet; shot through the left forearm; wounded in the right leg below the knee with a saber; wounded on top of the head with the butt of a musket; shot just below the outer corner of the left eye; shot in left side; shot in the back. I have killed many Mexicans; I do not know how many, for frequently I did not count them. Some of them were not worth counting.

"SOME OF THEM were not worth counting." Geronimo's choice of words is shocking in its ferocity—yet the sentence reflects the driving force in his life. Unlike Sitting Bull and Chief Joseph, who sought freedom and independence for their people, Geronimo was a leader devoured by his personal torments, torments he sought to ease with warfare.

In 1861, his attention was diverted from the hated Mexican enemy to a new foe: white American soldiers. The United States had formally taken possession of New Mexico and Arizona from the republic of Mexico in 1848, but for most of a decade the scarcity of white settlers had left the region almost untouched by the change. The conflict could not be put off indefinitely: Americans were relentless in their search for new lands to mine and homestead—and when they arrived in the Southwest, they were bound to come to blows with the raiding, warrior culture of the Apaches. The impending war erupted in 1861 when Cochise, a proud warrior chief, disputed charges made by an unyielding army lieutenant stationed at the remote post of Apache Pass.

In the passage that follows, Geronimo provides a swift-moving account of his wars with the blue-coated American soldiers. In a blend of incidents and anecdotes rather than a coherent historical narrative, he occasionally errs as he recalls the particulars of a given event. His story, however, captures the bitter fighting between the small Apache bands and the organized military units, the long odds faced by warriors still armed with arrows and spears going against rifle-carrying troopers, and the cruelty of common soldiers and generals alike.

What comes to life in Geronimo's story is the revolution wrought by the coming of the Americans. The blue-coats transformed the traditional Apache-Mexican warfare of raid and counter-raid into a comprehensive campaign of conquest, designed to confine and control the seminomadic Native Americans. The United States government, unlike the Mexican, sought nothing less than systematic control of the war-torn region.

As happened elsewhere on the frontier, the whites did not simply fight to take away lands from the Indians—they sought to force their enemies to dispose of the whole way they thought of themselves and their environment. The Apaches had different ideas about control of territory than the Lakota of the Northern Plains, who fought to guard their hunting grounds; unlike Old Joseph of the Nez Percés, they did not plant poles to mark their terrain. Yet their culture depended upon village mobility, hunting, and gathering (even with their limited agriculture); and such a way of life could not coexist with private exploitation and ownership of the landscape. Nor would the Americans be satisfied with mere counter-raids to fend off the Apache war expeditions that bedeviled the Mexicans.

Though Geronimo hardly knew it when he first met white men, the Apaches faced the end of their existence as an independent nation of armed warriors. Free movement through the mountains was to be replaced with confinement to miserable reservations; self-sufficiency with a welfare system of government rations, supplied through contracts put out to local ranchers and businessmen. The Apaches thrived on war with their neighbors; but these new neighbors came in greater force than anything they had ever seen. And when the Indians reluctantly accepted the reservation system in the early 1870s, further trouble was sure to follow.

The inevitable conflict, however, erupted out of a stupid, brutal misunderstanding. In February 1861, Lieutenant George Bascom of the Seventh Infantry came to the mistaken conclusion that Cochise and his Chiricahua band had stolen cattle and a half-Indian boy named Mickey Free from a nearby ranch. Bascom refused to believe Cochise's honest denials, and bloodshed soon followed. Even the coming of the Civil War that year changed nothing. The Apaches continued to fight under the leadership of Cochise and his ally Mangas Colorado, with Geronimo as a key warrior. Freshly raised regiments of local white Westerners joined the battle under the command of General James Carleton and Colonel Kit Carson. As Geronimo relates below, both sides fought viciously, freely torturing and murdering captives and hostages.

In 1871, General Carleton was replaced by George Crook, a veteran division commander who had fought under General Sheridan in the Shenandoah Valley in the Civil War. Crook was a fighter of such ferocity that the Apaches dubbed him *Nantan Lupan*, the Gray Wolf Chief. Crook's campaign was to be a successful one; indeed, it was here that he won the reputation as an Indian fighter that would propel him to an important command in the Great Sioux War of 1876. Geronimo's account takes us through these years of hardship and bloodshed, until 1872, when he followed Cochise's lead and finally accepted the reservation system.

## The Coming of the White Men
*by Geronimo*

About the time of the massacre of Kaskiyeh we heard that some white men were measuring land to the south of us. In company with a number of other warriors I went to visit them. We could not understand them very well, for we had no interpreter, but we made a treaty with them by shaking hands and promising to be brothers. Then we made our camp near their camp, and they came to trade with us. . . .[8] Every day they

[8] These men were probably surveyors for the planned transcontinental railroad.

measured land with curious instruments and put down marks which we could not understand. They were good men, and we were sorry when they had gone into the west. They were not soldiers. These were the first white men I ever saw.

About ten years later some more white men came. These were all warriors. They made their camp on the Gila River south of Hot Springs. At first they were friendly and we did not dislike them, but they were not as good as those who came first. After about a year some trouble arose between them and the Indians, and I took the warpath as a warrior, not as a chief. I had not been wronged, but some of my people had been, and I fought with my tribe; for the soldiers and not the Indians were at fault.

Not long after this some of the officers of the United States troops invited our leaders to hold a conference at Apache Pass. Just before noon the Indians were shown into a tent and told that they would be given something to eat. When in the tent they were attacked by soldiers. Our chief, Mangas Colorado, and several other warriors, by cutting through the tent, escaped; but most of the warriors were killed or captured. Among the Bedonkohe Apaches killed at this time were Sanza, Kladatahe, Niyokahe, and Gopi. After this treachery the Indians went back to the mountains and left the fort entirely alone. . . .[9]

In a few days after the attack at Apache Pass we organized in the mountains and returned to fight the soldiers. There were two tribes—the Bedonkohe and the Chokonen Apaches, both commanded by Cochise. After a few days' skirmishing we attacked a freight train that was coming in with supplies for the fort. We killed some of the men and captured the others. These prisoners our chief offered to trade for the Indians whom the soldiers had captured at the massacre in the tent. This the officers refused, so we killed our prisoners, disbanded, and went into hiding in the mountains. . . .[10]

In a few days troops were sent to search for us, but as we were disbanded, it was, of course, impossible for them to locate any hostile camps. During the time they were searching for us many of our warriors (who were thought by the soldiers to be peaceable Indians) talked to the officers and men, advising them where they might find the camp they sought, and

[9] Geronimo has confused the individuals involved in this episode: on February 4, 1861, Lieutenant George Bascom seized Cochise and a number of his relatives in a tent at Apache Pass, demanding the return of a boy named Mickey Free who had been kidnapped from a local ranch. Only Cochise escaped, in the manner described (he and his people had nothing to do with the kidnapping); the rest were taken prisoner and held hostage.

[10] The army lieutenant refused to exchange prisoners, so an exchange of atrocities followed. The soldiers hung their prisoners and left them up to rot; the Apaches tied some of their hostages to the wheels of a wagon and set it on fire. This incident effectively set the tone of hostilities for the next ten years.

while they searched we watched them from our hiding places and laughed at their failures.[11]

After this trouble all of the Indians agreed not to be friendly with the white men any more. There was no general engagement, but a long struggle followed. Sometimes we attacked the white men—sometimes they attacked us. First a few Indians would be killed and then a few soldiers. I think the killing was about equal on each side. The number killed in these troubles did not amount to much, but this treachery on the part of the soldiers had angered the Indians and revived memories of other wrongs, so that we never again trusted the United States troops.

Perhaps the greatest wrong ever done to the Indians was the treatment received by our tribe from the United States troops about 1863. The chief of our tribe, Mangas Colorado, went to make a treaty of peace for our people with the white settlement at Apache Tejo, New Mexico. It had been reported to us that the white men in this settlement were more friendly and more reliable than those in Arizona, that they would live up to their treaties and would not wrong the Indians.

Mangas Colorado, with three other warriors, went to Apache Tejo and held a council with these citizens and soldiers. They told him that if he would come with his tribe and live near them, they would issue to him, from the government, blankets, flour, provisions, beef, and all manner of supplies. When he came back to our settlement he assembled the whole tribe in council. I did not believe that the people at Apache Tejo would do as they said and therefore I opposed the plan, but it was decided that with part of the tribe Mangas Colorado should return to Apache Tejo and receive an issue of rations and supplies. If they were as represented, and if these white men would keep the treaty faithfully, the remainder of the tribe would join him and we would make our permanent home at Apache Tejo. I was to remain in charge of that portion of the tribe which stayed in Arizona. We gave almost all our arms and ammunition to that portion of the tribe going to Apache Tejo, so that in case there should be treachery they would be prepared for any surprise. Mangas Colorado and about half of our people went to New Mexico, happy that now they had found white men who would be kind to them, and with whom they could live in peace and plenty.

No word ever came to us from them. From other sources, however, we heard that they had been treacherously captured and slain. In this dilemma we did not know just exactly what to do, but fearing that the troops who had captured them would attack us, we retreated into the mountains near Apache Pass. . . .[12]

[11] Another Apache method of throwing off pursuit was to set up dummy camps; the warriors went to great lengths to make them seem real, and they often succeeded in deceiving other Apaches working as scouts for the army.

[12] It was at this time that General James Henry Carleton took over the Department of New Mexico, and assigned Kit Carson and the First New Mexico Cavalry to attack the Apaches.

On this retreat, while passing through the mountains, we discovered four men with a herd of cattle. Two of the men were in front in a buggy and two were behind on horseback. We killed all four, but did not scalp them; they were not warriors. We drove the cattle back into the mountains, made a camp, and began to kill the cattle and pack the meat.

Before we had finished this work we were surprised and attacked by United States troops, who killed in all seven Indians—one warrior, three women, and three children. The government troops were mounted and so were we, but we were poorly armed, having given most of our weapons to the division of our tribe that had gone to Apache Tejo, so we fought mainly with spears, bows, and arrows. At first I had a spear, a bow, and a few arrows; but in a short time my spear and all my arrows were gone. Once I was surrounded, but by dodging from side to side of my horse as he ran I escaped. It was necessary during this fight for many of the warriors to leave their horses and escape on foot. But my horse was trained to come at call, and as soon as I reached a safe place, if not too closely pursued, I would call him to me. During this fight we scattered in all directions and two days later reassembled at our appointed place of rendezvous, about fifty miles from the scene of this battle.

About ten days later the same United States troops attacked our new camp at sunrise. The fight lasted all day, but our arrows and spears were gone before ten o'clock, and for the remainder of the day we had only rocks and clubs with which to fight. We could do little damage with these weapons, and at night we moved our camp about four miles back into the mountains where it would be hard for the cavalry to follow us. The next day our scouts, who had been left behind to observe the movements of the soldiers, returned, saying that the troops had gone back toward San Carlos Reservation.

A few days after this we were again attacked by another company of United States troops. Just before this fight we had been joined by a band of Chokonen Indians under Cochise, who took command of both divisions. We were repulsed, and decided to disband. After we had disbanded our tribe the Bedonkohe Apaches reassembled near their old camp vainly waiting for the return of Mangas Colorado and our kinsmen. No tidings came save that they had all been treacherously slain.[13] Then a council was held, and as it was believed that Mangas Colorado was dead, I was elected Tribal Chief.[14]

[13] Mangas Colorado was indeed dead. He had come in to a military post to negotiate his band's surrender, when he was taken prisoner. General Joseph West ordered that he should not live through the night. Two soldiers heated their bayonets over a fire and burned the chief's feet as he slept. When he leaped up, they butchered him for "attempted escape."

[14] It is highly unlikely that Geronimo was made tribal chief, which was a hereditary post. He was occasionally prone to exaggeration; his importance at the time was nothing like what legend has since made it out to be.

For a long time we had no trouble with anyone. It was more than a year after I had been made Tribal Chief that United States troops surprised and attacked our camp. They killed seven children, five women, and four warriors, captured all our supplies, blankets, horses, and clothing, and destroyed our tepees. We had nothing left; winter was beginning, and it was the coldest winter I ever knew. After the soldiers withdrew I took three warriors and trailed them. Their trail led back toward San Carlos. . . .[15]

My people were suffering much and it was deemed advisable to go where we could get more provisions. Game was scarce in our range then, and since I had been Tribal Chief I had not asked for rations from the government, nor did I care to do so, but we did not wish to starve. . . .

When I went to Apache Pass [Fort Bowie] I found General Howard in command, and made a treaty with him. This treaty lasted until long after General Howard had left our country. He had always kept his word with us and treated us as brothers. We never had so good a friend among the United States officers as General Howard. We could have lived forever at peace with him. If there is any pure, honest white man in the United States army, that man is General Howard. All the Indians respect him, and even to this day frequently talk of the happy times when General Howard was in command of our post. After he went away he placed an agent at Apache Pass who issued to us from the government clothing, rations, and supplies, as General Howard directed.[16] When beef was issued to the Indians I got twelve steers for my tribe, and Cochise got twelve steers for his tribe. Rations were issued about once a month, but if we ran out we only had to ask and we were supplied.

━━━━━

THE PEACE WAS not to last. First came the death of Cochise in 1874. He had commanded universal respect among his people, and had successfully kept them quiet. His eldest son and successor Taza could not keep his followers united, and the traditional raids resumed. Then came the transfer of General Crook to fight the Sioux. Relentless in war, Crook had also been fair and firm as an administrator. His departure opened the way for interference by civilians in the administration of rations to the reservation.

With the discovery of copper in Arizona in the 1870s, the desert territory began to attract white settlers and industry. In 1877, the influx

---

[15] With the end of the Civil War, General Carleton left the region, and the government put out peace feelers to the Apaches. Geronimo's narrative apparently leaps ahead to 1872, when General Oliver O. Howard arrived and made an agreement for peace with Cochise; General George Crook then launched a relentless campaign through 1873 to force the remaining holdouts to accept the reservation.

[16] The agent was Tom Jeffords, known as Taglito, the Red Beard. Jeffords was a stage owner whose bravery had won Cochise's friendship; Cochise insisted to General Howard that Taglito serve as their agent, and both Howard and Jeffords agreed.

was boosted by the Desert Land Act, which encouraged pioneers to establish stakes in the region. Then a true boom erupted when silver was discovered in Tombstone, and the country saw a new wave of ranchers, miners, and merchants. Power and wealth in this bustling territory was concentrated in the hands of a greedy, ambitious network of businessmen and power brokers known as the Tucson Ring.

The members of the Ring proved effective in pressuring Washington to respond to their demands in regard to the Apaches—demands that usually masked schemes for making money. The contracts for feeding the Apache reservations provided a particularly lucrative source of graft, leading to elaborate frauds. And the Ring agitated constantly for opening the Indian agency lands to white settlers—an agitation that took on added weight with the Tombstone boom.

The U.S. government had already begun to shrink the Apache reservations in 1875. After Cochise's death it planned to consolidate the various Apache agencies, eliminating Cochise's at Apache Pass and moving his Chiricahua band to the White Mountain, or San Carlos, reservation. San Carlos was a stretch of 2.5 million acres that already hosted seven often-hostile Apache bands, but Taza took most of his people there. Geronimo rebelled and fled to Mexico. In 1876, Taza died and his brother Naiche became chief.

The federal agent at San Carlos was John Clum, a fair-minded man who forced the military to withdraw and installed a system of Native American police and courts. But when Clum discovered that Geronimo had appeared on the Warm Springs agency in New Mexico, he had him arrested. He also arrested Victorio, leader of the Warm Springs band and Geronimo's old friend. Victorio was soon released, but he was deeply embittered.

In 1877, Clum resigned and the San Carlos reservation slipped into crisis. The Tucson Ring reached its hands ever deeper into the Indian agencies' funds, and the Apaches often went without critical rations. Frustrated and angry, Victorio led repeated outbreaks from the reservation until, in February 1879, orders were given to have him arrested. He escaped and embarked on an epic guerrilla campaign, ambushing U.S. cavalry detachments and raiding settlements through Arizona, New Mexico, Texas, and Mexico (where J.B. Gillett took part in the chase after his band). Finally, on October 14, 1880, Mexican soldiers trapped him and exterminated his people; only thirty warriors under the aging Nana escaped to wander the Mexican mountains.

Most of the other Apaches by this time had returned to the San Carlos reservation, where things went from bad to worse. The new agent, J.C. Tiffany, was openly corrupt, stirring further resentment. In 1881, a mystic named Nakaidoklini (who had studied at a Christian school in Santa Fe) introduced a new religion, similar to the later Ghost Dance of the northern Great Plains. Tiffany tried to have Nakaidoklini arrested. The result was an ambush of the army column sent to do the job, the death of the mystic, and a year of crisis—including yet another outbreak by Geronimo and others.

In 1882, the army restored the Department of Arizona to the command of *Nantan Lupan*, General George Crook. He had been off fighting the Sioux; now his knowledge of the Apaches was badly needed. Crook immediately set about two pressing tasks: reforming the reservation administration (including getting rid of Tiffany, who was indicted for massive corruption), and bringing in the renegades, including Geronimo, now raiding throughout the region. For this second chore, Crook quickly recruited hundreds of Apache scouts to do the tracking and fighting.

One of the young officers engaged in both tasks was Lt. Britton Davis. A thoughtful man of high principles, he was the son of Edmund J. Davis, the Republican Reconstruction governor of Texas hated by John Wesley Hardin. Davis was a remarkably open-minded man (one of the few in this book who seem not to have been particularly racist, even by today's standards); as he helped reform the San Carlos reservation, he became a keen student of the Apaches. He would need every bit of that knowledge when he went to the Mexican border to bring in Geronimo.

---

## Bringing in Geronimo
*by Lieutenant Britton Davis*

On September 4, 1882, General Crook took command of the Department of Arizona. He had previously subdued the Apache, in 1871–73, and knew them better than any other man in high command in the army. . . . As Bourke [his aide-de-camp] often said of him, "He was more Indian than the Indians themselves."

Immediately after taking command of the Department, Crook went to Fort Apache to learn from the Indians there the condition of affairs from their point of view. He met the principal chiefs, heard their complaints, promised to do what he could to rectify unjust conditions, and told them what in return he expected of them in the essentials of living at peace and going to work with a view to becoming self-supporting.

Continuing on to the Agency at San Carlos the General there prepared for business. He had been given full disciplinary control of the Indians of the entire Reservation, their rationing alone remaining under the jurisdiction of the agent, and this subject to the supervision of the military. The following officers had been ordered to report to the General at San Carlos: Emmet Crawford, Captain, 3rd Cavalry; Charles B. Gatewood, First Lieutenant, 6th Cavalry; and Britton Davis, Second Lieutenant, 3rd Cav-

alry. . . . San Carlos won our unanimous designation of it as "Hell's Forty
Acres."

A gravelly flat in the confluence of the two rivers rose some thirty feet or
so above the river bottoms and was dotted here and there by the drab
adobe buildings of the Agency. Scrawny, dejected lines of scattered cotton-
woods, shrunken, almost leafless, marked the course of the streams. Rain
was so infrequent that it took on the semblance of a phenomenon when it
came at all. Almost continuously dry, hot, dust- and gravel-laden winds
swept the plain, denuding it of every vestige of vegetation. In the summer a
temperature of 110 degrees in the shade was cool weather. At all other
times of the year flies, gnats, unnameable bugs—and I was about to say
"beasts of the air"—swarmed in millions. . . .

Everywhere the naked, hungry, dirty, frightened little Indian children,
darting behind brush or into wickiup [Apache lodges] at sight of you.
Everywhere the sullen, stolid, hopeless, suspicious faces of the older Indians challenging you. You felt the challenge in your very marrow—that
unspoken challenge to prove yourself anything else than one more liar and
thief, differing but little from the procession of liars and thieves who had
preceded you. . . .

Of us four, only Gatewood knew anything of the Apache. Graduated
from West Point in 1877, his experiences with them began two years later
in the fight with Victorio's band in the Black Range of New Mexico.
Thereafter, until I met him, he was almost continuously engaged in campaigns and scouting expeditions against them. Tall, spare, of extraordinary
endurance, patient, and fearless, he was the ideal selection for the job of
managing the White Mountain at Fort Apache. . . .

Of the five thousand Indians on the White Mountain Reservation about
four thousand were at or near the Agency at San Carlos, depending for
food on the government rations doled out to them there. Some two
hundred of the chiefs and principal men assembled for a conference with
the General. He heard their complaints, assured them he would have
abuses corrected as far as possible for him to do so, and told them what he
expected of those who wanted to live at peace and what the malcontents
might expect of him if they "started anything."

The Indians had just cause for complaint. Some of the reservations
originally assigned to them had been taken from them after they had
established themselves there. Other reservations had been cut down and
the hunting grounds, on which they depended for a large part of their
subsistence, greatly restricted. They had been driven onto this barren
waste at San Carlos with no provision for self-support. A nomad people
who had lived off the country, subsisting on game, wild fruits, nuts, and
certain herbs, they had not the faintest idea how to subsist by agriculture
and no means to that end had they known how.

They did know, however, that rations provided for them by the government were being openly sold to neighboring towns and mining camps. That beef on the hoof, forming the principal part of their rations, was so thin that it was hardly skin and bone. That the weekly issue of flour, the principal portion of the ration, would hardly suffice a family for one day. That other components of the ration were almost negligible when issued and frequently not issued at all.

There is nothing equal to idleness as a breeder for discontent. Here were five thousand restless, nomadic people who all their lives had roamed unrestrained throughout the Southwest, with many generations of nomadic blood behind them, herded now into a small tract of desert land and told to sit down, fold their hands, and be "good Indian" no matter how much we lied to and robbed them. . . .

The Bureau of Indian Affairs of the Department of the Interior at Washington had turned over to the army the task of controlling the Indians on the reservation and of returning to the reservation those still out; principally the Chiricahua and Warm Springs in Mexico. The Bureau, however, continued its agent at the agency to distribute the Indian rations. [The agent assigned to San Carlos, however, soon left.] His place was filled by his clerk, Colonel Beaumont, a fine old gentleman, an ex-officer of the Civil War, and an immediate buddy of ours. He gave every assistance and cooperation in his power, saw that the Indians got what was due them, and conducted his business in an irreproachable manner. . . .

To me was assigned the command of the Apache scouts [Indian warriors working for the army] at San Carlos, the quartermaster and commissary duties at the post, and command at San Carlos in Crawford's absence. . . . Al Sieber was appointed chief of scouts with Archie MacIntosh and Sam Bowman as his assistants. Mickey Free[17] was enlisted as a scout with the pay of a first sergeant, but his role was that of interpreter. . . .

Al Sieber, six feet one, about 190 pounds of bone and muscle, a little past forty years of age, was of Pennsylvania Dutch stock. He had been for eight years in the employ of the government as scout and in various other capacities against the Apache. Capable and courageous, the Indians feared and respected him. A better selection for chief of scouts could not have been made. . . . If there was ever a man who actually did not know physical fear, that man was Al Sieber! He never hesitated when it became necessary to throw caution aside. He was in constant danger of assassination as many of the Indians had personal grudges against him; but he went about his work as though all the world were his friends. . . .

Some years before I knew him[18] he was out with a troop of cavalry

---

[17] Mickey Free was the boy whose abduction led to the start of white warfare against the Apaches in 1861.

[18] This anecdote has been moved for continuity.

hunting hostile Apache. The command had a brush with a small band of them, the principal result of which was the capture of one lone Indian. The command had been out quite a while on the scout, were at a considerable distance from any source of supplies, and rations were very low. As they were breaking camp the morning after the capture, Sieber heard the officer who had command express regret that they had a captive who had to be fed and guarded until they reached a military post. "Don't mind him. I'll take care of him," offered Sieber; and the command moved out leaving Sieber, the captive, and a trooper who had been on night guard to follow.

The trooper was crouched by the embers of the cook's fire, eating his breakfast; the Indian, his breakfast finished, was crouched beside him smoking a cigarette. Sieber walked up behind the Indian and shot him through the head. As the body pitched forward into the fire the trooper merely glanced up at Sieber with the protest: "Say, Al, if you were going to do that why in hell didn't you do it before he got his belly full of grub!". . .

Such was the callousness with which the white man had come to regard the taking of the red man's life. Exasperated, our senses blunted by Indian atrocities, we hunted and killed them as we hunted and killed wolves. . . .

The administrative personnel completed, our first care was the organization of our scout companies and pack trains. In speaking of scouts I refer only to Indians. We used no civilians as scouts. Five companies were enlisted under the designations of Companies A, B, C, D, and E. Each company ordinarily comprised a first sergeant, a second sergeant, two corporals, and twenty-six privates. . . .

With just rationing, fair prices in the trader's store, and a little money [earned by a program of the army buying hay from the Apaches] to buy the simple things they craved, the rancor of the Indians quickly faded away. Little children no longer fled from us. The women began to appear in fresh, clean clothes; laughing, joking, jollying. . . . The men sought us for talks and cigarettes. We were getting their confidence, of all things the most necessary to our control of them. . . .

In March 1883, the General began organizing for an expedition into Mexico to rout the hostiles out. Permission to cross the border had been granted by the Mexican government. . . . With about two hundred Apache scouts enlisted from among the friendly Indians of the reservation, a troop of cavalry, and two pack trains, the General entered Mexico early in April. Under the guidance of Tzoe [a prisoner from the hostile band], the expedition penetrated the Sierra Madre mountains without their presence becoming known to the hostiles. About sixty miles northeast of the town of Nacori in Sonora the main body of the expedition was halted and Crawford, with Gatewood and forty or fifty of the scouts, went forward with Tzoe to reconnoiter. They surprised the camp of Benito while most of the men were away with a war party raiding Mexican settlements, killed several of the occupants of the camp, and captured several women and children. . . .

Through the Indian women that Crawford had captured, communication was established with the other camps of the hostiles and the chiefs were induced to come to the General's camp for a talk. The hostile camps were scattered over a tract of mountainous country some fifty miles square, much of it impregnable for troops. Two years later I spent three months scouting in it and found it hopeless for any sort of campaigning other than with Indians afoot.

The hostiles assured the General that they were tired of constant warfare. The fact that American troops with Indians of their own race had routed them out of their fastness in these Mexican mountains was a stunning blow to them. They wanted peace—in capital letters, so their sentiments might not be mistaken . . . "But," said the chiefs, "many of our people are scattered through the mountains in a dozen camps. It will take time to get word to them that peace has been declared. It will be especially difficult to get this word to them now as the alarm of the attack on Benito's camp has spread throughout the mountains."

It was finally agreed that the General should return to the United States with as many of the old men, women, and children as could be gotten together at once; some of the men to accompany them. The others to come in as soon as they could get word to the various rancherias and gather up their livestock. This they estimated would take about "two moons."

On June 23, the General arrived at San Carlos with 325 of the Chiricahua and Warm Springs bands; 52 men and 273 women and children. . . . Those who had come in were mostly Warm Springs. The greater portion of the Chiricahua still remained in Mexico under their hereditary chiefs, Mangas and Nachite [Naiche, or Natchez], the subchiefs Chatto and Zele, and the troublemaker, Geronimo. . . .

The difficulties of subduing the Apache were so unique that they were not understood even by many of our superior officers in Washington. . . . The Apache was unlike any other Indian tribe the whites have ever fought since civilization began to creep over the North American continent. His mode of warfare was peculiarly his own. He saw no reason for fighting unless there was something tangible and immediate to be gained. To satisfy his pressing needs for arms, ammunition, food, or clothing he would raid isolated ranches, the suburbs of small Mexican towns, or ambush travelers. But he had no such sense of bravado as animated other Indian tribes who, resisting encroachments on the Indian's domain, fought us man to man in the open. His creed was "fight and run away, live to fight another day." Corner him, however, and you would find him as desperate and dangerous as a wounded wolf.

Only when cornered, or to delay pursuit of his women and children, would he engage a force anywhere near the strength of his own. To fight soldiers merely in defense of his country, he considered the height of folly; and he never committed that folly if he could avoid it. . . . Defeat was the invariable portion for the Mexican troops, regulars or irregulars, who attempted to invade the Indian stronghold; and they had quit the game as not worth the candle, leaving the hostiles free to raid their own towns, New Mexico, and Arizona at their sweet wills. The Indians would frequently enter the Mexican towns, declare an armistice, and go on a high old drunk with the citizens of the town to celebrate it. A month later they might be at war with that town and at peace with another not twenty miles away. . . .

[Lt. Davis was then assigned to wait at the border with a detachment and escort the remaining hostile bands to the San Carlos Reservation.]

## GERONIMO ARRIVES

[After escorting the hostile band led by Chatto from Mexico back to the reservation,] I returned to the border to await Geronimo, of whom we had had no news. A dreary wait of six weeks followed with no sign of him. My scouts, almost all Chiricahua and Warm Springs, became impatient. The services of my old friend, the medicine man, were called for to determine where Geronimo was and when he would appear.

Preparations for the offices of the Reverend Doctor were elaborate. First a brush hut was built on a plot of ground a little remote from the camp, so he might be undisturbed. The hut was covered with canvas from the pack trains, only a small opening being left. With the pouch of "medicine" the Doctor entered the hut and the opening was closed.

There he remained all that day and into the night uttering incantations and from time to time burning a pungent powder, the odor of which we could smell a dozen yards away. Toward nine or ten o'clock he came out of the hut; but the incantations were not yet finished. From his right hand depended a thin buckskin thong with a hole in it. Twirling this around his head it gave out a shrill, whistling noise, not unlike the call of a bird.

Around and around his hut he went, then around the camp and through it, north to south, east to west, swinging his call and uttering incantations. The scouts, squatting in a circle, awaited his decision. The camp and all points of the compass properly incanted, he stopped at the scouts' camp fire, threw on it his pungent powder, and raising his face to the stars in a singsong chant made many gestures with his waving arms; then suddenly he ceased and, bathed in sweat, tottering a little with weakness, announced that he had found Geronimo.

Entering the circle of the scouts, he prolonged the suspense for several minutes while he gazed at the stars and mumbled a final incantation. Then he announced that Geronimo was three days away, riding on a white mule, and bringing a great lot of horses.

I was sending daily three or four scouts to patrol south and west along the border as we were not sure at just what point Geronimo might come in. Some four or five days after the Reverend Doctor's prophecy the patrol came in with a report that Geronimo was nearing the border and would arrive that afternoon; also, that he was riding a white pony.

How did the medicine man come so close to it? A signal from Geronimo's party? Not likely, as the Doctor was of the Tonto-Mohave tribe, bitter enemies of the Chiricahua. . . .

The only livestock Zele and Chatto had brought with them were ponies, a hundred or so with each band and stolen, of course, from the Mexican ranches below the border. Geronimo was more provident. As I sat on my mule at the international line watching the Indians coming up through the valley, I was surprised to see a great cloud of dust following them at an interval of two or three miles. My first thought was of a large force of Mexican troops in pursuit. But the Indians in advance, now plainly visible, showed no signs of haste or excitement.

In a few minutes Geronimo and fifteen or sixteen of his men and some seventy women and children arrived at the line. I had sent two of my scouts to meet them below the line and explain who we were and our reason for being there; a necessary precaution, taken also with Zele and Chatto, as the Indians were as wary and suspicious as so many wild animals.

Riding up to me and checking his pony only when its shoulder had bumped the shoulder of my mule, his first words were an angry demand to know why there was need of an escort for him and his people to the reservation. He had made peace with the Americans, why then was there danger of their attacking him?

I explained that there were some bad Americans just as there were some bad Indians and that on passing near a town some of these bad men, full of whiskey, might try to cause trouble. That the scouts were now American soldiers and if an American killed one of them the man would himself be hanged by the Americans. This satisfied him; he shook hands with me and assured me that he and I were thenceforth brothers.

That settled, I called his attention to the cloud of dust that was slowly approaching. "*Ganado*," he explained, laconically, in Spanish. And cattle they were, 350 head of beeves, cows, and half-grown calves stolen from the Mexican ranches just below the international line.

My heart beats went up to a record!

On my two previous trips to the reservation I had avoided attack from the excited citizens of the southern Arizona towns by rapid marches of forty or fifty miles daily, keeping away from the traveled routes and attracting the least attention possible from any of the ranches near which we had to pass. We made the 175 miles to the reservation in four or five days. But with this herd of slow-moving cattle, at their normal gait of twelve or fifteen miles daily it would take us two weeks. . . . To add to my woes, Geronimo's next demand was for a three-day halt then and there to rest the cattle in the luxuriant grass of the valley, explaining that they had been driven hard for fear of pursuit by the Mexican owners.

More time for the enraged citizens to organize and put their threats into execution! I vetoed the proposal emphatically and compromised on a start the following afternoon. . . .

We were traveling only eighteen or twenty miles a day, less than half the distance I had covered on my two previous trips, but Geronimo was not satisfied. Every night he would come to my tent with a protest against such long marches—we were "running all the fat off the cattle and they would not be fit for trading when we reached the reservation." . . .

I had been holding in reserve one argument . . . and now I sprang it on him. He had seen General Crook in Mexico with American troops. The Mexicans had the same right to come into the United States. We were too near the border to risk stopping, as the Mexicans might be following us.

"Mexicans!" he snarled. "Mexicans! My squaws can whip all the Mexicans in Chihuahua."

"But the Mexicans have plenty of cartridges, and you have practically none," I argued, as I pointed to his nearly empty cartridge belt.

"We don't fight Mexicans with cartridges," he replied contemptuously. "Cartridges cost too much. We keep them to fight your white soldiers. We fight Mexicans with rocks." I capitulated and compromised on a halt for one day. . . .

[Along the way, the party was overtaken by a customs inspector and a U.S. marshal, who had a warrant for the arrest of Geronimo on murder charges. The marshal also served a subpoena on Davis, ordering him to assist in the arrest. Davis was at a loss. Fortunately, he was then visited by a friend and fellow officer named Blake. The two men concocted an escape plan to get the hostile band back to the reservation. The two officers got the officials roaring drunk, sent them to bed, and then went to present their plan to Geronimo.]

I had decided to tell Geronimo neither the whole truth nor the exact truth; either would have sent him scurrying back to Mexico if the scouts did not kill him in the attempt. I did not know what my scout sergeant had in mind, but I did know that he was of a tribe hostile to the Chiricahua and that he hated Geronimo from the depths of his soul.

I told Geronimo that the two men he had seen talking to me in the afternoon were civilian officers of the government in Washington. That when anyone brought cattle in the United States they had to pay for them and these officers were there to collect the money. That the charge on his cattle was about a thousand dollars, which the collector demanded that I pay, or that I take the cattle to Tucson for sale. That I had refused to do either and they intended to take the cattle away in the morning and send them to Tucson with the cowboys at the ranch [located nearby, where the two officials were sleeping off their drunk].

To this I knew that he, Geronimo, would not consent, and to avoid trouble we had better start for the reservation immediately and get so far on the road by morning that pursuit would be useless. My brother [Blake, the visiting officer] would go with him and I would remain at the ranch to throw the officers off the trail if they tried to follow him.

As I talked to him he stood staring me straight in the eyes, his anger mounting and his lips twitching as he shifted his rifle from arm to arm. My sergeant was standing silently beside him, the other scouts and Geronimo's men forming a circle around us; Blake, with his pistol drawn but concealed under his coat, was backing me up. The whole group was tense and waiting.

As I expected, Geronimo's answer was an angry and emphatic "No!" Then he went on to say that he had come in peace but had found only trouble and threats. He was tired of it. . . . Here my Indian sergeant took a hand and words shot from him like the rattle of a machine gun in action as he faced Geronimo. What he said I never knew. The moment was too tense for Mickey Free to interrupt and interpret.

Geronimo's feathers began to droop. He glanced at his men and at the scouts. Nothing in them seemed to encourage him. After one or two ineffectual attempts to break in on the sergeant with arguments of his own, he confined himself to grunts and monosyllables. I saw that he was weakening and suggested that probably he was afraid his people were not smart enough to get away without the men in the ranch knowing.

This touched him in a tender spot and he instantly resented it. "His people could leave me standing where I was and I would not know that they were gone." I followed up my advantage by pointing out what a joke it would be on the officers in the ranch if they woke up in the morning and found that the Indians with all the cattle and ponies had disappeared.

Geronimo almost smiled, hesitated for a moment, looked inquiringly at his men, saw no opposition from them, and the battle was won. . . .

[That night, Blake led the Apaches as they safely stole away. Davis remained behind and explained to the officials—now with terrible hangovers—that he had been ordered by his superior officer, Blake, to stay and comply with the subpeona. The marshal and customs officer rode home, angry at being outmaneuvered by the young lieutenant.]

After two days of hard riding I overtook Blake a few miles south of the reservation line and we delivered our charges to Crawford at San Carlos without further incident. Geronimo's theft of the cattle profited him little. They were taken from him and turned in to the agency for beef, the Mexican owners being later compensated by our government. The loss of his prized possessions, after all he had gone through to obtain and preserve them, became a thorn in Geronimo's side and one of the main factors in the outbreak a year later, when . . . he left the reservation and made history in the Southwest by what has become known as the Geronimo campaign.

GERONIMO WAS NOT the only war leader to persist in his resistance to confinement—nor was he even the leading chief, or even a hereditary chief at all. But, aging though he was, his inability to accept defeat long after almost every other Indian leader had surrendered made him the personification of the Apache warrior in many eyes.

His return to the reservation took on symbolic meaning as well. After the death of Cochise, intransigent warriors such as Geronimo had turned the reservations into safe havens as they continued their traditional raids. Year after year, fresh outbreaks occurred, as small parties struck across the Southwest (skirmishing, occasionally, with rangers such as J.B. Gillett); occasionally, major crises led to larger breakouts, as such gifted commanders as Victorio took their people on the warpath. But the attack of *Nantan Lupan* in 1883 changed the old rules. The Mexicans had opened their border to pursuit by the U.S. Army, and General Crook's use of Apache scouts allowed him to penetrate the Sierra Madre fortress. Geronimo found he had nowhere left to hide.

The clash of cultures was far from over, but the clash of arms was almost at an end. After long resistance, the Apaches were just about beaten. As far as the American government was concerned, the Southwest was truly conquered territory. But it would take one final, climactic campaign—drawing in thousands of troops and destroying scores of lives—to truly break the independence of these proud, ferocious warriors.

# 12

# THE LINCOLN COUNTY WAR

Even before the final defeat of the Apache guerrillas, the nation's attention was drawn across the border to Lincoln County, in the New Mexico Territory. For most of 1878, the people of Lincoln County fought a ferocious civil war—an epic battle of economic domination and resistance, of frontier values and ethnic hostilities. What began as a feud between two would-be kingpins transformed (in the eyes of most of the local population, at least) into a fight between small ranchers and farmers on one side and monopoly power on the other, between the ruling political ring and rural Anglo and Hispanic communities.

In the late 1870s, Lincoln County was a vast, empty tract of southeastern New Mexico—an area about the size of South Carolina, with only two thousand residents.[19] The population was overwhelmingly Hispanic, mingling with a few white ranchers along the Ruidoso, Hondo, and Feliz rivers. To the west, just outside the county line, was the Mescalero Apache Agency. To the east, near the town of Roswell on the Pecos River, lived John Chisum, the greatest cattle baron of the Southwest. A group of Anglo small ranchers dwelt farther down the Pecos, at the Seven Rivers settlement. These independent cowboys (mainly former Texans) raided Chisum's vast herds to build their own; not surprisingly, Chisum and the Seven Rivers cowboys were sworn enemies.

The center of economic and political life, however, was the town of Lincoln and the nearby military post, Fort Stanton. With only five hundred people, Lincoln contained a quarter of the county's population, and served as its rudimentary seat of government. Almost all business in the county flowed through Lincoln—and everything in Lincoln flowed through Lawrence G. Murphy & Company, known as "The House." After arriving in Lincoln at the end of the Civil War, Murphy had established a monopoly over commercial transactions in the county. Through the skillful use of debt and political connections, Murphy forced ranchers off their land at will, single-handedly set produce and cattle prices, and controlled the

[19] This comparison, and almost all of the information in this section, can be found in the works of Robert Utley, the foremost authority on the Lincoln County War (in particular, see *High Noon in Lincoln* and *Billy the Kid*).

results of almost every election. The supply contracts for Fort Stanton and the Mescalero Apache Agency were all funneled through the dictatorial Murphy, and his mercantile store provided the only real retail outlet in the county. His only rival was John Chisum, who largely kept to himself over on the Pecos; the Seven Rivers cowboys, however, linked arms with The House in their hostility to Chisum.

Murphy's power was enhanced by his close connections to the Santa Fe Ring, the circle of Republican politicians who ran the New Mexico Territory like a private fief.[20] Most important was the U.S. district attorney, Thomas Benton Catron (who, historian Robert Utley tells us, "reigned as kingpin"). The other key players included Governor Samuel Axtell, district attorney William Rynerson, and district judge Warren Bristol; locally, Murphy had the firm support of Sheriff William Brady. The last—but not least—weapon in the Murphy arsenal was a band of gunslingers under the command of Texas badman Jesse Evans.

Murphy's most important subordinates were two fellow Irish Catholics named James Dolan and John Riley. Riley was a skilled political schemer, while Dolan was a hard-nosed tyrant like Murphy himself. Just about the time the Lincoln County War erupted, Murphy retired (the victim of advanced alcoholism) and put Dolan in charge of The House, with all its connections and gunmen.

Dolan proved an energetic, underhanded leader of what was now James Dolan & Company, but he suffered from the burdens of overextended credit and extravagant spending. Economic crisis drove Dolan to desperation; by the time the fighting started, he had mortgaged everything—including the store, his own ranch, and his cattle—to Santa Fe kingpin Thomas Catron.

Even as Dolan's economic monopoly teetered on the brink of bankruptcy, a rival appeared in the form of a young Englishman. John H. Tunstall arrived in Lincoln County at the end of 1876, determined to build his own ring and take over domination of the area for himself. Tunstall was no altruist: he told his parents in London that he aimed "to get the half of every dollar that is made in the county *by anyone.*" He acquired an ally in another recent arrival, a lawyer named Alexander McSween. Tunstall acquired livestock and a ranch, and together with McSween created a store to rival the Murphy-Dolan company. Chisum—interested in breaking The House's monopoly—also put some money into the operation.

As Dolan and Riley watched uneasily, Tunstall recruited his own gunmen among the Anglo ranchers of the western part of the county. Most important was Richard Brewer, a man who was deep in debt to The

---

[20] Murphy himself was a Democrat, probably less from conviction than from a need to control politics in the firmly Democratic Lincoln County (as seen in his easy cooperation with the Republicans who dominated the Ring). Power, not political sentiment, determined the relations of the Santa Fe Ring.

House and bitterly resented it. Another cowboy was a teenager on the run after killing a notorious bully. The youngster had a fanatic devotion to firearms, constantly practicing with his Winchester rifle and .41-caliber "self-cocker" revolver, the Colt Thunderer. He went by a number of names, including Billy Bonney, "Kid" Antrim, or just the Kid.

Most of the county residents reacted with joy to Tunstall and McSween's venture. Unaware of the Englishman's plan to create a monopoly for himself, they eagerly supported his side in the looming duel with Dolan. Especially hopeful were the Hispanics, who were sorely oppressed by the financial manipulations of Murphy and his heirs. The Anglo ranchers of the western part of the county aligned with Tunstall and McSween for many of the same reasons. These men would soon form the core of a fighting band known as the Regulators.

When the fighting between the two sides finally exploded, the war subtly changed into a struggle against the territory's political and economic powers. McSween and Tunstall might have been angling for personal gain, but men fought for them out of a desire for freedom and independence— the lure that had drawn them to this corner of the frontier in the first place. As a result, the Lincoln County War became the archetypical frontier battle, a war between the rugged individualist (or, more correctly, the rural community) and the encroaching tentacles of the political and economic kingpins—the wirepullers, corporations, and big businessmen. In origin, it was a feud between ambitious men; in the minds of the fighters, it was a battle against power.[21]

One of the stalwarts of the Regulators was a white rancher named George Coe, who with his cousin Frank ran a successful ranch in Lincoln County. George had run up against the power of The House more than once, and he eagerly joined the McSween side. Unfortunately, his story (extensively edited here to restore chronological continuity) misses much of the elaborate legal maneuvering behind the scenes, as each side struggled for the cover of law. But Coe vividly captures the rising competition that led Dolan to unleash his gunmen on Tunstall, and the fighting that climaxed in a five-day battle in the town of Lincoln.

## A Civil War in New Mexico
*by George W. Coe (as told to Nan Hillary Harrison)*

Now, to go back to my entrance into this Ruidoso Valley, March 18, 1876.[22] . . . The Coe boys [including George and his cousin Frank] were

---

[21] In fact, The House partisans saw it in a similar light, depicting themselves as the guardians of decent society, and the Regulators as riffraff and outlaws.

[22] This and the following paragraph have been moved for chronological continuity.

recognized as the best-equipped farmers who had ever entered Lincoln County. We brought in the first mowing-machine, and our principal products were potatoes, corn, and wheat. There was a flour mill on the ranch and an old tavern where travelers were taken care of. In the fall of '76, part of our outfit remained on the ranch while others took the mowing-machine and went out on the plains and cut hay to supply Fort Stanton. The prairie grass grew rank to a height of three or four feet. We sold this hay at sixty dollars a ton on contract.

From the time that we had settled here, there were two decided factions. One was the Lincoln crowd, and the other lived along the Ruidoso.[23] We were friendly with the Lincoln contingent, but were not intimately associated with them. . . . For some time we had no church services or schools, but we had our social gatherings, occasional dances, and picnics. At the dances Frank Coe and I were the official fiddlers, and I'm tellin' you we had as much wholesome fun as any bunch of cow punchers out West. There were vivacious, native [Hispanic] ladies who attended these *bailes*, and they were just as decorous as they are today. The majority of white settlers at that time were bachelors. Prominent among whom were the Coe boys, Doc Scurlock, Charlie Bowdre, Johnny Hurley, and Dick Brewer. . . .

Conditions in Lincoln County at this time were very unsettled. Fort Stanton was a four-company post established in 1852, and the only town of any importance besides Lincoln. It contained a post trader who kept a clubhouse for the soldiers and also handled merchandise. His and the store of the Murphy-Dolan firm were the only general stores in the county. . . .

[Fort Stanton, together with the Mescalero Apache Agency,] was really the only market for produce in the Southwest. Of many articles, such as beef, hay, and grain, the supply was not nearly sufficient to meet the demand. . . .

In 1866, at the end of the Civil War, a company of California volunteers was ordered to Fort Stanton and discharged. Prominent among the number was Major Murphy, Colonel Fritz, Jim Dolan, Johnny Riley, and Major Brady. Besides these, there were a large number of private soldiers. The officers at once recognized the great possibilities for money-making that this new Territory offered. Such men as Murphy, Dolan, Fritz, and Riley were not slow in taking advantage of an opportunity such as comes to few men. They embarked in a big mercantile business in Lincoln, and during the first few years they accumulated large wealth. They enjoyed every luxury that the age could supply, in spite of their remoteness from civilization. They became the dominant power politically, financially, and socially

---

[23] There were also two other factions along the Pecos River: cattle baron John Chisum, and a group of small ranchers located near Seven Rivers (who built their herds from Chisum's cattle).

on the Western frontier. They were capable, educated, and experienced. This gave them preference and advantage not accorded to the ordinary pioneer. They obtained from the Government the exclusive right to furnish Fort Stanton with supplies. This in itself was a strong financial asset.

Politics at this time seemed of no real importance to the natives. This gave the Murphy-Dolan company a better chance to gain a controlling interest in every line of industry. . . .

The concern began to totter before the ravages of extravagant spending, too much business done on credit, and bad collections. But in spite of all warnings, the owners kept to a pace far in excess of their incomes. Major Murphy, the financial head of the company, dissipated so recklessly that in later years he became merely a figurehead in the firm.[24] To make matters worse, a rival store began to take away a large share of the trade. The leaders of this enterprise, which was to break down the Murphy-Dolan monopoly, were Alexander McSween and John H. Tunstall.

## MCSWEEN AND TUNSTALL

Some ten years after the arrival in Lincoln of Murphy and his crowd, Alexander McSween, a brilliant young attorney from the East, started westward in search of health. He was accompanied by his young bride. They had already entered New Mexico, when, one evening, while enjoying their campfire, they discovered another camper nearby and made his acquaintance. This stranger was none other than Attorney Miguel Otero of Santa Fe, who advised McSween to go to Lincoln, as there were golden opportunities there for one of his type. McSween's meeting with this genial citizen and his acceptance of his advice to locate in this seeming utopia proved to be the most unfortunate event of his life.

McSween had been educated to be a Presbyterian minister and he was a Christian gentleman. After his arrival in Lincoln, he was soon employed by the Murphy-Dolan company as their legal adviser. . . .

Mrs. McSween was a polished and cultured lady. She was also a fine musician. Hers was the only piano in this part of the world, and it created no little excitement as it was being freighted through the country from St. Louis into this wild territory. After its arrival, McSween's home naturally became the center of social activities.

My personal opinion is that McSween was the most admirable character that ever came to this part of the country. My reason for this is that, amidst all the outlawry, injustice, and vice, Mr. McSween and his sister Mrs.

[24] The company was actually called L.G. Murphy & Co., until Murphy retired and protege James Dolan (with partner John Riley) took over, when it was renamed Jas. Dolan & Co. Murphy, suffering the ravages of alcoholism, sold out to Dolan in March 1877.

Shields kept up their faith and continued their Christian living and teaching. . . . He was never known to pick up a gun during all his terrible experiences in the Lincoln County War. He lived in a hornet's nest and was never stung. He stood alone and the mob respected his fearlessness. . . . He retired from the Murphy-Dolan company's employ when the affairs of this firm got to be so deeply involved and became John Chisum's attorney. . . .

About the time that McSween was retiring from the Murphy employ, there arrived in Lincoln a wealthy, cultured young Englishman from London, named John H. Tunstall. He was an attractive and rather striking figure, dressed as a Britisher, with a distinctive English accent, and he created quite a sensation as he mingled good-naturedly with the crowd. He soon won people to him, and they interested and pleased him. He decided at once to make this new wonderland his home.

His first business venture was to buy the ranch on the Río Feliz and stock it well with cattle and horses. He made his home in Lincoln. It was quite natural that he and McSween, with so much in common, should become friends. Tunstall proposed a partnership mercantile business in Lincoln, which was eagerly accepted by McSween. However, Mrs. McSween, with a woman's intuition and divination, argued against the proposition. She declared it would lead to jealousies from the Murphy-Dolan faction with unpleasant possibilities ahead.

The store was built and well stocked at a heavy cost, and was from the first a flourishing rival of the Murphy-Dolan Mercantile Company. When this venture was well under way, Tunstall, McSween, and John Chisum incorporated a partnership bank in one end of the store, and success seemed to be crowning their efforts. But the Murphy faction was looking on jealously, waiting its chance to overthrow this dangerous rival.

The chance came in the quarrel over the estate of Colonel Fritz.

It was while McSween was in the employ of this firm that Colonel Fritz, who had previously had an interest in the Murphy-Dolan company, returned to Germany and died there. He left an insurance policy in favor of his brother Charlie Fritz and his sister Mrs. Sholland. As McSween was the attorney for the firm, he was the logical person to collect the policy. In order to do this, he paid his own expenses to New York City, for which service he was to receive a commission. After his return, owing to the fact that [he was not paid his fee], he refused to pay all of the policy to the two contending heirs. This created considerable friction because of the fact that Major Murphy [actually James Dolan] held papers against the policy. He claimed that Colonel Fritz had deposited these as collateral for a debt.

The collecting of the ten-thousand-dollar Fritz insurance money by McSween furnished the Murphy faction an opportunity to issue an attachment on McSween's property, and also the property belonging to Tunstall, on the grounds that they were partners and therefore both were liable. Otherwise there would have been no way in which Tunstall could be drawn into the controversy as they wished. . . . It did not really matter whether the attachment issued against [Tunstall] was on account of the insurance money or some other charge. The point to consider is this: Why did it take a posse of fifteen or twenty men to serve an attachment on a peaceable citizen when it ordinarily takes but one man to perform this duty? My theory is that it was a frame-up to kill Tunstall.[25]

### A REMARKABLE FRIENDSHIP

Sometime before the [attachment] was issued for Tunstall's [property], he had met William H. Bonney, who was known as "Billy the Kid." By chance Tunstall became acquainted with this dramatic figure immediately after Billy made his first appearance in Lincoln. To Tunstall, a foreign, city-bred gentleman, Billy represented a new and interesting type, and with kindly feeling he was drawn toward the boy and invited him to lunch. This was the beginning of a most unusual and sincere friendship. Billy was looking for a job, and inquired of Tunstall whether or not he could give him some ranch work to do. Before they separated, Tunstall promised to find a place for him if possible.

Billy then came down to the Dick Brewer Ranch on the Ruidoso. He was the center of interest everywhere he went, and though heavily armed, he was as gentlemanly as a college-bred youth. He quickly became acquainted with everyone, and with his humorous and pleasing personality grew to be a community favorite. In fact, Billy was so popular there wasn't enough of him to go around. He had a beautiful voice and sang like a bird. One of our special amusements was to assemble every few nights and have a singing. The thrill of those happy evenings still lingers—a pleasant memory—and tonight I would give a lot to live through one again. Frank Coe and I played the fiddles, and we all danced and here Billy, too, was in demand. . . .

It was early in the year 1878 that he went to work for Tunstall. This was the first time in his life that he had ever drawn a cent of wages, and the only opportunity he had to make good. . . .

### THE MURDER OF TUNSTALL

On the evening of February 18, 1878, Tunstall was riding from the Feliz Ranch, accompanied by Billy the Kid and Dick Brewer.[26] As they entered the canyon, a flock of wild turkeys ran out of the timber in front of them.

[25] Jim Dolan and John Riley also had Judge Bristol issue a warrant for McSween's arrest on charges of defrauding the Fritz heirs of their insurance money.

[26] Tunstall had spent the day recruiting gunmen for his fight against James Dolan, the mastermind of what Coe calls the "Murphy-Dolan" faction. Dolan (who commanded his own army of fighters, under Jesse Evans) had engaged in elaborate legal maneuvers to undo McSween and Tunstall, taking over their store and, as Coe tells, sending a posse after Tunstall's property.

Tunstall never carried a gun, but the other two decided to have a turkey dinner next day, and lit out after the flock. It is my impression that the boys knew nothing of Tunstall's predicament until they heard the shooting. They immediately turned back to see what was happening and discovered a posse of men in the valley. They felt sure that Tunstall was dead. Knowing there was danger ahead, they hid in the brush until the posse, shouting and swearing, rode away. Then they rode down to where Tunstall's dead body lay, his face turned to the sky and his coat under his head. His horse lay beside him with the man's hat under his head. Man and horse had gone to sleep together. . . .

Many conflicting stories are told regarding this murder, but I am giving the facts as I know them and as told me by Brewer and Billy the Kid.

We brought the body to the Brewer home, placed it in a carriage, and drove into Lincoln. The entire community was aroused, and, gathering in a body, followed the procession into town. The Reverend Mr. Shields, the Presbyterian minister and brother-in-law of Mr. McSween, performed the last rites. Frank Coe, Billy the Kid, Dick Brewer, and myself carried the coffin from the house to the grave, about fifty yards distant. . . . It was noticeable at the funeral that not one of the Murphy-Dolan faction was there. . . .

So far as the Coe boys were concerned, there had existed a very kindly feeling between them and Riley and Dolan up to that time. However, after this event the bond of friendship was severed. Bad feelings had been brewing for some time over cattle rustling and such minor details, but the killing was the last straw and the immediate cause of the Lincoln County War.

Billy was not given to outward demonstration. In fact, I never saw him shed a tear. But after Tunstall's death there was a faraway, lonely look in his eye which I had never seen there before. He would walk rapidly back and forth, then suddenly remark: "George, I never expect to let up until I kill the last man who helped to kill Tunstall, or die myself in the act.". . .

Dick Brewer[27] organized a party of Tunstall's cowboys, took out a warrant for the arrest of Morton and Baker [members of the posse that killed Tunstall], and followed them to Seven Rivers on the Pecos. They stubbornly resisted arrest and put up a heroic defense, but after an exciting skirmish they were captured by Brewer's men, who started with them to Lincoln. The first night they stopped at the famous John Chisum Ranch.

[Teenaged Sallie Chisum,] who was the housekeeper of her uncle, Mr. Chisum, at this time, in giving an account of the incident said:

---

[27] This incident has been moved for chronological continuity. Brewer's posse reflects McSween's legal counterattack against Dolan: to counter Dolan's control of Judge Bristol, McSween obtained a warrant from Justice of the Peace "Squire" Wilson for the arrest of Tunstall's killers. This posse formed the core of the Regulators, the men who fought on McSween's side.

"They put the prisoners in my room for the night because it was the only room in the house that did not have an outside exposure. None of us slept. We did not discuss it, but we knew that the boys were doomed. A guard, armed to the teeth, watched them all night to prevent any possibility of escape. They were nice-looking young chaps with the unmistakable marks of culture. The next morning, young Baker gave me a bunch of keepsakes including a pretty gold watch, and requested me, in case anything happened to him, to send them to his sweetheart, Miss Lizzie Lester, in Syracuse, New York. . . ."

All the mention that Billy ever made to me about this tragedy was: "Of course, you know, George, I never meant to let them birds reach Lincoln alive."

He did not seem to want to talk about it and the subject was closed after he gave me to understand that these boys had paid the penalty for the part they took in the killing of Tunstall.

The accepted theory is that when the posse left the Chisum Ranch they rode to Ash Upson's store, which was also the post-office, and the prisoners asked permission to write a note to relatives. Morton said to the postmaster as he was departing: "When you hear of my death, please notify my cousin, Attorney H.H. Marshall, at Richmond, Virgina."

In reply to this request, McLoskey, one of the possemen, declared: "They will have to kill me if they kill you two boys."

For that remark it is said McLoskey paid with his life, the first to be shot. No one knows the details, but it is evident that, as the party jogged along the road late in the afternoon, someone of the party shot McLoskey, and as he fell dead from his horse, Baker and Morton, realizing they would get theirs next, did what any sane person would have done under like circumstances. They put spurs to their horses and made a desperate attempt for liberty only to fall, riddled by bullets, a few seconds later, about fifty yards apart. . . .


### THE KILLING OF SHERIFF BRADY

Billy the Kid made no idle boasts or bets. [On the night of March 31,] accompanied by Henry Brown, Fred Wait, John Middleton, and Jim French, he rode into Lincoln. At a late hour they stationed themselves behind an adobe wall which surrounded Tunstall's store. They knew it was Sheriff Brady's custom to ride in from his ranch, three miles out, to his office every morning. It happened that on this occasion Brady had remained in Lincoln. They waited there, and when he did not come according to schedule, they sent a man down to Uncle Ike Ellis's place. He was to pretend that he was drunk and shooting up the town. The trap worked like a charm. Someone sent a message to Brady saying that one of McSween's men was in the lower end of town, drunk and raising hell.

Sheriff Brady, Deputy Sheriff George Hindman, and Circuit Court Clerk Billy Mathews started out in a rush to locate the disturbance. . . . They were now passing Tunstall's store [as Brady talked loudly about how the Kid needed hanging]. From their place of hiding Billy's quick ear heard his sentence being sounded. Zip! Bang! went a round of shot. Brady's little speech was never finished. . . .

Immediately following the shot that killed Brady, the four McSween men accompanying Billy the Kid rose up from behind the adobe wall and showered the remainder of the sheriff's party with lead, killing Hindman and wounding Billy Mathews. This accomplished, the Kid jumped over the fence, turned Brady over off his gun, which was a new Winchester, and got away with it, while Billy Mathews was shooting at him.[28] Then the McSween men, having completed their program, rode rapidly out of town. This story was told to me by the men who did the deed, and I know it is true.

I craved peace more than anything else in the world, and possibly this restless, unhappy state of mind would have worn off with time if conditions had been different. Frank Coe and I had sent for a new threshing machine, costing six hundred dollars. It was the only machine of its kind in the [territory], and meant rich rewards if we could get time to use it. I had also acquired other valuable holdings, all of which I should have to sacrifice if I became a quitter as a citizen and joined the gang. I had too much at stake to be foolish.

While I was coming to these conclusions and endeavoring to carry calmly on, the report reached me that Sheriff Brady had been killed. This tragedy aroused as much excitement in the community as had the murder of Tunstall, and left Lincoln County without any semblance of law. It was now an open "free-for-all," and no one could figure on a day's peace ahead. . . .

That night previous to this, "Buckshot" Roberts, reputed to be a desperate gunman, had spent the night with Frank Coe. He had been given the name "Buckshot" because of the daring shooting scrapes he had engaged in. He claimed that he had once run into a regiment of Texas Rangers, and killed several of them single-handed in making his escape. His record as a desperado would probably win for him a high-paying job as a man-hunter. He was aware that these Ruidoso boys, with the exception of the Kid and Charlie Bowdre, were inexperienced youths who had never taken part in any kind of warfare. Roberts and Frank Coe discussed this situation freely.

28 Billy was probably looking for the warrant Brady carried for McSween's arrest on embezzlement charges. He actually dropped the rifle when Mathews put a bullet through his thigh.

The next day, as Frank rode over to my place, Roberts rode to Lincoln. On the way, his mind was busy formulating his plan of action. His design was daring, but Roberts was no coward. Rumor had it that the law was offering a hundred dollars a head for the men who slew Brady and their associates. The offer held good, dead or alive, but preferably dead, as dead men were easier to handle. . . .[29]

Our gang was assembled at my ranch. Our plan was to keep on the alert, but also to keep in the background. We were not going out hunting for scraps, but positively meant to be on the job if anything started.

There was an outlaw in the settlement by the name of George Davis. He had been stealing our horses from time to time, and we heard that he had a rendezvous across the mountains on the Tularosa side at Rincanalla. We decided that, as we had nothing of importance to do at this time, we would blow in on him and blot him off the map. . . .

## THE BLAZER'S MILL BATTLE

Of course, we had no idea that "Buckshot" Roberts was on our trail, waiting for an opportunity to catch us off guard and kill as many of us as he could on the first round. We wandered around on the Tularosa side and reached Blazer's Mill[30] about eleven o'clock in the morning. Frank Coe, Dick Brewer, and myself were well acquainted with Dr. Blazer. He was running what was known as a roadhouse.

He greeted us warmly and said: "Stay for dinner, boys. I'll have the cook fix you dinner and get your horses fed."

However, he added that Roberts was following close on our beat and we had better keep an eye on the trail, as the soldiers would likely take up the hunt also.

Dick Brewer was our captain at that time. He said: "Well, if that's the program, we'll be prepared for them, fellows.". . .

We remained on guard, sitting out on the porch with our guns cocked in our laps, chatting and watching the trail. In about thirty minutes, true to our expectations, "Buckshot" Roberts came riding up on his bay mule to within twenty or thirty steps of where we sat. He offered no word of greeting, but crawled off his mule, armed with two six-shooters, a rifle, and a twelve-inch belt full of cartridges. He set his rifle on his foot and stood motionless as he recognized that we had the advantage over him at that time. The boys, having finished their dinner, walked out onto the porch.

[29] Roberts had been one of Dolan's gunmen from the beginning, having been a member of the posse that killed Tunstall.

[30] This site was usually called Blazer's Mills (with a plural "s"), and appears on the map with that spelling.

Roberts at once recognized Frank Coe, and said: "Coe, I want to speak to you a moment."

They walked around the house and sat down in an open doorway. Middleton and I then went in and ate our dinner. We finished the meal in silence and went out. The fellows had held a conference and decided that Roberts was there for no good, so just to save further trouble we would go around and arrest him. After quizzing him, Frank suspected that he was not going to be easy to handle. Therefore, he advised him to give himself up. . . .

"I'll be damned if I do," was his emphatic retort. "I give up to no bunch like Billy the Kid's. He and his pals have just killed Morton and Baker, and I'll fight 'em to the last ditch before I surrender."

Frank still sat trying to reason with him, but made no headway.

Dick Brewer's mind was fully made up to take Roberts regardless of consequences. He counseled with us, saying: "Boys, he's a bad hombre, well-armed, and I ain't going to ask for anyone to go around the house and get him, but who will volunteer? Anybody?"

"You bet I'll go for one," Charlie Bowdre spoke up.

"I'll be another to go, Dick," said I.

And then Billy the Kid stepped forward and said: "I'd sure hate to miss the frolic, so I guess I'll go with you."

"Good!" said Brewer. "If he kills that little bunch, the rest of us will take a hand."

We three bucked up, cocked our guns, and started around the house, Bowdre taking the lead. We took the dare, but we knew some of us were playing our last card. Roberts had his cocked rifle lying in his lap as he and Frank talked, and as Charlie Bowdre turned the corner of the house, he dropped his gun on Roberts and commanded him to throw up his hands.

"Not much, Mary Ann," answered Roberts vehemently.

Bowdre had the drop on Roberts, as the latter had to raise his gun from his lap. With his refusal to throw up his hands, they fired simultaneously. Bowdre's bullet struck Roberts right through the middle, and Roberts's ball glanced off Bowdre's cartridge belt, and with my usual luck, I got there just in time to stop the bullet with my right hand. It knocked the gun out of my hand, took off my trigger finger, and shattered my hand which still bears record of the fight. The wound did not seem to affect me, but I was stunned, not knowing just what to do. Instead of offering my back as a target for his bullets, I ran forward right in front of Roberts. He shot once at John Middleton, and the bullet entered his breast. He fired three times at me, but missed.[31]

---

[31] According to Robert Utley, Frank Coe later reported that he had never seen a man work a Winchester as fast as Buckshot Roberts did during those furious seconds. The Kid apparently tried to rush him as soon as his ammunition ran out, but Buckshot jabbed him with the muzzle of his rifle and sent him flying. Later he grabbed a rifle off the wall, once he retreated inside, and kept firing.

Dick Brewer was enraged and swore vengeance against Roberts, declaring: "I'll get him now at any cost."

We were ready to a man to fight to the bitter end.

After Roberts was shot, he fell back into the room. He pulled himself together and got to the bed. He pulled a feather bed onto the floor, lay down on it, and cocked his gun ready to battle to his last breath.

Just how he accomplished this in his dying moments, one cannot imagine, but he proved worthy of his nickname, "Buckshot," and never weakened.

Dick Brewer got Roberts's location in the house, went around by the sawmill and fortified himself behind some big logs. Thus concealed, he could look into the door. He saw an object indistinctly, and took aim and fired at it. Roberts, too, was watching, and noted the direction from which the bullet came. When Brewer stuck his head up just above the log for one second, Roberts cut him down with a bullet between the eyes and he fell over dead. We had lost our captain, but we had lost none of our thirst for revenge, and intended to get Roberts at all costs.

Dr. Blazer suggested: "Boys, I'll go around where I can see him, and try to find out how badly he is wounded." He then called out to Roberts, "I am Dr. Blazer, the man of the house. May I come in and help you in any way?"

"No," answered Roberts weakly. "I'm killed. No one can help me. It's all over."

Blazer then entered the room, and saw that there was nothing to be done. Roberts, gritty to the last, was dying. Blazer returned to us and said: "Boys, there's no use in fighting any longer. That fellow won't live an hour."

A telegraph line extended from Fort Stanton to Las Cruces, and the Indian Agency was about a mile from us on this line. There was a detachment of soldiers stationed there. About the time Blazer came out and gave us this information, we looked up the road and saw a squad of soldiers riding hurriedly toward us. We knew too well what that meant, and our business "laid rolling" about that time. We ran up the hill and hid in the mountains in the timber. We then circled around the Agency, got onto the main trail, and started back to our own stamping ground. . . .

After we got back into our own territory, there was another matter to be settled. We had to have a new sheriff. The Murphy and McSween parties each had a candidate. The Murphy candidate was George Peppin, a man in the Murphy employ. This did not please the McSween sympathizers, so they put up a man by the name of John Copeland, who was supposed to be neutral. Both petitions were sent to Governor Axtell. Copeland received quite a majority of signers on his petition, and was installed as sheriff. The Murphy faction wanted him to step into Brady's shoes and follow the latter's policies. That meant arresting Billy the Kid's gang. It took a full-grown man to accomplish that, and Copeland, recognizing the fact, was a little backward about getting on the job.[32]

He remained in office only a month. Then the Governor appointed George Peppin of the Murphy faction as sheriff and deputy United States Marshal. This appointment smacked of the control of the old "Santa Fe Ring," and caused much comment. The Murphy party now enjoyed the same power as they had under Brady. . . .

## THE FRITZ RANCH SKIRMISH

Everything rocked along this way for a month or so. The Seven Rivers squad, located sixty miles southeast of us, but still in the county, had bragged that they were coming to "clean up Billy the Kid's gang." That sounded funny to us. Since neither the soldiers at Fort Stanton nor any other civil or federal authority had been able to get the fellows who killed Brady, it hardly seemed likely that the Seven Rivers outfit could take the prize.

Intense feeling had subsided to such an extent that we dared to go into Lincoln when necessity demanded. Frank Coe, Ab Saunders [Frank's brother-in-law], and I had some important transactions in town, which we planned to transact through Ike Ellis, our old neighbor and friend. . . . When we reached Lincoln, Uncle Ike told us that everything was quiet there. After finishing our business, Frank Coe and [Frank] McNab decided to go home with Ab Saunders for a little visit. The rest of us later concluded that we would return to the Ruidoso.[33]

McNab, Coe, and Saunders rode leisurely along as far as the Fritz Ranch. There was a nice spring brooklet that crossed the road, and, not apprehending any danger, they stopped to get a cool drink. It so happened that the Seven Rivers crowd, making good their threat, had also reached the Fritz Ranch. They saw the boys approaching, and, knowing the custom of drinking there, waited until they stopped at the spring. Ab Saunders and McNab had dismounted, and Frank Coe was in the act of doing so, when they were surprised by a volley of shots. Both Ab and McNab were mortally wounded. Frank put spurs to his horse and attempted to ride out of it at full speed. He was making good his escape when a stray bullet hit his horse in the head, and the horse dropped dead, leaving Frank afoot. This gave his pursuers the advantage. He took shelter under an embankment and had used about all his shells when they ordered him to throw up his hands and come out, promising not to kill him. Having no choice, he did

---

[32] Copeland openly sympathized with the McSween faction.

[33] McNab had succeeded Brewer as commander of the McSween Regulators.

go out. They then arrested him . . . and took him to the Fritz ranch house, where they informed him that his brother-in-law, Ab Saunders, was mortally wounded and that McNab was dead. . . .

As we were preparing to leave Lincoln, the report reached us that all three of the boys had been killed by the Seven Rivers gang. That settled our trying to make a move out of Lincoln. We remained there at Uncle Ike's home, and when the mail carrier arrived that afternoon he brought the correct account of the tragedy.

I was still carrying my hand in a sling, but it wasn't my wound that was disturbing me now. A burning desire possessed me to avenge the wrongs inflicted on me and mine. That was another night of watchful waiting. Next morning the Seven Rivers bunch started with Frank Coe, as their prisoner, to Lincoln. They traveled in two divisions. One came straight into town and landed Coe at the old Murphy house, while the other surrounded the town. The [second] bunch stopped down at the lower end of Lincoln, and concealed themselves in order to find out what was going on. We were also keeping watch from behind a four foot wall on top of Uncle Ike's house. From there we observed a moving object down the river, but we were unable to distinguish whether it was animal or human. We sent downstairs for Ben Ellis's spyglass, and discovered that it was a man who had his field glasses focused on us. Uncle Ike had asked us not to shoot unless it was absolutely necessary, and we wanted to respect his wishes. But I was doing the spying, and turning to the boys, I said: "Men, this is absolutely necessary. We've got to pick that plum off guard."

I was still carrying my prize Winchester. It had never harmed a man yet, but was sure death on deer.

"Now watch me get that fellow right through the middle," I told them, and pulled the trigger.

Down he rolled out of sight, but we had no way of knowing whether he was hit or just scared. However, it was a signal for the posse in the background to make a break for the hills, the better to fortify themselves. As they ran across the field, we bombarded them, and they made for the river for protection.

In the meantime, the group which was assembled in the Murphy house guarding Frank Coe heard the shooting and in the excitement forgot their prisoner. As they all ran outside to see what was happening, Frank lost no time in taking advantage of his opportunity to escape. . . .

A short time later we were happily surprised to see Frank walk in unharmed, ready to take his place with his friends again.

The Murphy-Dolan faction, reinforced by the Seven Rivers gang, believed that [McSween's] entire outfit was assembled in the Ellis stronghold. They knew that if this were so, they were not equal to handling the situation, and decided to send to Fort Stanton for a detachment of soldiers, their motive being to get both factions arrested. This was a clever trick to get Brady's killers into custody without danger to themselves, though the apparent reason for these wholesale arrests was to stop the Lincoln County warfare.[34]

Toward noon the ambulance arrived from Fort Stanton bringing Ab Saunders, who had been wounded at the Fritz Ranch. They had stopped at the edge of town to pick up ["Dutch Charlie" Kruling], the man whom I had caught spying on us a short time before, and curled off his perch on the beef-head. [Kruling] was not badly injured, for my bullet had struck through both legs without breaking a bone. However, it did tear off quite a slice of ham. The distance of this shot was afterward measured and found to be 440 yards, or a little more than a quarter of a mile.

[The soldiers arrived and arrested everyone but George Coe, who feigned incapacitation, with his hand as evidence. Once everyone arrived at Fort Stanton, Copeland convinced Lieutenant Colonel Dudley to put them into his custody, and then released them.]

With all the soldiers which the Murphy faction kept scouting up and down the Ruidoso, and reinforced by their prizefighters from Seven Rivers, they had never yet captured a man or broken into our stronghold. . . .

During the time we were not in actual conflict with the Murphy faction, we amused ourselves at target practice until we were acknowledged as the most expert gunmen in the land. We did not intend to be found lacking in any crisis. To Billy the Kid went the honor of being the most skillful six-shooter or two-gun man in that part of the West, while I was considered the best marksman. I had to practice constantly, as my right hand had been put out of commission and it was imperative that I train the left one to take its place.

———

OVER THE NEXT several weeks, McSween's Regulators—now commanded by "Doc" Scurlock—fought a number of inconclusive skirmishes with The House gunslingers and the Seven Rivers cowboys: Scurlock led a raid on one of Dolan's herds, and The House fighters launched unsuccessful attacks on the Regulators at San Patricio and at John Chisum's ranch. Ironically, Dolan went bankrupt under the burden of the war and heavy debts; The House's holdings were foreclosed on by Santa Fe kingpin Thomas Catron, who now firmly aligned the territorial authorities against McSween's Regulators. McSween and his men were indicted on multiple counts. Local juries, however, supported the Regulators; they ignored the blatantly biased intervention of Judge Bristol and cleared the McSween men. They went further, in fact, returning indictments for Dolan, Jesse Evans, and several others.

In another key development, Congress passed a law making it illegal

———

[34] Copeland (still sheriff) actually sent for the troops.

for U.S. soldiers to be used in civil disputes. Lieutenant Colonel Dudley of Fort Stanton—despite his sympathies for Dolan—had to sit back and let the Lincoln County War run its course. And that course was about to take a dramatic plunge toward its final, epic conclusion: the Regulators decided that the time had come for a final showdown.

## The Five-Day Battle
*by George W. Coe*

We could see no hope of a peaceful settlement, and decided there was but one thing for us to do. That was to organize our forces, go into Lincoln, and fight it out to a finish. Our sympathizers were still backing us up. We assembled and all agreed to a decision. . . .

War was imminent. The next question was the selection of a leader. Martin Chavez, a prominent native, lived at Picacho. We knew him to be one of our sympathizers, though he had never entered actively into any engagement. . . . We requested him to accept the leadership of our band, and promised to abide by his decisions and follow his plans. He readily consented, and began to draw up a plan of attack. His idea was to go into Lincoln, post our friends as to our proposition, and make arrangements to gain a toehold before any resistance could be offered.[35]

The date was set for us to assemble by night, and we rode into Lincoln, fifty men strong, without being discovered. There was no moon. The townspeople were enjoying the peaceful July night undisturbed, as we worked in silence. [Scurlock and McSween] placed us in different sections of the town. Fourteen of the most daring fighters were located at the McSween home, for we knew that this would be the center of the battle to come. . . .

The remainder of our men were natives and new recruits. These were placed at Uncle Ike Ellis's house in the lower end of town. It happened that I accompanied Chavez to the old Montano store, which stands near the center of town. He now had all his men in the positions desired without having fired a gun.

The Murphy gang little dreamed what was going on until the next morning. The majority of them were stationed just above the McSween house, but held no part of the town except the old Murphy building.[36] They figured that the Kid and his allies in the McSween home would have to surrender.

[35] Coe is mistaken here; Chavez was leader only of the large Hispanic contingent; Scurlock and McSween were overall commanders, and made the decision to ride into Lincoln for a showdown.

[36] The Dolan men also held the old Indian tower, the Torreon.

There was a saloon adjoining one end of the Montano store. It was operated by Ike Stockton, a McSween sympathizer. This was a popular meeting place where many of the townspeople stopped for their morning appetizer. I was on guard when I noticed a couple of fellows approaching the saloon.

"Get your gun," I whispered to Chavez. "This is as good a time as any to start the fight."

We grabbed our guns and started for the door. Two or three native women who were in the room became hysterical at the sight of our weapons, clutching at us, begging us not to shoot. [At about this point, Sheriff Peppin and a posse rode into town through a howling dust storm and fired on the McSween home. Some of the men in the Montano store ran out after them.] The boys in the Indian Tower had also spied them and opened fire, as did our men at the McSween home. . . . The incident caused a panic, and everyone in town began to get busy. They realized that the ball had started rolling. By this time the whole town was aroused and bullets were coming from every quarter, but, since all of us were under cover, there were no immediate casualties. After the first flurry of this attack had subsided, the day dragged by with only an occasional exchange of shots to hold us at attention.

I became restless, feeling that we were hampered by the inmates of the house. Time was passing and we were getting nowhere. I told Chavez, when night came, that I would like to change my position. Accordingly, under cover of darkness, I withdrew from the Montano house and went up to the McSween citadel. During the night the Murphy party placed a group of men behind the McSween place and along the hillside. They also sent a squad of four or five men to the lower end of town, where they were stationed behind some big boulders. These fellows had fired into a body of our men, thus informing us of their location.

The next day Murphy's men on the hillside began bombarding the McSween house, and at the same time the five men in the lower end of town got a little too bold. Herrera, one of the Mexicans with Chavez at the Montano house, was a crack shot and had a big gun. He had been watching their maneuvers for some time, and, catching one of them exposed, pulled down and killed him. The boys at the Ellis place then took a shot at the bunch dodging around the boulders, which left both sides of the rock fortification exposed. The fugitives made a dash for safety in the timber on the hillside, making easy targets as they ran. Bullets flew thick and fast from both our quarters. Two men were killed, and we believed that a third was wounded.[37] Up to this time, we had slain several of their men, though not

---

[37] Among the men the Regulators fired on were some soldiers from Fort Stanton; this incident enraged Lieutenant Colonel Dudley, leading him to violate both the law and explicit orders by sending his troops into town on the last day of the battle.

one of ours had been touched. The fighting continued for three ghastly days without further casualties. We had the town completely bottled up, while they held only the Murphy building. There was no possible chance, unaided, of their getting the advantage. They realized the fact and called the military for help. . . .

Everything was quiet. But by some strategy they succeeded in getting a messenger through to the fort, and about ten or eleven o'clock on the third [fifth] day, Colonel Dudley and his command of soldiers arrived. This command consisted of one company of infantry, one of cavalry, and one of artillery. The Colonel also brought a twelve-pound cannon [a howitzer] and a Gatling gun. . . .

"I'm planting my Gatling gun right here," [Colonel Dudley] called out, "and at the first shot from the house, I'm going to blow up the whole works. Do you get that?" he added.

Meanwhile, it had been arranged between the soldiers and the Murphy party that, while the former held our attention, the latter were to bring coal oil and shavings to the rear of the house, saturate the window sills, and set the building afire. When the soldiers retired, we discovered that the house was burning and that there was no possibility of extinguishing the blaze.

Then the military removed to the center of town, where they erected their camp and threw out a picket line which reached clear across the town. This cut off our men in the lower end, and rendered them powerless to give us any assistance. Our men at the Ellis place were next ordered to evacuate their position or the house would be shot up. The majority of these men at Uncle Ike's were natives and had no leader. They became terror-stricken, and, without hesitation, took to their heels, leaving only Uncle Ike and his family to hold the fort.[38]

The McSween party realized that they were doomed. The house was constructed in an L. It was a twelve-room adobe building with four rooms in the front, four in the east, and four in the west wing. The wind luckily was coming from the east, which was a temporary assistance. There was no chance for the enemy to get our boys until the fire had burned around that L. The little band within took up floors, moved furniture, and fought desperately to hold out if possible until nightfall, when there would be more hope of escape.

Mrs. McSween's treasured piano, which had been such a joy to the community, became a burden as the hours wore on. . . . The piano was moved from place to place in an effort to save it from the flames, but it

[38] Lieutenant Colonel Dudley decisively altered the battle's outcome by shielding Dolan's men from gunfire. He also aimed his howitzer at the various McSween strongholds (apart from McSween's house), terrifying the resident gunmen into fleeing—since they honestly believed that Dudley was about to fight on Dolan's side.

burned at last with the rest of the furniture. . . . The Kid and O'Folliard[39] did play the piano occasionally between battles, and with their irrepressible high spirits tried to dispel the gloom settling around the survivors. It was almost uncanny to hear, at long intervals, during that memorable day, the weird notes pealing forth from the famous music box. Added to this were the suppressed whisperings of a prayer constantly being uttered by Mr. McSween as he passed from room to room with his Bible in his hand, his faith never forsaking him to the last.

About thirty steps across the alley from the main building was a warehouse. This had been used for a bedroom and loafing-place for us boys. It so happened that when the soldiers arrived, Henry Brown, a man by the name of Smith, and myself were in the warehouse, which was also exposed to the battle. This had been used by Tunstall for storing grain, which was piled up five or six feet high on the side toward the main house. There were several ventilators in this side, which came in handy as portholes for us. In our concealment we were anxiously watching for a chance to get a shot at the enemy. None of the soldiers knew that we were in there.

There were three women in the McSween party—Mrs. McSween, her sister-in-law, Mrs. Shields, and Miss Gates, the school teacher. They were almost hysterical, for they knew that we were making our last stand; that this was to be the end. When the women left the burning building, they came to the warehouse. At the same time a fellow by the name of Jack Long came running with a can of oil, intent on setting the warehouse afire. The women intercepted him and pleaded with him not to burn the building. I had been watching, and was holding my gun cocked on him, but dared not fire, as Mrs. McSween was standing between us. I prayed that she would move just one step. Just as she stepped aside, he bent over to pick up the oil can. As he stooped, I fired and missed. An outhouse stood nearby, and into this he darted for protection. All day, when we had nothing else to do, we made that our target and shot it full of holes. The result was that he was forced to crawl down into the pit rather than meet certain death. He afterwards remarked that it was the most gruesome experience of his life, but beat dying all hollow at that. . . .

By a terrific struggle the McSween outfit had kept the fire from reaching them until nightfall, but at last the moment had arrived to move. Their only choice was to burn with the building or make a break for liberty. It was no time for talk, but action.

Billy the Kid turned to McSween and urged him to join the fight. "Come on, Gov'nor, it's time to lay down your Bible. Your gun will talk faster than your religion right now." But McSween remained firm, holding to his faith and convictions. Billy the Kid had held on faithful to his trust,

---

[39] Tom O'Folliard was a tall young fighter who idolized the Kid and was his constant companion.

inspiring his comrades with good cheer to the last moment. They must now break out and meet the firing squad or perish in the flames.

The men were leaving the building between volleys. By rushing out just after a round of shots was fired, several escaped safely, though four or five dropped before a rain of enemy bullets.

The Murphy faction supposed that only a few of the defenders remained in the house, and suddenly charged the place. The Kid shot Bob Beckwith down as he entered the door, and, faithful to the last, called to McSween to follow him. With a six-shooter in each hand, firing as he went, he strode over Beckwith's lifeless body and McSween followed him. Through a veritable rain of bullets, as guns spat lead and fire and death, Billy ran, a target for twenty guns. Flames seemed to envelop him, lead tore through his clothes and hat. He picked his perilous way over the corpses of his friends. On he fled, a gun in each hand, popping out salutes to his enemies. In addition to killing Beckwith, he wounded two others.[40]

Again the Kid had cheated death. Not so McSween. He offered no resistance, but stepped from his doorway, faced the bloodthirsty gang, and said calmly, "Gentlemen, I am McSween."

As the words left his lips, he fell shattered by numberless bullets, but with his Bible still clenched in his hand. . . .

About the time McSween and the Kid were leaving the burning building, Brown, Smith, and I decided that it was wiser to make a break for safety than to remain and face the entire army. An eight-foot wall stood between us and escape, but luck was with us. A row of old barrels stood beside the wall and we used these as stepladders. As we went over the top, the bullets poured around us from every direction, but once on the other side we were swallowed up in the darkness of the night. . . .

In order to celebrate their victory properly, the Murphy faction drank, sang, and danced the gruesome hours away. McSween had two negro servants, Sebrian Bates and George Washington. They were both good musicians, and the revelers forced these two innocent victims to sit up on an adobe wall and play their violins through the long hours of that sad night. . . .

Among other disgraceful scenes enacted by the Murphy faction was the looting of the McSween store after the battle. Merchandise was carried away in every conceivable manner. They made a thorough cleanup while they had the power.

---

THE FIVE-DAY Battle, as it was called, ended in complete defeat for the McSween forces, and the death of McSween himself. As Robert Utley has noted, neither side displayed much leadership in the fight, but the

---

[40] The Dolan men did not charge, and the evidence suggests that the Kid broke out before Beckwith (a Seven Rivers man) was shot.

McSween forces had the definite advantage until Colonel Dudley intervened. Despite his sympathy for the Dolan side, Dudley was sincerely
concerned about the women and children in the town; his very appearance, however, shifted the balance decisively in favor of The House
gunmen.

Ironically, Dolan lost his empire in the fighting. Driven to financial
collapse, he had his mortgage foreclosed by Thomas Catron. Catron was
perhaps the real victor in the conflict, extending his already considerable
control over the New Mexico economy. Undoubtedly the forces of resistance had lost a major battle in the Western Civil War of Incorporation.

The Lincoln County War, however, was not quite over. Chaos reigned in
the county for a time. A group of Texas gunmen recruited to aid The
House coalesced into a ruthless gang of terrorists known as the Wrestlers.
Led by John Selman (the same man who later murdered John Wesley
Hardin), the gang swept through the county in August and September,
pillaging ranches, raping, torturing, and murdering. They burned both the
Coe and Tunstall ranches, and even plundered the town of Lincoln. The
Wrestlers' atrocities utterly terrorized the county; for weeks, the fields and
roads were left deserted, as settlers remained out of sight from pure fear.
On October 7, President Hayes announced that Lincoln County was in a
state of insurrection, and the army was free to put down the anarchy.

Meanwhile, the Regulators broke up, though a remnant remained under
William Bonney. The Kid had begun the war as a common soldier, no more
noted than any others; by the end, he was an acknowledged leader, despite
his youth. He sought revenge for the defeat by raiding Dolan's herds—
only now they were Catron's, and so Billy drew down the wrath of the
greatest power in the territory. He also fell out with John Chisum, who had
given up in his feud with the Seven Rivers cowboys and had begun selling
off his huge herd. The Kid declared that Chisum owed him wages for his
services in the fight against The House, which the cattle king denied.
Chisum also took a sour view of the Kid's blossoming romance with his
teenage niece, Sallie.

In the months after the end of the war, the Kid and his remaining
confederates turned increasingly to gambling and simple outlawry, devot-
ing themselves mainly to cattle stealing. In a land where fences were few
and cattle often wandered loose, however, rustling was not seen as much of
a crime by most of the population. In addition, the young bandit commanded tremendous loyalty among Hispanics, who saw him as the avenger
of their lost cause (he also spoke fluent Spanish, wore a huge sombrero,
and had numerous Hispanic girlfriends). As Utley has pointed out, Billy
was one of the few Anglos who never condescended to Spanish-speaking
New Mexicans.

The aftermath of the war also led to a new governor, Lew Wallace (who
was busy writing the novel *Ben-Hur*). Wallace, eager to look good in

Washington, prematurely issued a general amnesty and declared that peace had arrived. But when the lawyer of McSween's widow was killed in the streets of Lincoln by Jesse Evans's gunslingers, it was clear that peace had not even come close.

The Kid had witnessed the killing, and he made a deal with Wallace to testify in return for a pardon, or at least non-prosecution on his many outstanding indictments. Unfortunately, many of the accused (including Jesse Evans) promptly disappeared, and District Attorney Rynerson—a Dolan loyalist—proceeded to prosecute the Kid despite the governor's promise.

Billy escaped, leading to the final episode in his volcanic life. He and his gang (really a loose association of friends and acquaintances) spent most of their time rustling horses around the towns of Fort Sumner and White Oaks, New Mexico (where gold was discovered in 1879), driving the animals to the Texas panhandle, where they sold the horses and rustled cattle for the return trip. All the while, newspapers turned the young gunman into the now-famous "Billy the Kid," the most notorious outlaw in the Southwest.

It was during this period that the Kid engaged in a gunfight that reveals the reality behind his myth. On January 10, 1880, Billy and a few Chisum hands were drinking at Bob Hargrove's saloon in Fort Sumner, when they were confronted by a Texas badman named Joe Grant. Drunk and belligerent, Grant swapped his six-shooter for the fine, ivory-handled revolver of one of Billy's frightened acquaintances. The Kid remarked on the beauty of the pistol; he calmly lifted it from Grant's holster and examined it, spinning the cylinder smartly before returning it. Later, Grant grew angry with the Kid, who quietly turned away. The Texan jerked his new gun, aimed it at the back of Billy's head, and squeezed the trigger. The hammer clicked on an empty chamber, thanks to the Kid's deft spin. Billy whirled and fired three quick shots from his self-cocker. All three bullets smashed through the same spot on Grant's chin; he probably died before he hit the floor. "Joe," Billy said, "I've been there too often for you."

Meanwhile, the powerful men of the New Mexico Territory demanded action. Governor Wallace issued a five-hundred-dollar reward for the Kid, and John Chisum recruited a friend of Bonney's to run for sheriff of Lincoln County. He was a tall Texan, a former buffalo hunter, and a dead shot named Pat Garrett. Despite being a wanted man, Billy actively campaigned for a rival candidate. But the tide was shifting in the county, and Garrett handily won the election. As the county sheriff and deputy U.S. marshal, his single most important assignment was to capture the Kid.

Garrett, with the assistance of Ash Upton, later wrote about Billy in a notoriously unreliable biography titled *The Authentic Life of Billy the Kid*. In the final chapters, however, Garrett shifted to an exciting, accurate, first-person account of his chase after the Kid's gang of ex-Regulators and outlaws. Immediately upon starting out as sheriff, the Texan discovered the depth of resistance among the local Hispanics, who viewed the Kid as a hero and a defender of their rights; they angrily confronted him, and refused to provide information that might lead him to the young fugitive. They resented the power and arrogance of immigrant white Texans such as the new sheriff (even before the Lincoln County War, the area had been the scene of bloody Texan-Hispanic feuding).

Garrett, however, knew the Kid personally, and he had a knack for making the right guess. He would not let his respect for Bonney's deadly gunplay stop him from bringing the outlaw to ground. But the hunt proved to be a wild, up-and-down ride before the two faced off for the last time in a darkened room in Fort Sumner.

---

## The Hunt for Billy the Kid
*by Pat F. Garrett*

In the month of October, 1880 . . . the author of this history first became in an official capacity actively involved in the task of pursuing and assisting in bringing to justice the Kid and others of his ilk. . . .

[Garrett began his duties by taking a posse and a Federal Treasury agent on a sweep of the county, capturing a number of wanted men. He took them to the town of Puerto de Luna, where sheriff's deputies took possession of the prisoners. Meanwhile, the local Hispanics angrily confronted the new lawman.]

While the deputies were gone with the prisoners to have them ironed, I happened to be sitting in the store of A. Grzelachowski, when Juanito Maes, a noted desperado, thief, and murderer, approached me, threw up his hands, and said that having heard I wanted him, he had come to surrender. I replied that I did not know him, had no warrant for him, and did not want him. As Maes left me, a Mexican[41] named Mariano Leiva, the big bully of the town, entered. With his hand on a pistol in his pocket, he walked up to me and said he would like to see any damn Gringo arrest him. I told him to go away and not annoy me. He went out on the porch, but there he continued in a tirade of abuse, all directed against me. I finally went out and told him that I had no papers for him and no business with him. I assured him, however, that, whenever I did, he would not be put to the trouble of hunting me, for I would be sure to find him. With an oath,

[41] As does almost every other writer in this volume, Garrett refers to Spanish-speaking Americans as "Mexicans," despite the fact that most of the Hispanics he refers to in this selection were probably born in the United States.

he raised his left arm in a threatening manner, his right hand still on his pistol. I thereupon slapped him off the porch. He landed on his feet, drew his pistol, and fired without effect. My pistol went off prematurely, the ball striking at his feet; the second shot went through his shoulder. Then he turned and ran, firing back as he went, very wide of the mark. . . .

We [Garrett and his posse] got away from Puerto de Luna about 3 o'clock in the evening with but one recruit—Juan Roibal. Of all the cowardly braggarts in the place, not one could be induced to go when the time came. They were willing to ride in any direction but that in which the Kid might be encountered. . . .[42]

The day before I had started a spy, José Roibal, brother of Juan, from Puerto de Luna to Fort Sumner. He was a trustworthy fellow, who had been recommended to me by Grzelachowski. He had ridden straight through to Fort Sumner without stopping, obtained all the information possible, and on his return reported to me at Pablo Beaubien's ranch, a mile above Gearhart's [where the posse had camped]. His appearance at Fort Sumner had excited no suspicion. He kept his eyes open and his mouth closed; when it was necessary to talk, he pretended he was a sheepherder looking for strays. He learned that it was certain that the Kid, with five adherents, was at Fort Sumner and that he was decidedly on the *qui vive*. . . . The Kid and his crowd, it was said, kept horses saddled all the time, and were prepared either to give us a warm reception when we should appear on the scene, or to run, as occasion demanded. After gaining all the information possible without exciting suspicion, José rode leisurely from Fort Sumner, crossing the river on the west. O'Folliard and Pickett followed him across the river, and asked him who he was, what his business was, etc. He replied that he was a herder and was hunting stray sheep. This satisfied his questioners, and they allowed him to depart.

After the Kid, O'Folliard, Bowdre, Rudabaugh, Wilson, and Pickett had all met at Las Canaditas, they had gone directly to Fort Sumner, and were putting in a gay time at cards, drinking, and dancing. . . .

With all this information from our faithful spy, we left Gearhart's ranch about midnight and reached Fort Sumner just before daylight. . . .

On the morning of the eighteenth of December, before anyone was stirring in the plaza of Fort Sumner, I left our party with the exception of Mason in concealment, and started out to make observations. . . . I was confident that the gang would be in Fort Sumner that night and made arrangements to receive them. There was an old hospital building on the eastern boundary of the plaza—the direction from which they would come. The wife of Bowdre occupied one of the rooms of the building, and I felt sure they would pay their first visit to her. So I took my posse there, placed a guard about the house, and awaited the game. They came fully

[42] What Garrett refers to as cowardice was most likely positive support for the Kid.

two hours before we expected them. We were passing away the time playing cards. There were several Mexicans in the plaza, some of whom I feared would convey information to the gang, so I had them with me in custody. Snow was falling on the ground, the fact of which increased the light outside. About eight o'clock the guard said cautiously from the door, "Pat, someone is coming!"

"Get your guns, boys," said I. "No one but the men we want would be riding at this time of night."

With all his reckless bravery, the Kid had a strong infusion of caution in his composition when he was not excited. He afterwards told me that as they approached the building that night he was riding in front of O'Folliard. As they rode down close to our vicinity, he said a strong suspicion arose in his mind that they might be running into unseen danger.

"Well," said I, "what did you do?"

He replied—"I wanted a chew of tobacco bad. Wilson had some that was good and he was in the rear. I went back after tobacco, don't you see?" and his eyes twinkled mischievously.

One of the Mexicans followed me out, and we joined the guard, Lon Chambers, on one side of the building, while Mason with the rest of our party went around the building to intercept them should they try to pass on into the plaza. In a short time we saw the Kid's gang approaching, with O'Folliard and Pickett riding in front. I was under the porch and close against the wall, partly hidden by some harness hanging there. Chambers was close behind me, and the Mexican behind him. I whispered, "That's him." They rode on up until O'Folliard's horse's head was under the porch. When I called "Halt!" O'Folliard reached for his pistol, but before he could draw it, Chambers and I both fired. His horse wheeled and ran at least a hundred and fifty yards. As quick as possible I fired at Pickett, but the flash of Chambers's gun disconcerted my aim, and I missed him. But one might have thought by the way he ran and yelled that he had a dozen bullets in him. When O'Folliard's horse ran with him, he was uttering cries of mortal agony; and we were convinced that he had received a death wound. But he wheeled his horse, and as he rode slowly back, said, "Don't shoot, Garrett. I am killed.". . .

During this encounter with O'Folliard and Pickett, the rest of our party on the other side of the house had seen the Kid and others of his gang. My men had promptly fired on them and killed Rudabaugh's horse, which, however, ran twelve miles with him to Wilcox's ranch before the animal died. As soon as our men fired, these four ran like a bunch of wild Nueces steers. They were, in truth, completely demoralized.

As soon as the outlaws had disappeared Mason came around the building just as O'Folliard was returning, reeling in his saddle. After we had laid him down inside, he begged me to kill him, saying that if I was a friend of his I would put him out of his misery. . . . Once he exclaimed, "Oh, my

God, is it possible that I must die?" I said to him just before he died, "Tom, your time is short." He answered, "The sooner the better; I will be out of pain then." He blamed no one and told us who had been in the Kid's party with him. He died in about three quarters of an hour after he was shot. . . .

The gang was now reduced to five who remained at Wilcox's ranch that night, depressed and disheartened. After a long consultation they concluded to send someone to Fort Sumner the next morning to spy out the lay of the land. They took turns at standing guard throughout the night to prevent surprise, and the next morning sent Wilcox's partner, Brazil, to the plaza. They had been suspicious of treachery on the part of Wilcox and Brazil when they were so effectually surprised at the old hospital building, but had been entirely reassured by them after returning to the ranch.

Brazil came to me at Fort Sumner on the morning of the 20th of December. He described the condition of the crestfallen band of outlaws and said they had sent him in to gather news and report to them. I told him to return, and, as a ruse, to tell them that I was at Sumner with only Mason and three Mexicans. . . . I told him that, if he found the gang still at the ranch when he arrived there, he should remain; but if they had left, or should leave after his arrival, he was to come and report to me. . . . Brazil went home and almost immediately returned, reaching Sumner about 12 o'clock in the night.

There was snow on the ground, and it was so desperately cold that Brazil's beard was full of icicles. He reported that the Kid and his four companions had taken supper at Wilcox's, then mounted their horses and departed. My party and I all started for the ranch immediately. . . . We reached the ranch, surrounded the house, found it vacant, and rode on towards Wilcox's. About three miles from there we met Brazil, who reported that the outlaws had not returned and showed me their trail in the snow.

After following this trail a short distance, I was convinced that they had made for Stinking Spring, where there was an old deserted house, built by Alejandro Perea. When within a half mile of the house, we halted and held a consultation. I told my companions that I was confident we had them trapped, and cautioned them to preserve silence. We moved quietly in the direction of the house until we were only about four hundred yards distant; then we divided our party, leaving Juan Roibal in charge of the horses. Taking one-half of the force with me, I circled the house. I found a dry arroyo, and by taking advantage of its bed we were able to approach pretty close. . . .

I had a perfect description of the Kid's dress, especially his hat. I had told all the posse that if the Kid made his appearance it was my intention to kill him, for then the rest would probably surrender. The Kid had sworn that he would never give himself up a prisoner, and would die fighting even though there was a revolver at each ear, and I knew he would keep his word. I was in a position to command a view of the doorway, and I instructed my men that when I brought up my gun they should all raise theirs and fire. Before it was fully daylight, a man appeared at the entrance with a horse's nosebag in his hand, and I took him to be the Kid. His size and dress, especially the hat, corresponded exactly with the description I had been given of the Kid. So I gave a signal by bringing my gun to my shoulder; my men did likewise and seven bullets sped on their errand of death.

The victim was Charlie Bowdre. He turned and reeled back into the house. In a moment Wilson called to me from the house and said that Bowdre was killed, and he wanted to come out. I told him to come out with his hands up. As he started, the Kid caught hold of his belt, drew his revolver around in front of him and said, "They have murdered you, Charlie, but you can get revenge. Kill some of the sons of bitches before you die." Bowdre came out with his pistol still hanging in front of him, but with his hands up. He walked unsteadily towards our group until he recognized me; then he came straight at me, motioning towards the house, and almost strangling with blood, said, "I wish—I wish—I wish—" then in a whisper, "I am dying!" I took hold of him, laid him gently on my blankets, and he died almost immediately.

As I watched in the increasing daylight every movement about the house, I shortly saw a movement of one of the ropes by which the horses were tied, and I surmised that the outlaws were attempting to lead one of the horses inside. My first impulse was to shoot the rope in two, but it was shaking so that I was confident I would only miss. I did better than I expected, for just as the horse was fairly in the door opening, I shot him and he fell dead, partially barricading the outlet. To prevent another attempt of this kind, I shot in two the ropes which held the other horses and they promptly walked away. . . . I now opened a conversation with the besieged, the Kid acting as spokesman. I asked him how he was fixed in there.

"Pretty well," answered the Kid, "but we have no wood to get breakfast with."

"Come out," said I, "and get some. Be a little sociable."

"Can't do it, Pat," replied the Kid, "business is too confining. No time to run around."

"Didn't you fellows forget a part of your program yesterday?" said I. "You know you were to come in on us at Fort Sumner from some other direction, give us a square fight, set us afoot, and drive us down the Pecos.". . .

About 4 o'clock the wagon arrived from Wilcox's with the provisions and wood, and we built a rousing fire and went to cooking. The odor of roasting meat was too much for the famished lads who were without provisions. Craving stomachs overcame brave hearts. Rudabaugh stuck out from the window a handkerchief that had once been white and called to us that they wanted to surrender. . . . In a few minutes all of them—the Kid, Wilson, Pickett, and Rudabaugh—came out, were disarmed, given their supper, and started in our custody to Wilcox's. . . .

The Kid and Wilson were taken from Santa Fe to Mesilla under charge of Tony Neis, a deputy United States marshal, where the Kid was tried at the March, 1881, term of the District Court, first for the murder of Roberts at the Mescalero Apache Indian Agency in March, 1878. Judge Bristol, who presided at the trial, assigned Judge Ira E. Leonard, of Lincoln, to defend the Kid, and the outcome of the trial was that he was acquitted. He was again tried at the same term of court for the murder of Sheriff Brady at Lincoln on the 1st of April, 1878, the outcome of this being a conviction. Judge Bristol sentenced the Kid to be hanged on the 13th of May, 1881, at Lincoln. . . .

Lincoln County did not then have a jail that would hold a cripple. The county had just purchased the large two-story building, formerly the mercantile house of Murphy & Dolan, for use as a public building, but a new and secure jail had not been constructed. Hence I was obliged to keep the Kid directly under guard all the time. For this duty I selected my deputy sheriff, J.W. Bell, and Deputy Marshal Robert W. Ollinger, and chose as a guard room one of the rooms in the second story of the county building, separate and apart from the quarters given the other prisoners. . . .[43]

On the evening of April 28, 1881, Ollinger took all the other prisoners across the street to supper, leaving Bell in charge of the Kid in the guard room. We have only the Kid's story and the sparse information elicited from Mr. Geiss, a German employed about the building, to determine the facts in regard to events immediately following Ollinger's departure. From all the circumstances and indications, the information from Geiss and the Kid's own admissions, the conclusions seemed to be as follows:

At the Kid's request, Bell accompanied him downstairs [down an external staircase from the second-story room] and into the back corral where was the jail latrine. As they returned, Bell, who was inclined to be rather easy-going in his guarding of the Kid, allowed the latter to get considerably in advance. As the Kid turned on the landing of the stairs he was hidden from Bell, and being very light and active, he bounded up the stairs, turned to the right, pushed open with his shoulder the door of the room used as an armory, which, though locked, was easily opened by a firm push, entered the room, seized a six-shooter, and returned to the head of the stairs just as Bell faced him on the landing of the staircase and some twelve steps

---

[43] Bell was an amiable, sociable man, and he developed a friendly relationship with the Kid, whom he found hard not to like. Ollinger, on the other hand, was a bully by nature and a veteran of the Dolan side in the Lincoln County War. He hated Bonney, and taunted him with a steady stream of insults.

beneath.[44] The Kid fired, and Bell, turning, ran out into the corral in the direction of the little gate, but he fell dead before reaching it. The Kid ran to the window at the south end of the hall, from which he saw Bell fall; then slipping his handcuffs over his hands he threw them at the body, saying, "Here, damn you, take these, too." He then ran to my office and got a double-barrel shotgun. This gun was a very fine one, a breech-loader, and belonged to Ollinger. He had that morning loaded it in the presence of the Kid, putting eighteen buckshot into each barrel, and had remarked, "The man that gets one of these loads will feel it." The Kid then went from my office into the guard room and stationed himself at the east window which opened on the yard.

Ollinger heard the shot and started back across the street, accompanied by L.M. Clements. Ollinger entered the gate leading into the yard just as Geiss appeared at the little corral gate and said, "Bob, the Kid has just killed Bell." At the same instant the Kid's voice was heard above, "Hello, old boy," said he. "Yes, and he has killed me too," exclaimed Ollinger, and thereupon fell dead from eighteen buckshot in his right shoulder, breast, and side. The Kid then left the guard room, went through my office into the hall and passed out on to the balcony. From there he could see the body of Ollinger as it lay in the projecting corner of the yard near the gate. He took deliberate aim and fired the other barrel, the charge taking effect in nearly the same place as the first. Then breaking the gun across the railing of the balcony, he threw the pieces at Ollinger, saying, "Take it, damn you, you won't follow me anymore with that gun."

He then returned to the back room and armed himself with a Winchester and two revolvers. He was still encumbered with his shackles, but hailing old man Geiss, he commanded him to bring a file. Geiss found one and threw it up to him in the window. The Kid then ordered the old man to saddle a horse. . . . When he left the house and attempted to mount the horse, the animal broke loose and ran down towards the Rio Bonito. The Kid thereupon called to Andrew Nimley, one of the prisoners who was standing by, to go and catch it. Nimley hesitated, but a quick and imperative gesture from the Kid started him. He brought the horse back, and the Kid remarked, "Old fellow, if you hadn't gone for this horse, I would have killed you." This time the Kid succeeded in mounting, and saying to those within hearing, "Tell Billy Burt I will send his horse back to him," he galloped away, the shackles still hanging to one leg. . . .

All the inhabitants of the town of Lincoln appeared to be terror-stricken. It is my firm belief that the Kid could have ridden up and down the plaza until dark without a shot being fired at him or any attempt made to arrest him. Sympathy for him might have actuated some of this, but most of the

[44] Robert Utley's theory is that the slender Kid slipped his handcuffs off one hand and whacked Bell, then seized his pistol.

people were doubtless paralyzed with fear when it was whispered that the dreaded desperado, the Kid, had slain his guards and was at liberty again. . . .

He stayed for some time with one of [Pete] Maxwell's sheepherders about thirty-five miles east of Sumner. He spent some time also at various cow and sheep camps; and he was often at Canaditas, Arenoso, and Fort Sumner. He was almost constantly on the move, living in this way about two and a half months, hovering in spite of danger around the scenes of his past two years of lawless adventure. He had many friends who were faithful to him, who harbored him, who kept him supplied with territorial newspapers and other valuable information concerning his safety. His end had not yet come, but it was fast approaching.

During the weeks following the Kid's escape, I was censured by some for my seeming unconcern and inactivity in the matter of his rearrest. I was egotistical enough to think I knew my own business best, and preferred to accomplish this duty, if possible at all, in my own way. I was constantly but quietly at work seeking trustworthy information and maturing my plan of action. I did not show my face in the Kid's old haunts, nor did I disclose my intentions and doings to anyone. Most of the time I stayed at home and busied myself about the ranch. If my seeming unconcern deceived the people as well as gave the Kid confidence in his security, my end was accomplished. I was strongly inclined to believe that the Kid was still in the country and probably in the vicinity of Fort Sumner, yet there was some doubt mingled with this belief. The Kid had never been taken for a fool; on the contrary, he was generally credited with the possession of forethought and cool judgment in a degree extraordinary for one of his age. It was therefore hard for me to believe that he would linger in the Territory in the face of all the elements in his situation—his liability to the extreme penalty of the law, the liberal reward for his detection and rearrest, and the ease with which a successful flight into safety might be made. My first task was to resolve my doubts. . . .

[After asking around fruitlessly for information,] I concluded to go and have a talk with Pete Maxwell, in whom I felt sure I could rely. We three [Garrett, Deputy Thomas K. McKinney, and a citizen named John W. Poe] rode in that direction, but when we were within a short distance of Maxwell's place, we ran upon a man who was in camp. We stopped to see who it might be, and to Poe's great surprise, he found in the camper an old friend and former partner by the name of Jacobs, with whom he had been associated in Texas. So we unsaddled here and got some coffee. Then on foot Poe, McKinney, and I entered an orchard which ran from where we were down to a row of old buildings, some of which were occupied by Mexicans, not more than sixty yards from Maxwell's house.

We approached these houses cautiously, and when within earshot heard the voices of persons conversing in Spanish. We concealed ourselves quickly and listened, but the distance was too great to hear words or even to distinguish voices. Soon a man arose from the ground, close enough to be seen but too far away to be recognized. He wore a broad-brimmed hat, dark vest and pants, and was in his shirt sleeves. With a few words which reached our ears as merely an indistinct murmur, he went to the fence, jumped it, and walked down toward Maxwell's house. Little as we then suspected it, this man was the Kid. We learned subsequently that when he left his companions that night, he went to the house of a Mexican friend, pulled off his hat and boots, threw himself on a bed and commenced reading a newspaper. He soon, however, called to his friend, who was sleeping in the room, and told him to get up and make him some coffee, adding, "Give me a butcher knife, and I will go over to Pete's and get some beef. I'm hungry." The Mexican arose, handed him the knife, and the Kid, hatless and in his stocking feet, started to Maxwell's house, which was but a few steps distant.

When the Kid, who had been thus unrecognized by me, left the orchard, I motioned to my companions, and we cautiously retreated a short distance. In order to avoid the persons we had heard at the houses, we took another route, approaching Maxwell's house from the opposite direction. When we reached the porch in front of the building, I left Poe and McKinney at the end of the porch, and about twenty feet from the door of Pete's bedroom, while I myself entered it. It was nearly midnight and Pete was in bed. I walked to the head of the bed and sat down near the pillow and beside Maxwell's head. I asked him as to the whereabouts of the Kid. He replied that the Kid had certainly been about, but he did not know whether he had left or not. At that moment, a man sprang quickly into the door, and, looking back, called twice in Spanish, "*Quién es? Quién es?* (Who comes there?)" No one replied, and he came on into the room. I could see he was bareheaded, and from his tread I could perceive he was either barefooted or in his stocking feet. He held a revolver in his right hand and a butcher knife in his left.

He came directly towards where I was sitting at the head of Maxwell's bed. Before he reached the bed, I whispered, "Who is it, Pete?" but received no reply for a moment. It struck me that it might be Pete's brother-in-law, Manuel Abreu, who had seen Poe and McKinney on the outside and wanted to know their business. The intruder came close to me, leaned both hands on the bed, his right hand almost touching my knee, and asked in a low tone, "Who are they, Pete?" At the same instant Maxwell whispered to me, "That's him!"

Simultaneously the Kid must have seen or felt the presence of a third person at the head of the bed. He raised quickly his pistol—a self-cocker— within a foot of my breast. Retreating rapidly across the room, he cried, "*Quién es? Quién es?* (Who's that? Who's that?)" All this occurred more rapidly than it takes to tell it. As quick as possible I drew my revolver and fired, threw my body to one side, and fired again. The second shot was useless. The Kid fell dead at the first one. He never spoke. A struggle or two, a little strangling sound as he gasped for breath, and the Kid was with his many victims.

HERO OR VILLAIN? The debate over the Kid's legacy has been waged for a century, more in popular culture than in serious history. Certainly Billy usually killed and stole for his own reasons, and not out of political motives. But the young gunslinger was a classic example of the "social bandit"—a concept created by English historian E.J. Hobsbawm to describe an outlaw celebrated by the general population for his defiance of wealth and power. As Robert Utley has noted, the Kid emerged as exactly this type of local folk hero: "In his own time, however undeservedly, Billy the Kid won this accolade from the Hispanic plowmen and herdsmen of New Mexico"—from everyone, in fact, who felt the pain of defeat in the Lincoln County War.

Self-serving bandit though he may have been, the Kid had also posed a political problem for the conservative interests ruling the New Mexico Territory. The instability fed by his lawlessness, his thefts from powerful men, and his status as a folk hero among the disaffected posed a challenge to the governor, Thomas Catron, and the Santa Fe Ring in general. That problem was eliminated—as were so many similar problems across the frontier—by a well-placed bullet.

The Kid was not the only source of resistance to the conservative powers in New Mexico. Shortly before the Lincoln County War, the Maxwell Land Grant Company defeated local gunslingers led by Clay Allison. In the 1890s, the Hispanic *Gorras Blancas* (white caps) fought back against wealthy Anglo and Hispanic landowners, usually by fence cutting and barn burning, but occasionally with gunfire as well. But the death of Billy the Kid was an important turning point in the conquest of the Southwest. Though another three decades would pass before New Mexico would become a state, the territory was quickly becoming conquered ground.

# V

## CONQUERED GROUND

LAST EPISODES ON THE
FRONTIER
1885 – 1892

| | |
|---|---|
| **1878–81** | · Cochise County War between Tombstone businessmen and rural cowboys in Arizona |
| **1880** | · Five homesteaders and two railroad gunmen die in Mussel Slough, California, as pioneers resist eviction by the Southern Pacific |
| **1883** | · Northern Pacific, Southern Pacific, and Santa Fe transcontinental railroads completed |
| **1883–84** | · Fence-Cutters War between small ranchers and big, corporate ranchers in Texas |
| **1885** | · Grover Cleveland (Democrat) takes office as president |
| **1885–86** | · Geronimo Campaign, the last offensive by Indian warriors |
| **1886–88** | · Tonto Basin War between large landowners and local settlers in Arizona |
| **1887** | · Dawes Act converts tribal lands to individual holdings, and opens resulting "surplus" Indian lands to settlers |
| **1889** | · Benjamin Harrison (Republican) takes office as president |
| | · Washington, Montana, and North and South Dakota admitted to the Union as states |
| | · The western Indian Territory opened to settlement, leading to land rush and crime wave |
| **1890** | · Wyoming and Idaho admitted to the Union as states; Mormons drop polygamy as a tenet of belief, clearing the way for Utah statehood |
| | · Western Indian Territory organized by Congress as the Oklahoma Territory |
| | · Census Bureau announces the extinction of the frontier line |
| | · Ghost Dance religion spreads to Sioux reservations; Sitting Bull killed while resisting arrest; army slaughters Lakota Ghost Dancers at Wounded Knee |
| **1890s** | · Hispanic *Gorras Blancas* ("White Caps") in New Mexico attack the property of Anglo and wealthy Hispanic ranchers |
| **1892** | · Farmer and labor groups form the Populist Party |
| | · Johnson County War: Invasion of fifty gunmen from the Wyoming Stockgrowers' Association defeated by local residents; Tom Horn hired as assassin |
| **1893** | · Grover Cleveland (Democrat) takes office as president |
| | · Historian Frederick Jackson Turner publishes his thesis that the Western frontier shaped American democracy |
| | · Great Northern Railroad completed |
| | · Dawes Commission initiates plan to convert last tribal Indian Territory lands to private plots |

|      | · Utah admitted to the Union as the 45th state |
|------|---|
| 1907 | · Oklahoma state formed by union of Oklahoma and Indian territories |
| 1912 | · Arizona and New Mexico admitted to the Union as states |

# 13

# THE GERONIMO CAMPAIGN

"Once I moved about like the wind. Now I surrender to you and that is all." When Geronimo spoke these words to General George Crook, the Apache leader was an aging man. He was approaching sixty, and his long life of ceaseless warfare showed in his hard, weather-beaten features. The year was 1886; Geronimo and his small band were the last Native Americans left who still resisted the U.S. Army. Everywhere the Indians had been crushed: the Bannock and Ute uprisings of the late 1870s had been ruthlessly suppressed, while the last great resistance to the reservations had ended in 1881, when Sitting Bull led his followers back from their Canadian exile. And yet, only a few days after Geronimo spoke those words of surrender, he refused to accept defeat and fled to the mountains once more.

How could the Apaches persist while others fell? Certainly the determination of other Indian tribes was not lacking; few leaders, for example, could match Sitting Bull in his iron-willed resistance to life on the reservation. The answer, rather, lies in two factors: the differing impact of the astonishing transformation of the West's natural environment, and the unique nature of Apache warfare.

From the Great Plains to the Northwest, from the Rocky Mountains to the California coast, a massive wave of white invaders had not only crowded in on Indian land but had remade the land itself, destroying the physical basis for the Indians' culture and independence. Chief Joseph summed up the problem succinctly: "We were content to let things remain as the Great Spirit Chief made them. They were not; they would change the rivers and mountains if they did not suit them." For non-agricultural Indians, the destruction of the game and the natural habitats that sustained them literally starved them into submission.

The march of land-changing Americans and immigrant Europeans had its most startling effect on the Great Plains. As we have seen, the buffalo had been almost the sole means of survival for Indians such as the Sioux, Cheyennes, Pawnees, Crows, and Comanches, and the immense herds required vast ranges of prairie to survive. And, as we have also seen, hunters such as Buffalo Bill Cody and settlers such as the family of Fanny Kelly attacked the buffalo in two ways, by directly slaughtering them and by plowing under their grazing grounds.

Buffalo Bill, though, was an underachiever compared to later hunters. Buffalo skins, it was discovered, made decent leather, and dozens of hunting parties began to scour the Great Plains in the 1870s. Between 1872 and 1874, hunters slaughtered well over four million bison—on top of more than a million killed by the southern plains Indians. Pat Garrett, for example, worked as a hunter on the Staked Plains of the Texas panhandle, where a good marksman could kill up to 3,000 animals a year. Carcasses rotted on the ground; about three were killed for every one that made it to a leather factory. Not surprisingly, the Native American warriors realized that their survival was at stake: the Red River War of 1874–75 began with an Indian attack on a party of buffalo hunters at Adobe Walls, Texas. Congress, too, woke up to the crisis, but President Grant vetoed a bill meant to protect the remaining buffalo. By the late 1870s, the southern herd had been exterminated.

The slaughter was repeated slightly later to the north, where the defeat of the Lakota Sioux and the Northern Cheyennes made big-time buffalo hunting possible. Sportsmen sensed the approaching extinction of the bison, and reacted by joining the massacre. When Sitting Bull decided to come back across the Canadian border and accept the reservation, he did so largely because there were no longer enough buffalo left to sustain his people's existence.

But despite the attention that has been paid to the killing of the buffalo, it is unlikely that they would have survived for long (in numbers sufficient to sustain the Indians), because their ranges were taken over by farms and cattle ranches. On the eastern half of the Great Plains, both American and foreign-born sodbusting farmers moved in. Kansas led the way: in 1860, there already were 107,000 settlers in the eastern section; by 1880, about 996,000 filled out the state, rising to 1,427,000 by 1890. Nebraska's white population rose from 29,000 in 1860 to 1,058,000 in 1890. The Dakotas went from a mere 4,837 white residents in 1860—not much of a competition for the Indians—to over 500,000 in 1890. These settlers plowed up the dry-land ocean swells described by Francis Parkman, completely changing the Western landscape within a generation. Cattle did the same for the land farther west. Within a decade after the first gold strike in the Black Hills, the open ranges of Montana and Wyoming began to teem with cattle, as did the Staked Plains of Texas after the elimination of the buffalo.

As Chief Joseph observed, the whites did indeed change the rivers and mountains to suit themselves, and traditional Indian culture could not survive the transformation. Once it had been possible for the native warriors to win temporary reprieves, to drive back white intrusions; Crazy Horse and Red Cloud, for example, forced the army to dismantle three forts and to abandon the Bozeman Trail. But the pace of American expansion and development eclipsed those times. The flow of settlers accelerated sharply after the completion of the first transcontinental railroad in 1869; by 1883, four separate railways spanned the West, with thousands of miles of branch lines, and goods and people moved faster and farther than ever before. Towns and true cities arose: Portland reached a population of 62,000 by 1890, while Denver hit 106,000 and San Francisco swelled to almost 300,000. By the time Geronimo met General Crook in 1886, the Indians could look out across the West and see nothing but conquered ground.

And yet Geronimo persisted. He was able to, in part, because Arizona lacked large numbers of white settlers and cities to crowd in his movements. The territory had only 40,440 white and Hispanic residents in 1880, while only 5,000 or so lived in the capital city of Tucson. Few pioneers reached the high mountains traveled by the warriors and their families. Even more important, however, was the nature of Apache ways. As we have seen earlier, the Apaches were long accustomed to living amid Mexican ranches and villages. The arrival of numbers of white Americans made less of an impact that it had among the Indians of the Northwest or the Great Plains. Geronimo's own account reveals how his people depended for survival on predatory raids on their more settled neighbors.

Those raids separated the Apaches from the Native Americans of the Great Plains and Northwest. Where the Sioux, Cheyenne, and Northwestern Indians often gathered in large numbers to wage war—as at the battles of Killdeer Mountain in 1864, Adobe Walls (during the Red River War) in 1874, and the Rosebud and Little Bighorn in 1876—the Apaches moved and fought in small guerrilla bands. They marched, often on foot, through the most forbidding mountains, raiding settlements and setting ambushes. As J.B. Gillett's earlier account revealed, they were a difficult foe to pin down and beat.

So when Geronimo and his fellow leaders—Chihuahua, Naiche (also called Natchez or Nachite, the son of Cochise), Nana, Josanie, and others—began to bridle at reservation life, fleeing to the mountains was a viable option. And ever since Lieutenant Britton Davis escorted Geronimo and his people back to San Carlos in early 1884, Apache resentment had been growing. General Crook had banned two practices dear to the warriors' hearts: the brewing of tiswin, their traditional alcoholic drink, and wife-beating. The dispute might seem petty and undignified, but it went straight to the heart of the Apaches' status. In their own minds, they were still an independent, undefeated people: they told Davis that they had made a truce, not made themselves slaves to General Crook. Crook's authority only extended to military matters, they argued. In other words, they were not yet conquered people.

In 1885, the dispute blew up into an open rebellion and the last great struggle of the Indian wars: the Geronimo Campaign. In the pages that follow, Davis describes the days leading up to that final Apache outbreak, and the

hectic, frustrating marching and fighting that followed. Davis was a sympathetic, fair-minded man, and he offers keen assessments of the Indians' predicament, the status of the various leaders, and the army's actions. Following the
pattern he had set earlier, General Crook enlisted other Apaches as scouts to
do most of the tracking, chasing, and fighting of the hostile bands. It was a
policy driven by necessity, for the rugged mountains of Mexico and the American Southwest were almost impossible for fully equipped U.S. troops to penetrate. It was also a policy destined to bear fruit. [1]

## The Final Outbreak
*by Lieutenant Britton Davis*

With every man, woman, and child of the hostiles back on the Reservation,
the General [Crook] permitted them to select the part of it they desired for
their home. They selected the vicinity of Turkey Creek, a small stream
seventeen miles southwest of Fort Apache and near that portion of the
Reservation occupied by the White Mountain bands, to whom several of
the hostiles were related by marriage or otherwise.

Crawford and I favored establishing them as a pastoral rather than as an
agricultural people. Turkey Creek had no water for agricultural purposes,
nor was there any vacant land near Fort Apache suitable to sustain any large
number of them. Nomads for generations past, their natural bent was the
acquisition and care of animals. We proposed that they be given sheep and
a few cows to start with, hoping in time they would become independent,
peaceful, and prosperous as the Navajo. I believe the General would have
accepted our view, but the Indian Bureau in Washington was again in the
saddle, and farmers they must be. . . .

The Indians scattered among the trees and began erecting their simple
homes of brush covered with cotton cloth, old shirts, pieces of blankets, or
any other available material. This work fell to the women, the men started
gambling games or lolling in the shade of the trees as they criticized the work
of the architects. . . . The more suspicious and intractable of the Indians
selected sites for their camps at a distance of several miles from mine. These
were Mangas, Chihuahua, Geronimo, and their bands. The followers of Ka-
ya-ten-nae did likewise; but he selected a site for himself on a ridge just above
my camp, where he could see everything that went on in it. . . .

With no outstanding chief of the type of Mangas Colorado, Cochise, and
Victorio, after the death of the latter the Indians fell apart under several

[1] For detailed information about this struggle, see *The Geronimo Campaign* by Odie
B. Faulk (New York: Oxford University Press, 1969), the source of most of the
information provided here.

separate subchiefs. The subchiefs were Chatto, Zele, Benito, and Chihuahua, all of whom seemed to have some hereditary rank that I never clearly
understood. . . . The rank and designation of these subchiefs was different
from, and in a social sense superior to, that of Geronimo and Ka-ya-ten-nae,
who had won their spurs in warfare, or by their skill as leaders of raids.

Geronimo was neither a chief or subchief. He had risen to the leadership
of a faction (about one-fifth) of the warriors, by sheer courage, determination, and skill as a leader. But he was feared and disliked by the great
majority of the Indians. This is shown conclusively by the fact that part of
the Indians came in with the General, part under their chief Zele, accompanied by Nachite, and part under Chatto. . . .

Like Geronimo, a much younger man, Ka-ya-ten-nae, about twenty-five
years of age, had acquired leadership of a faction of the unruly and dissatisfied young men, thirty-two in number. His ambitions I nipped in the
bud, narrowly escaping being nipped myself in doing it.

In my talks with the Indians they showed no resentment at the way they
had been treated in the past; only wonderment at the why of it. Why had
they been shifted from reservation to reservation; told to farm and had
their crops destroyed; assured that the Government would ration them,
then left to half starve; herded in the hot, malarial river bottoms of the Gila
and San Carlos, when they were a mountain people? These and other
questions I could not answer. . . . We have heard much talk of the treachery
of the Indian. In treachery, broken pledges on the part of high officials,
lies, thievery, slaughter of defenseless women and children, and every
crime in the catalogue of man's inhumanity to man the Indian was a mere
amateur compared to the "noble white man." His crimes were retail, ours
wholesale. . . .

Geronimo never came to my tent unless he wanted something, and this
in four months was not more than eight or ten times. . . . Nana, Chihuahua, and Ka-ya-ten-nae held aloof. Chihuahua came once, to protest
the General's edict that the making of tizwin [or tiswin] must cease. . . .
That the General was entirely right in his effort to prohibit tizwin drinking
was proved the following spring, when a tizwin drunk in defiance of this
order was the culmination of dissatisfaction that finally caused the malcontents to leave the Reservation. . . .

## THE OUTBREAK

A little before sunrise on the morning of May 15, I came out of my tent to
find all the chiefs and subchiefs with about thirty of their followers, waiting
for me. They said they had come for a talk. Not a woman or child was in
sight, a sure sign of something serious in the air. Near my tent was a small
knoll from the top of which any movement of troops from Fort Apache

could be seen as soon as they left the post. Two or three Indians had climbed the knoll and were watching the post. These men and a number of others were armed with rifles. . . .

Loco began a slow and halting harangue. Chihuahua impatiently interrupted him and springing to his feet, said: "What I have to say can be said in a few words. Then Loco can take all the rest of the day to talk if he wishes to do so."

Chihuahua then went on to repeat his previous arguments on the subjects of wife beating and tizwin drinking. They had agreed on a peace with Americans, Mexicans, and other Indian tribes; nothing had been said about their conduct among themselves; they were not children to be taught how to live with their women and what they should eat or drink. All their lives they had eaten and drunk what seemed good to them. The white men drank wine and whiskey, even the officers and soldiers of the posts. The treatment of their wives was their own business. They were not ill treated when they behaved. When a woman would not behave the husband had a right to punish her. They had complied with all they had promised to do when they had their talk with the General in Mexico; had kept the peace and harmed no one. Now they were being punished for things they had a right to do so long as they did no harm to others. . . .

I began something in regard to the wife beating. Old Nana got up, said an angry sentence or two to Mickey Free, and stalked out of the tent. I asked Mickey what Nana had said and Mickey tried to dodge the answer. When I insisted, he translated: "Tell *Nantan Enchau* (stout chief; Crawford and Gatewood were both rawboned) that he can't advise me how to treat my women. He is only a boy. I killed *men* before he was born."

That was a solar plexus blow to my dignity, and from the grunts of approval I saw that it was futile to pursue the matter further. . . . Chihuahua resumed the argument, if one-sided statement of a bill of rights may be called an argument.

"We all drank tizwin last night," he continued, "all of us in the tent and outside, except the scouts; and many more. What are you going to do about it? Are you going to put us all in jail? You have no jail big enough even if you could put us all in jail."

Since the replacement of Crawford by Pierce, the Indians, especially Geronimo, had frequently asked me if *Nantan Lupan* (Gray Wolf chief, the General) was still in charge of them. . . . Naturally the Indians inferred that *Nantan Lupan*, the man they most feared but upon whom they most relied for protection, had also left them. . . . And at that I am sure that some of them did not believe me, for one of the arguments Geronimo used to induce them to leave the Reservation was that Crook also had gone away.

I told Chihuahua that what to do about the drink was too serious for me to decide. I was simply carrying out the General's orders, which he had given for their own good. I would wire him at once and request instructions, which I would make known to them as soon as I received them.

[Lieutenant Davis promptly sent a telegram to Captain Pierce, who was responsible for passing it on to General Crook. The inexperienced Pierce, however, failed to pass it on, thinking it did not warrant the General's attention.]

Friday, Saturday, and most of Sunday passed without a reply from the General. I inferred, of course, that he was making preparations to deal with the situation and that I would have his orders when he was ready. I could not conceive that Pierce had not forwarded my wire. . . .

Sunday afternoon there was a baseball game between two post nines that I was asked to umpire while I was waiting at the post for a reply to my telegram. In the midst of the game, about four o'clock in the afternoon, Mickey and Chatto [a former hostile Apache, now an army scout] came to me with the report that a number of Indians, they did not know how many, had left their camps and were on their way to Mexico.

I attempted at once to send a telegram to Captain Pierce advising him of this, but the operator found that the wires had been cut. It was not until the next day near noon that the break was found. The Indians had cut the line in the fork of a tree and tied it with a buckskin thong. My telegram then went through, and was forwarded to the General, but too late for him to put into effect any plans he might have had in mind.

Captain Wade, in command of the troops at Fort Apache, immediately ordered them to prepare to take the field, but it was dark before they were ready. I returned to my tent to prepare my scouts to accompany them. The scouts were drawn up in front of my tent to have additional cartridges issued to them. On the Reservation they were allowed only four or five each, as cartridges passed as currency at twenty-five cents each and the temptation to sell or gamble them was great. I had a thousand rounds in my tent. . . .

First and last, during the Geronimo campaign, over five hundred Apache, including nearly one hundred Warm Springs and Chiricahua, were enlisted as scouts. [The] three who deserted that night were the only ones who proved unfaithful to their trust; and some excuse might be made for them on account of the pressure brought to bear on them by their blood relatives, Geronimo and Chihuahua.

With the troops from Fort Apache we marched all night, my scouts and a dozen of Gatewood's White Mountain following the trail, a slow proceeding at night. A little after sunrise the following morning we came out on the crest of a ridge bordering a valley some fifteen or twenty miles wide. In the distance, on the opposite side of the valley, we could see the dust raised by the Indian ponies ascending another ridge.

Realizing that further pursuit by troops was useless and that we were in for a long campaign in Mexico, I reported to Captain Smith in command of the troops that I would return with my scouts to Fort Apache and wire the General again, asking for instructions. . . .

The leaders who took part in the outbreak were Geronimo, Chihuahua, Nachite, Mangas, and old Nana. Chatto, Benito, Loco, and Zele with three-fourths of the Chiricahua and Warm Springs refused to take part in it. Almost immediately after they left their camps dissension cropped out among the hostiles. Nachite and Chihuahua charged Geronimo and Mangas with having lied to them to get them to leave by telling them that Chatto and I had been killed and that troops were coming to arrest all the Chiricahua and Warm Springs and send them away. Nachite and Chihuahua threatened to kill Geronimo. This caused a split in the camps. Mangas and his small band left at once for Mexico and never rejoined the others. Chihuahua and his band stopped in the Mogollon Mountains northeast of Morenci, Arizona, uncertain whether to go on to Mexico or return to the Reservation.

Coming out with my scouts the second time, about ten days after the outbreak, I ran into Chihuahua's party. We opened fire on them at a distance of six or seven hundred yards but the hundred or so shots exchanged with them did no damage other than causing them to lose the breakfast of a fat cow they were preparing. The meat was hot on the coals when we got to their camp, and was appreciated by us, as we had had no breakfast. We also captured a dozen ponies and a little camp plunder they left in their haste to be on their way to Mexico.

[Lieutenant Davis's skirmish, however, led nowhere, except to more frustration. Chihuahua decided to rejoin Geronimo. Meanwhile, Josanie— the younger brother of Chihuahua—took nine warriors on a 1,200-mile trek through the American Southwest. On November 23, Josanie struck the San Carlos Reservation, killing twenty White Mountain Apaches, along with two white civilians. He continued on through Arizona and New Mexico, raiding ranches, ambushing troops and civilian posses, and finally returning to Mexico at the end of December. Arizona and Eastern newspapers published screaming headlines, demanding the extermination of the hostiles. Meanwhile, Davis resigned in favor of a much easier job (as manager of a mining operation in Mexico), as did the often-wounded civilian chief of scouts, Al Sieber. A new pursuit column of Apache scouts formed up under the command of Captain Emmet Crawford.]

On December 19, Lieutenant Fountain's command, pursuing a hostile band [Josanie's] that had come up on a raid into Arizona, was ambushed. The surgeon, Doctor Maddox, and four men were killed and several wounded. The Indians suffered no loss as far as was known.

About December 18, Crawford reentered Mexico with a force composed only of scouts and pack trains. Lieutenant Maus had taken my place, with Lieutenant Shipp as assistant. Sieber started with the command, but was later recalled by the General, and Tom Horn, who had been taken along as Spanish interpreter, took his place as chief of scouts.

OFFICIALLY NAMED THE Second Battalion of Indian Scouts, Crawford's unit added up to a hundred Apache warriors, divided between Lieutenants Marion P. Maus and W.E. Shipp, with Tom Horn as civilian chief of scouts. Shortly after Crawford entered Mexico, Captain Wirt Davis led a similar group, designated the First Battalion of Indian Scouts, through New Mexico on a chase after Josanie's tiny band. It was Crawford, however, who was destined to finally fight a decisive engagement against the agile Apache warriors under Geronimo and Chihuahua.

Shortly after the New Year, Crawford began moving up the Arras River in the rugged Sierra Madre of Sonora, Mexico. On January 8, 1886, Crawford's scouts found fresh signs of Geronimo's trail. It was an almost impossible feat: the hostiles were marching through rocky, mountainous country, often leaping from rock to rock. The captain decided not to waste the opportunity, and he pushed his men on a ferocious two-day march to catch the fugitive band. Early on the morning of January 10, the scouts managed to surprise the camp of the wily Geronimo.

Lieutenant Maus, a tough, professional soldier, later wrote about that hard chase through the mountains at night—made all the harder by the decision to wear thin-soled moccasins to hide the sound of the march. Chief of Scouts Tom Horn also wrote about the ensuing mountaintop battle. Horn, though still fairly young, was an experienced Apache hand—by his own account a protege of Al Sieber, a former drover for a company that supplied cattle to the San Carlos Reservation, and a speaker of the Apache language. Though his memoirs (written while he awaited hanging for contract killings in Johnson County, Wyoming) often prove unreliable—sometimes grossly inaccurate—here he provides a brisk, believable account of the surprise attack. It was to be the critical fight of the campaign, but one with a tragic end. Little more than twenty-four hours after the first shots, Crawford would be dead, Horn wounded, and Maus in command.

## The Chase
*by Lieutenant Marion P. Maus*

The march was now conducted mostly by night. We suffered much from the cold, and the one blanket to each man used when we slept was scanty covering. Often it was impossible to sleep at all. At times we made our coffee and cooked our food in the daytime, choosing points where the light could not be seen, and using dry wood to avoid smoke. Our moccasins were thin and the rocks were hard on the feet. Shoes had been abandoned, as the noise

made by them could be heard a long distance. The advance scouts kept far
ahead. Several abandoned camps of the hostiles were found, the selection of
which showed their constant care. They were placed on high points, to
which the hostiles ascended in such a way that it was impossible for them to
be seen; while in descending, any pursuing party would have to appear in
full view of the lookout they always kept in the rear. . . .

At last, after a weary march, at sunset on the 9th of January, 1886,
Noche, our Indian sergeant-major and guide, sent word that the hostile
camp was located twelve miles away. The command was halted, and as the
hostiles were reported camped on a high point, well protected, and apparently showing great caution on their part, it was decided to make a night
march and attack them at daylight. A short halt of about twenty minutes
was made. We did not kindle a fire, and about the only food we had was
some hard bread and some raw bacon. The medical officer, Dr. Davis, was
worn out, and the interpreter also unfortunately could go no further. We
had marched continuously for about six hours and were very much worn
out and footsore, even the scouts showing the fatigue of hard service.
These night marches, when we followed a trail purposely made over the
worst country possible, and crossing and recrossing the turbulent river,
which we had to ford, were very trying. But the news of the camp being so
close at hand gave us new strength and hope, and we hastened on to cover
the ten or twelve miles between us and the hostiles.

I cannot easily forget that night's march. All night long we toiled on,
feeling our way. It was a dark and moonless night. For much of the distance
the way led over solid rock, over mountains, down canyons so dark they
seemed bottomless. It was a wonder the scouts could find the trail. Sometimes the descent became so steep that we could not go forward, but
would have to wearily climb back and find another way. I marched by poor
Captain Crawford, who was badly worn out; often he stopped and leaned
heavily on his rifle for support, and again he used it for a cane to assist him.
He had, however an unconquerable will, and kept slowly on.

At last, when it was nearly daylight, we could see in the distance the dim
outlines of the rocky position occupied by the hostiles. I had a strong
feeling of relief, for I was certainly very tired. We had marched continuously eighteen hours over a country so difficult that when we reached their
camp, Geronimo said he felt that he had no longer a place where the white
man would not pursue him.

## Surprise Attack
*by Tom Horn*

We got to the camp all right, and [Crawford] broke the command up into
four bunches. I took the east side and [Crawford] sent Shipp to the west
side. The east side was next to the mountains and the west side was about a

mile from the Arras River. [Crawford] placed Maus to the south side, [which] left Crawford on the north side. We were approaching the camp from the north. . . .[2]

We were all in position before daylight, and all we had to do was wait; the longer we could wait the more light we would have and the better would be the shooting. One thing that was against me was the eagerness of the scouts. I talked to them, and warned them to try to keep from starting the fight as long as possible, to give us better light, but they were all mad because of the raid that the renegades had made on the Reservation. . . .[3]

There were dozens of horses scattered around everywhere, and just as it was getting light we could begin to see the women and children working around among the horses, and others beginning to build fires. Minutes were worlds to me just then, as it was still too dark to do any good shooting.

[According to Maus, the fight was brought on by the braying of burros in Geronimo's camp, who smelled the waiting scouts. As the hostile warriors came out to investigate, firing erupted.]

No one spoke, but everybody seemed to fire at once. . . . Well, there were big doin's in that camp for the next half hour! Geronimo jumped up on a rock and yelled, "Look out for the horses!" And a minute afterwards he yelled: "Let the horses go and break toward the river on foot! There are soldiers and Apache scouts on both sides and above us. Let the women and children break for the river and the men stay behind!" Toward the river they all ran, and I was thinking that Lieutenant Shipp had not got into [his] place. . . . I could hear old Geronimo giving his orders as plainly as though he had been by my side.

I knew that my scouts could hear and understand also. Geronimo kept on yelling to his people: "Towards the river! Towards the river!" . . . Time was very short, but it seemed ages to me. I knew that a scared Indian could outrun a mad one; that my long, hard work was about at a close, and I was thinking it was too bad. I was just saying to myself: "If Sieber were here what a scientific lot of swearing there would be!" Then my thoughts came to a close, for I found Shipp, and he was the "rightest" man in the world.

Shipp had a boy with him that could speak English. I don't know how much he could speak, but I don't think it was much. I think it was the opposite of much that he could speak. Anyhow, this boy, Charley, could of course understand the renegades, and when the fight started, and Geronimo commenced to yell to his people to go towards the river, Charley made Shipp understand it some way or other, and Shipp and his men lay

[2] Horn was prone to exaggerate, and here he took credit for directing the entire attack; his account has been edited to reflect the more likely case, that Captain Crawford organized and led the assault himself.

[3] Horn is referring to the attack by Josanie on November 25, 1885.

still till the renegades got up within ten feet of them before they opened fire. Then they did good work and lots of it.

Instructions to the scouts did not amount to anything. They shot everything in sight. Women and children and everything else! When I saw the renegades were all going directly away from me, I told my men to go rounding in the horses, and to yell to all the scouts to look out for the horses.

I ran down the way the renegades had gone. With me was the boy, Chi-kis-in, the son of old Pedro, my first friend among the Apaches. He was a man now, and was called a good warrior.

Shipp and his men came up in front of the renegades, and as they did, stopped them short, for the renegades did not know how many scouts there were in front of them. They checked up for a few minutes, but Maus and Crawford were still giving them a good, heavy fire from both sides. Then Chi-kis-in and I ran right into them all, and that did settle it! They scattered like quails. "Scatter and go as you can!" yelled Geronimo.

I lost some good shooting by running over a little ridge to where I heard him, to try to get a shot at him. I could not tell one Indian from another they were so thick, and all running, and it was sure enough run, too! So I could not distinguish Geronimo. Crawford had told me to try to kill him if I possibly could, and I knew him so well that I thought I could recognize him at any distance. . . .

When I saw that I could not pick out Geronimo, I followed along, shooting whenever I could see a buck to shoot at, but I was getting down to where the women and children were, and things were pretty badly mixed up. Shipp was right in front of a big lot of women and children, and could have gotten all of them, but they could not surrender, as the scouts kept killing them so fast, and when that was stopped they were beginning to stampede.

Then I tried old Sieber's way. I ran down to my scouts and yelled and cursed and swore, and said some awful things, so Shipp said; but I was not on exhibition. I don't know what I did say. Shipp said I would yell in Apache and then swear in English, then more Apache and then more swear! . . . Well, whatever I did do, it had the desired effect. I got the scouts to stop shooting the women and children, and I got a lot of the women and children to surrender. I think we got only sixteen to surrender; the rest of them wanted to but were stampeded by my scouts.

───────

GERONIMO WAS INDEED convinced that there was nowhere now that the U.S. Army would not follow him—especially as long as the units that did the chasing were composed of other Apaches. He sent word to Crawford that he wanted to talk.

That talk never occurred. The day after the mountaintop battle, Mexican militia—mostly Tarahumara Indians, deadly enemies of the Apaches—approached Crawford's camp. The militia wanted Apache scalps, for which the Mexican government was still paying bounties, and they did not care whether the Apaches who provided them were renegades or U.S. soldiers. A sharp skirmish took the life of Captain Crawford and wounded Tom Horn.

Geronimo, however, still wanted to talk about surrendering. Maus arranged a conference, and on March 25, 1886, General Crook came down to Canyon de los Embudos—the Canyon of the Tricksters—to talk to the Apache chief. General P.H. Sheridan, the army's commanding general, wired Crook from Washington that he was to offer no terms but unconditional surrender, *"unless it is necessary to secure their surrender."* Not surprisingly, Crook found it necessary; he offered two years of exile in Florida, followed by a return to Arizona. First Chihuahua, then Geronimo accepted the terms. "Now that I have surrendered I am glad," commented Chihuahua. "I'll not have to hide behind rocks and mountains; I'll go across the open plain." Geronimo remarked, "Two or three words are enough. I have little to say. I surrender myself to you." Then he shook Crook's hand and said, "Once I moved about like the wind. Now I surrender to you and that is all."

As the troops and the Apaches marched back, however, Geronimo's band fell in with Bob Tribollet, a bootlegger and a member of the Tucson Ring. Tribollet was making a fortune from selling liquor to the Indians and supplies to the army; he had every interest in prolonging the campaign. He promptly got the Apaches drunk (on whiskey sold at inflated prices) and convinced them that they would be assassinated once they returned to Arizona. Chihuahua's band had gone on to the reservation, but Geronimo and thirty-eight followers decided to turn back.

The result was months more fighting and scores more deaths—and the end of General George Crook's command. Sheridan had always been uncomfortable with Crook's use of Apache scouts; now Crook had defied his demand for an unconditional surrender, and Geronimo had escaped on top of it all. The stocky, pugnacious commanding general was fed up with the complaints from Arizona settlers and businessmen, and distrustful of the scouts' reliability. After goading Crook into resigning, Sheridan placed General Nelson Miles in command. He ordered Miles to protect American life and property, keep hounding Geronimo's band, and to rely on U.S. troops, not Indian mercenaries.

While these events unfolded, two men observed with interest. One was former lieutenant Britton Davis, who still lived nearby in Mexico. Here he provides a critical account of the campaign that followed—from the American side. On the other side was Geronimo himself. Never actually defeated in battle, the aging warrior kept up the never-ending raids, ambushes, and escapes. After Davis's account, he provides the Indian perspective on events from the surrender conference to the moment he decided that the chase finally had to stop.

---

## Miles Takes Command
*by Lieutenant Britton Davis*

Crook was convinced that the only way to complete the subjugation of this small remnant was relentless pursuit with the scouts until they were all killed, or so weary of being chased from pillar to post that they would be disposed to surrender on terms Crook felt he could expect to extract from them. We have seen that Sheridan disagreed with this plan and Crook was relieved, Miles taking his place April 12. . . .

Miles adopted a policy midway between Crook's and that demanded of Crook by Sheridan. He garrisoned all water holes and ranches he thought might be subject to attack and established twenty-five or thirty signal points on prominent mountain peaks, using heliostats for signaling.[4] The scouts were dismissed, except a few used for trailers with the various cavalry and infantry commands who were to pursue the hostiles.

A principal pursuit column was organized under Captain H. W. Lawton, Fourth Cavalry. The command as at first was composed of infantry, mounted cavalry, and about a dozen Indian trailers [commanded by Tom Horn], and had orders to operate only south of the American border. . . .

While these preparations were going on the hostiles were not idle. During the last days of April a party of them came up from Mexico, raided over a large part of central and southern Arizona, pursued constantly by various commands in futile efforts to destroy or capture them, and finally escaped back into Sonora after killing near a score of people with no loss to themselves.[5]

On May 5, Captain Lebo[6] overtook and fought them in the Pinito Mountains of northern Sonora with a loss of one of his men killed and one wounded. No damage was done to the hostiles so far as known. Ten days later, on May 15, Hatfield's troop[7] struck them in a small mountain range

---

[4] This was a notable innovation, since the heliostat—a device for flashing visual signals—could not be interrupted by the Apaches, who regularly cut telegraph lines (splicing the cuts with leather thongs, making them harder to find).

[5] See Geronimo's description of these events in the next selection.

[6] Captain Lebo commanded Company K of the Tenth Cavalry, the famed "Buffalo Soldiers"—a unit composed of African-American troops. Lebo and his men chased Geronimo about 200 miles before this sharp fight—perhaps the finest performance of any unit of U.S. troops in the entire campaign.

[7] Captain C.A.P. Hatfield and a column of the Fourth Cavalry. See Geronimo's description of this fight in the next selection.

between Santa Cruz and San Pedro rivers, and captured their ponies and camp equipage. As Hatfield was making his way out of the mountains through an unknown country, back to water for his men and stock, the Indians ambushed his scattered command in a box canyon, killed his blacksmith and cook, wounded the first and second sergeants, and recovered the ponies. So far as known they suffered no loss themselves. . . .

Being deprived of their ponies and scant camp equipage meant little to the hostiles. Seven times in fifteen months this happened to them, and seven times within a week or ten days they reequipped themselves through raids on Mexican settlements or American ranches. . . . Conditions were very different from what they had been when our troops fought these Indians ten and twelve years before. . . . It was now no longer a question of fighting them but purely one of wearing them down.

## On the Run
*by Geronimo*

We started with all our tribe to go with General Crook back to the United States, but I feared treachery and decided to remain in Mexico. We were not under any guard at this time. The United States troops marched in front and the Indians followed, and when we became suspicious, we turned back. . . .

General Miles was made commander of all the Western posts, and troops trailed us continually. They were led by Captain Lawton, who had good scouts.[8] The Mexican soldiers also became more active and more numerous. We had skirmishes almost every day, and so we finally decided to break up into small bands. With six men and four women I made for the range of mountains near Hot Springs, New Mexico. We passed many cattle ranches, but had no trouble with the cowboys.[9]

We killed cattle to eat whenever we were in need of food, but we frequently suffered greatly for water.[10] At one time we had no water for two days and nights and our horses almost died from thirst. We ranged in the mountains of New Mexico for some time, then thinking that perhaps the troops had left Mexico, we returned. On our return through Old Mexico we attacked every Mexican found, even if for no other reason than

[8] These were the handful of Apache scouts, commanded by Tom Horn, who were retained as trailers.

[9] In reality, Geronimo's band attacked the Peck Ranch in the Santa Cruz valley, killing several cowboys. He was chased back into Mexico by Captain T.C. Lebo's company of the all-black Tenth Cavalry. Shortly afterward Geronimo returned to the mountains of Arizona, which he calls "New Mexico."

[10] As Davis mentioned above, General Miles garrisoned the main water holes.

to kill. We believed that they had asked the United States troops to come down to Mexico and fight us. . . . We were reckless of our lives, because we felt that every man's hand was against us. If we returned to the reservation we would be put in prison and killed; if we stayed in Mexico they would continue to send soldiers to fight us; so we gave no quarter to anyone and asked no favors.

After some time we left Gosoda and soon were reunited with our tribe in the Sierra de Antunez mountains. Contrary to our expectations, the United States troops had not left the mountains in Mexico, and were soon trailing us and skirmishing with us almost every day. Four or five times they surprised our camp. One time they surprised us about nine o'clock in the morning, and captured all our horses (nineteen in number) and secured our store of dried meats. We also lost three Indians in this encounter. About the middle of the afternoon of the same day we attacked them from the rear as they were passing through a prairie—killed one soldier, but lost none ourselves. In this skirmish we recovered all our horses except three that belonged to me. . . .[11]

Soon after this we made a treaty with the Mexican troops. They told us that the United States troops were the real cause of these wars, and agreed not to fight us anymore provided we would return to the United States. This we agreed to, and resumed our march, expecting to try to make a treaty with the United States soldiers and return to Arizona. There seemed to be no other course to pursue.

## The Last Surrender
*by Lieutenant Britton Davis*

While at Fort Apache, July 1 [1886], to inspect the condition of the Chiricahua and Warm Springs bands who had refused to leave with Geronimo and Mangas, Miles learned from the Chiricahua Ki-e-ta [or Kayitah], who had deserted on the hostile raid in May, that some of the followers of Geronimo and Nachite were, like himself, tired of warfare, and that the entire band might be persuaded to listen to reason and agree to surrender if two or three men they knew were sent to talk to them. Ki-e-ta consented to be one of the emissaries, and an influential Chiricahua known as Martine was selected as the second member of the ambassadorial party.

But it was essential that some officer with authority should be the bearer of Miles's tender of terms; and this officer must be known to Geronimo,

---

[11] This was the fight of May 15 with Captain C.A.P. Hatfield's column of the Fourth Cavalry, also described by Davis.

and [one] who knew him, if anything tangible was to result. Any strange officer attempting to enter Geronimo's camp would be shot on sight.

Crawford was dead. I had resigned and would doubtless not have been selected for the duty even if I had remained in the service. Gatewood had been relieved from duty at Fort Apache the previous December, and had rejoined his regiment at Fort Stanton, New Mexico. He had met Geronimo and other chiefs occasionally during the winter we were in camp near Fort Apache. What was of more importance, Geronimo knew of the high esteem in which Gatewood was held by the White Mountain Apaches, who had been under his care for more than three years. Miles sent for Gatewood.

Cool, quiet, courageous; firm when convinced of right, but intolerant of wrong; with a thorough knowledge of the Apache character and conversant with the causes leading to the outbreak, he was the ideal selection. . . . Through the courtesy of his son, Major Charles B. Gatewood, U.S. Army, Retired . . . I am able to give from his father's personal memoirs a brief account of his experiences as bearer of the flag of truce. . . .

Gatewood continued on to Lawton's command on the Arios River, two hundred miles south of the border, with his small command organized at Bowie. . . . Lawton knew nothing of the whereabouts of the hostiles, and Gatewood remained with him until about the fifteenth of August, when word was received that Geronimo's party was near Fronteras, a Mexican town of northern Sonora. . . .

Taking the trail of the women [who were returning to Geronimo's camp from Fronteras] six miles east of Fronteras, Gatewood and his party followed it for three days, a piece of flour sack on a stick being held aloft as a flag of truce. As he was going into camp on the Bavispe River about sundown of the third day, Martine, who with Ki-e-ta had been in advance, returned to him with the information that the hostiles were in camp about four miles away on a lofty peak of the Torres Mountains. . . .

Both of the Indians had been in Geronimo's camp, and had informed him of their mission. Geronimo had detained Ki-e-ta and sent Martine back with the message that he would talk to Gatewood only . . . that only Gatewood and his small party would be permitted any nearer the place designated for the conference. This was a little glade on the bank of the Bavispe about two miles from Gatewood's camp.

Gatewood thus describes the meeting: "By squads the hostiles came in, unsaddled, and turned out their ponies to graze. Among the last to arrive was Geronimo. He laid his rifle down twenty feet away and came and shook hands, remarking on my apparent bad health and asking what was the matter. The tobacco having been passed around, of which I had brought fifteen pounds on my saddle, he took a seat alongside as near as he could get, the others in a semi-circle, and announced that the whole party was there to listen to General Miles's message.

"It took but a minute to say, 'Surrender, and you will be sent with your families to Florida, there to await the decision of the President as to your final disposition. Accept these terms or fight it out to the bitter end.' A silence of weeks seemed to fall on the party. They sat there with never a movement, regarding me intently. Finally Geronimo passed a hand over his eyes, made his hands tremble, and asked me for a drink."

Geronimo was greatly disappointed when he found that Gatewood had no liquor with him and explained that the hostiles had been on a drunk for three days with mescal purchased from the Mexicans of Fronteras. . . .

Geronimo's first reaction to Miles's demands was an emphatic refusal. He and his people would leave the warpath only on condition that they be allowed to return to the Reservation, reoccupy their farms, be furnished with the usual rations, clothing, and farming implements, and be guaranteed immunity from punishment. The discussion continued all day, neither party gaining a point.

"Take us to the Reservation or fight," says Gatewood, "was his ultimatum as he looked me in the eye." Gatewood returned to his camp with an agreement to meet the hostiles again the next morning and continue the argument. As he was about to leave, he had the opportunity to tell Nachite, who had inquired about his mother and daughter, who had gone in with Chihuahua's party six months before, that they with all of Chihuahua's party had been sent to Florida and that all the Chiricahua and Warm Springs at Fort Apache were being sent there. . . .

When Gatewood returned to the council he found the hostiles more inclined to listen to his arguments. Nachite was anxious about his family and leaned now to Gatewood's side. Geronimo, seeing that he was losing ground, began to inquire what kind of a man Miles was, having never known anything of him. Gatewood described Miles in glowing terms; but fear and suspicion on the part of the Indians prolonged the discussion till near sunset. Gatewood was preparing to return to his camp, where Lawton had arrived that day, when Geronimo suddenly said to him:

"We want your advice. Consider yourself not a white man but one of us. Remember all that has been said today and tell us what we should do."

Gatewood replied: "Trust General Miles and surrender to him."

The next morning the pickets passed a call for "Bay-chen-day-sen"—Long Nose—Gatewood's name among the Apache. Gatewood met Geronimo, Nachite, and several more of the hostiles half a mile from his camp. They told him that they had decided to take his advice to go to the border, and surrender to Miles. . . .

The principal reason that Nachite, in particular, decided to surrender, and that caused him to influence Geronimo, was the desire and belief that he was soon to see his family again. But instead of being sent to Florida *with their families*, as they were led to believe, the men of the hostile party were confined in the dungeons of Old Fort Pickens at Pensacola and their families at St. Augustine in Fort Marion, several hundred miles away. Nor was this the only outrage perpetrated on these people. At Fort Apache were some seventy-five men and about 325 women and children who had resisted all efforts of the hostiles to induce them to leave the Reservation. Moreover, almost every adult male . . . had served at some time as a scout in pursuit of the hostiles. . . . [Yet] the men were disarmed and they with the women and children sent to Fort Marion; the same punishment that was meted out to the hostiles themselves.

———

BETRAYAL WAS THE only reward for the Apache scouts, who were the main weapon the government had wielded against their rampaging relatives. Mass exile, of course, solved the persistent problem of Apache breakouts and raids; but the government could have found a far more beneficial solution. The Navajo, for example, had successfully navigated from a background of warfare to flourishing sheep herding, thanks to intelligent policies and the absence of pressure by white settlers on their traditional homeland. But for the Apaches, banishment was the final, tragic conclusion to decades of struggle.

Even in defeat, Native Americans suffered further encroachments. Land-hungry settlers greedily eyed reservation lands, held in trust by each tribe as a whole. The Dawes Act of 1887 divided most of these holdings among individual Indian families; the resulting "surplus" lands were opened to white settlement.

For the army, it was difficult to imagine that the long war of conquest was finally complete. Since the end of the Civil War, it had fought more than a thousand separate engagements with hostile Indians. The official death count of almost 950 soldiers only hints at the scope of the conflict, which tied down two-thirds of the U.S. Army. Uncounted are the dead among Indian auxiliaries, who fought bravely in countless places—the Crow and Shoshone who saved Crook's army from catastrophe at the Rosebud, for example, or the Apache scouts who eventually brought Geronimo down. Uncounted are the settlers and emigrants who suffered Indian raids on trails and homesteads. Uncounted, too, are the thousands of casualties—men, women, and children—among the Native Americans who resisted.

One last burst of resistance led to a final tragedy. The Ghost Dance religion, taught by a Paiute Indian named Wovoka, caught fire among Native Americans. In South Dakota, Sitting Bull took up the new faith, which held that believers could bring about the return of the buffalo, the resurrection of the dead, and the end of white rule. Driven to needless panic by the popularity of the dance, government agents on the Sioux reservations called in troops. In 1890, Sitting Bull—as he himself had prophesied—was killed by his own people, members of a reservation police force, as he resisted arrest. The army then tracked down a large contingent of dancers at Wounded Knee; a tense standoff ensued as the soldiers tried to disarm the Lakota. A shot erupted, and the troops promptly gunned down hundreds in the snow. It was a pointless fight; by 1890, the Indians had long since lost the war for the West.

## 14

# THE DALTONS RIDE FOR THE LAST TIME

When Billy the Kid fell to the ground with a bullet in his chest in 1881, the Western frontier seemed to stagger along with him. Both as a symbol and as a flesh-and-blood, revolver-wielding gunman, William Bonney had epitomized the resistance of frontier communities to the growing, conservative power of government, capital, and political power brokers. His death seemed to bring the absorption of the frontier into mainstream America one step closer—but few at the time would have predicted that the conquest of most of the West would be complete within a decade.

At that same moment, independent frontier communities across the West were falling to the forces of incorporation. Far to the north, Stuart's Stranglers—the hired gunmen of cattle baron Granville Stuart—were sweeping eastern Montana, exterminating rustlers, misfits, and rifle-carrying malcontents. The Wyoming Stockgrowers' Association—heavily weighted with wealthy English absentee landowners—also began to enforce its interests with deadly force, working together with gunslinging officials such as Frank Canton. To the east, both famous and little-known Kansas town lawmen such as Wild Bill Hickok[12] and Wyatt Earp had succeeded in clamping down on the wild Texas cowboys, who increasingly took their herds to more accessible railheads or new markets farther West. A more stable society filled in the Kansas plains; in 1880, the state took the once-unimaginable step of banning alcohol.

Within Texas, the Rangers steadily wore down the violent ways of frontier communities—stamping out the endemic bloody feuds and scouring the long-time havens of rustlers, thieves, and backcountry dissidents and malcontents. New conflicts arose between local frontiersmen and big corporations, which purchased (or, more often, simply staked out) vast ranches to cash in on the cattle boom. The XIT ranch, for example, was owned by a syndicate of Chicago investors, while the Prairie Cattle Company spanned lands in Colorado, New Mexico, and Texas. These big operations began to string barbed wire across the open range, only to

[12] Hickok was shot in the back of the head by a drifter named Jack McCall in Deadwood, the prime boomtown of the Black Hills, in 1876—not long after the death of his old patron, George Custer.

have it cut down by small ranchers. After the Fence-Cutters' War of 1883–
84, the Texas legislature made fence cutting a felony—further undermin-
ing the resistance of isolated frontier settlements.

Across the West, state and territorial legislatures and public offices were
often dominated by wealthy kingpins and corporate interests, frequently
organized into stockgrowers' associations such as those in Montana and
Wyoming or political rings such as those in Santa Fe and Tucson. On the
shrinking expanse of frontier, these wealthy interests enforced a new respect for property and authority—like that found in the East, but with the
heavy hand long familiar in the West.

Of course, most of the men who fired their guns in anger in the 1860s,
'70s, and '80s did not see themselves as defenders of the downtrodden or
as political crusaders against the power of government. Much of the
violence erupted between men who were drunk, angry over money, or
acting out of personal whim. But Richard Maxwell Brown has shown that
the frontier *was* highly politicized: often gunslingers fully realized the
political implications of what they were doing—as young Texan and Democrat John Wesley Hardin did when he described his hatred of Republicans, the North, and the federal government.

Furthermore, frontier violence was a political problem for the authorities even when the killing was done for personal reasons. It was violence, after all, combined with weak government power, that made the
frontier something different from just another undeveloped area. The
frontiersman's willingness to kill and his disregard for property and authority made it difficult for legal and economic institutions to function
and grow—especially when whole communities looked the other way or
even celebrated the outlaws. If America was to truly expand into the
West, the frontier had to be tamed—new rules had to be rammed into
place.

By the start of the 1890s, these new values had begun to take root. Of
course, the work of gun-wielding lawmen and vigilantes might never have
succeeded except for the growth and development of Western society. For
every cattle baron and political string-puller, there were hundreds of thousands of solid farmers and small businessmen, happy to be earning a living
in peace and quiet, voting for sheriffs who promised to enforce the letter of
the law. With the completion of four major transcontinental railroads in
1883, economic expansion boomed: people and money poured into regions as diverse as Idaho and Arizona, the Dakotas and Colorado, building
a network of railroads, ranches, farms, towns, banks, and local government. This growth undermined the social basis of the Code of the West—
the belief in settling things man-to-man, without attention to legal
niceties. Now rural farmers took to politics—forming first the Greenback
Party and in 1891 the Populist Party—concerning themselves with the
availability of credit, the regulation of railroads, and tax reform. Prosperity

and social stability—along with steady law enforcement—eroded frontier resistance.

A few areas, however, remained to be conquered. Johnson County, Wyoming, swarmed with small ranchers and the occasional outlaw— dissidents against the might of the wealthy Wyoming Stockgrowers' Association. There, in that remote corner of a still sparsely settled territory, juries refused to convict men accused of rustling. Fed up with local resistance, the Association organized lynchings of suspected cattle thieves in 1889 and 1891. Ex-sheriff Frank Canton, now working directly for the big ranchers, set about hiring gunmen from Texas. On April 5, 1892, the Johnson County War erupted in open battle as Canton and a team of fifty killers rode into the county with a death list. They succeeded in shooting down two hard-fighting local men before they were surrounded by more than 200 cowboys and small ranchers. After a three-day siege, the U.S. cavalry rode in to stop the fight. The frontier resisters had won a rare victory in the war against the powers of the West.

Then there was Oklahoma. Ever since its original incarnation as the Indian Territory, the area had been used as a dumping ground for defeated tribes. Even so, pressure from white settlers continued. Bowing to what seemed to be the inevitable, the government opened much of the western half to white settlement in 1889, sparking the famed land rush. Thousands of wagons and horses lined up on the border, rushing across at high noon on the designated day to mark out choice claims. In 1890, the western half of the Indian Territory was officially designated the Oklahoma Territory; the Native Americans were now crowded into only the eastern section.

Oklahoma turned into one of the last frenetic hives of the frontier—a land of quickly constructed shanties and ramshackle towns, where the law was an ad hoc institution at best. Bandit gangs wandered the territory, holding up banks and trains—and often winning local support and admiration along the way. One of the most famous (and popular) was the Dalton Gang, a band built around three brothers: Bob, Grat, and Emmett Dalton. They were born into a family of "sooners," or pioneers who settled in the territory before it was officially opened to settlement. The boys had even worked as deputy U.S. marshals, until an older brother, Frank, was killed and the survivors found themselves accused of rustling.

The accusations might well have been accurate. Not long after leaving law enforcement behind, they embarked on a crime spree, together with Bill Doolin, another famous outlaw. Specializing in train robberies, the gang wandered the south-central plains for almost two years, often returning after their holdups to a dugout that Emmett had built as a hideaway. Interestingly, the Daltons had originally lived in western Missouri, where former Confederate guerrillas (notably Jesse and Frank James and the Younger brothers) had turned to outlawry decades earlier; Emmett wrote that the brothers identified strongly with bandits such as the James boys, who were popular—and highly political—heroes in much of Missouri. In Oklahoma, the Daltons won similar popular acclaim for their exploits against the powerful railroad corporations.

In October 1892, the Daltons decided on their most daring raid yet: to hit two banks in the same day, in Coffeyville, Kansas. The three brothers and two confederates (Dick Broadwell and Bill Powers—Doolin had split from the group) planned the raid carefully, but they little realized that their time had almost passed. The law-abiding citizens of Coffeyville were not about to stand idly by.

## The Final Reckoning
### by Emmett Dalton

The three of us, Bob, Grat, and I, said farewell to official arms at a time when the entire Western country was passing through a singular pandemic of lawlessness. It was not alone in the law enforcement agencies that laxity and inefficiency were evident. The fiber of the whole country was growing flabby. . . . There was widespread corruption in business and government. Predatory rings multiplied. Legislatures abetted notorious pillage. A time when men were inclined to take back their delegated powers, turning again to the personal force of wit or gun. It was an outstanding example of how easily crime can become democratic. . . .

In the West it incubated a large nest of outlaws. On the one side railways, banks, and great corporations, many of which were lawlessly maneuvering for privileged booty; on the other side train and bank robbers who lobbied with six-shooters. Here in the Indian Territory the infection was rife. . . .

### ON THE EDGE OF THE ABYSS

Bob Dalton squatted on the ground. He had a stick in his hand. With the stick he was drawing a crude map in the dust. Grat, Powers, Broadwell, and I huddled around him. The glow of a tiny campfire laid a brimstone tinge on our faces. It was one o'clock in the morning of October 5, 1892. The frosty night nudged in close about us, peering over Bob's shoulder as he sketched the plot of Coffeyville, to which we would go up with the next light of day.

The scene was Onion Creek, where the water ran still and dark along the edge of a farm two miles from town. Late as it was, the little fire was kept carefully banked down lest it attract suspicion from the nearest farm dwellings or from some tardy homecomer on the road.

"Here's the way we'll go in," said Bob, illustrating with a scratch of the stick. The instructions were chiefly for the benefit of Powers and Broad-well. They were strangers in this region. Grat, Bob, and I were familiar with every hog trail, for we had come often to Coffeyville in other days. In fact, the farm where our parents had once lived lay only a mile away. "Here," resumed Bob, "is Union Street. We'll go along as far as the old Opera House and tie our horses right there." He made another designating mark.

"The Condon Bank stands at this spot on the plaza. And there is the First National." For a moment the stick made marks and indentations to impress relative positions. Bob paused and looked at me. "I'm taking Emmett with me," he announced. "We'll handle one of the banks. You three can take the other. Which do you want?"

"Whatever you say, Bob," spoke Grat.

"You name it," added Powers.

"We'll flip for it," Bob announced.

The First National would probably be a shade more dangerous because it was farther from the place where the horses would be tied. I produced a coin. "Heads," I said, "will take the First National. And I'm laying my luck on heads this time." . . .

"Heads it is," read Powers. We were all satisfied.

We warmed our hands at the fire. "Colder'n hell," said Broadwell.

"Probably be a lot warmer tomorrow," retorted Grat significantly. . . .

"Before we hit the blankets," interposed Bob, "we'll turn ourselves inside out." We performed the customary protective ritual. Every man searched himself for any evidence which might serve to identify himself or incriminate his fellows or innocent persons in case of disaster. Into the embers of the fire went letters and mementoes. Every man had something to contribute. . . .

We mounted our horses and rode up out of Onion Creek bed at sunrise. We were timing ourselves to reach town just after the two banks had opened at nine o'clock, and before the merchants might withdraw consid-erable deposits. Grat, Bob, and I had been in both banks many times. We knew their personnel. We were also acquainted with all the prominent merchants and with every law officer of the town. For a moment it seemed strange and unreal to be headed in to sack a place where so often we had come on peaceful missions. . . .

## THE FINAL RECKONING

We were coming in now on Union Street, the main residential avenue. A few belated children were hastening to school. A woman was digging up some flower bulbs. The blacksmith shop was melodious with anvil music. Somebody getting a horse shod. Folks going about their business.

"I'll be damned!" suddenly spoke Bob. "Look, the hitch rack's gone.

Torn down to fix the street where them darkies are workin'." This was the
rack where we had intended tying our horses beside the Opera House.
"This street'll be bad to get out of," added Bob. "Horses might stumble.
Got to find another place." He peered around quickly, estimating. "Back
yonder in the alley," he indicated. We turned and cantered in behind the
blacksmith shop and the lumber yard. There the alley widened to considerable area. And there folks often hitched their horses to a fence rail while
they did their trading. . . .

Half past nine now.

Looking east through the alley, which opened on the triangular central
plaza, we could see the front of the First National Bank. Adjoining it, and
also plainly visible, was Isham Brothers' hardware store. As events turned
out, we could not have placed the horses in a more dangerous spot. . . . At
our left as the five of us strode swiftly out of the alley, walking east, stood
the Condon Bank, located in the Luther Perkins Building. It occupied the
north end of the plaza, fronting south. On three sides were plate-glass
windows. It was like a showcase into which the sun streamed brightly. It
was perhaps fifty paces from the First National. On our left also, in order
from the alley, were McKenna & Adams's clothing store, Wells Brothers'
general merchandise store, and the old Opera House. At our right on this
side of the plaza were Slausson's drug store, a furniture shop, the post
office, and Reed Brothers' clothing store. Another tier of stores occupied
the southern end of the plaza, and on the eastern frontage flanking both
sides of the First National Bank and Isham's place, stood Boswell's hardware store, Rummell's drug store, and Brown and Cubine's shoe shop.
These places, then, formed the gallery from which the deadliest street
battle in the West was to be viewed and from which it was to burst in a
tornado of fire within a few minutes.

The plaza, thus encompassed by buildings, was paved entirely with
brick. Our feet made a scuffling noise on it as we advanced—Bob and I
ahead, Grat, Powers, and Broadwell just behind. Hitching racks lined the
sides of the open area. Several teams were there. Draymen were wont to
stand in the plaza with their wagons, awaiting business. Drayman Charley
Grump was the first on hand this morning. He looked at us with idle
curiosity as we neared the banks.

Eighty feet from the alley mouth, Grat, Powers, and Broadwell wheeled
sharply and entered the Condon Bank. Bob and I proceeded without
looking back, toward the First National. There was a scattering of people
on the streets. But thus far we had attracted no special notice. Men walking
with rifles in hand was not of itself a suspicious circumstance.

Charley Grump's eyes bulged. From where he sat sunning himself on his
dray wagon he could look straight into the Condon Bank. He saw the first
move of the holdup by Grat, Powers, and Broadwell—saw it like a show
from a reserved seat. In a flash he knew.

"The Daltons!" shrilled drayman Grump, leaping from his wagon. Now Bob and I, as we went swiftly toward the First National, had also become significant. Once more he cried out the alarm—"Look out! The Daltons!" It wasn't a matter of recognition but of correct assumption. His startled outcry echoed across the plaza. . . .

Bob whirled and fired at Grump in an effort to check the alarm. The bullet took him in the hand. He scuttled into the store. . . . Awakened suddenly to danger by Grump's affrighted yell, the citizenry were held numb with shock and indecision in the stores and along the streets. For minutes no one raised the mustering call to arms.

In the Condon Bank, Grat covered cashier Charley Ball with his Winchester. Charles T. Carpenter, the vice president, also stood with hands raised. Broadwell and Powers held guns on T.C. Babb, the bookkeeper, and on one other man in the bank. The outlaws scooped fifteen hundred dollars of counter cash into the sack Grat carried. "Open the safe and open it quick!" Grat commanded the cashier with rifled threat.

Ball hesitated—Ball, the sickly man of cool nerve and rigid discipline. "It's a time lock," parleyed Ball with courageous wit. "Doesn't open until nine forty-five." He slanted a shrewd look at Grat.

Grat hesitated, indecisive. The statement surprised and momentarily baffled him. The moment for swift, unerring decisiveness had come. But Grat, Powers, and Broadwell let it slip. Nine forty-two now. . . . "We'll wait three minutes," said Grat. If he or his two companions suspected a ruse, none of them made any effort to verify the cashier's statement or call his audacious bluff . . .

Nine forty-three. Ball's strained face turned a shade whiter. Outside somewhere along the plaza a gun cracked. Another. The sweat broke out on the cashier's forehead. Doggedly Grat, Powers, and Broadwell waited.

I have dwelt at some length on Ball's behavior. His was the decisive act in Coffeyville that day. His shifty falsehood about the vault—which all the time was open to any hand—was to save his bank eighteen thousand dollars. It was also to cause the death of eight men within the next five minutes.

Meantime Bob and I had entered the First National. I was a few feet ahead. In the bank at the time were Thomas G. Ayres, cashier, Bert S. Ayres, his son, and assistant cashier W.H. Sheppard, the smiling and gracious teller, and a bookkeeper whose name I have forgotten. These composed the official force. In addition, three customers were present: J.H. Brewster, a prominent contractor; C.H. Hollingsworth; and Abe Knott, a deputy sheriff of Montgomery County.

Knott had just cashed a four-dollar check. He stood with his back to me as Bob and I came through the door. I recognized him as he turned in surprise at my command of "Hands up!" . . .

"Keep 'em high!" I warned, striding closer toward Knott. He grinned with cool effrontery. But he made no more suspicious moves. "I don't want your chickenfeed," I said. Tom Ayres had dodged down behind the counter at my first command. I expected him to come up shooting. I had to watch him as well as the deputy sheriff for a tense moment. But Bob, who had entered right behind me, edged around and covered him. The others were standing as ordered.

Throwing Ayres a sack, Bob ordered him to put the money in it. He started dumping in trays of silver. "Keep that silver out," Bob spoke. "It's too heavy to bother with. The vault!" he rapped. "The big stuff!"

Tom Ayres opened the vault and threw the currency into the sack. Things were going like clockwork here at the First National. Not more than a minute had elapsed since Bob and I came through the front door. Here, too, a clock was ticking on the wall.

In the stores along the plaza the citizens were coming out of their coma of fright. If they had been slow to start, they were now making up for lost time. There was a scurrying toward the first concentration of resistance. A stealthy mustering. Word of the raid was being flung all across the town: "The Dalton gang—they're holding up both banks! Already wounded Charley Grump!"

The First National vault had been emptied. Bob and I were marching the bank officers and the three customers toward the front door. Bob was ahead. I brought up the rear, lugging the weighty money sack. Bob stepped out and peered quickly about.

Whang! came the first opposition shot. The bullet smashed into the door casing. Bob jumped back into the bank, grinned, and said, "Bum shot!" We herded the bankers and the customers out through the door—all except Sheppard, the teller. Knott was watching like a hawk for a chance to shoot. We hadn't disarmed him. But he edged out, and his chance was gone.

A glance through the front window revealed men scurrying this way and that, everyone acting on his own, like a squad of deploying soldiers without an officer. Some were hastening to arms. Others were running to cover. There was a scattering of shots toward the First National as soon as the men we had sent through the front door had gotten in the clear. Those shots the group in the Condon Bank had heard as the minute hand on the wall hung at nine forty-three.

The battle had opened.

"Can we get out the back way?" I asked Sheppard, whom I had kept covered while Bob watched the front door for a possible rush.

"The back door's open," calmly announced Sheppard. He had remained coolly unruffled throughout the holdup. Even in these circumstances he could be polite. A fragment of his celebrated smile still clung to his lips. "It leads to the alley."

"You come and show us," I insisted. He led us to the rear door. It was open. I finished tying the money sack in the middle so that it would hang securely over my arm. We ordered Sheppard back into the bank. Then Bob and I stepped out into the alley. Out front the crackle of guns was increasing. But here for a moment everything was clear.

"You look after that money sack," said Bob. "I'll do the fighting." Lucius Baldwin, a young clerk in Boswell's hardware store, emerged from the store into the alley. He came trotting toward us with a revolver in his hand.

"Hold up there!" Bob called, withholding his fire. But the clerk kept on coming at a dog trot. He did not fire, and he did not speak. Some strange confusion was upon him. Like a somnambulist he moved, gun leveled at us.

Bob fired. The ball struck Baldwin in the breast. He crumpled up, the revolver skittering from his hand. . . .

We hastened north through the alley behind the bank, turned left on Union Street, and within a few yards had come around to where we were exposed to the gathering storm in the plaza. Now for the first time the citizens saw us and had us a few moments in the clear against the sights of their rifles. On the instant the hitherto desultory and rather aimless shooting burst into a crescendo of fire. Within the sounding box of the store-flanked plaza it bellowed in thunderous crashes. The din became terrific. Teams hitched along the square and in the adjacent streets broke loose and ran helter-skelter. . . .

The shooting was as yet still wild and spasmodic. The townsfolk were still in the first jumpiness of buck fever. For a moment it seemed inexplicable that Bob and I should be the target for so much flailing lead and yet remain unsinged. Then I realized that while some of the shots were coming in our direction, most of them were being directed into the front of the Condon Bank. Without catching the significance of that, I had a swift sense that Bob and I were being favored by the flip of the luck at the morning campfire which now seemed ages remote. . . .

Now two of Coffeyville's brave, embattled citizens stepped into the open: George Cubine and Charles T. Brown. They were partners in business. Cubine was an expert bootmaker. He catered to the cowboys' tastes in fancy footwear. Years before he had made boots for Bob, Grat, and me. He knew us well.

Cubine came out of his shop with Winchester in hand. Brown followed at his heels, himself unarmed. Cubine swung down on us. As he did so, Bob took a flash shot. Cubine fell dead before he could fire. Brown, undaunted, stooped down and took the rifle from the dead man's hands. He leveled at us. No buck fever in Cubine and Brown. Bob shot again. Brown died beside his partner.

At the moment I was slightly ahead of Bob. Hampered by the heavy money sack, I had reached cover behind the corner of the Perkins building.

It was for the death of Cubine that I was later convicted, although I had not fired a shot at him.[13]

"Go slow," Bob said as he came to my side. "Take it easy—I can whip the whole damn town!" We jogged around into the alley behind Wells Brothers' general store, momentarily secure. We did not yet know how thoroughly aroused and determined the citizens were. Even their hectic fire hadn't greatly alarmed us, although it was the first time we had met such general resistance. . . .

We were surprised not to find Grat, Broadwell, and Powers at the hitching rack. A thundering crash of shots resounded from the plaza. "What's keeping the boys?" Bob muttered anxiously as I tied the money sack to the saddle.

The Isham hardware store, adjoining the First National Bank, afforded the best cover for the fighting citizens, and there a crowd had gathered. From the show cases they had armed themselves with rifles and revolvers. They had spotted us as we came to the horses. The open alley gave them an unimpeded range. Bullets were whining about our ears even before I had made the money sack secure. Bob began pumping his Winchester, swinging it this way and that in rapid arcs, still believing that he might be able to terrify the opposition. But this time the citizenry were beyond intimidation. A fog of acrid gunpowder smoke began to swirl lazily in the October sunshine. And still no sign of our three comrades.

"The boys must be in trouble," exclaimed Bob. "We better go and help 'em out." Here we were, Bob and I, with good assurance of safety only a few yards down that alleyway. All we had to do was fling a leg to saddle and make a dash for it. The shooting was still inaccurate, although we were fair targets from the Isham arsenal. "Come on," said Bob, walking into the line of fire. "We'll go and help 'em." I don't believe it was a test of Bob's loyalty, in the sense that test implies deliberation. . . . I went by his side. For myself I recall no definite sensation of fear or anxiety. We were still on the swelling tide of battle.

The fight burst once more with a sudden crash in front of the Condon Bank as we came toward the head of the alley on the plaza. It was Grat, Powers, and Broadwell coming out.

With foolish but magnificent courage Grat had been counting the ticks of the clock on the bank wall. What was happening in that deadly showcase had been as plain as day to a hundred hidden and squinting eyes on three sides of the plaza. Despite the danger to the bank officials, lead had poured like hail against the bank front, shattering great windows, pitting the

---

[13] Emmett Dalton actually confessed to shooting Cubine. He worked on this memoir much later in life, after he had become a peaceful citizen, banking on his reputation as a reformed outlaw; it is not surprising that he distanced himself from the bloodshed in Coffeyville.

woodwork. At the first crash Grat had ordered all except cashier Ball to flatten on the floor.

"Get down, or you might get killed," he roared. Grat himself stood behind a window casement, partially protected. Broadwell and Powers were under precarious cover. Broadwell had in his hand the sack with the counter cash, about fifteen hundred dollars—the meager silver measure of his life and of Grat and Powers's.

Ball stood by the safety vault, continuing his magnificent bluff. He too watched the hands of the clock. Half a minute more. The sickly, taciturn man who had closed his mind against everything except that rigid conception of his duty did not flinch. And Ball won his grim gamble.

Before the clock had ticked off the few remaining seconds the fire had become so intense and the rally of the citizens so ominous that even Grat, for all his reckless nerve, considered it best to make a desperate retreat. Glass was falling about them, wood splintering—bedlam and inferno. Death was fanning hot and close. Eighty bullet holes were later counted in Condon Bank Building. Suddenly all the gold in the Condon vault had no value to the outlaw trio. They drew together for the rush.

And now they were coming out. From our exposed position in the alley we saw them break for cover. They came out shooting. Their guns talked fast.

For a moment the attention of Bob and myself was distracted. The firing zone had spread. . . . Bob pumped his gun at the doors and windows, and at every sign of mobilizing menace, partly to protect himself and me, and also to keep the way of retreat clear from possible enfilading fire for Grat, Powers, and Broadwell. They were now backing across the sixty feet of exposed plaza toward the alley in which we waited.

They came very slowly, it seemed to me, but their Winchesters kept pouring a leaden hail toward the Isham store. They were in turn receiving more than they sent. It was during this hot exchange that cashier Ayres of the First National fell wounded. He and the others who had been in the bank had taken refuge in this store after we had turned them loose. . . .

The kaleidoscope was gyrating in swift detonating flashes. Movements and attitudes of ourselves and our swarming antagonists, whenever they showed themselves, stood out in sharp, looming pictures. Everything seemed crystal clear. My brain registered multiple images. I could see the boys reloading their Winchesters. I could see the swing of the glistening barrels. The somber strained faces of my companions. The dull gleam of the shadowy plate glass under the overhanging sidewalk porch of Isham's store, whence flashed lances of flame.

Powers had come perhaps twenty feet into the alley mouth when he was hit in the arm. I saw him return the shot, after he had regained the balance from the violent impact of the bullet. For a moment he took refuge in a doorway of the McKenna-Adams store, reloading.

I suddenly realized this was to be a fight to the death. All the time I had expected the firing to die away, to feel myself on the back of my horse plunging away, presently, with the others—expecting relaxation from this terrible tension.

But there was no let-up. The terrible frenzy of an aroused citizenry was now upon us in full avalanche. . . . Bob and I covered the retreat while Grat and Broadwell hastened toward the horses in our rear. Powers too passed us after he had recovered from the first shock of his wound. We were all together at last. In those few seconds it must have been incredible—some devil's miracle—to the citizens that we were all still on our feet and by way of escaping after so much lead had been flung at us. Powers had been hit and was still alive. Broadwell had been hit, and he too was still in the fight. . . . The firing lulled. Then it broke out again with renewed fury.

A team hitched to a Standard Oil wagon, one of the runaways, broke into new panic at the crash. . . . It stampeded straight for the spot where our horses were tied. Our own horses reared and plunged. Any instant they might break loose and leave us afoot. But Grat was thinking fast and straight now. In a flash he shot one of the oil-wagon horses in the head, bringing him down and halting the runaway.

The firing from Isham's store was accurate now. The range was about one hundred yards.

I saw Bob stiffen and reel a little. An instant later, as I had my gun up at aim, a Winchester ball took me through the upper arm, shattering the bone. The blow knocked the rifle from my hand. I stooped over and picked it up with my left hand. My right hung useless. Bob sagged down against a pile of rocks in the alley, against a high board fence. He didn't say anything.

As I turned in a temporary daze to reach the horses, I got a second rifle bullet. It smashed through the back of my hip, between two shells in my cartridge belt, and passed out through the groin. For a moment it paralyzed my leg. I had taken only a few limping strides when I saw Grat fall, almost opposite the horses at the rear of the blacksmith shop lot. He did no more shooting, dying within a few moments. He had been shot through the chest.

Meantime City Marshal Charles T. Connelly had maneuvered around into the alley behind us toward the west. Connelly was a brave man. He came right out into the open among us. When he was shot and by whom I do not know. . . .

Although I had been twice wounded, I felt no pain: just a numbness which hampered me as I started untying my horse. I recollect it made me furious. Somehow I got the horse loose. All the animals were snorting and skittish. Powers, who was starting to mount beside me, was having trouble controlling his big dapple-gray. Just as he got his leg over the saddle, I saw him pitch headlong. A second bullet had killed him instantly.

Broadwell and I were up together. For the moment every man was thinking of himself. Broadwell reeled in his saddle. "I'm hit bad," he muttered. Clutching the saddle horn he put spurs to his horse and clattered down the alley westward. I followed him a few yards. Suddenly I realized Bob wasn't with us. I didn't know he had been so badly wounded. Looking back I saw him still huddled there against the rocks.

"You go on," I called to Broadwell, "I'm going back." The alleyway was screaming with shots from Isham's and the plaza—from everywhere, it seemed. Bob's and Powers's horses were killed. Our own firing had left a drifting fog of smoke. It hung over the inert figures of Grat and Powers and the huddled form of Bob. Two of us dead now. One mortally wounded. Myself hard hit.

I had trouble getting my horse to face the smoke. The money sack still hung there on the saddle, ironically. I had no thought now of shooting. Had no thought of anything except to reach Bob. To haul him up behind me, if he still lived, and try to break clear from that inferno. . . . My wounds were bringing on nausea. It was all I could do to control my animal. Bullets were still singing. That I was not riddled in that short zigzag ride to Bob was a miracle.

Meantime Carey Seaman, the barber, had come into action. Seaman had returned from a hunting trip in the Indian Territory just before the battle began. He was unhitching his team at his stable, a block away, when the firing started. In his buckboard was a shotgun, loaded with buckshot. Grabbing it up, he had skirted back through an open lot to the alley. There he was screened from our view by a high board fence. During the deadly volley through the alley he had reached the cover of an outhouse. There he must have been standing as I wheeled to ride back toward Bob. Now he stepped out into the alley, hammers cocked above a double load of buckshot.

"Don't mind me, Emmett," Bob whispered as I leaned down toward him. "I'm done for. Don't surrender, boy. Die game!" He seemed to realize, although already far gone, that it would be impossible for me to get away now. . . .

Behind me a crashing roar resounded above the thinner din of rifles. Twice it sounded. Carey Seaman had pulled his triggers.

It was all over. With eighteen buckshot in my back, from hip to head, I slid down. The double impact had taken me as I was bending down to catch Bob's last admonition. I clutched at the money sack in my agony. It came loose. I fell on it in a huddle beside Bob. In his last throe, Bob turned laboriously on his side, propped himself weakly on one elbow. With his eyes already glazing he fired one last wild shot. And so he died.

Sieved with twenty wounds. I still managed to cling to consciousness. But the world swam far away. For a moment longer the sound of guns continued, faint and monotonous, as if the frenzy of the citizens could not be surfeited. Then the detonations ceased. The quarry was all down. For a moment everything was deathly quiet.

Then rose a dreadful yelping of dogs. Many dogs. Howling an eerie dirge. And through the lifting smoke fog they began to come—the citizens of Coffeyville, the men who had exterminated the Dalton band. Their feet scuffled hesitantly across the brick plaza and down the alley. Vaguely I saw them in a swimming haze. Coming to count the dead. Coming to recover the sacked loot, some twenty thousand dollars.

Dick Broadwell, fatally wounded, had ridden a mile from town, where he toppled dead from the saddle.

Less than ten minutes had elapsed from the time the five of us had entered the banks. The shadows of the buildings across the alley hadn't shifted more than an inch. The clock in the Condon Bank had moved its black hands but a brief span since Grat had first glanced at it. In that short interval, eight men had died: Bob and Grat Dalton, Dick Broadwell, and Bill Powers of the outlaw band; Cubine, Brown, Baldwin, and Connelly, among the citizens. Four had been wounded: three citizens—Thomas G. Ayres, of the First National Bank; T. A. Reynolds, a clerk at Isham's; Charley Grump, the drayman—and myself. . . .

The curtain had come down on the most deadly street battle in the West.

———

FROM BEGINNING TO end, this book has been about conflict—the sprawling, diffuse, vicious conflict that spanned half a continent and culminated in the streets of Coffeyville. Fifty years before, young Jesse A. Applegate and Francis Parkman had set out across the same plains that Emmett Dalton almost died on; but that fifty years had made all the difference. During that span, the West had been invaded by a new people, in numbers never before seen there—millions of people with new values, a new culture, new political institutions, and a new way of using the land. As we have seen, the invaders crushed and swept away the old inhabitants, changed the environment itself, then fought among themselves over power, property, and community. It was a twice-conquered West that swallowed the Daltons whole that cold October morning.

That conquest had not necessarily been a heroic battle, either: few of the characters who have appeared in these pages, either as subjects or speakers, survive in the imagination as romantic figures. Among the various resisters, for example, John Wesley Hardin was a racist, trigger-happy murderer who happened to have strong political convictions, while Geronimo was a man disliked by many of his own people, who nursed a scalding hatred of Mexicans, and who went to war to preserve such traditional ways as wife-beating and predatory raids. Among the conquerors, William Break-enridge happily took part in a cold-blooded massacre; Buffalo Bill Cody helped drive a species into near extinction; General P. H. Sheridan openly despised Indians as savages; and even Texas Ranger J. B. Gillett once shot a fleeing, unarmed man in the back.

On the other hand, the war for the frontier witnessed enough heroism and drama to sustain a century of myth—and its mayhem was tragically real, with a death toll in the thousands. Today, it is hard not to feel the poignancy of the apocalypse that struck the Indian peoples, and admire the truly principled resistance of Chief Joseph, Crazy Horse, Sitting Bull, and others. And it is easy to identify with those who fought against the abuses of power by groups like the Murphy Company, the Santa Fe Ring, and the Montana Stockgrowers' Association.

But the struggle to incorporate the frontier into American society was driven not only by the kingpins and lawmen, but by millions of peaceful farmers, ranchers, and small-business owners. The same social and economic expansion recounted in the last chapter, which transformed the natural world and ringed the Indians in on their reservations, also served to undercut the isolation of frontier settlements. The same wild Kansas prairies described by General George Custer, where Wild Bill Hickok ruled with his pistols, unhampered by legal niceties, changed by the 1890s into well-developed counties, with school districts, prospering towns, banks, and businesses, with rail and telegraph service. Lynchings and main-street walkdowns were things of the past. Even the political schemers and big corporations had to give room as the rising tide of population and economic development eroded their sway (seen in the rise of the Populist Party, for example).

Frontier conditions persisted in a few areas. In Oklahoma, ex–Dalton gang member Bill Doolin pursued his profession with a new band, before taking a shotgun blast to the chest in 1896. Wyoming in particular continued to be a battleground after the small ranchers' victory in the Johnson County War of 1892. The big stockgrowers quickly struck back by signing up Tom Horn as a paid assassin. Where open invasion had failed, Horn succeeded with ambush and sniper fire. Supposedly earning six hundred dollars for each kill, he systematically murdered suspected rustlers and noncriminal troublemakers. By the end of the decade, resistance in Johnson County was broken—though Horn was swung from the gallows in 1903, when he was executed for shooting the fourteen-year-old son of one of his intended victims. The Hole-in-the-Wall country, too, continued to host outlaws such as Butch Cassidy and the Wild Bunch, who roamed the northern plains during the late 1890s before departing for South America in 1902. They were lucky to have survived for so long.

Crime and violence, of course, have never been eradicated. They continue to plague the West, where the legacy of the frontier lives on in the remoteness of the country, the independent mind-set, and the high rate of gun ownership. By the 1890s, much of Western society had undergone a critical change. Where juries once refused to convict men for rustling, robbery, and even murder, where vigilante groups enforced the law with lynchings, Westerners now clamor for even more stringent law enforcement and fewer rights for the accused. The violence of frontier resistance to wealth and power has largely disappeared. Despite lingering Western hostility to the Federal government, residents in Montana, Wyoming, Arizona, and elsewhere earn wages in U.S. currency, borrow from banks, vote in elections, support the police, celebrate their patriotism, and in general take part in the same social and economic system as the rest of the country.

Perhaps the most telling sign of the successful incorporation of the West lies in Emmett Dalton's own account of the climactic Coffeyville raid. Emmett confessed to shooting and killing George Curbine, and he served many years in prison as a result. Indeed, it would be hard to imagine him wading through the torrent of bullets that took the lives of every other gang member without firing back as rapidly as possible. But he glides through his own retelling of the battle, never actually squeezing off a round. Why? By the time he prepared his memoirs (together with a professional writer), he had long since lived a peaceful life—as a real estate agent, building contractor, and even a Hollywood screenwriter. After being pardoned in 1907, Dalton sought to distance himself from his past, except to the extent that he could cash in on it; he even campaigned against crime. He was no killer, he implied, he was just another productive citizen with a colorful past. The conquest of the West, it seems, had even reached to the heart and mind of one of its last outlaws.

# EPILOGUE

## The Writers, in Order of Appearance

**Francis Parkman, Jr.** turned south after his stay with the Oglala, and eventually returned to the East along the Santa Fe Trail. His eyesight failed rapidly after his return, and he was forced to dictate much of his classic work on his journey. He went on to become one of the first great American historians, establishing himself as an authority on European-settled North America before 1763. His book *France and England in North America* became a classic. He died in 1893.

**Jesse A. Applegate** lived his life out in Oregon, a respected member of a celebrated pioneer family. After working for a time as a lawyer, he eventually became a teacher and writer. He died in 1918. His uncle of the same name (who had helped lead the Great Migration) also wrote about the 1843 trek, in *A Day with the Cow Column*. The uncle achieved legendary stature as a leader in the newly opened territory, emerging as a statesman in the turmoil of Oregon's early history.

**William T. Sherman** resigned from the army after his service in California, and became head of a military academy in Louisiana. Upon the outbreak of the Civil War he returned to the army, where he emerged, after a few setbacks, as one of the great generals of the war. He commanded the U.S. Army from 1869 to 1884, leading it during most of the final cycle of Indian warfare. He died in 1891.

**Chief Joseph** never succeeded in his lifelong quest to return to the Wallowa Valley, despite his travels to Washington and the widespread sympathy he attracted. He was held as a prisoner of war first in Kansas and then in the Indian Territory, that dumping ground of defeated Native Americans. He was eventually transferred to the Colville Reservation in Washington, where he died in 1904.

**Fanny Kelly** returned to Kansas after her captivity, and with her husband, Josiah, opened a hotel in Ellsworth. He died of cholera in 1867, leaving her with three children; in 1870 she moved to Washington. In an effort to win government compensation, Kelly obtained notarized statements from several soldiers and Lakota chiefs (including Red Cloud and Spotted Tail) and published her book in 1871. Congress responded with a $5,000 payment. In 1880, she married again, and in 1904 she died in Washington.

**Henry H. Sibley** capped off a distinguished career as a Minnesota frontiersman by crushing the Sioux uprising of 1862. Sibley had served in Congress and as first governor of the state, 1858–60. After defeating the Santee revolt and punishing their western Dakota friends, Sibley was made major general of volunteers in 1865 (the army distinguished between officers of volunteers and officers in the regular army—the latter were career officers, and had far more prestige). He helped negotiate new treaties with various Indian bands, then became president of the Minnesota Historical Society in 1879. He held that office until his death in 1891.

**Alfred Sully** joined in further campaigns against the Lakota and Cheyennes in 1865, with no success. The crusty, irascible officer continued to serve on the frontier after the Civil War ended, taking part in the Sand Hills battle, a major fight at the beginning of the Southern Plains War of 1868–69. Custer strenuously criticized him during the preparations for the winter campaign in that war, and Sheridan removed Sully from command of the main attacking column (which Custer then led to Black Kettle's camp on the Washita). Sully was named commander of the Twenty-first Infantry regiment in 1873. He died at Fort Vancouver, Washington, in 1879.

**William M. Breakenridge** took to a wandering life in the years after the Sand Creek Massacre. He worked first as a train brakeman, then as a store clerk in Nebraska in 1867, then as a deputy sheriff in Phoenix, Arizona Territory, in 1878. A year later he landed in booming Tombstone, where he pinned on the badge of a deputy sheriff. As a Democrat, Breakenridge was an uneasy bystander during the Cochise County War, when Republican Wyatt Earp and his brothers broke the power of the rural, Democratic cowboys, smugglers, and small ranchers. Breakenridge continued his career as a fighter for the growing frontier establishment after leaving Tombstone, working as a deputy U.S. marshal and special officer for the Southern Pacific Railroad. He died peacefully in Tucson in 1931.

**William F. Cody** was immortalized as **Buffalo Bill** in 1869 by the dime novelist Ned Buntline. In that year Cody was still working for the army during the Southern Plains War. He became a scout for the Fifth Cavalry, commanded by Major Eugene A. Carr, and helped find the camp of Tall Bull and the intransigent Dog Soldiers band on July 11, 1869. He joined in Carr's surprise attack on the Indians' camp, which led to the death of Tall Bull and the end of the Southern Plains War. In 1883, Cody built on his fame to organize his famed Wild West Show. The show was a tremendous success; Cody even persuaded Sitting Bull to join the troupe for a season, and the two men became good (if improbable) friends. When the Ghost Dance took hold on the Lakota reservations, the government agents became frightened and wanted to arrest Sitting Bull. General Nelson Miles recruited Cody to talk to the venerable chief and bring him in peacefully, but he was deflected by agent James McLaughlin, who wanted his own Sioux police to do the job. The result was a tragedy. Cody lived out the rest of his life peacefully, dying in 1917.

As described by J.B. Gillett, **John Wesley Hardin** continued to burn a trail of death after the events described in his own account. He married Jane Bowen, landed in jail, and was broken out by his cousin Mannen Clements. Hardin and the Clements family took part in the Sutton-Taylor feud in the early 1870s. In 1874, he shot down Deputy Sheriff Charles Webb, and fled with his wife and daughter to Florida. Texas posted a $4,000 reward for his capture, and Hardin lived under the name J.H. Swain, Jr. In 1877, Ranger John Armstrong and three others caught up to Hardin on a train in Florida and wrestled him to the ground. Tried and convicted of murder, Hardin went to prison and began studying law. His wife died while he was in prison. In 1894 he was released, and he soon set up office as an attorney in Gonzales. Eventually he moved to El Paso, where he again took up his old ways, gambling and drinking. On August 19, 1895, Hardin was throwing dice in the Ace Saloon when John Selman (leader of the notorious Wrestlers who had devastated Lincoln County after the Five-Day Battle) walked in and shot him in the back of the head. Selman (inexplicably a town constable) was acquitted, and a year later was shot to death by George Scarborough, a fellow lawman.

**J.B. Gillett** retired from the Texas Rangers in 1881. Before he quit, he engaged in one final exploit, crossing the Mexican border illegally to bring back a man wanted for murder. Gillett took charge of a group of railway guards for a time, then became El Paso's city marshal. In 1885, Gillett hung up his guns and turned to ranching. He established a 30,000-acre operation at Barrel Springs, Texas. He died peacefully in Temple, Texas, in 1937.

**Wooden Leg** was only nineteen when his people surrendered to General Miles in 1877. The large, powerful warrior traveled with the rest of the Northern Cheyennes to exile in the Indian Territory, where they were placed with the Southern Cheyennes. He did not join in Dull Knife's breakout from the reservation (see the entry on Dull Knife, below), but he was eventually sent back to a reservation on the tribe's homeland in Montana. Wooden Leg rose in prominence in the decades that followed, taking part in the Ghost Dance in 1890 and becoming a judge of the tribal court. He was baptized as a Christian at age fifty, and died peacefully—a highly respected old man—in 1940.

**John F. Finerty** continued his career in typical Gilded Age fashion. The Irish-born reporter went on to further adventures in the years immediately following the Great Sioux War, becoming the first newspaperman to interview Porfirio Díaz, the newly triumphant Mexican dictator. He also joined in the campaign against the Utes in Colorado, Miles's patrol of the Canadian border in pursuit of Sitting Bull, and General Carr's campaigns against the Apaches. Finerty soon turned his attention to Washington, becoming a correspondent in the capital, 1879–81. He then served in Congress, 1883–85, as—being an Irishman in Chicago—a Democrat.

**Two Moons** was catapulted to prominence after the Northern Cheyennes surrendered: General Miles lifted him from being one of the nine lesser chiefs of the Fox warrior society to become the army-designated head chief of the entire tribe. Miles may have confused Two Moons with his uncle of the same name, who was a legendary warrior and a victor in many battles with the Cheyennes' Indian foes. Nevertheless, Two Moons carried out his government-imposed duties well, and became a leading spokesman for adapting to the new ways being thrust upon his people. He returned with his people to a reservation in Montana, and died peacefully around 1917.

**Nelson A. Miles**, a volatile mixture of vanity, ambition, and ability, reached the peak of his career with the surrender of Geronimo and his fellow hostile Apaches. Miles tried to claim sole credit for the surrender, publishing a blatantly fraudulent description of the event in his memoirs. Afterward, he was the toast of the nation, and newspaper tycoon William Randolph Hearst promoted him as a presidential candidate. The hostility this created prevented him from being promoted to major general (his old rival George Crook got the post), but he was named commander of the army's Division of the Pacific in 1888. In 1890, Crook died, and Miles pulled political strings to get himself promoted, and was named head of the Division of the Missouri. It was in this post that he ordered the assault on the Lakota Ghost Dancers at Wounded Knee in 1890. In 1895, he took command of the entire U.S. Army, which he kept unprepared for the outbreak of the Spanish-American War. During the conflict, Theodore Roosevelt won glory in battle in Cuba, as Miles captured Puerto Rico in an uneventful campaign. In 1901, he was promoted to lieutenant general. In 1903, President Roosevelt unceremoniously forced Miles to retire. The general died in 1925 while attending the circus in Washington.

**Theodore Roosevelt** returned from the Dakota Territory to marry Edith Kermit, his second wife (he had taken up ranching after the death of his first wife, Alice Hathaway). He quickly rose in the Republican party, serving as a civil service commissioner (1889–95), New York City police commissioner (1895–97), and Assistant Secretary of the Navy (1897–98). In each post he won attention as an energetic reformer. During the Spanish-American War he organized a cavalry regiment known as the Rough Riders (composed largely of Westerners), which he led in a famous charge up San Juan Hill in Cuba. After the war he rose to the governorship of New York (1899–1900) and the U.S. vice presidency under McKinley immediately afterward. When McKinley was assassinated, Roosevelt served out most of his term as president and was elected to another four years in 1904. Throughout his life he was associated, and associated himself, with the frontier, and he wrote the award-winning history *The Winning of the West*.

**Frank M. Canton** left the office of sheriff of Johnson County in 1886, returning to work as a cattle detective for the Wyoming Stockgrowers' Association. He was a key figure in hiring as many as fifty gunmen (mostly Texans) for the Association, helping to lead them on a raid into the county in 1892. Known as the Johnson County War, the raid was an all-out attempt by the cattle barons to kill off their opponents, including both rustlers and homesteaders. Canton and his men shot down two hard-fighting resisters before they were surrounded by their foes. The local men were preparing a final assault on the Association gunslingers when the cavalry (including Lieutenant Charles B. Gatewood) intervened. After these events, Canton drifted down to the Oklahoma Territory, where he again took up work in law enforcement. Canton helped put down the territory's outlaw bands (including the remnants of the Dalton gang) and killed a man named Bill Dunn in a main street walkdown in the town of Pawnee. He found work as a deputy U.S. marshal in Alaska, then returned to Oklahoma. In 1907 he was named adjutant general of the Oklahoma National Guard. He died peacefully in 1927.

**Geronimo** and his fellow hostiles were sent as prisoners of war to Fort Pickens, Florida, and forced into hard labor for almost two years. They were not allowed to see their families until May 1887. Later they were transferred to Mount Vernon Barracks in Alabama. In Florida and Alabama, disease struck the Apache warriors and their families, killing scores of them. Many of the former scouts were allowed to return to New Mexico, but Geronimo was transferred to Fort Sill, Oklahoma, in 1894. Geronimo tried to "take the white man's road," and worked as a farmer. In 1905, he rode in the inauguration parade of Theodore Roosevelt in Washington, D.C., along with chiefs of many other tribes. Like Chief Joseph, he spent his days trying to win permission to return to the land where he was born. Like Chief Joseph, he failed. He died at Fort Sill in 1909. Historian Odie Faulk reports that his wife was prevented from killing his favorite horse at his funeral, even though "Apache custom held that a warrior would need a horse to ride in the afterworld."

**Britton Davis** retired from the army in 1885, in the midst of the Geronimo Campaign, and became the manager of the Corralitos Mining and Cattle Company in Mexico. He ran the firm's sizeable operations for twenty years. He moved to New York State in 1912 and took up farming. In 1924 he sold off his lands and moved to San Diego, where he died in 1930, at the age of seventy, shortly after completing his classic book *The Truth About Geronimo*. Along the way, he managed to marry twice and leave behind three children.

**George W. Coe** and his cousin Frank did far better than most veterans of the Lincoln County War. After the end of the fighting, they left for San Juan County. They received pardons from territorial governor Lew Wallace, and returned to Lincoln County in 1884. Frank established a ranch and lived peacefully until his death in 1931, survived by his widow and six children. George built the Golden Glow ranch, where he lived until 1941. His descendants (who are fully aware of their ancestor's role in the Lincoln County War) still operate the ranch to this day.

**Pat F. Garrett,** like most of the fighters in the Lincoln County War and its aftermath, met a violent death. After killing off the Kid and most of his gang, the former buffalo hunter and cowpuncher failed to win a second term as sheriff of Lincoln County (he was even forced to hire a lawyer to get the reward money for Billy Bonney's death). Garrett spent the next twenty years drifting between ranching and law enforcement, until President Theodore Roosevelt appointed him customs inspector in El Paso. Later he established a ranch outside Las Cruces, New Mexico, where he was soon locked in a bitter feud with Wayne Brazel, who had leased some of Garrett's land. Brazel turned to a noted badman and contract murderer, Jim "Killer" Miller. On February 29, 1908, Miller ambushed Garrett and shot him in the back of the head as Brazel watched. A year later, Miller himself was lynched for a contract killing in Ada, Oklahoma.

**Tom Horn** left government service after the Apache wars to follow, as Odie Faulk writes, "a path of violence." He fought in the Pleasant Valley War (a fight between factions of settlers) in Arizona in 1887; served as deputy sheriff in the territory's Yavapai County; and worked for the Pinkerton detective agency. After the Johnson County War in Wyoming, he found work with the Wyoming Stockgrowers' Association as a "cattle detective." His job was to assassinate rustlers and troublesome homesteaders. He left in 1898 to serve in the army during the Spanish-American War as chief packer, then returned to continue his deadly work. After mistakenly shooting down the teenage son of one of his intended victims, he was arrested for murder on January 13, 1902. Tried and convicted, he wrote his memoirs on death row. He was hung on November 18, 1902, as two cowboy friends stood by and sang "Life's Railway to Heaven."

**Emmett Dalton**, the former farmer, lawman, and sole survivor of the Dalton gang's raid on Coffeyville, Kansas, confessed to killing George Cubine during the foiled robbery and was sent to the Kansas State Penitentiary. Pardoned in 1907, Dalton married his longtime girlfriend and took up work as a building contractor and real estate agent. In 1920, he moved to Los Angeles and wrote for various movie studios, helping to create the mythology of popular entertainment that would soon overshadow the real history of the frontier. He also campaigned for prison reform and against crime. He died peacefully in 1937.

## Others Who Appear in This Book

**John M. Chivington** was investigated and castigated by one military and two Congressional panels after he instigated the Sand Creek Massacre. Chivington resigned from the army in 1865, and was never punished. He took to freighting in Nebraska in the late 1860s, traveled widely, then returned to Denver in 1883. In 1894, still arguing that he had won a glorious triumph at Sand Creek, Chivington died of cancer.

**James B. "Wild Bill" Hickok** killed Phil Coe in a walkdown in Abilene shortly after John Wesley Hardin left town. The enraged Texans allegedly put a price on his head; Hickok served out the year, then quit to become a guide and a performer with a wild west show. In 1874, he returned to the West, and he fell in love with and married Agnes Lake Thatcher, a noted circus manager and performer. His days as a gunfighter were over, however; his eyesight was failing rapidly. In 1876 he made his way to Deadwood, a burgeoning mining town in the Black Hills. On August 2, 1876, Hickok sat down to play poker in the Number Ten saloon; normally he sat with his back to the wall, but this day was an exception. An obscure gunman named Jack McCall walked up to Hickok and blasted him in the back of the head. Hickok's hand—two aces and two eights—became known as "the dead man's hand." When asked why he hadn't shot Hickok from the front in the usual fashion, McCall reportedly said, "I didn't want to commit suicide." McCall was hung for the murder on March 1, 1877.

**Crazy Horse** and **Sitting Bull,** paralleling the history of their people's independence, both died while resisting arrest. For Crazy Horse, the end came soon after he led his people onto the reservation in defeat. He was regarded as a troublemaker by Red Cloud and Spotted Tail, the leaders of the agency Indians, and Red Cloud maneuvered to prevent Crazy Horse from gaining influence among the Lakota. During the Nez Percé war, Crazy Horse refused repeated requests that he help the army track down Chief Joseph's people. Through a combination of intrigues on the reservation, Crazy Horse's own intransigence, and General Crook's own fears, a cloud descended on him; Crook ordered him arrested. On September 6, 1877, as the soldiers were putting him into a guardhouse, Crazy Horse turned to escape, and they stabbed him with their bayonets. He died soon after in his father's arms.

After returning from Canada in 1881, Sitting Bull was imprisoned at Fort Randall in the Dakota Territory until 1883. He then settled at the Standing Rock Reservation, where he clashed repeatedly with the government agent, James McLaughlin. Sitting Bull understood the changes that had swept over the land; he took up farming, and made sure his offspring went to school. But he insisted on Lakota autonomy—a stand that clashed with government plans to break up the reservations into family plots, thus reducing the Indian lands and allowing white families to settle the resulting "surplus." As described previously, Sitting Bull also joined Buffalo Bill's Wild West Show, and befriended him. Later he took up the new Ghost Dance religion; when the government grew fearful that the faith would lead to an outbreak of violence, it ordered that Sitting Bull be arrested. General Miles sent Buffalo Bill to do the job; agent McLaughlin diverted him, and sent in his own force of Indian police. In the struggle that ensued, Sitting Bull was shot to death by Lieutenant Bull Head and Sergeant Red Tomahawk in 1890. A few days later, the army slaughtered scores of Ghost Dancers at Wounded Knee.

For **Dull Knife**, the aging leader of the Northern Cheyennes, his surrender to Miles in 1877 brought on a devastating end to everything he had always known. The tribe was quickly shipped off to the Indian Territory for internment with the Southern Cheyennes. Dull Knife, however, could not bear to be so far from the Big Horn Mountains and the Powder River: in September 1878 he led 300 men, women, and children on a 1,500-mile flight back to their homeland. They were caught and returned to the reservation, only to break out again in January 1879. This time, one-third of them died under armed attacks and the winter weather. Dull Knife himself made it to the northern plains, and he was given a home with Red Cloud's people. In 1883 he died, bitter and broken, by the Rosebud River.

**George Crook** was forced out of command in Arizona by General Sheridan in 1886, and was reassigned to head the army's Department of the Platte. Crook, once a trusted subordinate of Sheridan during the Civil War, continued to fight for better treatment of Geronimo and the other hostile Apaches after their surrender, and to campaign for dignified treatment of the Indians in general. In March 1888, Alfred Terry retired from the army, and Crook and his old rival Miles fought to be promoted to the now open major generalcy. Crook won, and he took command of the Division of the Missouri. He died of a heart attack in 1890, while fighting to get Congress to move the Apache prisoners from Florida to a better location. According to Odie Faulk, Lakota leader Red Cloud declared, "He, at least, never lied to us."

**Marcus Reno** and **Frederick Benteen**, the two ranking officers to survive the Little Bighorn defeat, led dramatically different lives after the disaster. Benteen—Custer's leading critic within the Seventh Cavalry (he started writing to newspapers attacking Custer soon after the Battle of the Washita)—fought bravely against the Nez Percés in 1877, and was promoted to brevet brigadier general. Ironically, his feud with Custer may have saved his life, since he was assigned the tedious duty of scouting to the south at the Little Bighorn, and arrived last on the field. He retired in 1888, and died in Atlanta in 1898. Reno, though cleared by a military court of any wrongdoing at the battle, was thrown out of the army in 1880 for drunkenness and making advances toward a subordinate's wife. He died in bitterness in 1889.

**Oliver O. Howard**, the general so loved by the Apaches and so hated by the Nez Percés, continued as commander of the army's Division of the Pacific after the Nez Percé war. He was transferred, in 1886, to command the Division of the East. He retired in 1894 and died in 1909 at the age of seventy-nine. Howard had been brimming with good intentions throughout his life: heading the Freedman's Bureau after the Civil War, founding Howard University, negotiating with Cochise, and generally trying to "civilize" and uplift the nonwhite races. Unfortunately, his good intentions struck many of those whom he tried to help as patronizing; tolerance and respect for the ways of others were not virtues of liberals in the nineteenth century.

**Granville Stuart** quit the ranching business after a particularly harsh winter savaged the cattle industry in Montana in 1886–87. As one of the most prominent citizens in the territory, however, his future was secure. He was named a state land agent in 1891; in 1894, President Cleveland appointed him U.S. minister to Uruguay, and later to Paraguay. He returned to Montana in the early 1900s and was commissioned to write the official history of the young state, which he never completed. He died in 1918 at age seventy-four.

**Josiah "Doc" Scurlock**, the one-time commander of the McSween Regulators in the Lincoln County War, did not have long to live after Pat
Garrett shot his friend, the Kid. Scurlock rode for a time with Billy after
defeat of the McSween faction, but he soon returned home and took a job
on Pete Maxwell's ranch (where Billy was killed in 1881). In 1882,
Scurlock ran into a man named Fred Roth on the Chisum ranch, and an
argument soon developed. Both men pulled guns, Roth ducking behind
the ranch house and Scurlock behind a wagon. Roth blasted three shots
through the wooden vehicle, hitting Scurlock with two of them. Scurlock
collapsed, saying, "That's enough. You've got me, Fred. Don't shoot any
more." He died on the spot.

**Charles B. Gatewood** was immediately transferred by General Miles to
Fort Stanton, New Mexico, after securing Geronimo's surrender. Miles, as
Odie Faulk writes, did not want the lieutenant to cast any shadows on the
general's glory. Miles soon changed his mind and made Gatewood his aide
de camp, where he could be watched more easily. In 1890, with his role
now forgotten by the press, Gatewood was allowed to rejoin his regiment,
and he took part in the Wounded Knee campaign. In 1892, Gatewood and
his men intervened in the Johnson County War, saving Frank Canton and
the other besieged gunmen of the Wyoming Stockgrowers' Association
from a final assault by the homesteaders they had come to attack. Gatewood was wounded in the aftermath of the struggle, and retired to Mary-
land, where he died of stomach cancer in 1896. Gatewood, a man
renowned in the army for his dignity and fearlessness, never engaged in the
debates over who was responsible for getting Geronimo to surrender.

**Henry W. Lawton** was promoted by Miles from captain to lieutenant colonel and commended for his role in Geronimo's surrender. In the Spanish-
American War he commanded the Second Division of the Fifth Corps,
fought in Cuba, and earned a promotion to full colonel in the regular army.
He transferred to the Philippines in December 1898, and was killed while
leading an attack on Philippine insurgents in San Mateo, Luzon. The guerrillas were led, ironically, by a man named Geronimo—and a persistent army
rumor had it that Lawton was shot by one of his own men.

**Martine** and **Kayitah**, the Apaches responsible for leading Gatewood to
Geronimo, were hauled off to Florida along with the hostiles as prisoners
of war. They and the other government scouts endured, in the words of
Geronimo's nephew, "the contempt and dislike of their people all that
time." After many years they returned to the Mescalero Apache Reservation in New Mexico. Through the help of Charles B. Gatewood's son, they
secured government pensions in 1926—the only reward they ever got for
their critical role in ending the last real Indian war.